ABOUT THE AUTHOR

Michael Latham was born in Leigh and brought up in Bolton, and has been a lifelong supporter of Leigh and Bolton Wanderers. A graduate of Bristol University, where he gained a degree in Economic and Social History, he now has his own accountancy business but has spent much of the last thirty years researching the history of Rugby League and writing for a considerable number of newspapers, magazines and sporting publications. He has been involved with National Sports Reporting, one of the foremost sports agencies in Britain and is Chairman of the Association of Sports Historians. A contributor to League Express since its inception, he writes regularly for Rugby League World and The Independent and hosts an hour-long weekly Rugby League programme on BBC Radio Lancashire. A self-confessed 'groundhopper' he has visited all the current English and Scottish Football League grounds and has seen professional Rugby League played on well over one hundred grounds. This is his seventh book on Rugby League.

BRITISH RUGBY LEAGUE
A GROUNDHOPPER'S GUIDE

LEAGUE
Publications Ltd

First published in Great Britain in 2005 by
League Publications Ltd
Wellington House
Briggate
Brighouse
West Yorkshire HD6 1DN

A CIP catalogue record for this book is available from the British Library
ISBN 1-901347-14-1

Designed and Typeset by Daniel Spencer, League Publications Limited
Manufactured in the EU by L.P.P.S. Ltd, Wellingborough, Northants

CONTENTS

PREFACE

When Tony Hannan, Tim Butcher and I sat down in the autumn of 2002 to discuss a monthly series of articles on grounds for Rugby League World magazine little did I realise that this book would be the result. From my first article on Hull's departure from the Boulevard the series, entitled Groundhopper's Guide, has since taken up most of my thinking time. Football and Rugby League grounds have always held a special fascination for me and in recent years I have been fortunate enough to complete the groundhopper's ambition of seeing a first-class game at each of the current Football League and Scottish League grounds. I have also completed the 'set' of Highland League grounds and have several more ambitions in the pipeline.

Hilton Park, Leigh was the first Rugby League ground I visited and it has retained a special place in my heart, strengthened during that wonderful season of 1981/82 when Leigh lifted the Lancashire Cup and then went on to win the Championship after a memorable last-game win at Whitehaven. John Woods remains my ultimate sporting hero.

I was fortunate enough, as a youngster, to see Leigh's 1971 Wembley Challenge Cup Final victory over Leeds and later became good friends with several of the players, including Kevin Ashcroft who is one of the game's true characters. Over a period of about 25 years I missed only a handful of Leigh games and edited the club's match-day programme for over a decade. In the past ten years or so my reporting commitments have meant travelling far and wide watching the greatest game of all.

In 1999 I was asked to present BBC Radio Lancashire's weekly Rugby League programme alongside Dave Swanton, following on from the pioneering work done at the station by Jason Harborow. Swanny's unfortunate defection to rugby union left me organising the programme single handed, for the best part of fifty-two weeks a year. Sports Editor Gary Hickson has been a huge help and gives me a free rein presenting what is currently League 2005, which has been enormously satisfying. I never cease to be amazed at how approachable and amenable are the vast majority of people in the game of Rugby League, and the great and the good have only been too happy to travel to Blackburn to spread the word.

While other students travelled the world, I spent three summers and subsequently a great deal of time researching the history of the game in dusty libraries. During the early 1990s I wrote six books on Rugby League, the last being a biography of John 'Buff' Berry of Tyldesley and England fame. 'Buff Berry and the Mighty Bongers' sounded like a sex manual and, if it had been one, it might have sold more copies.

When League Express started publication in 1990 I began by contributing the Leigh match reports and that created a new 'career' as a sports journalist. Looking back, the memorable 1995 World Cup was my breakthrough year and I have been very fortunate to see most of the big games first hand since the switch to a summer season. In the process I have clocked up well over one hundred Rugby League games a year and made visiting new grounds a priority wherever possible.

This book would not have been possible without the help of numerous individuals, many of whom are listed below:

Kevin Ashcroft, Tony Ashcroft, Eric Ashton, Mark Aston, Timothy Auty, Maurice Bamford, Hilary Barlow, Dean Bell, Keith Bell, John Blair, Jeff Bowron, Carl Briscoe, Tim Butcher, Phil Caplan, Brian Cartwright, Jon Clarke, Tony Collins, Gina Coldrick, John Cornwell, John Cox, Ken Dalby, Alan Davies, Roland Davis, Ernie Day, Trevor Delaney, Bob Eccles, John Edwards, St John Ellis, John Etty, Jack Fennell, Dave Fletcher, Raymond Fletcher, the late Trevor Foster, Alan Galloway, Paul Gamble, Len Garbett, Mike Gardner, Robert Gate, Richard Gay, Eppie Gibson, Geoff Gunney, Mike Haddon, Dave Hadfield, Tony Hannan, Andrew Hardcastle, Chris Harte, Norman Hazell, John Helm, Gary Hetherington, Gary Hickson, David Hobbs, Terry Hollindrake, Andy Howard, David Howes, Eric Hughes, Mike Hulme, Trevor Hunt, John Huxley, Michael Inman, Robin Isherwood, Ian Jackson, Harry Jepson, Maurice Jones, Neil Kelly, Simon Knox, Ian Laybourn, Mark Lee, Graham Lovett, Phil Lowe, Peter Lush, Tom Mather, Andy Mitchell, Piers Morgan, Graham Morris, Ray Myers, Kevin Nicholas, David Oxley, Chris Park, Dave Parker, Stewart Piper, Darrell Platt, Mick Rhodes, Paul Rowley, Mike Rylance, Martyn Sadler, Tommy Sale, Roy Sampson, Irvin Saxton, Bob Shuttleworth, Alan Smallshaw, Mike Smith, Peter Smith, Andy Sneddon, Daniel Spencer, Graham Steadman, Mike Stephenson, Dave Swanton, Mark Taylor, Mike Ulyatt, Brian Walker, Gareth Walker, John Walsh, Billy Watts, the late Tom Webb, Denis Whittle, Steve Wild, Dave Williams, Graham Williams, Andy Wilson and Nigel Winnard, and the late Harry Woods. Apologies to anyone I have missed out.

Five books, in particular, have been inspirational especially Trevor Delaney's outstanding 'The Grounds of Rugby League' (Delaney, 1991) and 'International Grounds of Rugby League' (Delaney, 1995). Simon Inglis's brilliant book 'Football Grounds of Britain' (CollinsWillow, 1996) and Kerry Miller's 'History of Non-League Grounds' (Polar Print, 1996) come highly recommended. In recent times, though, my favourite book is 'The Ultimate Directory of English & Scottish Football League Grounds' by Paul and Shirley Smith (Yore Publications, 2002).

The pioneering research carried out especially by the late Tom Webb, Robert Gate, Trevor Delaney, Raymond Fletcher and Irvin Saxton on the history of Rugby League leaves me hugely in their debt.

Most of the photographs in this book are my own, with other contributions from Andy Howard and Dave Williams. I apologise to copyright holders if there has been any accidental infringement.

Thanks to Tim Butcher, Martyn Sadler, Daniel Spencer and Tony Hannan for their expertise, encouragement and help over many years at League Express Towers and for seeing the results of my labours committed to print. I sincerely hope that you, dear reader, get as much enjoyment out of this book as I did writing and compiling it. Finally, thanks to my father, Derek, for introducing me to the wonderful world of Rugby League and to the wider world of other sports at an early age. My groundhopping days certainly started young.

Mike Latham, September 2005

BARROW

The longest cul-de-sac in England is how some describe the long road from the M6 to Barrow-in-Furness. But those who seek to make fun of the town for its comparative isolation do so at their peril.

A trip to Barrow for the initiated Rugby League fan is one of life's true pleasures, especially if combined with a stop-off in the delightful town of Ulverston or a few moments savouring the view from Rampside, along the coast road. Just a few miles from Barrow, it is one of the most atmospheric spots in the kingdom with its panoramic view across the wide expanse of Morecambe Bay. In the late 1890s, Fleetwood used to take a boat across for their games in Barrow to save on a long railway journey.

The writer defies anyone not to be uplifted after those detours and, on arrival at Craven Park, the pulse quickens for here is a wonderful, traditional Rugby League ground where you can feel the pride of the townsfolk in its heroes of the past.

Those memories, of five Wembley finals and great players like Willie Horne, Bill Burgess (senior and junior), Jimmy Lewthwaite, Phil Jackson and Billy Little, to name but a few, have helped sustain Barrovians from the feeling of being cast off since the formation of the all-singing and dancing Super League. Think of the millions squandered in ventures far away from the game's heartland and ponder awhile just how much better spent it would have been in the game's traditional areas.

Despite it all Barrow has survived, albeit at a modest level. The current board of directors, in situ since the mid-1990s, has been determined to ensure that the game continues to be played in the town, in a ground that is one of the best appointed outside the top flight. Maintained to a high standard, Craven Park boasts a fine playing surface and cover on all four sides, with the new Willie Horne grandstand, costing £340,000, of which £200,000 was grant funded, seating 950, named after the town's favourite son and opened in 1999, the centrepiece.

In the space of forty years in the nineteenth century, Barrow grew from a tiny hamlet to the biggest iron and steel centre in the world and a major shipbuilding port with a population of over 70,000. Its prosperity grew with the developing industries and rugby was established in the town from 1875 onwards when the Barrow club was formed.

Initially the fledgling club had two home grounds with one, the old Parade Ground, situated just a stone's throw from Craven Park, eventually abandoned in favour of the other, Cavendish Park. The latter ground, situated on Barrow Island, and now used by amateur soccer and rugby teams, was Barrow's permanent home from 1883 until 1914.

Cricket, athletics and cycling events were also held at Cavendish Park and the rugby club erected two grandstands, one in 1887 at a cost of £50, the other, 70-yards long, six years later to accommodate the increasing number of spectators. The ground enjoyed one of its finest days in March 1889 when the visit of the touring Maoris to play a District XV

The Willie Horne Stand and *(inset)* the great man himself

attracted a crowd of 6,000 (£120) and saw the locals win by a goal to nil.

Originally, Barrow's nickname was the Boilermakers and later the Shipbuilders, reflecting the importance of that industry to the town's prosperity. The Barrow Ship Building Company had been formed in 1870 and in 1897 - the year that the rugby club joined the Northern Union - the company was bought by the Vickers family steel business of Sheffield. The first submarine was built in 1901 and by 1914 Britain had the largest, most advanced and best-supported submarine fleet in the world, with Vickers supplying all but four of the 74 built.

The Barrow shipyard, later owned by Vickers Armstrong, now controlled by BAE Systems and containing a highly-skilled workforce, continued to be at the forefront of developments in maritime design and build of all sorts of sea going vessels. It has supplied 309 Royal Navy submarines, including every nuclear submarine, with names like Dreadnought, Astute and Trafalgar currently in service and battleships, cruisers, destroyers and aircraft carriers, together with the SS Oriana, the finest passenger cruiser of its day when it undertook its maiden voyage in 1960.

Much of the workforce played for or supported the Barrow club and one of the leading figures in Barrow's shipbuilding history, as we shall see, was behind the formation of Craven Park.

Cavendish Park, overlooking the shipyard, was the scene of many of the finest moments in Barrow's early history. The club earned senior status in 1900 after beating Tyldesley at Lancaster in a Promotion-Relegation test match (re-introduced by the RFL in the National Leagues for 2003) and played the first New Zealand and Australian tourists at the ground. The highest attendance at Cavendish Park was 12,000 for a Challenge Cup-tie against Hunslet in March 1908, producing receipts of £308.

But in 1914, with war clouds looming, Cavendish Park was requisitioned with its strategic position deemed essential for the war effort. Barrow had to find a new home and they moved to Little Park, Roose, situated a good three miles from the town centre.

Little Park had been the home of Barrow AFC prior to their move to Holker Street in 1909, and was purchased by the rugby committee from Lord Richard Cavendish for the sum of £3,000 in 1920/21. A new 66-yard long stand, built at a cost of £2,650, was opened in September 1921 and another stand, seating 500 with standing room for another 4,000, was erected three years later.

Barrow's record crowd at the venue was recorded in March 1923 when 12,214 saw a Challenge Cup third round tie against Oldham, but the latter part of the 1920s saw declining attendances and a move back to nearer the town centre was considered imperative.

Commander Charles Craven OBE, the chairman of Vickers Armstrong Limited, was the driving force behind the funding and construction of the new ground. Fittingly, when it opened in 1931, Barrow's new ground was named after him. The identified location of the new ground appeared at first rather unpropitious, the location of a derelict jute works, five reservoirs, a mission hall and railway track. But Mr Craven, assisted by the Mayor, Alderman John Whinnerah, secured the site for £2,500 and the first of 40,000 tons of fill and banking were tipped in October 1929 when a third of the site was under water, part of it to the depth of 13 feet.

Vickers Armstrong Limited provided the tipping materials and, later, free transport for the 92,000 sods of turf with grandstand and shelters transferred from Little Park in 1931. With its steel frame, brick walls and 14 rows of steep wooden box seating the stand survived until it was demolished in 1998. Fund raising efforts raised all but £300 of the total cost of the project (£7,500), the balance being made up by club funds.

It was a major operation, much of it achieved with the help of voluntary labour from the ranks of the unemployed, who received free season tickets as recompense. But it was a real red-letter day for the town of Barrow when the first match at Craven Park was staged against Swinton on 29 August 1931, even though the visitors won, 30-7, before a crowd of 16,167. Mr Craven was given the honour of making the first kick-off.

Little Park, meanwhile, was used briefly for speedway after Barrow's departure but objections over the bumpy track ended hopes of establishing the sport. Greyhound racing was also briefly staged there but the site was built upon after 1932 and now forms part of the Holbeck housing estate, though the Ship Hotel, which Barrow used as changing rooms, still stands.

Craven Park was soon host to some huge crowds - 21,555 attending a Good Friday game against Salford in 1934. Four years later Salford, Barrow's opponents in the 1938 Wembley Challenge Cup Final, attracted a slightly bigger crowd - 21,651 - for the cup final dress rehearsal on Good Friday 1938. That record looks set to stand for all time, with Craven Park's current capacity little more than one-third of the record crowd.

Barrow's third-round victory over Leeds had produced then record receipts of £1,084 from a crowd of 20,007, but Albert Gear's last-gasp try for Salford ruined Barrow's first Wembley final and it was to be 17 years later before the club finally secured their one and only success in the capital.

The post-war years provided Barrow with a glorious spell of success, ending with their defeat in the 1957 Cup Final. At the forefront was Horne, who became a legend in his own lifetime. Between 1943-59 he played 461 times for Barrow and scored 112 tries, kicked 741 goals for 1,818 points, captaining the club in three Wembley finals, of which the 1955 one was won. He died in 2001, six years after being made a Freeman of the Borough of Barrow-in-Furness.

For a decade Barrow was one of the leading clubs in the game, regularly contesting the major honours and producing some great players, many of them local lads. Local journalist Mike Gardner captured the era brilliantly in his widely acclaimed biography, entitled, simply, "Willie".

"It was a wonderful era and many Barrovians still remember it to this day," Gardner says. "They had a good team in the late 1930s but the team in the Horne era was exceptional. At times there were ten internationals in the 13 - you can't believe it now. Living Barrovians point to it as the greatest point in the town's sporting history. We had the GB captain in Horne and all the backs were internationals.

"Those times, realistically, will never come back but the people are so proud of it. Sport, and life itself, has changed so much and whether the younger generation is proud, or even aware of it, I'm not sure. But it was a glorious time.

"Barrow is a unique place, a big town with a population of around 70,000, but an insular place that people won't leave. There are two great traditions - shipbuilding and Rugby League. At one time everyone worked in the shipyards, where there were dozens of trades, now long forgotten, all with their own trade unions and they built great ships like the Oriana, and later the Trident and Polaris submarines.

"The team of the 1950s was hero-worshipped. All of them were Barrovians or Cumbrians and going to Craven Park was like a religion. Barrow men built the greatest ships in the world and they mirrored that pride in their wonderful team. They used to say that if you worked at Vickers Armstrong, you could work anywhere in the world."

Gardner trawled through the nostalgia and produced one of the finest sporting

The view of the Craven Park pitch from the players' tunnel

biographies ever written. Spend five minutes leafing through its pages or studying the atmospheric photographs of a bygone age and you are in a time warp. "The world was a different place then but Willie Horne was Barrow's David Beckham," he says. "When he died there were hundreds at the funeral and the flag on the Town Hall stood at half-mast. The memorial service at Craven Park was an incredibly emotional occasion. It's hard to think of anyone held in the same affection as Willie Horne is in Barrow."

Nostalgia, though, isn't what it used to be and Gardner contrasts those glory days with the current state of Barrow trundling along in the lower leagues, 15 years out of the top flight and counting.

"In 1917 there were 33,000 working in the shipyards," he says. "At the height of the Trident programme in the late '80s there were 10,000 and now it's about 2,000. The heart has been ripped out of the town and that has been mirrored in the decline of the team.

"Willie's era was like a different age. I remember a tale he told me about the first time that he was picked to play for England. A journalist telephoned the ground with the news and Willie was summoned from training to answer the call. It was the first time he had ever used a 'phone.

"Everyone knew Barrow in the 1940s and '50s for its shipbuilding and rugby team. From the age of three Willie would play rugby in the street until sometimes 10 o'clock at night and then practise for hundreds of hours on the playing field at his passing and kicking. Nowadays kids train one hour a week and spend the rest of their free time on their computers. Sportsmen may be bigger, faster and stronger than ever before but they are not as skilful.

"Willie was the kindest, most gentle person I ever met and the reverence with which he was held in Barrow extended far beyond him being a very good player."

Since Horne retired, Barrow have gradually slipped from the limelight, though their

14

Lancashire Cup success of 1983 is still remembered with great affection in the town. So, too, are players of recent generations like Eddie Szymala, David Cairns, Ian Ball and Steve Tickle, just as were Charlie Carr, Jim Lewthwaite, Frank Castle.

The 1938 Challenge Cup Final ball

Floodlights were switched on at Craven Park in November 1966, the £7,000 cost funded by a supporters' group. Barrow returned to Wembley in 1967 but lost, to Featherstone, for the fourth time in five visits and have not returned. In 1970 they attracted 11,500 for a cup-tie against Castleford - their highest gate since 1957 and the last time a Barrow home gate has been over 10,000.

After the re-organisation of the leagues in 1973 Barrow became an archetypal "yo-yo" club between the two divisions, with some memorable promotion campaigns often followed by relegation. In 1989/90 they won only one game in the first division, were relegated and have not played in the top flight since.

The local council granted a £60,000 seven-year loan in 1986 that effectively saved the club from extinction and three years later plans to sell Craven Park to developers and move in with Barrow AFC at Holker Street were abandoned after a boardroom split.

In the early 1990s the club's history was marred by poor results, turmoil in the boardroom, top players leaving and attendances for home games often falling below the 1,000 mark. Since then the situation has stabilised and Barrow has survived, earning a notable landmark when they staged one of the games in the 2000 World Cup.

In the years of the Cold War, the Russian generals in the Kremlin would doubtless have a map of the UK on their walls with the town of Barrow firmly circled for its military significance. It was ironic, therefore, that Russia played Fiji in the first ever international at the ground - a crowd of 2,187 seeing the Fijians win, 38-12.

Nowadays Barrow, briefly re-titled the Braves and then the Border Raiders after their "merger" with Carlisle, are simply the Raiders. Their team largely comprises local talent and the game of Rugby League still figures prominently in the town's sporting scene. Keith Nutter's excellent history of the club, published as part of the Tempus series, puts into perspective the importance of the club to the town.

Old men may occupy the newspaper microfilms in the splendidly appointed local

library, reliving their youth and the great deeds of Horne and Co or the years (until 1972) when Barrow boasted a Football League team. But the present board is determined not to live in the past and plan for the future, though it is hard to imagine Barrow ever regaining the standards they reached in the immediate post-war years.

The heart of the greatest game of all still beats soundly in Barrow and, with a statue of Horne *(left)* unveiled in May 2004 after sponsorship from the North-West Development Agency and Barrow Borough Council, its glorious past is unlikely to be forgotten either. Of three possible sites identified for the statue the chosen one was on Duke Street overlooking Craven Park - a fitting place for the ultimate local hero.

BATLEY

"Mount Pleasant is a rare example of a Yorkshireman with a sense of humour," is the way that New Zealand legend Kevin Tamati, then coach of Lancashire Lynx, famously used to describe a ground once renowned as one of the bleakest places in the kingdom.

But were Tamati to return these days he would find the place transformed. It all began in the summer of 1989 when the Heritage Stand was constructed after Mount Pleasant's main stand had been condemned.

Partly financed through a public appeal and a daily draw, the project came to fruition because of the bravery of then Batley chairman Stephen Ball who put up his house as security in order to obtain bank loans needed to finish the project.

Officially opened on 11 September 1990 by John Etty, a distinguished former player, when Batley marked the occasion with a 40-0 victory over Carcassonne, the stand was the first project in the regeneration of the ground.

So named because special plaques are mounted on the walls in memory of former supporters, the Heritage Stand is 33 metres long and of a propped cantilever design and contains 685 seats.

The current Batley chairman, Kevin Nicholas, took over with a new board in November 1997 and takes up a story that demonstrates his driving force and intuition. "The club was desperately short of money and there were so many things that needed doing," he says. "The new stand had used second-hand seats from Elland Road and underneath was just builder's rubble. The idea had been to have the changing rooms under the stand but the club had just run out of cash.

"On the other side the roof had come off the long stand and it did not fulfil the safety criteria. At the bottom end of the ground, where the grassed hill was located, the local council were not happy about safety aspects. When the ground was originally being built the hill had been constructed out of ash from the mills in Batley. The ash was transported up to the ground by way of horse and carriage. In summer weather you could have mistaken it for the Sydney Cricket Ground but in bad weather it was dangerous. In the top left hand part of the ground was just a void where the old terrace had been and this had been cleared for safety reasons."

By astute use of resources and tapping into all available sources of finance, Nicholas and his fellow directors set about the job of changing the face of Mount Pleasant. "Around 1995 they had the City Challenge in Batley and a lot of government money came into the town," he says. "That set me thinking about schemes that we could use. The government then brought in a sports ground initiative and I made enquiries of Stephen Ball, who thought there was still something left in the pot. We got £70,000 to fill in the void at the top of the ground and built a terrace. The total cost was £90,000, the balance made up of directors' loans. I knew the builder who did the work - he had a small building firm and his overheads were small.

16

"When we completed that, out of the blue I heard about another scheme that had some surplus money for rugby and cricket grounds. If we could get any project to them within one month we would get up to a maximum of £250,000. We got the plans together and eventually received £180,000 to do the bottom terrace. Initially the plan was to drill in to the bank which was all ash. But then I realised you could get money for ash and a contractor cleared the site for nothing and paid us £10,000 for the ash. The rest of the money came from directors' loans and I thought that was that, because the grant scheme then finished.

"But then the wooden seats in the Heritage Stand were past their sell-by date. We got supporters to sponsor new seats at £20 per seat and raised £12,000 through fund raising. The builder did us a favour and cleared out under the stand and got a shell of a building up. One of our directors is a plasterer and he constructed the bar and kitchen under that stand. We got a brewery loan for £20,000 to kit out the bar and kitchen which is being repaid off barrelage. The director's wife runs the kitchen and for the first time we then had our own catering outlet and bar because the Taverners' Club at the entrance to the ground (formerly the Batley Miners' Welfare) is not under our control."

Nicholas then met with Kirklees education department. "They had opened study centres at Huddersfield, Leeds United and Headingley and there was still money in the kitty," he says. "They agreed to come on board to use the boardroom in the top stand. We got funding for three years initially but then, with some help from the junior education secretary they got permission to build a much bigger classroom costing £100,000. This was in the top stand and included some extra hospitality boxes with one side looking out onto the field with a viewing gallery. On match days we use this as a vice-presidents lounge and bar.

"A new government initiative was concerned with safer sports grounds and we got £200,000 towards the project on the long stand.

As the scheme came to an end we heard that some clubs had not been taking up the money so we approached them again and got some more funding for the bottom end which was all rubble and rough ground. We managed to tarmac the bottom end and build a grassed play area which we are hoping to change into a training area in the future. Then we also were able to smarten up behind the Heritage Stand and in front of the turnstile approach. They were both £50,000 projects and we had to find £10,000 towards each. No one else was taking them up because they were put off by having to find money but we wanted to improve the ground as much as we could, so we found the extra. Ultimately, we want to stage things like pop concerts and boxing matches at Mount Pleasant."

Nicholas looks back with justifiable pride at the achievements of his board and thinks that they were fortunate that there were so many government schemes around at the time. "From what I can gather there are no new initiatives in the pipeline and so the club is now totally reliant on local authority help," he says. "The directors have shown a tremendous amount of commitment and foresight. The money could have gone into the playing side of things but we have always preferred to look long term. It has been frustrating to miss out on players at times, as we want the best team in the league as much as anyone. But if you look around the ground now we feel it has been worthwhile.

"The only problem is that the people of Batley probably don't appreciate what they have got. Our core supporters are absolutely fantastic and have a great passion for Rugby League and away supporters who come to the ground are always very complimentary about the changes they have seen since their last visit. But our gates are still disappointing. In the next few years it looks as though we will only be able to do small things to the ground, but we aim to finish the long stand and raise money for a new club shop and electronic scoreboard. Mount Pleasant is now an ideal ground and the spectators are very close to the pitch which creates a very intimate atmosphere. We hope in future that we will be staging representative games here.

"Our directors work very hard on the maintenance of the ground and we have two back-room staff that work all day on the ground, painting and repairing. A lick of paint goes a long way to maintaining what we have got. There is a huge community aspect to rugby in Batley and we have got a ground of which we can all be proud."

John Etty, who now lives on the Fylde Coast, looks back with affection at his time with his hometown club when Mount Pleasant was a far different place to the ground it is today. He played 345 games for Batley, between 1944 and 1955, and scored 97 tries. "I played my first game there as a 16-year-old in a schools tournament," he says.

"The slope was daunting and a lot of players considered Batley to be a poor ground because of that, but the current directors have made a great job on the ground and it is a vastly-changed place these days.

"We had to change in the old pavilion that was also used by the cricketers and it was very primitive and cramped. We had to walk across the cricket field to the pitch. A lot of players found running up the slope difficult but, once you got used to that, it was much better, though it was still easy to lose your balance.

"When I started it was still wartime and we had to train in the black-out. We would run around the cricket field and had to be careful not to run into the roller. I preferred playing up-hill to down as I always kept my balance easier. Bill Riches was my centre and we formed a good combination. In those days there was one league and we played all the Yorkshire clubs and relied on clubs like Leeds and Bradford bringing supporters. We had 17,000 on once for a game against Leeds, which is vastly different to the crowds they get today.

"But we had a weak team in the '50s and some supporters went to watch other teams or even to watch Leeds United. I got a bit dispirited at times because as a winger I did not see much of the ball. I was transferred to Oldham completely out of the blue, and in my second season there scored 43 tries. That was the difference - I was suddenly playing with better players.

"But they were happy times at Batley and I certainly developed as a defensive player because I had plenty practice at that. A lot of our supporters were marvellous and stuck by the club through thick and thin and in all weathers. I remember the terrible winter of 1947 when there was very heavy snow. Some supporters stayed up all night lighting braziers to thaw out the pitch so that we could play. They put a tremendous amount of effort into the club and there was a real community spirit."

One of the highlights of Etty's time at Batley was a tour game against New Zealand in 1947. "We won, 19-18 and that was a huge thrill," he recalls. "Eric Hesketh had a great game at stand-off for us that day but he was sold to St Helens, Riches went to Hull, Bill Hudson to Wigan and me to Oldham, Sadly, we became a feeder club to the bigger clubs.

"I remember another game that sticks out was in 1946 when Jim Sullivan played what proved to be the final game of his career at Mount Pleasant. We beat Wigan that day, 13-2. Another all-time great, Gus Risman who had come with us to finish his career played his final game at Mount Pleasant against Dewsbury in 1954.

"The derby games against Dewsbury were always special ones. They were always hard-fought and I remember they had lots of scrums because of the rules at that time. Most of the games were very tight and very well supported. Although there was a keen rivalry between the two clubs they always seem to be played in a good sporting manner. I remember after one game we all went to hospital to visit a Dewsbury player that had been injured playing against us.

"Another game that I remember was playing for Yorkshire against the 1948 Australians when we beat them. Early in the game I went past one of their players and he then whispered in my ear that if I did that again he would rearrange my teeth. That was the first time I had really encountered gamesmanship. He tried to frighten me but it didn't work. By then I was quite experienced and had played around 100 games so I couldn't care less.

"Mount Pleasant's glory days were at the turn of the twentieth century when Batley won the cup three times between 1897 and 1901. I remember a reunion in 1946 at the Batley ground when the mayor, Alderman Wilf Auty, a former player, came with some of the survivors from those days. As a little boy I remember meeting Jim Gath, a forward who played in the first cup final and he was an inspiration to me. It's amazing to think that I knew players that had played in those pioneering days."

One of Etty's lingering frustrations was that many of the Batley teams in which he played never utilised the slope effectively. "Most of the coaches we had discouraged kicking and that was a mistake," he says.

"I remember the Yorkshire Cup semi-final against Castleford in 1950 which ended in a 2-2 draw. That day we stuck to the ball whereas if we had used an attacking game and kicked a lot more I am sure we would have won. That annoyed me for a long time afterwards, that we stuck the ball up our jumpers, as anyone who kicked the ball was frowned upon."

Rugby was first played at Mount Pleasant in 1880 after the formation of the Batley Cricket, Athletic and Football Club. Batley Cricket Club, formed in 1863, took the lease of eleven acres of bleak and exposed land at Mount Pleasant, just off Purlwell Hall Road about one mile from the town centre and moved from their previous ground known as "Billy Wood's Croft" near the ruins of Howley Hall, where the famous WG Grace had once played.

A local rugby club, Batley Athletic, joined the cricketers, much to the chagrin of the town's other rugby team, the Mountaineers. The first rugby game was played on 2 October 1880 when Bradford Zingari were defeated, the Batley captain Jake Parker having the distinction of scoring the first try. At that stage the club's headquarters and dressing rooms were at the Royal Hotel on Bradford Road, described as being eight minutes walk from the ground, later moving to the George Hotel.

Both cricket and rugby grounds have an appreciable slope, from west to east, with the rugby field being sited to the east of the cricket ground. The only first-class cricket game to be staged at Mount Pleasant was in September 1883 when RG Barlow's XI defeated T Emmett's XI by 202 runs.

The rugby field initially had just one small covered stand, on the site of the present day Heritage Stand, when Batley lifted the Yorkshire Cup in 1885 and when, in 1887, Yorkshire played Surrey in a county game at the ground. Two Batley players, Tom Elliker and Herbert "Dodge" Simms were in the Yorkshire ranks that day.

In December 1888 Batley hosted a team from overseas for the first time when the touring Maoris earned a draw with a late score. In the early 1890s a huge open grandstand, formerly used for the Yorkshire Agricultural Show at Dewsbury, was constructed down the popular side. The ground improvements came just in time to host the golden era of Batley, one of the Northern Union's founder members, as they won those three Challenge Cup

Finals in the space of five seasons. Despite such success the ground was in danger of being used for building land until Alderman JW Blackburn, the club's first president, and Mr Oldroyd MP purchased the land and then sold it to the club for £2,300.

Mount Pleasant attracted a crowd of 18,000 (£666) for a third round cup-tie against Bradford in 1902 when every available space was taken up. The players entered the field by way of a ladder at the rear of the stand over the heads of spectators.

Two years later the ground was suspended for one month after referee JH Smith, one of the foremost officials in the early days of the Northern Union, was hit by a missile thrown from the crowd. Batley played "home" games at Bradford Park Avenue and Wakefield.

In 1909 Batley defeated the first Kangaroos, 12-5, and repeated that success three years later with a 13-5 victory.

A barrel-roofed stand was built on the south side at a cost of £700 in 1913. This stand survived until the Safety of Sports Ground Act came into being following the Bradford City fire in the mid-1980s and in 1929 half of the terraces on the popular side were covered after assistance from the supporters club.

The 1920s was a successful decade for Batley, who won the championship in 1924 after defeating Wigan in the final at Broughton. They did so without their star forward and captain, Frank Gallagher, who was away with the tour party, but Wigan lacked five players for the same reason.

In 1925 a new ground record was established when 23,989 (£1,693) saw the third round Challenge Cup-tie with Leeds. The following year Batley continued their fine record against touring teams, defeating New Zealand, 19-17.

A television documentary in the late 1960s highlighted the derelict, weed-strewn ground that Mount Pleasant had become and it was not until 1969 that new dressing rooms were opened under the main stand, saving the players from having to change in the cricket pavilion which had become dilapidated.

Hunslet ground-shared Mount Pleasant for two years from 1980 after losing their tenancy at the Elland Road Greyhound Stadium and Batley had the strange experience of occupying the away dressing room for Hunslet's "home" game. Batley lost their "home" game but won "away" later in the season.

In the same campaign a crowd of 3,200 saw Batley defeat Rugby League new boys Fulham, 10-8, in the club's official centenary match. Bradford Park Avenue FC also ground-shared Mount Pleasant for three seasons between 1993-96, before they re-located to Horsfall Stadium.

They may be the Bulldogs these days but for most people involved in Rugby League Batley will always be the Gallant Youths. They have a rich heritage at Mount Pleasant and there are enough people around with the spirit of the club at heart to ensure that the greatest game of all will continue to be played there long into the future. A trip to Mount Pleasant highlights just what community pride, intuition, dedication and foresight can achieve.

BLACKPOOL

Brash, breezy and entertaining - the seaside resort of Blackpool could have been made for Rugby League.

The town's link with the sport goes back to the early days of the Northern Union and Blackpool again boasted a professional club following the formation of the Panthers, playing at Blackpool FC's Bloomfield Road stadium, in 2005. "The Boys are back in Town," belted out the public address system as Paul Gamble made the ceremonial kick-off at the friendly against St Helens on Sunday 6 February 2005.

Gamble made 340 appearances for the old Blackpool Borough club - a record - and still lives in the town. "I never thought I'd see the day when professional Rugby League came back," he said later. "It has been a fantastic occasion and hopefully will be the start of something special. When I played for Borough it was a real family club and a huge part of my life. Even when we were losing it was still enjoyable to play for the team because we had a good team spirit and a good friendly atmosphere."

Gamble last played at Bloomfield Road in Borough's last season in 1986/87, after they were forced to leave Borough Park due to ground safety regulations.

"The stadium is vastly different today and looks a real picture," he said. "It has always had a really good playing surface but the new stands are terrific and it will be a lovely ground when it's completed. They've improved the ground tremendously.

"There is a base of interest in the town. The supporters' club kept going and there are two open-age teams, the Scorpions and Stanley and the Sea Eagles who play in the summer conference, so there is a foundation there."

The then St Helens coach, Ian Millward, was also impressed. "The first thought that comes to my mind is that it is fresh," he said. "It is a great stadium and I am very envious of it. The area has a certain vibrancy about it and hopefully Blackpool will fulfil their ambitions."

Though Panthers defeated a youthful Saints side, 20-16, before a crowd of 852, they experienced a season of struggle on and off the field, raising doubts about their long-term future. Their first senior game back in the resort ended in a 24-34 defeat to Swinton Lions in a Northern Rail Cup-tie before a crowd of 512 on Friday, 18 February 2005 and many of their subsequent home crowds were around the 350-mark in their first season.

Panthers also had to play three "home" games at Preston Grasshoppers RUFC (a venue previously used for Rugby League by Lancashire Lynx) when Bloomfield Road was unavailable. The staging of the Northern Rail Cup Final at Bloomfield Road on Sunday 17 July 2005, however, was a huge success. A capacity crowd of 9,400 saw Hull KR prevail against Castleford, 18-16, after a thrilling game and the ground, re-developed on two sides, was well received, raising hopes that more big games would be staged there in the future.

An early effort to establish the game by the seaside ended ignominiously late in the nineteenth century, when Blackpool folded after one season in the Lancashire Second Competition in 1898/99. Playing initially at Raikes Hall Gardens, an entertainment complex that included a theatre and boating lake, Blackpool were rooted to the bottom of the table, suffering some heavy defeats and eventually losing every league game. Disappointing attendances caused the directors of Raikes Hall to withdraw their support, forcing Blackpool to finish the season playing at the athletics track in Whitegate Lane, before closing with debts of around £120.

In the early 1920s the town's Bloomfield Road soccer ground staged some charity RL games in aid of the Shipwrecked Mariners Society. Blackpool's first application to join the Rugby League came in 1950 when the Town Council approved in principle a 50-acre site on the old Stanley Park airport to include a Rugby League ground and speedway track. The prime mover behind the scheme was Councillor JH Shoesmith, who became the first chairman of the future Blackpool Borough, but the proposed stadium never materialised.

Blackpool Borough in action under the shadow of the famous tower in the 1970s

Blackpool Council promoted a summer knock-out competition for professional teams at The Oval, Stanley Park over a fortnight in June 1952 and interest was such that a Supporters' Club was formed in 1953, starting with 70 members, even though there was no team to support. After raising an initial share capital of £5,900, Borough's application to join the RFL was accepted in time for the 1954/55 season. For many years, until the formation of Fulham in 1980, Borough were the "Babes" of RL.

Borough's first home was at the South Shore Greyhound Stadium on St Annes Road. The stadium was long established: greyhound racing was first held in July 1927 and speedway was briefly staged at the venue in the following two years before petering out.

The stadium was home to Borough from 1954 to 1963 after passing an inspection from the authorities concerned that, due to the position of the inside hare rail, the pitch was little more than the minimum width allowed for Rugby League. Subsequently, players frequently complained over safety issues due to this anomaly.

After frenzied activity over the summer months of 1954, including the preparation of the pitch, dressing rooms and the building of a team, under the direction of Chris Brockbank, the former Warrington manager, Borough made their bow with a 3-40 defeat at Salford.

Other RL clubs readily welcomed Borough into the fold, allowing players to join the new club on free transfers or for small fees.

Borough's first home game was a midweek encounter against Batley, staged on Tuesday 17 August 1954 when the visitors ran out 10-7 winners before a crowd of 3,000.

The following Saturday, the visit of St Helens attracted a gate of 8,000 (a figure not to be surpassed at the ground) with Borough going down to a 2-34 defeat.

Borough had to wait until late November of that year before their first win, defeating Hull KR, 19-3, at home, and they went on to record seven victories in their inaugural season.

A real red-letter day for the fledging club came when they were invited to host the New Zealanders in the first match of their tour in 1955/56. The interest in the game was such that it was quickly realised the tiny St Annes Road Stadium was too small and the venue was switched to the town's soccer ground, at Bloomfield Road. A crowd of 12,015 saw a thrilling 24-24 draw with Borough's Aboriginal winger Wally McArthur the star with a try and six goals.

Bloomfield Road was also called upon after Borough reached the quarter-finals of the Challenge Cup in March 1957. Despite atrocious weather a crowd of 20,946 (reported elsewhere as 22,000) - the highest ever to watch a Borough home game - saw Leigh run out 24-13 victors.

By the late 1950s, though, gates for home matches began to fall to disappointing levels and several of the best players were sold, including Peter Fearis, Lionel Emmitt, Jackie Brennan and McArthur, to help make ends meet.

Borough survived, relying mostly on the financial support of club directors, and re-built their side that now included an up and coming scrum-half, Tommy Bishop, RL legend Brian Bevan (who saw out his playing days at the seaside) and a former American gridiron player, Chuck Wiseman.

Borough's future was threatened when the South Shore Greyhound Stadium site was sold for housing and the club was given until the end of the 1962/63 season to find a new home. The last greyhound meeting was held there on 30 October 1964 before the site was developed. A road named Stadium Avenue is the only remaining link. The ground went largely unlamented by RL fans as viewing was far from ideal and spectators were not allowed to stand behind the posts.

Notice to quit their home could have sounded a death knell to Borough but for the determination of the directors, led by chairman Gordon Emery, to find a new home.

After careful consideration, a decision was taken to develop a derelict site, previously home to the town's gas works, bordered by Rigby Street and Princess Street and close to the centre of town. The site, leased from the Corporation to a local coach firm, was empty during the winter and used as a coach park during the summer months. When approached, the coach firm agreed to release half of the site, from the Rigby Road side, to Borough and a 21-year lease was agreed with the Corporation.

The club president, Sir Frederick Emery, loaned the club £50,000, and outline planning permission was finally granted after several delays. The project was a hugely ambitious one and the total estimated cost was £67,000 - the balance being made up by a loan from the RL, an increase in the share capital and other fund-raising ventures.

Developing the site proved to be far from straightforward, and plans to build the main stand on the south side were abandoned when surveyors discovered a large gas main. The concrete foundations of the old gasworks had to be dynamited out and an old tar pit cleared.

Terracing was built from 40,000 tons of hardcore from the site of the Palace Theatre, which was demolished at this time to make way for a department store. The ground was finally built at a cost of £40,000 above the original estimate.

Borough Park was described as "the last word in new stadia" by one national journalist when it opened on 31 August 1963.

Borough marked the occasion in style, with a 36-16 victory over Salford before a crowd of 5,000.

Chief interest lay in the concrete, cantilevered main stand, seating 1,200, which gave a tremendous panoramic view over the playing area. The paddock for 1,000 was protected by the overhanging pitched roof, but the rest of the ground was made up of shallow, uncovered terracing with a greyhound track between the spectators and the pitch.

Later that season, Borough's 4-25 defeat to Castleford, in a third-round Challenge Cup-tie on 14 March 1964, attracted a record crowd of 7,614, despite heavy rain and the game being televised by the BBC.

The fact that the ground construction costs had vastly exceeded expectations, largely financed by loans, weighed heavily on the club and, to general consternation, Bishop was sold to Barrow.

Many supporters vowed never to set foot inside Borough Park again after a move that set a precedent for other promising players being moved on to earn transfer fees.

In their second season at their new ground, Borough finished bottom of the RL and they continued to struggle despite recruiting several well-known players at the end of their playing careers such as Ray Ashby, Billy Boston, John Stopford and Dave Bolton.

But many felt that the club did little to help itself, making no apparent effort at promotion in the town, while the loyal supporters that turned up were treated, week after week, to depressing articles in the programme over the club's battle for survival.

The club's fortunes briefly revived in dramatic fashion in 1976 when Jim Crellin was recruited as the latest in a long line of coaches. Crellin's astute work in the transfer market, that included the key signings of hooker "Smiler" Allen and scrum-half Jackie Newall, built a strong side and Borough earned a famous run through the Player's No.6 Trophy rounds, on their way to the club's first ever appearance in a final.

Borough's 15-5 semi-final victory over first division Leigh, played at Borough Park in front of 2,500 and a national audience on BBC Grandstand, on a day of unremitting rain and fog, has become part of Borough folklore. The club gave a fine account of itself in the final, against Castleford at Salford, before losing 25-15.

Sadly, though, the momentum was not maintained and financial problems again reared their head. Players were sold and Crellin resigned as the team ended the season second-bottom of the second division.

For long-suffering Borough fans, however, there was another glorious, if brief, era on the way as Borough, under the direction of manager Albert Fearnley and player-coach Bak Diabira, enjoyed a promotion season in 1978/79. The campaign had begun auspiciously for Borough, when they hosted the Australians for the first time in the opening game of their tour. Despite going down, 1-39, before a crowd of 2,700, Borough's battling performance was said to have done the town proud.

The events of that momentous season (for Borough fans at least) have been recorded for posterity in outstanding fashion - Dave Hadfield was then a burgeoning reporter and he "wrote the team to promotion" as set out in one of the chapters (entitled 'A Tangerine Machine') to his book, 'XIII Winters'.

Sadly, though, Borough were immediately relegated, though they enjoyed their brief flirtation with the top flight, winning five games, and average gates rose to 1,576 - the highest for many seasons.

In April 1982 Borough were put into liquidation, but a new company, Savoy Sports and Leisure Limited, bought the club and the RFL accepted it into membership.

The biggest blow, though, came after the tragic Valley Parade fire of May 1985 when a local registration scheme for all sports grounds came into operation and stringent new safety measures were introduced. For a club forced to operate on a hand-to-mouth existence virtually since its formation, that was the final straw.

Lancashire County Council ordered £65,000 of work for Borough Park - front staircases identified as being the main requirement - and reduced the stand capacity to 100 and that of the ground to 200 - with an ultimatum to complete the work by 1 February 1987. Many felt the Council decision was a huge over-reaction, especially as the stand was made of concrete and of relatively recent construction, but it must be viewed in the context of the times.

With no grant aid forthcoming, Borough's days at the ground were over. Their final first-team game at Borough Park was on 4 January 1987 when they lost 5-8 to Whitehaven before a crowd of 386, though the second team continued to play at the ground for a considerable time afterwards. Borough Park also hosted greyhound racing, local amateur RL, gridiron and was also a brief home to Blackpool (Wren Rovers) AFC and was only recently demolished. A cinema complex and a chain public house now occupy the site.

Borough staged their final seven remaining home games at Bloomfield Road, attracting a best crowd of 823 for the visit of Wakefield Trinity in the Challenge Cup, before the news came out that a consortium had taken over the club and intended moving out of Blackpool.

At their meeting on 15 May 1987, the RL Council gave the club permission to relocate to Wigan - the worst decision, many felt, and not just with the benefit of hindsight, they ever made. Wigan is a true RL town, but Wiganers watch Wigan and the newcomers got a frosty and largely disinterested reception.

And so, for season 1987/88, Springfield Borough was born, playing at the Springfield Park home of Wigan Athletic AFC.

Originally built as part of a huge sporting complex that incorporated an athletics, cycling and trotting track, the ground had briefly been home to Wigan in 1901/02 between them leaving their Prescott Street ground, off Frog Lane and taking up residence at Central Park.

Billy Boston performed the celebrity kick-off before the opening game, against Barrow on a Friday 4 September 1987. The crowd that evening, 2,431, was bettered only twice during the season (with the highest 3,894 for Leeds' visit in the John Player Trophy).

The following January, with the pitch apparently suffering from over-use, the club was given six months notice to quit by their soccer landlords, resulting attendances never going above 550 in the last eight home games. Borough's final game at Springfield Park saw them defeat Sheffield Eagles, 11-10, in a Premiership tie on 24 April 1988, before a crowd of 530.

For the 1988/89 season the club was renamed Chorley Borough and played at Victory Park, Chorley - a well-appointed venue that had been home to the Magpies, then a Conference outfit, since 1920. A gate of 1,030 was recorded for Workington Town's visit in the opening home game and surpassed only once, when the Boxing Day visit of Leigh attracted 1,506. Gates fell to as low as 188 for the game against Mansfield.

A further boardroom spilt occurred during the season over a decision to relocate to

Altrincham for the following season. Five directors resigned and formed a new Chorley club, whose turbulent, if brief, history is a story of its own.

Another season, another name change: in 1989/90, re-branded as Trafford Borough, the club began a ground-sharing arrangement at the Moss Lane ground of Conference side Altrincham AFC, playing their first home game against Swinton on 6 September 1989 when the crowd was 1,089. Moss Lane, whose main feature was a cavernous main stand, was another well appointed ground and the Robins at that stage had realistic hopes of earning a Football League place.

The club played at Moss Lane for three seasons, often playing before hugely disappointing crowds. Halifax's visit in their second season at Moss Lane attracted 2,284 but gates slumped to as low as 138 for the Scarborough game in the third, when the club recorded just two league wins.

Borough staged their final three "home" games at Huddersfield, their final game at Moss Lane in March 1992 being against Keighley when 456 saw the home side go down to a 7-30 defeat.

There was to be another sting to the tale. After leaving Moss Lane behind, they moved back to Blackpool under a new title of Blackpool Gladiators. Their new home at the seaside was as a ground-share with non-league soccer club Blackpool Mechanics AFC, in Common Edge Road.

Bloomfield Road

The ground had undergone dramatic changes in recent seasons with the construction of three areas of covered standing and terracing added but was still considered rudimentary compared to the standards of other RL grounds of the day, and the Chorley and Altrincham grounds they had left behind.

The seats for the main stand came from the old Derby Baths in the town centre, where they were used in the spectators' gallery. The ground was later re-named Jepson Way in honour of the soccer club's late founder member and secretary, Walter Jepson.

Gladiators attracted 736 for their first game back in the town, for a Lancashire Cup-tie against Workington, but bettered that only once, when the visit of well-supported Keighley the following March drew 1,214.

With only four wins all season, the Gladiators faced an uphill struggle and their problems intensified when a special meeting of clubs on 10 March 1993 voted by 28-6 to scrap the three-division system, introduce two divisions of 16 clubs and demote the bottom three clubs. Alongside Chorley Borough and Nottingham City, Blackpool's league status was lost. Their final home game saw an ignominious 5-90 defeat against Dewsbury before 486 spectators, their final senior game a 0-56 defeat at Dewsbury in the return.

Professional RL was thus lost to the seaside town, though the Blackpool club struggled on for a few seasons, playing in the National Conference from 1993/95 and then in the Alliance competition until folding at the end of 1997. Their final game against a senior club was a Regal Trophy tie at the McAlpine Stadium in November 1994 when Huddersfield ran in the incredible tally of 26 tries in a 142-4 victory.

There was plenty to be proud of in-between, and some great and lasting memories, but inglorious failure is where this seaside tale started and ended - until Blackpool Panthers bravely set about writing a new chapter.

BRADFORD

Christmas 2002 came early for Trevor Foster MBE with news of his beloved Bradford Bulls' return to Odsal in time for the 2003 Super League season after two years in the wilderness at Valley Parade.

"Wonderful news, absolutely wonderful," said Trevor, unable to hide his enthusiasm and relief. "We are going back home."

Home was exactly what Odsal was to Trevor ever since he came north from Newport in 1938 to sign for Bradford Northern. He went on to make over 400 appearances for the club and earned a reputation throughout the game as one of the best and fairest forwards of all time. When his playing days were over he served his adopted club in virtually every role: as coach, director, chairman of the floodlight fund and president of the supporters' club and remained the club's timekeeper and a life member until his death in April 2005 at the age of 90.

Trevor first set eyes on Odsal as war clouds loomed. It was just four years after Northern had left their old ramshackle ground at Birch Lane, having signed a ten-year lease at what was the largest ground in England outside Wembley.

Odsal was a former quarry used for waste disposal and, before the ground officially opened, Mr Ernest Call, Bradford's Director of Cleansing, supervised the controlled tipping of household waste. An estimated 140,000 cart-loads of material formed the bankings and the capacity of the ground was thought to be in the region of 150,000.

Bradford took control of the ground in January 1934 and nine months later a crowd of 20,000 (producing receipts of £803) saw the opening game when Huddersfield's Australian winger Ray Markham scored four tries in his side's 31-16 victory.

The Northern club was now responsible for the boundary fencing, dressing rooms and seated accommodation.

The clubhouse and dressing rooms were opened in February 1935 and, for 50 years, the players and match officials had to descend the steeped terraces through the spectators to reach the pitch below. Many a tale has gone down in folklore of harassed referees and opposing players running the gauntlet of spectators before they reached the sanctuary of the dressing rooms after a game.

The banking at the Rooley Avenue end was not formed until mid-1936 and most of the terracing, constructed with the aid of railway sleepers, was added later. There were continual problems with the state of the playing area, while a grandstand erected on the south-west terrace was poorly designed and hindered the view for thousands of spectators at either side of the ends, or those positioned higher up on the bankings.

Trevor remembered seeing Odsal for the first time. "I was immediately struck by what a huge complex Odsal was," he recalled. "The ground still needed an awful lot of work doing to it but I loved the open space and feeling of being able to move around at your

RIGHT: The late, great Trevor Foster MBE carries out his timekeeping duties at Odsal Stadium

leisure. There were no social rooms to any extent but the potential was obvious that it could be an outstanding football ground. That potential came to fruition after the war when we had huge crowds. 30-40,000 crowds were commonplace right up to the 80,000 we had for the 1960 Championship Final and then of course there was that amazing evening when the Challenge Cup final replay between Warrington and Halifax saw a crowd of 102,000."

That occasion, on 5 May 1954, has gone down in Rugby League history with an official crowd of 102,569 (£18,623) as Warrington lifted the cup with an 8-4 victory. An estimated crowd of 120,000 actually witnessed the match and the incredible scenes are wonderfully captured for posterity in Robert Gate's book, suitably entitled: "There Were A Lot More Than That."

Trevor soon settled into his new environment, took up digs with two old spinster ladies, the cousins of the Bradford chairman Harry Hornby, and stayed there for ten years. "It was very homely and I was treated like I was one of the family," he said. "The supporters went out of their way to wish me well. The warmth of the Bradford people was wonderful and it was just like being at home in Wales."

Trevor soon adapted to the new game, quickly learning the new techniques. His game prospered with the extra space of League, played with six forwards instead of eight in rugby union. "I was so keen that I worked on the ground for about twelve years and Odsal was soon in my blood," he said. "I used to help in the office, work on the ground, mow the grass, mark out the pitch, tidy the dressing rooms and wash and iron all the playing strips. I was very happy just being near football all the time.

"All the players were proud to play there and we had a very close-knit team.

29

Everyone knew that Odsal was going to be home to us for a long time and that the future was bright. It was a wonderful feeling on match-day, looking out of the dressing rooms and seeing the crowds coming to the ground in their thousands. There was that incredible walk down the steps to the pitch with spectators wishing you well on the way down and either congratulating or commiserating on the way back up. At half-time the players just sat on the touch-line for the team talk.

"You would see the same people at every home game and build an affinity and a relationship with the supporters. The players felt part and parcel of their lives. There was a bar on top of the dressing rooms (now called the Trevor Foster lounge) and the spectators loved to be with you and to talk about rugby."

Apart from a break for war service in the Middle East, Trevor gave unstinting devotion to Bradford's cause and remembered the late 'forties as a golden era. "It was wonderful to play with world-class players like Ernest Ward, who was a great captain, Eric Batten and the great Willie Davies," he said. "Willie was an icon and watching him was like seeing poetry in motion. He was a magnificent player and a great friend. He had the incredible ability to run very fast with the ball in his hands – Willie was a master, and not many players can do that."

Odsal was now an established ground and able to accommodate with ease the huge crowds that flocked to see Rugby League after the desolation of the war years. "The team was headed by a wonderful former Welsh player, Dai Rees, and, with Mr Hornby, he created a wonderful family atmosphere around the club," Trevor said. "He was a great tactician and in many ways a man ahead of his time."

With three successive Wembley trips and a string of Yorkshire Cup successes the good times came to the Bradford club and Odsal was regularly chosen for representative football. But a reminder that the ground, situated in a deep channel thought to have been gouged out during the fourth Ice Age ten thousand years ago, had its own micro climate

came in December 1948. The third Test against Australia was postponed with fog at ground level while the rest of the stadium, 100 feet above was bathed in sunshine.

Bradford also pioneered floodlit football in the north and staged a tour game under the new lights against the 1951 Kiwis that attracted a crowd of 29,072. "That was a fascinating experience and I really enjoyed it," Trevor said. "We went down to the pitch in the darkness and then the lights came on. It felt like being in another world.

"By then there were stands on either side but none at either end," Trevor added. "It was an accepted fact that if it rained you got wet. People used to stand on the terraces in huge numbers often despite atrocious conditions."

Finally, Trevor took the hard decision to retire as a player and played his final home game against Hunslet in April 1955. The redoubtable Australian forward Arthur Clues was in the opposing team and carried Trevor off the field at the end. "Arthur and me had been great rivals," Trevor recalled. "We became great friends and that moment when I had played my final game was very poignant. It was a hard decision to make but my body had had enough."

Within years of Trevor hanging up his boots, however, the Bradford club was in a steep decline and recorded their lowest ever crowd of 324 when Barrow visited Odsal on 23 November 1963. Just over a fortnight later the club went out of existence after 841 saw Northern lose 5-33 to Leigh in what looked at the time to be Odsal's final game.

But Trevor Foster was determined to re-build a new club from the ashes. "It was a terrible affair when the club closed down," he remembered. "A new regime had come into the club but the directors were not getting anywhere and gates went down very badly. That last match against Leigh was just so sad. But quickly I, amongst others, got people together and we started organising weekly meetings of supporters. We built up a strong committee and then called a public meeting at St George's Hall. There were a thousand people there and on the night we collected £1,000. I signed a letter to the RFL asking for the club to be reinstated and off we went again.

"Interest had dropped off and we had a poor team and people had simply got out of the habit of going to games. But I was confident that Bradford was still a rugby town." Happily, a new Bradford club was formed in time to re-commence for the 1964/65 season. A crowd of 13,542 saw the first home game, against York, on 22 August 1964.

The events of 1964 were almost matched in 2000 when Bradford again left Odsal to share Valley Parade while a planning application for redevelopment of the ground was submitted. "That day was very sad, one of the saddest of my life," Trevor said. "After playing there for 17 years and spending the rest of my time since at Odsal, it was my home."

Trevor still retained an enormous enthusiasm and love of Rugby League and was totally behind the switch to summer and the advent of Super League, with the Bradford club emerging as one of the leading lights in the new game.

"In the early 1990s crowds had gone down again and that centenary season they were under 5,000," Trevor said. "But with the start of Super League the club gained a tremendous momentum sparked by the wonderful vision of our chairman, Chris Caisley, and set things in motion to become the premier club in Rugby League football. Odsal was a great place to be on a warm summer night and the youngsters flocked to watch all the exciting events on and off the field. It was tremendous to see so many families coming to the games that wouldn't have come in the depths of winter.

"Odsal is so huge that it takes in all the elements and the cold in winter was so hard to bear at times. But so many people have a great attachment to the place and lots of supporters have had their ashes scattered at the ground."

Odsal has also staged so many other sporting events, notably speedway. Hornby linked with promoter Johnnie Hoskins and 20,000 saw the first meeting on 23 June 1945. In 1946, crowds for speedway at Odsal averaged 31,000. The speedway team collected six nicknames over the years, starting as the Boomerangs, then the Tudors, Panthers, Northern, Barons and Dukes. The final speedway meeting at Odsal was held on 11 October 1997.

Bradford City played a total of 21 Football League fixtures at Odsal while Valley Parade was being rebuilt following the tragic fire in 1985, recording a highest attendance of 13,831 for the visit of Leeds United in September 1986, a game marred by crowd trouble. Odsal has also hosted trotting, professional cricket, wrestling, show jumping and the Harlem Globetrotters, while in September 1956 Trevor Foster played Jesus Christ in a floodlit pageant staged by the Bradford Charity Players entitled "The Life of Christ".

Like so many people who were there Trevor's abiding memory of Odsal remained that 102,000 crowd in 1954. "It was a wonderful atmosphere that night and to see the crowds piling in from every quarter," he said. "The traffic from Lancashire was bumper to bumper and so many people either missed the game completely or were unable to get a proper view of the game. Mr Harry Hornby was the man who made Odsal. He was a great managing director. I remember that night about 10 o'clock, when he came into the social club. He took off his glasses because of the tears in his eyes and announced with great pride the following words: "Gentlemen, I have some great news for you. Tonight's gate is 102,569."

"Next morning the telephone never stopped ringing and all of the world's press wanted to know about Odsal Stadium."

As well as his playing contemporaries, Trevor reserved special praise for the Paul brothers, Robbie and Henry, current coach and former long-serving player Brian Noble and that great Northern stalwart, Keith Mumby: "the best tackler I've ever seen."

"Players have come and gone but Bradford has always been a very happy club with wonderful staff and I feel that we are on the verge of a great new era," he said shortly before his death.

One of Trevor's proudest possessions was a programme for the opening match at Odsal when the Black Dyke Mills Band played selections before kick-off. "The band was invited back for the first game back at Odsal and that was a wonderful day," he said. The return to Odsal on 9 March 2003 attracted a crowd of 20,283 with local pop idol Gareth Gates performing the ceremonial kick-off. The Bulls marked the occasion with a 22-10 victory over Wakefield. Two months later a new structure was opened behind one end with a restaurant housing 400 people and 19 hospitality boxes. Odsal was barely recognisable from the day Trevor Foster first saw the ground but his enthusiasm never wavered in the intervening years and he left an indelible impression on those fortunate enough to know him.

One of the fastest growing cities in Europe during the Victorian era due largely to its association with the wool trade, the original Bradford rugby club was formed in 1863. Their first ground was as a ground-share with the cricket club on Great Horton Road, a venue used for eight first-class Yorkshire CCC games, the last being the 1874 Roses Match.

After complaints about damage done by the rugby players to the turf Bradford moved after two years to a new site at Laisteridge Lane and then across the city to a new ground at North Park Road in the Manningham district. Further grounds on Peel Park, in Girlington

102,569 fans pack Odsal for the 1954 Challenge Cup Final replay between Warrington and Halifax

and at Apperley Bridge were fleetingly used before Bradford rugby acquired a major stage after that string of unsatisfactory venues.

In the late 1870s a new company, the Bradford Cricket, Athletic and Football Club was formed at Park Avenue, within easy reach of the city centre and with a railway line link running alongside the ground. The rugby club merged with the new organisation and staged their first game at Park Avenue on 25 September 1880 against Bradford Rovers. This game was played on part of the cricket field as the rugby enclosure was not fully developed until four years later. They soon built up a strong fixture list and won the Yorkshire Cup in 1884. In the years up to the formation of the Northern Union they were one of the leading clubs, playing on the premier rugby ground in Yorkshire and two of their foremost players, JT Toothill and TH Dobson, won international honours. The ground had two magnificent pavilions; the larger one on the southern side of the cricket ground and a smaller, double-fronted one served the football ground. Park Avenue, which staged its first first-class cricket game in 1880, soon became one of Yorkshire's three main venues, alongside Headingley and Bramall Lane.

After attracting a crowd of 5,000 for their opening game against Wakefield Trinity on 7 September 1895, when the first league games were played following the "split", Bradford went on to achieve considerable success. After being crowned champions of the Yorkshire Senior Competition in successive seasons around the turn of the century they won the Championship in 1903/04 and the Challenge Cup in 1906. One of the early internationals, England against Other Nationalities, was staged at Park Avenue on 2 January 1905 before 5,500 spectators. With two large open stands behind both posts and a covered stand that

33

ran almost the length of the Horton Park Avenue side, the ground could accommodate large crowds. A record was set in 1906 when 28,000 (£761) saw the Challenge Cup-tie against Halifax that ended in a scoreless draw.

But in season 1906/07 crowds began to fall in comparison with the Bradford City soccer club at Valley Parade (formed 1903, after the demise of Manningham RFC). At the end of that season, after a loss of £600 was reported, a decision was taken to form an association club and Bradford (Park Avenue)A FC came into being. They initially played in the Southern League before attaining Football League status in 1908. In the 1960s the club entered a terminal decline and lost its League status after the 1969/70 season after failing in their fourth successive re-election attempt. Their highest attendance at the ground was for a war-time game against Blackpool in 1944 when 34,810 spectators were present but just 2,563 saw their final home league game, against Scunthorpe United. The ground then fell into dereliction and decay and was taken over by Bradford Metropolitan Council in 1990. Though cricket is still played there it has not been a regular venue for Yorkshire for many years and the ground is a pale shadow of its former glories.

A new rugby club, meanwhile, was formed by a breakaway group and they spent the 1906/07 season playing at the six-acre site at Greenfield Athletic Ground in Dudley Hill, adjacent to School Street, off Cutler Heights Lane. They rented the ground for £8 per annum from Whitaker's Brewery. They spent around £500 on levelling the pitch, fencing and building a new stand. The venue, with its pear-shaped running and trotting track around the pitch, was considered far from ideal for rugby. Their opening game was against Huddersfield on 7 September 1907 and attracted a crowd of 4,000 - the visitors winning, 8-5. The "Northern" tag was added three days later to inform the sporting public of the city that Northern Union football was still being played locally. When the first New Zealanders visited that season the crowd was restricted to 2,000 by torrential rain and the pitch was described as a "sea of mud". The venue became a trotting, athletics and greyhound stadium before the site was sold for industrial warehousing.

In 1908 Northern moved to a new ground at Birch Lane after the committee decided it would be better to have a ground nearer the city centre. Huddersfield again provided the opposition for the first home game, again spoiling

Family day out...Bradford have enjoyed a crowd boost in the summer era

the party, this time with a 14-11 win. Northern played the inaugural Kangaroos in only the second game of their tour and their first on English soil on 7 October 1908, losing 11-12 before 4,000 after a last-minute conversion attempt was missed. But Birch Lane had only rudimentary facilities - its main feature an open stand of 12 terraces built in the summer of 1908. This stand was finally covered only in January 1929. Shallower terracing made up the rest of the spectator accommodation.

The ground was the previous home of Bowling Old Lane rugby club, whose field was on part of the cricket club's grounds. The rugby club folded in 1906 after turning to soccer. The site of the rugby pitch is now covered by housing and one corner of a school.

In the early 1920s, despite a new embankment that raised the capacity of the ground to 15,000 Northern began a search for a new home venue. Their search eventually ended with the opening of Odsal Stadium and St Helens Recs provided the last opposition at Birch Lane on 7 April 1934, winning 8-7. The highest crowd at Birch Lane was 10,807 for a Challenge Cup-tie against Dewsbury on 16 February 1924.

On occasions Northern hired Valley Parade for big games, commencing with a Challenge Cup-tie against Oldham in February 1920 which attracted a crowd of 20,318. They played six games there between 1920 and 1937, returning in April 1988 for a game against Wigan. Valley Parade, then known as the Bradford & Bingley Stadium, then housed Bradford's home games in 2001 and 2002 while Odsal was being re-developed.

Valley Parade - home to the Bulls
for the 2001 and 2002 seasons

CASTLEFORD

A trip to the Jungle in mid-summer is enough to revitalise even the most jaded of spirits. Castleford, quite simply, make the best of what they have got and the place is awash with colour and has a great community feel.

Three bars, a selection of food outlets, including the best jacket potatoes in the "Northern Union", kids' games as a curtain-raiser, dancing girls and an entertaining side with a host of emerging young English players presented Super League in the most positive of lights. Even after relegation in 2004 the Jungle remained a vibrant place to watch National League football.

Yet it was not always so. Castleford were slow to embrace the benefits of the summer game and, until a young, untried Australian coach, Stuart Raper, arrived in 1997, might easily have lost their place in the elite for good. Little more than two years later Raper took the Tigers to within one game of the Grand Final.

The following year, 2000, saw Castleford sign up an innovative sponsorship deal with an internet trading company, jungle.com, and Wheldon Road, their home since 1927 was renamed. In mid-summer of that year a fleet of coaches sponsored by the company ferried 5,000 Castleford fans to a match in London in an innovative move and a terrific example of community spirit.

Richard Gay, the former Tigers fullback was at first sceptical over the reputation that Castleford enjoyed as a family club when he moved from Hull. "I wondered what they meant and how they went about it," he recalls. Soon, he knew.

"The supporters really do get involved at Cas. No sooner than the match is over, the players are mingling over a drink in one of the bars and there is a great deal of interaction between the players and the fans. If you win they celebrate with you and if you lose they commiserate and buck you up. They seem to have built a loyalty that isn't just dependent on results. And there is a terrific spirit about the whole club."

Looking around the well-maintained Wheldon Road ground today, with its old main grandstand and with standing on three sides, it is hard to believe that soccer was once the dominant game.

Castleford Town AFC played at Wheldon Road but their fortunes declined after they failed to earn election to the new Division Three (North) in 1921 at a special meeting of the Football League in London on 7 March 1921. There were 28 applicants of which half were elected en bloc. A ballot was then taken to admit four more. It was a close-run thing with Town getting more votes (18) than any other of the non-selected clubs, with Wigan Borough (34), Halifax Town, Stalybridge Celtic and Southport (25 each) getting through.

Town played in the Midland League from 1909/10 onwards, alongside future Football League clubs such as Doncaster Rovers, Rotherham, York City, Chesterfield, Lincoln City, Halifax Town and Scunthorpe United. But after finishing bottom in 1925/26

the club did not seek re-election. Had that vote gone differently in 1921 who knows whether Castleford would ever have become a senior RL club?

There had long been a rugby tradition in the town with a club, formed as a split from the first Castleford RU organisation, operating under the auspices of the Northern Union from 1896-1907 before disbanding. The club played its home games on a patch of ground known initially as Mr Hunt's Field and latterly as the Sandy Desert on the opposite side of Lock Lane to where Lock Lane ARL club play today. The playing area still remains. In their first senior game Castleford lost 3-12 at Wakefield Trinity on 12 September 1896 in the Yorkshire Senior Competition. They lost 4-6 at home to Brighouse Rangers the following week and earned their first win against Holbeck at the seventh attempt. They finished a respectable ninth out of 16 clubs in their first season and lost to eventual beaten finalists St Helens in the Challenge Cup. In their final season as a senior club Castleford finished 28th out of 31 clubs in the combined league in 1905/06. Their last senior game resulted in a 0-25 defeat at Pontefract on 16 April 1906. The roots of the present Castleford club go back to 1912, when a new club was formed, and ten years later, playing at the Sandy Desert, the club entered the Yorkshire Senior Competition.

In 1926 Castleford were elected to the Northern Rugby Football League after failing with two previous attempts. They had sent a letter to all of the League's member clubs as part of their application process headed "Distinction or Extinction" and pleading for support for their "third and last" application to join. The letter worked. Castleford played their first season at the Sandy Desert, entertaining Rochdale Hornets on 1 September 1926 (lost 0-3) after losing 0-22 at Hull four days previously, before taking over Wheldon Road from the soccer club in time for the 1927/28 season. The Rugby League loaned £800 towards the purchase of the ground. Castleford had lost 12-18 to St Helens Recs in a first-round Challenge Cup-tie staged at Wheldon Road in February 1926 and they lost 0-3 to Huddersfield in their first league game there on 27 August 1927 before 5,000 spectators.

Len Garbett has been involved in virtually every capacity at Castleford, signing for the club as a player in 1935, later becoming coach, secretary and director and eventually club president for services rendered. Len remembers those early days when a fledgling professional club sought to make its way in the game.

"Sandy Desert was just an open place on the main road," he recalls. "The move into the RL did create some interest but there hadn't been much support for the club before that. The ground wasn't up to senior standards, especially when the River Aire overflowed its banks and flooded the playing area. But everyone worked hard to improve things. The playing area was re-turfed, fencing and turnstiles were erected and two ex-army huts served as dressing rooms. The club bought an old double deck bus and used the top half as a press box and the bottom half as a team room.

"When they moved to the present ground, that's when Rugby League really took off in Castleford, though when the club moved in, the ground was very run-down and there was just one small stand with leaky dressing rooms behind it. The two ends were much smaller, too. The current training ground and car park were all allotments and people paid so much a week to grow their own vegetables.

"Castleford is a recognised RL area now and soccer is limited to amateur sides. There are a good few amateur RL teams but these only developed when the professional side was formed."

Len was born on Princess Street and his bedroom overlooked the ground. "They nailed hoardings round the ground and hung rugs up to stop people getting a free view," he recalls.

Gradually, interest in the club built up and a then-record attendance of 13,327 was set for the visit of St Helens for a second round Challenge Cup-tie in 1931. In that year the supporters club funded a part covering of the popular side backing on to Princess Street and the main stand was later extended.

In November 1934, though, the main stand was destroyed by a fire, the cause attributed to an unattended coke stove. "Many of the old club records were lost in the fire," Len recalls. From the ashes rose the current steel-framed and wooden main stand, 50 yards long with seats for 1,400 and a further 1,000 paddock spaces. The stand was completed in time for the visit of Hunslet in a third-round cup-tie in March 1935 when a ground record crowd of 25,449 was recorded.

Within a decade of becoming members of the RL, Castleford reached Wembley in 1935 and "the Babes", as the press termed them, carried off the Challenge Cup with an 11-8 victory over Huddersfield. Their captain was Arthur Atkinson who had made his debut in

Sandy Desert as it is now

**Castleford fans
go "down the
lane" in the 1980s**

Cas's inaugural season as a senior club. Atkinson was born, Len recalls "just 200 yards off Wheldon Road." Now, a solid oak gate at the ground commemorates one of Castleford's finest. "Jim Croston and Arthur Atkinson was the best centre pairing I've ever seen," Len adds.

"Most of the players were local and that has remained the case to this day," Len says. "Castleford has always been a homely club and it has never lost that, even in the modern era of Super League."

In the late 1930s the ground developments continued. The old wooden fencing was replaced by iron railings and the Wheldon Road end was terraced. The ground staged its first representative match in October 1936 when Lancashire beat Yorkshire, 28-6, before a crowd of 7,648 when Croston, wearing the red rose, and Atkinson were on opposing sides. Wheldon Road has since staged another six Roses clashes, the last in 1981 when just 1,222 turned up to see Yorkshire beat Lancashire, 21-15. In 1950 Castleford used the land behind the main stand, previously rented to allotment holders, for a training pitch and car park.

Castleford enjoyed a glorious period in the 1960s, especially after floodlights were installed in 1965. "Classy Cas" as they became known were regulars on television, enjoying success in the popular BBC2 Floodlit Trophy with the second half of games televised live on Tuesday evenings. Cas lifted the trophy three times in succession and beat Salford and then Wigan in consecutive Wembley finals in 1969 and 1970.

"That was when we had our best team," Len says. "Malcolm Reilly, who I signed for Cas, was a terrific footballer. Alan Hardisty and Keith Hepworth, the "H bombs" were two great halfbacks and we had to let another, Roger Millward, go because he couldn't get a regular place. They've only had one better halfback but I can't swank." That was Len jocularly referring to his own career, like so many effectively ruined by the war. He joined up at 20, served for nearly seven years, was involved in the Normandy Landings and was "lucky to come home" to carry on watching his beloved Cas.

The scene at Wheldon Road in the early 1960s as Castleford take on Leeds

Castleford went close to setting a new ground record when an official attendance of 22,582 saw a second round Challenge Cup replay against Hull KR in March 1967. An estimated 8,000 further spectators gained free admittance after parts of the ground's original wooden perimeter fencing were torn down.

The Wheldon Road end was covered in the late 1960s and the Princess Street stand was rebuilt and extended the full length of the touchline, while the main stand was improved and made all-seater in 1970 and the pitch drainage was improved.

Improved bar facilities also made the ground an attractive venue for representative games. In 1969 Wheldon Road hosted the Great Britain under-24s as they beat their French counterparts, 42-2 and, in 1970, an encouraging crowd of 8,958 saw Great Britain beat France, 6-0, in a floodlit World Cup game played in continual pouring rain. In 2000, the Jungle staged a World Cup quarter-final tie as New Zealand defeated France, 54-6, before 5,158 spectators.

In 1971, Wheldon Road staged a Test for the first time but only 4,108 turned up to see New Zealand beat Great Britain, 17-14, and so clinch the series. Fullback Derek

A frosty Wheldon Road before a match with Wigan in 1969

Edwards was the only Castleford player on view. The crowd was actually higher than the 3,764 figure recorded for the first Test at the Willows in what was a poorly supported tour but neither ground has staged a Test match since.

Wheldon Road's capacity was halved following the Popplewell Report in 1985 and the main stand's capacity temporarily reduced to 800. With the help of loans from Wakefield council and the RFL, Castleford carried out essential fireproofing and cladding work on the stand to enable it to be fully used and the floodlights were also upgraded.

Further ground improvements in 1989 included the addition of eight hospitality boxes at the railway end and the erection of an elevated scoreboard to leave the well-maintained ground very similar to that of today.

Rugby League fans like the ground for the ability to move freely around, the large amount of cover, its facilities and its closeness to the pitch. The current capacity is 11,750 with seating for 1,500. Castleford's highest attendance of the summer era was recorded as 11,702 to witness a Super League game against Leeds in May 2000.

"It's still the same atmosphere as 50 years ago," Len says. "The locals are still there and though the faces change, they make the same row. So many walk to the ground, "down the lane" as Wheldon Road is called.

"It might be called the Jungle but it's Wheldon Lane to me. Always has been, always will be. There are so many other counter-attractions these days but Rugby League will keep going at Cas. We've got a good crowd and a good club. We've always been a local side, we've never been bankrupt, we've won the Cup four times, we've had some wonderful footballers and a few picked for Great Britain. You can't do much better than that.

"And you can't beat going 'down the lane' to the match."

41

CHORLEY

There were times when Chorley's Victory Park home seemed inaptly named. But 15 years after joining the Rugby League they were still there, flying the flag as the only professional side in Lancashire. Until, that is, the shock news came on the eve of their final game of the 2004 campaign, that the club's backers had withdrawn support from the end of that season.

Victory Park - so named as it was opened immediately after the First World War - has been home to Chorley FC since 1920 and the soccer and Rugby League sides appeared from a distance to co-exist quite happily under the banner of Chorley Sporting Club, a company thought to be controlled by multi-millionaire businessman Trevor Hemmings.

It is a ground that changes character with the seasons. In the depths of winter it can seem the coldest place on earth but in the midst of summer, with fans sprawled out on the grassy bank opposite the main stand, it takes on an entirely different feel. "Just like being at Manly," said the last Chorley coach, Mark Lee, with barely a hint of irony.

Described as "a magnificent brooding ground with an unmistakably Lancastrian atmosphere about the place" in Kerry Miller's wonderful book, "The History of Non-League Football Grounds" Victory Park is synonymous as home to the Magpies, as Chorley FC are known due to their long standing colours of black and white stripes. Much of the land, formerly the site of the Duke Street Brick Works and the disused Ranglett Pit, had subsequently been used as a rubbish dump and ashes tip, hence the Ashby Street that runs parallel to the ground. The record attendance was set in 1929 when 9,679 saw an FA Cup-tie against Darwen. The present-day main stand dates back to 1947 after the previous one was destroyed by fire.

"When empty, Victory Park is one of the most awesome stadia in England," the estimable Miller writes. "And curiously feels far more intimidating in that state than when filled with hundreds of spectators on match day."

Chorley was a rugby town before it became dominated by the soccer code. Major John Lawrence, a Chorley man who played for the fledgling Wigan club, decided to form a club in his own town. The first meeting took place on 15 October 1875 and in the first season six matches were played, including one against Wigan. They played at Dole Lane, the site now occupied by the Coronation Recreation Ground, and Lawrence organised a strong fixture list, with Swinton, Rochdale Hornets and Salford among their early opponents.

In October 1878 he organised a floodlit game against Swinton at Dole Lane, scheduled to be the first floodlit rugby game in Lancashire. The event generated tremendous interest and attracted a curious crowd of 8,000. As a good businessman, Lawrence was keen to ensure that everyone paid. "To prevent persons entering the field by other means than the gates the walls were plentifully besmeared with gas tar," reported the Chorley Guardian. "Several police constables were engaged to guard the hedge of the adjoining field".

The evening ended in disappointment, however, as the contractors, Messrs Parker and Bury of Manchester, were unable to get the Siemens Lights working and after a two-hour wait in pouring rain the game was abandoned. The crowd became so agitated that two members of the club's committee had the foresight to run off with the night's takings and hide them under a bed at the club's headquarters at the Rose and Crown Hotel. The game took place a few weeks later before a much smaller crowd at which the public was admitted free of charge.

Chorley won the North of England Challenge Cup, defeating Rossendale in the final at Blackpool in 1879, and the magnificent trophy is currently held in the archives at Astley Hall. But the rugby code began to decline in popularity and at the AGM, held in June 1883, it was decided to dissolve the club and an association club was formed in its place. Describing the soccer code prior to the first practice game, the Chorley Guardian explained: "The game differs from the rugby system mainly in that while all that is skilful in regard to passing the ball and dodging runs is retained, the practice of collaring the players and touching the ball with the hands is rigidly eschewed."

So Chorley FC was born and about to embark on a path that has at times seen them among the top rank of non-league clubs in the country, though they are currently in the First Division of the Unibond League, the lowest level of senior football under the recently reorganised non-league structure.

Rugby returned to Chorley in 1988 as a consequence of Blackpool Borough leaving the seaside town. Carl Briscoe, who went on to become Chorley's appearances record holder, remembers it well.

"The Blackpool team had a large contingent of Wiganers and we used to travel over for training and matches in a minibus," he recalls. "There was a great team spirit and though we weren't the best team in the league we more than held our own in the mid-1980s and had some terrific players like Tommy Frodsham and Hugh Waddell. It was very sad when Borough Park was closed down due to safety reasons and we played out the rest of the 1986/87 season at Bloomfield Road before leaving Blackpool for good.

"A new club was set up at Springfield Borough, playing out of Springfield Park, then home to Wigan Athletic. We had a successful playing season, reaching the play-offs and giving Leeds a big run for their money in the John Player Trophy. But as the second team in Wigan, no matter how hard we tried, the gates were small and the directors decided to move on again after one season. One faction favoured a move to Altrincham, another wanted to remain in Lancashire and there was a kind of uneasy truce as we settled at Chorley in 1988."

The first game staged at Victory Park was on 4 September 1988 when the visitors, Workington Town, won 22-8 before a crowd of 1,030. The visit of Leigh on Boxing Day attracted 1,506 - the biggest of the season - and the seasonal average was 512, down 410 on the campaign at Springfield but marginally up on the last season in Blackpool.

"After one season, though, the club split in two - one half moving to Altrincham to play as Trafford Borough and the other half remaining at Chorley and forming a new club," Briscoe continues. "The players were split roughly 50-50, too, but I decided to stay at Chorley."

Former long-serving Blackpool Borough officials Syd Secker and George Lunn took the posts as first chairman and secretary respectively and Stan Gittins was the first coach. Ironically, the new season threw up an early meeting of the rival clubs, Chorley defeating Trafford 12-6 in their opening game - a Lancashire Cup preliminary round tie that attracted

a crowd of 628 on a late August Wednesday evening. John Duffy scored Chorley's first try and ex-Blackpool Borough stalwart Billy Price added three goals and two drop goals in a game that simmered with animosity throughout. As the final hooter sounded a joyful Secker ran on the pitch and held Price in a bear-hug in an emotional scene that lingers in the memory.

Chorley's reward was a money-making tie at home to glamour club Wigan but safety reasons meant the tie was switched to Leigh's Hilton Park ground. On a Friday evening the star-studded Wigan side ran out 50-4 winners, Kevin Iro scoring four tries. Chorley's reward was their share of a 5,026 gate – which remained a record for a Chorley "home" game.

Later in that inaugural season the visit of Oldham attracted a crowd of 2,851 which remains a record for a Rugby League game at Victory Park. The Roughyeds, it will be remembered, had a tremendous travelling support in those days.

Briscoe enjoyed his time at Chorley even though there were times of struggle. "We had some good players, bolstered by a few Kiwis and Australians who came over," he recalls. "Of those, Aaron Whittaker was a classy stand-off and went on to play Test rugby, while Karl Benson was another good player who's now coaching at a high level in New Zealand.

"Then we had Mike Smith, a fullback from Wigan St Pats who could kick goals for fun and David Jones, an ex-BARLA international on the wing. But there were times when you'd be lining up for the kick-off and you had to ask the name of the player on your right. Quite often we'd have to bring in players at the last minute to make up the numbers. But that was the harsh reality of life in the lower division in those days.

"The "derbies" against Trafford were always the closest and hardest fought games of the season and produced some infamous contests. There was an intense rivalry between the clubs, in the boardroom and among the players as well. No one from either side wanted to lose those."

After three seasons at Victory Park the club received an ultimatum to quit when a faction of the soccer board decided that they could do without a Rugby League tenant. So, for season 1992/93 Chorley moved a few miles down the road to the Grundy Hill ground of Horwich RMI. The contrast was stark.

Grundy Hill dated back to the early 1900s and by the time Chorley moved in was showing its age. The soccer club's origins were as a sporting section of the Railway Mechanics Institute, with Horwich a noted railway town following the decision of the old Lancashire & Yorkshire Railway Company to construct the Locomotive Works in 1885. The main stand was a fascinating historical artefact but with its eight struts that supported the roof the view of the pitch was far from ideal. On the same side was a social club with a scratching shed opposite and a tea hut in the corner that consistently served the best Lancashire hotpot in the Northern Union. On cold days the hut generated a sizeable head of steam such that it was almost possible to imagine that an old locomotive had rolled up to be attended to by the mechanics.

Grundy Hill also boasted the most unbelievable playing surface. Wherever you viewed on the ground it looked as though you were looking uphill. It was compared by one ground-hopping expert to "an inverted crown green bowling rink tipped at an angle for good measure."

With its views over the West Pennine moors Grundy Hill would have been made for summer rugby, but in the depths of winter was one of the bleakest places in the kingdom.

"Victory Park was a nice, compact ground with not a bad playing surface, even though there were a few undulations," Briscoe recalls. "Grundy Hill was an entirely different prospect, built on the side of a hill with a pitch that not only sloped from one end down to the other but from side to side as well. In winter, with the wind whistling down from Rivington Pike, it was bitterly cold and the ground took some adapting to. You'd see opposing teams come to Grundy Hill for the first time and look open-mouthed at the pitch. At the top end, playing up the slope you were gasping for breath because of the altitude but at the other end, where the dressing rooms were situated in a wooden hut, it was like being below sea level.

"There was a 16-foot drop from one side to the other and you could really peg in opposing sides in the bottom corner, like the old ground at Dewsbury or at Batley. I remember one match against Blackpool (Trafford had now returned to the seaside to become Blackpool Gladiators) when it was the coldest conditions I can recall for a rugby match. The pitch was covered in about a foot of snow and it took the players about two hours to thaw out afterwards."

Even though summer rugby was a distant dream there were changes in the Rugby League hierarchy and late that season, after a meeting of clubs on 10 March 1993, dubbed "Black Wednesday" by its critics, came the bombshell news that three clubs would be ditched at the end of the campaign, ending the three-division system and reducing the number of member clubs from 35 to 32. "We were suddenly fighting for our lives and involved in a desperate struggle to stay in the league," Briscoe recalls. "It was worse for me because, even though I'd taken over as caretaker-coach I'd broken my jaw and couldn't play. It was so frustrating."

Chorley looked to have secured their league place with late-season wins over fellow strugglers Nottingham City and Highfield at Grundy Hill, prompting a champagne soaked celebration on the pitch after the latter game. Chorley's tense 18-8 win, before a season's best crowd of 767 with Smith contributing 14 points, appeared the most vital in the club's short history. "But then Highfield somehow won their last two games, both away, including one at Barrow, and though the directors fought tooth and nail to keep us in the league, we were down," Briscoe says. "It was the lowest point of my career."

Victory Park

Chorley

The average attendance at Horwich was 434, up a modest 40 on the previous season at Chorley. To their great credit Chorley fought on, playing against the country's best amateur sides in the newly-formed National Conference alongside Blackpool Gladiators and Nottingham City. But unlike the others Chorley managed to return to the professional ranks, rejoining the league in the Centenary Season of 1995/96. The opportunity arose because of the demise of the old Doncaster club, with Chorley reminding the Rugby League that when they were demoted to the Conference a pledge was given that if any of the existing members dropped out they would automatically be offered back their place.

"Initially I went to play for Bramley but I soon returned and played for Chorley in the Conference," Briscoe says. "It was a great credit to the directors that they kept the club going and never lost the belief that we'd get back. Lindsay Hoyle (now the town's MP) was a driving force behind the club at that time, a massive influence and was figurehead for the club in its return to the League. A lot of the Conference clubs really raised their games when they played Chorley - it was like their cup final."

Chorley left Grundy Hill after playing there for two seasons, returning to Victory Park for the 1994/95 season.

During that campaign, Grundy Hill was sold for a housing development and the money used to buy Leigh's Hilton Park from administrators. With new standards for pitches in senior non-league football, Horwich RMI could not retain their status by playing at Grundy Hill and so had to find an alternative, as the cost of levelling the ground was prohibitive. With Leigh in financial difficulties the opportunity presented itself to move to a ready-made ground that would conform to all regulations. Grundy Hill Estates Limited thus now own Hilton Park and the soccer club, renamed Leigh RMI, are co-tenants, playing in the Conference North League, two levels below the Football League. Ironically while one team moved out of the railway town another was making plans to move in, Bolton Wanderers selling their Burnden Park home and opening their £30m Reebok Stadium as part of the Middlebrook development on the Red Moss site, close to the motorway, in 1997.

Chorley celebrated their return to the professional ranks as Briscoe scored two tries in their first win - at old foes Highfield - and then by defeating Barrow, 15-12, before 550 at Victory Park.

In a Regal Trophy tie in October they defeated hapless Nottingham City, sadly rapidly sliding into oblivion, 92-0 with Martin Holden scoring four tries and Smith contributing a try and ten goals. They finished a respectable ninth in the second division with 11 points from 20 games and home gates averaged 501.

Then along came summer rugby and, early in September 1996, another bombshell. The club had been bought by Preston North End and would move to Deepdale for the 1997 season, playing under the title Lancashire Lynx, after the nomenclature Central Lancashire was briefly adopted.

No stone was left unturned as Lynx, with former Kiwi legend Kevin Tamati in charge of playing affairs, took on a wholly professional outlook with the aim of securing a Super League place. For Briscoe, used to life with a struggling club, it was a real eye-opener. "At Chorley and Horwich we'd trained where we could, on dimly-lit school pitches, on astro-turf and on supermarket car parks in the depths of winter," he recalls. "Suddenly it was party time - everything was done professionally. We had our own training kit, fantastic training facilities and playing at Deepdale was the highlight of my career, very rewarding. I've only played on one better surface and that was at Elland Road."

One of soccer's most atmospheric grounds, and one of only three remaining as soccer

Preston Grasshoppers' Lightfoot Green

Preston North End's Deepdale

grounds from the first season of the Football League in 1888 when North End were one of the dozen pioneers (Turf Moor, Burnley and Anfield, then home to Everton, are the others), Deepdale was undergoing huge change with the development to build the three new stands that now grace the Preston skyline. As an aside, Victory Park and Deepdale can both be viewed from the top of Healey Nab, the hill on the outskirts of town that can be seen clearly from the main stand at Chorley.

Horwich RMI FC's Grundy Hill

A pre-season friendly against Wigan attracted an encouraging crowd of 3,716 and there was an attendance of 713 for a Challenge Cup fourth-round tie against London Broncos in the first official game at Deepdale, the Broncos winning 48-5.

But it soon became evident that it would be a struggle to attract support in a soccer-dominated town. Despite the excellent venue - a great view from the Tom Finney Stand, first-class social facilities and that enviable playing surface, Lynx's average gates in 1997, games often played on a Friday evening, were 413 (down three from their last season at Chorley) and long before the 1998 season ended in triumph, with Lynx winning the second division title, there were rumours that PNE had lost enthusiasm for the venture.

So it proved - a sunny Sunday afternoon when then RFL Chief Executive Neil Tunnicliffe came to town to present Lynx with the championship trophy after a game against Batley proving to be the last RL game staged at the ground. Deepdale looked a picture and 1,079 fans revelled in the late summer sun. But the die was cast.

Lynx had played three mid-summer home games up the road at the Lightfoot Green home of Preston Grasshoppers RU club (ironically one of the original Chorley club's last opponents in the 1882/83 season) when Deepdale was undergoing pitch repairs. The Oldham game at Lightfoot Green, played on the last day of May, attracted a season's best crowd of 1,351. When the Treize Tournoi was staged at the end of the campaign Lynx played French sides Villeneuve and St-Esteve at the Grasshoppers.

"The club had used up its budget for the season and told the players they'd have to play for nothing in the competition," Briscoe recalls. "Most of us did and we really did ourselves proud. We started with a fine win away at St-Esteve and beat them and Villeneuve at home to qualify for the final. We played Villeneuve, again, before a crowd of over 10,000 in Toulouse. It was a great experience and the match was shown live on French television. Though we lost narrowly (10-16) we gave a great account of ourselves."

Briscoe retired after the final and in 1999 there was a reality check - a return to Victory Park and the departure of some of the best players, like Phil Jones who was transferred to Wigan. At least Chorley had the distinction of playing the last professional game of the old Millennium - their home game against the re-born Sheffield Eagles taking place on a Tuesday afternoon, 28 December when a crowd of 888 saw the Eagles earn a famous 33-20 win.

The 1999-2000 season was an unmitigated disaster, as Lynx ended the year with a run of 24 straight defeats, having used 72 players. The club was eventually sold by PNE who decided to cut their losses and the intervention of the Chorley Sporting Club ensured that there would be a future for Rugby League in Chorley.

Under new management, and the coaching of former Kiwi and Wigan great Graeme West, the re-branded Chorley Lynx endured a miserable start that included a cup defeat by amateurs Woolston. But the first victory was as sweet as it was emphatic - York hammered 78-8 in mid-March, with former Wigan reserve halfback Stuart Fisher scoring five tries and kicking nine goals. How the club stalwarts in the 254 crowd - ironically the lowest of the season - enjoyed that one.

Chorley had experienced the tough times and, epitomising what was once a universal spirit of Rugby League, were only too keen to help out clubs in distress. Swinton played one game at Chorley in-between leaving Gigg Lane and moving to Moor Lane and in 2003 Lynx hosted two Oldham games while Boundary Park was unavailable due to re-seeding.

In 2003, under the coaching of ex-Lynx centre Darren Abram, they enjoyed a fine campaign on a tight budget, finishing second in the newly-formed National League Two before running out of steam in the play-offs. Winger Eric Andrews scored at least one try in 15 consecutive games but still the crowds could not be enticed - averaging just 434, ironically down by 60 on 2002.

But a trip to Chorley remained one of the hidden pleasures of Rugby League, especially in the summer. If you got there early enough and you would have seen chairman Henry Morris putting out the corner flags or Sporting Club manager Dennis Ramsdale constructing the goalposts. You could have enjoyed a drink in the spacious social club and watched the game from the grassed bank or the stand, or just taken advantage of the opportunity to wander around the well-kept ground and watch the play from a host of different angles. It was Rugby League in the raw but there wouldn't be a game without clubs like Chorley and there was a real community feel generated by a small but dedicated band of supporters.

They didn't have to besmear the walls with tar any more to prevent people entering the ground without paying. But when Mark Lee compared it to Manly he was, for once, wrong. It was far better than that!

And the final game went down in folklore, Lynx recovering from 16-0 down to beat York, 21-20, Brian Capewell hitting a match-winning field goal *(right)* from inside his own half with the last kick of the game. Grown men and women cried. Through the tears Lee managed another classic quote: "It isn't over till the fat stand-off scores."

DEWSBURY

A huge piece of history went the way of the bulldozers the day the builders moved in on Crown Flatt, at the time of its demolition to make way for a housing development the oldest rugby ground then in use within the Rugby League.

Situated on a plateau above the famous mill-town, Dewsbury's home, originally known as Crown Flatts, owed its name perhaps because it was sited on what had been Crown land. It was a plateau of sorts - the ground had a pronounced slope, known as the "nine 'ole" perhaps as much as nine feet from corner to corner, which generations of Dewsbury players used to great advantage.

Rugby was first played there in 1876 when Dewsbury Athletic leased the field from the Lord Savile Estate for the sum of £20 per annum. Athletic later amalgamated with Dewsbury and Savile and Dewsbury United Clerks Cricket Club and the club was known as Dewsbury and Savile.

The club's rise was rapid - they won the Yorkshire Cup for the first time in 1881 and also hosted Yorkshire's game against Cheshire in that year. The first stand was constructed three years later and, in 1885, a 130-yard long construction, known as the "Noah's Ark Stand", was erected on the south side at a cost of £250, covering the entire length of the field. The ground then had a capacity of 5,000 seats, remarkable for the time, and was easily the best equipped in the county.

Crown Flatt's stature was recognised in 1890 when it hosted a rugby union international. Saturday 15 February 1890 was a famous day in Welsh rugby history. Wales beat England for the first time in a game played in a snowstorm on a quagmire of a pitch, the foul weather restricting the crowd to only 4,000, which proved a blow to a number of ticket touts. One had bought one thousand tickets at eight pence each on the Friday prior to the game and had to resort to trying to sell them for two pence each leading up to the kick-off. Dewsbury's Welsh halfback Bill Stadden, a butcher in the town, scored the only try of the match, early in the second half.

Stadden feigned to throw the ball into a line-out but then bounced the ball, re-gathered himself and went over the line. The Dewsbury fans present supported Stadden and Wales and afterwards AE Stoddart, the England captain, said the ground "was an insult to both teams." The Yorkshireman newspaper commented: "It will be a very far cry indeed to the next international at Dewsbury. The bitter invective of Stoddart against the ground may have been partly inspired by the unpatriotic attitude of the crowd. Certainly England has a right to expect greater encouragement from her own supporters."

Stadden never appeared for Wales again and committed suicide at the age of 45 in 1906.

Eight years later the original Dewsbury club abandoned the handling code and moved to Savile Town to play soccer. A new Dewsbury rugby club was formed in April 1898,

The final game at Crown Flatt - Dewsbury v Barrow, 14 April 1991

joining the Northern Union Yorkshire Second Competition in 1898/99 and playing at Crown Flatt having negotiated a 999-year lease. The old club disposed of all its equipment, fixtures and stands and the new organisation had to start from scratch after playing their first game in September 1898.

Dewsbury joined the senior ranks in 1902 and the ground was sufficiently re-developed to hold 15,200 spectators for a third round Challenge Cup-tie against neighbours Batley in 1912. A combined Dewsbury-Batley XIII lost 8-18 to the first New Zealand tourists in November 1907 before 7,000 but eleven months later Dewsbury beat the first Kangaroos, 15-0, with only 2,000 in attendance.

The first stand to be covered was erected at the ground in 1914 two years after Dewsbury won the Challenge Cup. The stand was of a distinctive barrel-shaped design and capable of seating 1,300 with a standing paddock for a further 2,000 beneath.

In 1920 a new ground record was established when 26,584 saw a Yorkshire Cup-tie against Halifax and Crown Flatt staged the 1934 Yorkshire Cup Final when Leeds and Wakefield Trinity drew 5-all before 22,598.

But by the time Dewsbury shocked the Rugby League world by winning the championship in 1973, the ground had remained unaltered for many years and was a shadow of its former self. The final turning point came on 13 September 1988 when vandals burnt down the ancient wooden grandstand. Three schoolboys, with a combined total age of 35, were found responsible. The fire destroyed the boardroom, changing rooms, equipment, records and archives and effectively spelt the end of the famous old ground.

Although a temporary main stand was erected, the character of the ground was lost forever and a year later the club members decided to sell Crown Flatt for nearly £2m to Duncan Developments Limited, a sponsor of the club. One of the most emotional games in

Dewsbury's recent history took place when Dewsbury overcame a 16-point deficit to beat Rochdale Hornets, 36-34, in the first home game after the fire.

Crown Flatt staged its final game on 14 April 1991 when Dewsbury drew, 19-19, with Barrow on a sunny Sunday afternoon before a crowd of 1,321. The spring-like weather was out of character with the melancholy many felt deep down in their hearts as they trudged up the hill from town on the Leeds Road for a final time. George Banks, a distinguished former Dewsbury player, made the kick-off.

After three years in exile at Mount Pleasant, Batley - ironically Dewsbury's greatest rivals - the new £1.5m ground at Owl Lane, a Jimmy Ledgard punt or three up the hill, was ready, after numerous planning delays.

The first game at the new Crown Flatt was also played against Barrow on 11 September 1994 when Dewsbury ran out resounding 76-8 winners before a 3,427 crowd. The local MP, Ann Taylor, officially opened the stadium and the ceremonial kick-off was made by Mick Sullivan, alongside Garry Schofield Great Britain's most-capped player who had begun his career at Shaw Cross Boys Club and ended it as player-coach at Dewsbury before moving to Australia.

Assistant coach Les Holliday marked the occasion by scoring three tries and kicking ten goals.

On Boxing Day 1994 a ground record was set when 3,995 saw Dewsbury beat Batley, 16-0. In the first season at their new ground Dewsbury averaged crowds of 1,859 compared to 955 in the final season at the old one. Built on the 17-acre site of the former Shaw Cross Colliery, the ground has a 4,500 capacity with seating for just over a thousand people in a main stand that also houses the Royal Suite, Ledgard Room and Bailey Bar plus seven executive boxes. A standing, covered terrace is situated opposite the main stand and the two ends are grassed over. There is a splendid view of the Gawthorpe Water Tower, also a landmark to be spotted from the old ground, which survived an attempted German bombing raid during the Second World War. The ground was renamed Ram Stadium in 1998, a year after Dewsbury took on the Rams nomenclature. In 2000 Ram Stadium hosted the Emerging Nations World Cup Final as BARLA GB & Ireland beat Italy, 20-14, before a crowd of 1,601. In 2005 the Ram Stadium was renamed the Tetley's Stadium after a sponsorship deal with the well-known brewers.

Mike Stephenson, better known throughout the game as "Stevo", is a Dewsbury legend. "Everyone who has played at Dewsbury can't escape the fact it was one of the worst slopes in the history of the Rugby League," says Stevo. "I believe that from one corner diagonally to the other corner there was a slope of about seven-and-a-half feet. They called it the "nine 'oil". Maybe that derives from it being approximately nine feet. I don't really know - I have never found out why.

"They also say that you could roll a ball on its side from one corner to the other. It was a wonderful attribute to us when we were playing. When I was captaining Dewsbury we would always try to play uphill in the first half then downhill in the second. We continually kicked the opposition off the park. A lot of opposing teams, you could tell, never fancied it.

Housing estate - Crown Flatt as it looks today

Dewsbury

"In my time we had two great kickers in our side, Allan Agar and my namesake, Nigel Stephenson. But sometimes the slope could work against you. I remember when Bradford signed Terry Price. He could kick from his own half and the ball would roll over the dead in-goal line. In those days it meant you had to drop-out from your own '20'. I think they changed the rule because of him. Bradford used to run the ball backwards at times, to enable them to pass it to Price inside his own half and the way he kicked it was like kicking down Everest."

Stevo's affection for the club began early. "I was born and bred in Dewsbury," he says. "I watched them as a kid and my aunties, Margaret and Doris, still go to watch Dewsbury. They are both in their 70s but have faithfully followed the club all their lives. I was initially dragged up there and at that time they rarely ever won. My hero was Johnny Bullock, a little halfback. As kids we thought the world of Eric Ashton, Billy Boston and Alex Murphy but Johnny was my real hero. I was introduced to him a couple of years ago and it was a real thrill. To me he was THE man. There was another player called Marchant, famous for, shall we say, his tenacity. In those days the disciplinary met once a month and he was sent off in three successive matches so he had a lot of explaining to do. I later played with him in my early days. If he was going to come short, he'd signal it by slapping the side of his thigh. All the kids in Dewsbury at time used to go around slapping the side of their thighs, his mannerism became that well known.

"By the time I played, the ground was quite dilapidated. It had staged some famous games but it was showing signs of age. Some really great players had played there and there was a great tradition attached to the place. I was very sad when they sold it. The great fire ruined it."

Stevo made an emotional return to the ground's former site lately. "They named one of the roads after Nigel and me, Stephenson Close," he says. "We went up Eddie Waring Way to reach it. Eddie was born in the town and he went to the same school as my mother. They used to go dancing together at the ages of 14 and 15. My mother was the pools person around Dewsbury in the '50s and '60s at a time when not many clubs had a commercial side. But though she used to sit in the bar at Crown Flatt she never watched me play after an incident when I was 15 or 16. I was playing at Thornhill in the juniors as a hooker and was getting a bit beaten up. Suddenly there was a hell of a commotion. My mother ran on the pitch shouting, 'Michael, stop it! Let someone else have a go in that position'.

"I've never been as embarrassed. After that she never watched me again, not even in the '73 Championship Final.

"It was nice of them to name a street after me but the occasion was tinged with sadness. On the one hand I felt very proud but I had taken a couple of friends with me as well as a television crew from Sky for Boots 'n' All. I was just showing them where the

halfway line used to be when one of the new residents came out of his house and told us all to clear off.

"My association with the club goes back even longer in the family. I remember relatives telling me about the olden days when couriers used to run down progressive scores to the market in the middle of town."

Long before summer rugby was even thought about Crown Flatt could be a daunting place to visit."Training was often rugged. The ground was at the top of the hill," Stevo says. "It was typical of the West Riding with the woollen mills situated in the valleys. Even in the summer months it was always freezing."

Dewsbury's '73 Championship triumph over Leeds at Odsal was Stevo's best memory. In the last of the top-16 play-offs before the league was re-organised into two divisions, Dewsbury came from eighth place in the table to earn a famous victory.

As captain, Stevo led from the front. He scored two tries and was a clear choice for the Harry Sunderland Trophy. He never played for Dewsbury again. "That was the club's greatest day," Stevo says. "I have to say that. They had won the Championship in the war years when Eddie was manager. He used to pester the authorities in the RAF, Army and Navy to get guest players like Roy Francis, Jim Sullivan and Vic Hey. But this was the first time they had won the championship in peacetime. My father used to regard the '47 championship final, when they lost to Wigan at Maine Road under Hey, as Dewsbury's greatest day before that. Coincidentally, that was the year I was born."

Stevo has been referred to as the first of the running hookers, a style that earned him a big money move to Penrith in Australia in 1973. "That's nonsense," he retorts. "I merely copied the style of Tommy Harris. He was the first, without a doubt. He was an absolute hero."

And he still harbours regrets over his move, even more than 30 years on. "Finances came into it," he says. "I left on a bad note to go to Australia. I was sold for £20,000, a world record fee at the time, and I was entitled to 10 per cent of that but never got it. In those days £2,000 would buy you a semi-detached house. The RFL backed Dewsbury but they were desperate to stop anyone going to Australia at that time. It left me with a sour taste because I had given a lot to the club, as many players did. Much later, when the club was going through bad times, there was a scheme for supporters to buy one-foot squares of the pitch. They wrote to me in Australia asking me if I would contribute. I had a wry smile over that but nowadays I just laugh at it.

"In '72/73 we had a very good side and it was getting better. Many of us had been together since we were a bunch of kids and we had a good team spirit. There were the likes of the two Bates, Alan and John, Allan Agar, Trevor Lowe and Jeff Grayshon - a really solid side. Most of us were together at Shaw Cross and we always felt we could give the big guns a run for their money, especially at our place. That season we lost to Bradford in the Challenge Cup semi-final at Headingley. They had professionalism that day and we didn't, but it gave us the spur we needed. I was the only international in the side, though many more went on to become internationals afterwards, and when the chance came again we were determined to take it. Bradford had battered us and we tried to match them physically instead of trying to play football. We had a list of moves as long as your arm - it wasn't unusual for us to try 15 moves in the first 15 minutes - and our coach, Tommy Smales, used to show them using pepper-pots and beer glasses set out on a table. The Bradford defeat was a bitter lesson and we went on to win against all the odds against Leeds."

Stevo's worst experience, one that still haunts him, was when his teammate, John

Davies, died in his arms during a game at Crown Flatt against Batley in April 1969. "It was a big, big shock," Stevo recalls. "He made a break and suddenly collapsed. I was nearest to him and rushed over. A lot of players needed counselling after that. It later transpired John's heart had exploded. When someone dies on a football field it takes an awful lot to be able to continue doing what you are doing. It was the worst time of my career as a professional Rugby League player. John was taken off and the tannoy announcer appealed for the assistance of a doctor. Playing the last part of the game, while John was on his way to hospital, was the hardest thing I've ever had to do. Most people were unaware of the severity of the incident but I knew. I knew he'd gone. John was a wonderful bloke and a wonderful servant to Dewsbury."

Stevo's better memories were the Boxing Day fixtures, especially one famous occasion. "With playing I never used to have a drink at Christmas but one year a hard frost had been around for ages," he recalls. "On the Christmas Eve there was snow on the ground and the pitch had been frozen for five or six days. There was no way the game would be on so, foolishly, I lumped in with a few of the lads for some beers and arrived home worse for wear. I fell asleep downstairs still in my work-clothes. Unbeknown to me some fans had spent two days working on the pitch with braziers and straw to get the game on and we played. The game was against Huddersfield and I felt awful. I vowed never to drink again. But I went on to score three tries and I won the man-of-the-match. Packing down the scrum smelt like a brewery. I wasn't the only one who'd been on the beer. But it was not the way to prepare for a game and my performance was a complete fluke."

Stevo was pleased with Dewsbury's new ground when he visited it for the first time. "Especially within the resources and money they had at the time," he says. "Sadly, it is an exposed area, though the change to summer must help. When they first went there they couldn't win for toffee and they got the Bishop of Pontefract to come and exorcise the ground, in front of the Sky cameras."

Neil Kelly was one of Dewsbury's longest-serving players and their most successful coach of modern times, including the 2000 NFP grand final win over Leigh. He was one of only two players to have played in the final match at Crown Flatt and the first one at the new ground, Nathan Graham the other, with Pat Trainor and Derek Hadley of Barrow also playing in both games.

His memories of Crown Flatt are divided pre and post-fire. "When I first went there it was a traditional Rugby League ground," he says. "I made my Dewsbury debut in 1982 and, inevitably, a lot of things have changed since. There was a Dutch barn-type stand, terracing on the far side and the famous slope. It was a bit like Batley playing there, a game of two halves. We always aimed to score enough points in the first half, playing down hill." Post-fire Crown Flatt was often a desolate place. "They had a temporary stand and the changing rooms were a converted shed," Kelly recalls. "The showers were like a sheep-dip. It was just a matter of time before they moved on.

"The people were fantastic - it was very much a close-knit family club, close to the heart of the community. One game that stands out, I remember, is playing in a 0-0 draw against Rochdale on a quagmire. But as a player you got used to the pitch and used it to your best advantage. In the last game the builders organised a competition among supporters to guess how much the slope dropped. There was a surveyor measuring it but some supporters allowed their emotions to get the better of them and thought they were measuring the ground ready to start building there and then. It took some calming down."

Kelly remembers clearly the final game, against Barrow, when that draw was secured

Ram Stadium

with a late Paul Hughes try, converted by Graham. "The game ran something like ten minutes over when Hughesy scored," he says. "It was emotional, rather more than I had anticipated. I had played more than 200 games there but there were supporters that had watched all their rugby at Crown Flatt. To leave the ground for the final time was a moment of great sadness.

"By the time we moved to the new ground a lot of things had changed. We had spent three seasons at Batley, which hadn't gone down too well. Throughout our time there the focus was on when we would go to our new ground. I actually worked on the construction of the new ground, alongside my brother Andy, as a bricklayer and saw the pitch being laid. It was intriguing seeing the ground developing as it did. It was built on the site of the old Shaw Cross Colliery, which was capped off, and the methane was measured. The first game, ironically against Barrow, was a big occasion. I actually worked at the stadium on the Saturday morning, applying a few finishing touches. I was sub that day and Paul Delaney captained the side. I was pleased for Paul - he was a Dewsbury lad and was part of the fabric of the place.

"We had a tremendous victory and the novelty was playing on a relatively flat pitch. A lot of people wanted us to recreate the slope at Crown Flatt but, quite rightly, they didn't. From '96 onwards, as I witnessed as a coach, it was a great place to be. We won minor premierships, the grand final and the Trans-Pennine Cup. There were some very significant games and victories.

"The new ground isn't held in the same affection as the old one was - it's not like the old ground at all. But the fact is, the ground was financed by the club's own money and they were proud of that. It wasn't as grandiose as the McAlpine Stadium or the KC Stadium, but it has character and room for development."

DONCASTER

Every time Stewart Piper drives down Bentley Road, like many people in Doncaster, he can't avoid casting a long, lingering look to his left to the overgrown wilderness that around ten years ago was staging top-flight Rugby League.

Tattersfield, a ground where he shed blood, sweat and tears and earned plenty of losing money in over a decade's service with his hometown club, is no more, though the playing pitch, now rapidly being reclaimed by nature, remains.

Doncaster moved out, ironically after their most successful season in history, spent in the old First Division in 1994/95, just before the revolution in Rugby League.

A financial crisis gripped the club, not for the first time, but of a magnitude that dwarfed all others. The club was said to be £1.4m in debt at the end and former coach Tony Fisher had to resort to issuing a winding-up notice to try and recover some of his wages.

Despite it all Doncaster, the great survivors of the game, performed one more trick of escapology. The loss of Tattersfield was one tragic bi-product of the crisis but, these days the future looks a whole lot brighter.

A new stadium on the near horizon, co-shared with Doncaster Rovers, and a few years of financial sobriety and realism under the shrewd leadership of chairman and benefactor John Wright has seen them establish themselves as a respected force in National League One. No more are they the club that sheds coaches as often as some people change their underwear - St John Ellis has been the incumbent since 1999.

Piper, whose association with the club began when, as a four-year-old, he helped his father at the old York Street Greyhound Track, couldn't be more delighted. "The new stadium's great - very good for the town," Piper says. "It's the best thing to happen to Doncaster for many a long year."

Doncaster Council have sanctioned a proposal to build a new 15,000-capacity stadium, at a cost of around £20m, that will be home to Rovers, Dragons and the Doncaster Belles Ladies Football team, about a mile-and-a-half to the south of Belle Vue. It is hoped the project will be completed by March 2006.

Piper's dad, Isaiah, a former Wakefield and Featherstone player, was the groundsman and kit-man when Doncaster entered the Rugby League in 1951. The game had long been played in the area, at an amateur level, introduced and popularised by men from Lancashire and other parts of Yorkshire who came to work in the big local collieries. Old timers still recall when Wigan came to play at Askern Welfare in the Challenge Cup in 1933, winning 46-0. The legendary Jim Sullivan kicked 11 goals for Wigan that day.

Formed as a company in September 1950, Doncaster were elected to the League on 30 April 1951 alongside Cardiff, who lasted just a single season. Upon Cardiff's demise Doncaster kept the title of the "Babes", traditionally given in those days to the newcomers, until Blackpool Borough joined in 1954.

Stewart Piper surveys the scene where the legendary Tattersfield ground once stood

The York Road stadium first hosted greyhound racing in 1928 and dirt-track racing was introduced a year later. When the newly-formed Doncaster club moved in it was estimated the capacity was 7,000, though it was felt there was room for development to accommodate up to 30,000.

An amateur county game between Yorkshire and Cumberland on 24 February 1951 christened the ground for rugby and in the first professional match there, on 18 August 1951, Doncaster beat Wakefield Trinity before a crowd of over 8,000 (600 of them seated). Ray Gunter, the MP for Doncaster, made the kick-off.

Only six turnstiles were in operation for the opening day and with the queues building prior to kick-off frustration set in. A section of the crowd broke down a perimeter fence and an estimated 1,500 gained free admission. Some sources give the attendance as 10,000.

One of the Doncaster players, scrum-half Jim Tynan, was delayed in traffic and the match started without him. The team photograph to mark the momentous day thus features only 12 Doncaster players. Tynan made his mark later, though, scoring one of the tries in a famous 10-3 win.

Doncaster's first season was a huge success results-wise. They finished 11th in the league, but crowds soon dropped below the optimistic break-even figure of 7,000 and only 2,200 were present for the visit of Castleford in early December. At the end of their first season "the Babes" had an average crowd of 3,200. Doncaster Rovers' average, by comparison, was 21,078.

The ground was disliked by many supporters, providing little shelter to ward off the winter chill and few good vantage points. Its comparatively remote location on the northern outskirts of town, and a poor bus service were other contributing factors, while the kick-off times of 2.30pm were felt to be too early for miners that had worked a morning shift.

The supporters worked hard and provided £300 worth of terracing, from ash-like materials, at the southern (town) end of the ground. The visit of Bradford Northern for a Challenge Cup-tie in February 1952 made their efforts worthwhile as a crowd of 10,000 was accommodated. But their hard work came to nothing as, after two years' occupation, the club received notice to quit when the stadium was sold to a Sheffield businessman.

Doncaster

Doncaster hosted a touring team for the first and only time in their last season at York Road, losing 13-41 to the Australians in a game played on a Thursday afternoon in late October 1952. The crowd was 2,600. In the previous season they abandoned plans to play the New Zealanders under lights at York Road as the cost of adapting the greyhound stadium lights for a "one-off" game was considered too prohibitive. By the end of the season the club slumped to 26th out of 30 in the league. For one home game, against Widnes, the crowd barely reached 500.

Speedway returned to York Road in 1969 and the team then acquired the Dragons moniker now adopted by the RL side. But after disappointing crowds the operation was transferred to Birmingham in 1971. Greyhound racing continued at the venue until 1986 when the provisions of the Safety of Sports Grounds Act effectively spelled the end. The site is now covered by housing.

"York Road was a busy place," Piper recalls. "They had stock cars and speedway there as well as greyhounds and a casino but it wasn't ideal as an RL ground. I remember when Doncaster played the Australians - I sat on my dad's shoulders to watch the game. After games my dad would send me around the perimeter of the ground, looking for coins that had been discarded. I picked up many an old sixpence."

Doncaster then moved to their new ground, around a half mile away, off the Bentley Road, buying the 11-acre site for £5,000. It was sold on the understanding that it was only to be used for recreational use. Two bridges over the approach dyke were made, a small amount of terracing on the popular side constructed and an agricultural stand, situated where the main stand was later built, was hired.

Keighley provided the first opposition at the new ground, returning home with a 34-11 victory. Life was going to be a struggle for the Babes. They finished the season third bottom but that was comparatively successful compared to later seasons. Between 1956/57 and 1960/61, for instance, they were rooted to the bottom for five consecutive campaigns. In all Doncaster have been wooden-spoonists on 15 occasions.

Despite that, ground improvements continued. The main grandstand was built in 1954 and a small stand on the popular side was finally completed by the early 1960s with corrugated iron sheets covering about 40 yards of the railway sleeper terracing. This latter stand became popularly known as 'Len's Lean-to.'

"Dad was involved in building the terracing from old railway sleepers," Piper says.

Belle Vue

"The pitch was an old flood plain and the River Don was re-routed as part of the project. But the pitch was always waterlogged, it was like a swamp. I once lost a boot in the quagmire in the corner and it resurfaced in the summer!

"As a kid, though, it was the place to be. All the players were my heroes - they were like gladiators. But many a time the players would run out down the tunnel from the dressing room to the field and forget the roof was built too low. I remember George Goodyear knocked himself out before one game - he always ducked after that."

Piper played amateur for the nearby Bentley Yarborough club, over the road on the council pitches, and it was one of the proudest days in his life when, at the age of 22, he turned professional. The terms were unusual - £35 in his hand, a blazer and a tie. The money is long spent but he still has the blazer and tie.

"As a Doncaster lad it was all I ever wanted to do to play for my hometown team," he says. "It felt like you were representing the town and all the local lads used to feel the same way. We'd have lads from, say, Castleford and Hull in the team and they formed a few cliques, but the Donny lads always stuck together.

"Playing-wise we suffered plenty of bad results, we shed plenty of blood, sweat and tears but as far as we were concerned we were keeping the Rugby League flying in Doncaster. As long as it kept going we'd have played for nothing. We had more coaches than Shearings but the nucleus of Donny lads stayed together for quite a few seasons and as long as we all gave 100 per cent everyone was happy."

The Doncaster spirit of the time was captured for posterity in the evocative and emotional film, "Another Bloody Sunday," filmed by Yorkshire TV as part of their "Once in a Lifetime" series of programmes which looked at people's struggles against adversity. Other programmes in the series featured the life of a life-boat crew and a woman who lived alone on the Yorkshire Moors.

The Dons were the whipping boys of the time, struggling along before pitifully small gates. But their only win of the season came when they beat those other perennial strugglers, Huyton, 6-3, at Tattersfield on 24 February 1980.

The giant prop Tony Banham scored a memorable, late match-winning try that day and, set to classical music, it remains one of the enduring images of a film that captured the heart and soul of grass-roots Rugby League.

Long-serving general manager Tom Morton and chairman John Barron also made

memorable contributions. Piper featured in the film and organised a 25th anniversary reunion. "Sadly two of the players, Tony and Keith Willett, are no longer with us," he says.

"The title of the film was down to me - one day I was filmed as I sat in the dressing room before a match. I said to the lads: 'Another Bloody Sunday, we've got to win.' The director, Barry Cockcroft, immediately said: 'That's it - that's the title.' You'd look forward to playing every Sunday, no matter the result the week before. Despite our losing run we were convinced our losing run had to come to an end one day - and it did.

"It was great being involved in the film and people still remember me for it," Piper says. "It won an award at the Montreux Film Festival as the best documentary of the year. And Doncaster had sold the film rights for £15! I was a car salesman then, just as I am now, and people still come to my garage or see me in the street and shout: 'Another Bloody Sunday!'

"At that time we were the real rubbing rags of the League. People used to stand in the same spot every week and shout the most incredible abuse. Playing on the wing I copped a lot of it. I once had a fight with a spectator as I was leaving the pitch at half-time. He'd been abusing me non-stop and made a lunge for me as I walked off and I clocked him one. But he was there again the next match, still shouting."

Originally known as Bentley Road, the ground was re-named Tattersfield, in honour of Leonard (Len) Tattersfield, who took over as chairman in 1954. It was never a place for the faint-hearted. "But the ground was sacred for us. We'd have social evenings there, trained on it, ran up the stand steps," Piper says. "And there was a fund of stories from all the characters about the place.

"One year they built a big bath in the changing room but they couldn't afford to tile it. So, instead, they got some tarmac and put that on the bottom. When the water was hot it reacted with the hot bitumen and all the players came out of the bath with black arses!

"Some teams never liked playing there. We always seemed to beat Whitehaven. When we played them we knew they'd had a long journey and we'd turn the heating off and take the fuses out of the light switches in their dressing room. Then we'd lock the toilet doors and put "out of order" signs everywhere. Their players would run out on to the pitch for the game bursting for a crap, and it always gave us a bit of an advantage.

"Looking after the playing surface was always going to be an uphill struggle but the pitch was very flat and wide and we never had any complaints until the winter set in. Then it would always be soggy. But there was always a good spirit about the place. Doncaster was always regarded as a bit of an outpost, not a real RL hotbed and a soccer town, not like the towns in West Yorkshire and parts of Lancashire where they were RL born and bred."

But Doncaster, like all the clubs at the time, had a hard core of supporters that never gave in, epitomised by one lady, Joan Martin, who won RL Supporter of the Year Award in 1986. The writer still remembers the indomitable spirit shown by a small group of travelling Doncaster fans at a game in faraway Cardiff in the early 1980s.

"I remember one game when we were due to play Halifax," Piper recalls. "It had been snowing hard for days and there seemed no chance of the game taking place. But the supporters rallied round, cleared the snow and brushed the lines. There were about 30 or 40 of them - you'd never get that now. As a reward the club gave them a pie each for doing the job."

As defeat followed defeat - the nadir being a 75-3 loss at Leigh in March 1976 when the bus driver was co-opted to make up the numbers as substitute - it must have been tempting for Piper and his mates to have chucked in the towel.

Another came in April 1984 when the home game against Workington Town was attended by just 105 people. The last four home games of that season, against Blackpool Borough, Kent Invicta, Workington and Huyton, attracted a total of only 542 spectators. The following season Doncaster recorded another five attendances of less than 200.

"Give up?" Piper says. "I felt like doing that every week, especially if I had to go to work with teeth missing or a broken arm. But you would never give in. The camaraderie was fantastic and if you had a hard away game coming up you could never duck out for fear of being called a cheat by your teammates. But after all these years I remember the victories more than the defeats."

Piper was once transfer-listed by the club after a fall-out. "They put me on the list at £1,500 but the local newspaper made a mistake and printed it as £150," he recalls, wryly. "Sadly, no one bothered to correct them as they assumed that was the right figure. But I played 12 years in total and had a testimonial that was well supported. It raised £5,500 and that was a record for quite some time. I still went down after I retired to watch, but it's awful when you can't play.

"They got Tattersfield looking really good by the time they reached the first division, with new floodlights and a brilliant playing surface. But then the wags would say it had to be - the pitch certainly had a lot of shit on it over the years. A lot of shareholders were not consulted over the sale of the ground - they were treated very badly and the ground disappeared with indecent haste.

"The playing area is still there, though everything around it has been demolished. Every so often, I'll go and have a wander and reflect. It's a sad and nostalgic feeling and you can still hear the crowd shouting things to me like: 'Piper, you're as much use as an ashtray on a motorbike!' They were always encouraging."

Though Doncaster went into liquidation in 1986 a new company was formed under chairman John Desmond and a transformation took place in the club's image, on and off the pitch.

The ground improvements at Tattersfield were such that it was awarded an under-21s international in 1990, a crowd of 4,596 turning up to watch Great Britain defeat France, 16-2, on a bitterly cold Friday, February evening.

The new £60,000 floodlights were inaugurated and Hull KR winger Anthony Sullivan, whose late father, Clive Sullivan MBE had briefly coached the Dons (when Anthony was the ball-boy), marked the occasion of his international debut with a try. Two players who later went on to play for Doncaster, Graham Southernwood and Rocky Turner, were also in the GB side.

The ground looked a picture that night, barely recognisable from a decade or so before - the main stand adorned by a huge painting depicting a rugby game, the pitch in superb condition surrounded by a post and rail perimeter fencing, covered in advertising hoardings from local businesses.

Around that time Doncaster had more land than any other RL club. They had bought the adjacent 1,400-seater social club and also owned a training pitch and huge car park.

Another memorable game was in January 1989 when the visit of Wigan for a Challenge Cup-tie attracted a crowd of 5,274, surpassing the ground record of 4,793 that had stood since Wakefield's visit in April 1962.

Though Doncaster lost, 6-38, they were a team that commanded respect and the improvement in fortunes initially inspired by the highly-respected coach John Sheridan in the mid 1980s was continued by Dave Sampson and then Tony Fisher, who won promotion in 1993. Doncaster also lent a helping hand to neighbours Sheffield Eagles in the true spirit of the sport. After their Owlerton Stadium was declared unsafe the Eagles played five "home" games at Tattersfield in the 1989/90 season, one of seven home venues they used, prior to their move to Don Valley.

Sadly no sooner had Doncaster reached the top-flight than the financial problems surfaced, culminating in the club again being wound-up.

Briefly, the long suffering Dons fans enjoyed their time in the sun as the club won four of its first nine games in the top flight. This included a memorable 29-20 win at St Helens and a 21-6 success over Widnes in front of the Sky cameras that saw them fleetingly top the table. The third game of the campaign, a home game with Leeds (lost 6-16) set a new Tattersfield ground record of 6,440.

But in December Fisher was sacked, reportedly after a personality clash with Desmond and the following month the club entered administration. Though the Dons won only one and drew one of their last 21 games the average league attendance was a highly impressive 3,495, up 1,847 on the promotion season and an unimaginable situation from the nadir of 1983/84 when the average was 255.

The final game at Tattersfield was against Workington on 23 April 1995 when a crowd of 2,975 saw the visitors record a 50-16 win. The occasion is remembered for a series of protests by fans at rumours of a merger with Sheffield to form a South Yorkshire club to enter Super League. Eventually Sheffield went it alone - there was nothing left to merge with once the season closed.

A devoted band of officials and supporters, led by chairman David Prime, ensured that the RL flag was kept flying and a new club was formed, even though a temporary refuge had to be found out of town. Doncaster were re-admitted ten days before the start of the season, starting from scratch in the second division and without a share of television money.

Despite this huge handicap there was a huge amount of enthusiasm and they made arrangements to play at the Meadowcourt Greyhound Stadium *(below)* in Stainforth, north east of the town. It was a vast open place but at least it was a home of sorts and gratefully accepted at the time. And the devoted fans were just glad that the team, now known as Doncaster Dragons, had been saved.

Doncaster played their first four games of the 1995/96 Centenary season at Belle Vue, attracting 1,813 for their opening game against Hull KR, before christening Meadowcourt with a 31-8 win over York on 19 November 1995 before a crowd of 1,240. The old Tattersfield groundsman, the long-serving Keith Hudson, worked wonders to create a suitable playing area at Meadowcourt, ploughing up the area in the centre of the dog-track and laying tons of topsoil. York provided the opposition for the record crowd at the ground - 1,449 in April 1996. Doncaster had to play one rearranged home game against Hunslet at Featherstone as their new home had no lights and in 1998 staged a Challenge Cup-tie against Featherstone Lions at Wakefield.

Finally Doncaster returned to the town in 1998, to formally ground-share Belle Vue with Rovers. Situated across the road from the famous Town Moor racecourse, home of the St Leger, it is a ground that has plainly seen better days. But the soccer club survived the

The main stand at Belle Vue

loss of their league status and after five seasons in the Conference won promotion back in 2003. After a second successive promotion Rovers now play in the newly-named League One, a remarkable resurgence.

Rovers' home since 1922, Belle Vue (initially known as Low Pasture) was considered a fine Football League venue until the 1980s, once claiming a capacity of 40,000 in the immediate pre-war years. Its record attendance was 37,149 for a game against Hull City in 1948. But mining subsidence necessitated the dismantling of the cover on the popular side and the removal of much of the terracing around the same time. The top portion of the 62-step Spion Kop behind the south goal was also lopped off, changing the ground's appearance.

Legislation following the Valley Parade fire also forced the demolition of the wooden Bennetthorpe Stand at the town end which had been brought from Rovers' previous home. The main stand was badly damaged by fire in 1995 during a period when there seemed no hope for Rovers. They slipped out of the League in 1998, gaining just 20 points from 46 league games before re-building in the Conference under new chairman John Ryan and gaining promotion via the play-offs in 2002/03.

Rugby League had been played fleetingly at Belle Vue before. In 1953 Doncaster staged an exhibition game under floodlights at the ground and in 1983 hosted Cardiff City there before a crowd of 1,323. The Dragons certainly made themselves at home, rising from bottom in 1999 to third in the NFP in 2000, when Belle Vue was temporarily nicknamed "The House of Pain" for opponents. The Dragons' season ended in a 17-24 play-off reverse at the hands of Oldham, their only home defeat of the campaign.

The spirit of Doncaster RL was captured in Peter Hilton's book, "50 Years of Bloody Sundays," published in 2001 to commemorate the club's 50th birthday. Now with the new ground more than a pipe-dream exciting times lie ahead.

But the memory of Tattersfield will live on for many people involved in the game, not just in Doncaster. If you find the time, take a detour off the Bentley Road and walk around the high-grassed wilderness that once hosted the greatest game of all. Piper did again recently, for some of the photographs accompanying this book, gazing nostalgically at the bottom corner where he scored many tries. "I've a square yard of Tattersfield turf in my back garden and I have in my will that I want my ashes scattered here," he said. "Just listen - I can fair hear the crowd now."

FEATHERSTONE

Post Office Road, Featherstone, is a name synonymous with the game of Rugby League and a ground where many stirring games have taken place and passions and emotions run high.

Time moves so quickly and it is amazing to think that it is over 20 years ago that Rovers lifted the Challenge Cup at Wembley for the last time with that 14-12 win over Hull. Two decades on, the ground and the area have undergone massive change.

David Hobbs, who returned to the club as coach in July 2005, lifted the Lance Todd Trophy that famous day in 1983, his two tries going down in Rovers folklore. "For little more than a small village, with a population of 15,000, the success that Rovers have had is incredible," Hobbs says. "Of the 15 players that played at Wembley that day, eleven of them were miners and lived within a two-mile radius of the ground.

"They used to say you could put a bubble over Featherstone. You lived there, worked there, boozed there and played or watched your rugby there. Within a three-mile radius of Featherstone, there would be a dozen collieries and lots of small communities. That helped produce a rivalry, at school, at rugby and in the pit. Rugby League was a way of life, a fierce passion for so many people. There would be hundreds of miners playing the game for local teams, in Sharlston, Glasshoughton and Castleford. Featherstone had three amateur open age teams plus a professional club and that was a huge proportion of the male population engaged in playing the game.

"The week started on Monday morning, 6am, going down the pit. Training would be Tuesday and Thursday and after the weekend match everyone would go down to the same boozer, run through the game and still be talking about it all the following week. It was a very male-dominated society 20 years ago in Featherstone but so many things have altered in the intervening period."

Hobbs did as many lads before him, leaving school to work down the pit. His father, Derrick, was personnel manager at the local colliery and used to turn a blind eye if players needed some time off a shift in order to fit in a training session before an important game.

"We had a local team and a local following but then Castleford and Wakefield were the same at that time," Hobbs says. "But now we're not producing players from these areas like we used to. When I signed professional forms for Rovers another half-dozen signed at the same time from my junior team. It was a numbers game and some would make it.

"At 17 or 18 years old, young players had the cushion of learning their trade in the 'A' team, playing alongside some seasoned professionals. Players, maybe on the way down or coming back from injury, would protect the younger lads and pass on their experience."

Hobbs learned his trade alongside players he had idolised from the terraces, notably the fearsome, balding prop, Jimmy Thompson. "My dad was secretary of Rovers for about twelve years and I was always up there in the school holidays, painting railings and so on,"

A snowbound Post Office Road

he says. "Jimmy was a real local hero and he helped give me a good grounding in the game. He also taught me that no player was bigger than the club, and that spirit spilled over."

Rovers' teams throughout the years have always used the peculiarities of their pitch to best advantage. "If we won the toss we'd always play uphill in the first half then downhill in the second," Hobbs says. "A lot of teams just couldn't cope with the size of the ground - always as wide as it was long - and failed to control the ball."

Life in Featherstone changed forever after the miners' strike of 1984/85. With Rovers suffering financially, Hobbs was sold to Oldham for the princely sum of £40,000 to help balance the books. Now the pits have gone and many of the spoil-heaps and mine workings have been grassed over.

Sitting in the main stand these days, on a pleasant summer afternoon with cricket being played on an adjoining field and undulating grass swards way into the distance, Featherstone could be mistaken for a rural idyll.

"Featherstone is still pretty much a small, local ground and holds enough for the people that want to come," Hobbs says. "But whereas 20 years ago any one of, say, 16 teams could win the cup, now it's four or five and Rovers, realistically, won't get into Super League. So a lot of the "floating" supporters from places like Ackworth and Pontefract go to watch Castleford instead.

"The challenge for the game is to recreate that situation again where more teams could win honours. I've been to Wembley with Featherstone, won the championship with Featherstone but it's hard ever seeing those days happening again. As a result the better kids went to Cas to play Super League and, as the transfer market is virtually a thing of the past there's not the incentive to put money into development."

But then Rovers have had many a fight against adversity and survived to tell the tale.

The Railway End

Rovers became a senior club in 1921, twenty years after their formation. The club's original headquarters was the Station Hotel and their first field was on the site of the present club car park.

Rovers soon built a reputation as one of the strongest of the junior sides, reaching the last eight of the Challenge Cup in 1905 but closing down a year later after losing most of their best players to senior clubs. But they reformed on Boxing Day 1908, went on join the Yorkshire Combination and spent the 1912/13 season playing on the Colliery Miners' Welfare Ground.

Rovers closed down during the First World War but made rapid strides when peace-time football resumed, re-establishing the ground at Post Office Road. After impressive performances in league and cup, Rovers were accepted into the Northern Rugby League in June 1921 and undertook major ground developments ready for their elevation. That summer work began on banking up the terraces, covering the stand and building new dressing rooms.

Rovers' home debut as a senior club ended in disappointment as Hull won, 21-4, before a 4,000 crowd on 2 September 1921 but few sides have since relished the trip to Post Office Road. The club's fortunes, though, depended to a great extent on the fortunes of the mining industry and they suffered more than most from the trade depression following the 1926 general strike.

Rovers' hard-earned status as a senior club was threatened several times - not least when a Newcastle syndicate was twice thwarted in attempts in the early 1930s to move the club to the north-east.

The 'thirties were a desperately difficult time for the club that occupied the lower reaches of the league as gates dropped off to alarming levels. The lowest crowd for a first-team game was 200 against Bradford in 1930, though the visit of neighbours Castleford (who became a senior club five years after Rovers) provided a temporary respite three years later when a crowd of 9,334 was recorded.

The ground was open to the elements, apart from the main stand, until the construction of a small, roofed-in children-only enclosure on the opposite side. This structure, opened by the club president, Abraham Bullock, in 1938, was later extended in the early 1950s and became known as the Bullock Stand, housing many of Rovers' most vociferous supporters in what was often an intimidating ground for opposing teams, especially for cup-ties.

Rovers have often depended on the good nature of their supporters and, as an example, the Supporters' Club contributed £1,200 towards ground improvements in 1952, in what became Rovers' first Wembley year. When Rovers beat Wigan, 14-11, in a third-round tie, the crowd of 14,344 (£2,308) set a new ground record. Fullback Freddie Miller was the match-winner with two drop goals. Sadly he passed away eight years later and the present gate at the main entrance, "in memory of a great player and a gentleman", was erected by supporters in his memory.

With Rovers recognised as a redoubtable side in cup football, two successive third-round ties against St Helens provided great memories. Rovers beat Saints, 5-0, in a snowstorm in March 1958 before 15,700 at Post Office Road. A year later the ground record of 17,531, higher than the town's population, was established when Rovers beat St Helens, 20-6, in far better conditions to again reach the Challenge Cup semi-final.

Jack Fennell was a regular in the Rovers side at that stage and recalls the atmosphere of the ground at the time. "I went to South Featherstone School and, for every home game, Rovers would distribute a couple of tickets," he says. "That's how I first got interested in the game.

"Most of the players worked down the pit. There were three shifts and, if you missed training through being on the night shift you had to make up for it by training the following morning. We used to train Wednesday and Friday mornings and the

water from the boiler in the dressing rooms was still warm enough to use.

"There were temporary lights on the main pitch and training pitch that we used at night. When Eric Batten was coach we used to run up and down the terraces and use skipping ropes when the field was unfit. We had sprint training on a narrow cinder track behind the main stand. It was between the tiers of the stand and the dressing rooms and we'd run down four at a time. The backs would all try to run with the forwards so they would look faster but Eric soon got wise to that.

"The hard manual labour and training twice a week kept you fit but, before big games especially, we'd do extra training in the daylight if we could fit it in. We'd do a fair bit of ball work and Eric used to let the backs work out their moves.

"Most of the supporters worked at the pit, too, so if you had a bad game on the Saturday they were waiting for you on the Monday morning. It was no good having Monday off, they'd be waiting for you on Tuesday instead. Today there's not the same pressure on the players to perform away from the ground."

Supporters groups took over ground maintenance completely and resurfaced the car park and built new entrances. In the mid-1970s ten acres of land were given to the club by the Supporters' Club for training purposes and for use by junior sides. Rovers have always retained their close links with the amateur game and continue to stage many local finals. Floodlights were finally erected in 1983 and switched on for the first time for the visit of Wakefield in October of that year.

The miners' strike heralded a period of great hardship for the local community and, if things were not bad enough, the social club was destroyed by fire in July 1984. Seven months later, an electrical fault in the main stand led to a major fire with the structure being condemned and later demolished.

Out of the ashes Rovers survived and the new propped cantilever main stand, including two hospitality boxes and a police control room, was officially opened in August 1986. This stand cost £275,000 and other ground developments following stricter guidelines in the wake of the Valley Parade fire left Rovers with a total outlay of over £400,000 in the space of two years. In addition to that, a new clubhouse, incorporating dressing and medical rooms and costing £160,000 was officially opened when Rovers hosted the PNG tourists in October 1987.

Keith Bell was the ultimate Rovers stalwart, playing for the club for nearly 20 years between 1971-90 and is now heavily involved at Featherstone Lions ARLFC. He also followed a family tradition as his father, Jim, played for Rovers before the war and was later the groundsman, while his three brothers also played for the club.

"I remember going down to the ground as a kid and earned my pocket money washing the seats in the stand or putting the kit out to dry," he recalls. "There was the big

The family stand, at the newly-named Lionheart Stadium

wooden stand with the changing rooms underneath and it was a bit of an adventure for a kid going inside. On match day you could tell if there was a big crowd by the noise coming down from the stand into the changing rooms. And the atmosphere under the Bullock Stand was fantastic. It was a special place.

"The pitch was the minimum length and the maximum width, nearly square and with the famous slope as well. A lot of teams just didn't fancy playing at Featherstone. They were intimidated before the game began. And we had some brilliant players, Steve Nash, John Newlove - the most under-rated player I ever saw - and forwards like Jimmy Thompson, Vince Farrar and Keith Bridges. No one messed with our pack and everyone in Rugby League knew about us.

"Rugby League was the be-all and end-all in Featherstone and the village lived and breathed the game. Every kid in Featherstone had one ambition - to play for Rovers. Most of the players worked together and walked to training still in their overalls. In the depths of winter the training field would be a foot deep in sludge. It's changed a bit now. There's not the same passion and Rovers are not in the top league. The village has changed so much, too. The closing of the pits had a lot to do with that and when summer Rugby League came in that changed a lot of things also."

In 1997 Post Office Road was renamed the Lionheart Stadium after a sponsorship link-up with RJB Mining. The ground today is one of the best appointed outside Super League with a smart main stand, seating 850, and an impressive family stand opposite where the Bullock Stand once stood, seating 1,650. The ground's capacity stands at 6,700.

The post office from which the road takes its name is long gone but Rovers remain - a fiercely proud club still with deep roots in the local community, still battling against recurrent financial problems and limited resources with indomitable spirit. The true heart of Rugby League still beats strongly in Featherstone and a trip down Post Office Road to the ground remains one to be savoured.

GATESHEAD & NORTH EAST

Sitting in the Thunderdome's main stand on an April 2005 afternoon watching Gateshead Thunder take on Blackpool Panthers in a National League Two encounter was an appropriate time to reflect on the history of the game on Tyneside - so much potential, so much enthusiasm, yet so many broken dreams.

But, despite it all, Rugby League was still being played in the north-east, not once but twice that afternoon, with Gateshead Storm also taking part in an NL3 encounter just down the road. Somebody must have been doing something right.

You have to go back over a hundred years to the early years of the Northern Union to discover the roots of the game's fascination with Tyneside. Far from being a glorious time for expansion and progress, as those pioneering years following the breakaway from rugby union are often portrayed, it was an era when so much harm was done to the roots for future progress. Many long-established clubs went to the wall, unable to cope with the headlong dash towards professionalism and only the strongest survived. Self-interest and greed ruled above the game as a whole.

Such a case in point happened in the north-east where South Shields' entry into the Northern Union was doomed almost before it had started. The area was a strong one for rugby union with Percy Park (North Shields), Rockcliff (Whitley Bay), Northern (Newcastle) and North Durham (Gateshead) all rivals of South Shields, along with Westoe, based at South Shields cricket club. The Durham clubs, particularly Hartlepool Rovers, West Hartlepool, Sunderland, Tudhoe (near Spennymoor) and Durham City were also growing in strength as the end of the 19th century beckoned. The north-east was a rich breeding ground for Northern Union scouts with several players joining clubs in Lancashire and Yorkshire.

South Shields was a thriving seaport at this time with a population of about 100,000. Situated on the south bank of the River Tyne, about ten miles downstream from Newcastle-upon-Tyne, it was a major rugby-playing town. In the mid-1890s South Shields' fixture list, though, was decimated by the sudden departure of many of the senior clubs in Yorkshire to join the Northern Union. That left them more dependent than ever on local fixtures. The South Shields club, mindful of the increasing popularity of association football, tried to get a county league started to maintain interest, but the RFU would not allow this.

Club president John Moralee had seen the success that Sunderland AFC had enjoyed since they joined the Football League in 1890. They won the championship four times in their first dozen years and enjoyed average attendances of around 12,000 by the turn of the century. He was confident that his club could emulate their achievements in the other code. After careful consideration South Shields eventually decided to join the Northern Union, being accepted into membership in July 1901. They were confident that the other major north-east clubs would join them. However, their plans were immediately placed in

jeopardy by two separate developments. The RFU suddenly had an about-turn and sanctioned the formation of a North-East League after all - a severe body blow to hopes of Northern Union expansion. The Northern Union was also in a state of turmoil, with bitter wrangling between member clubs over the breakaway by fourteen of the leading clubs in forming a Northern Rugby League and distancing themselves from the Lancashire and Yorkshire Senior Competitions.

As a result the Yorkshire clubs would not sanction fixtures against the newcomers and South Shields had to resort to playing friendly fixtures in their first season, 1901/02. South Shields' first opponents were Warrington for a friendly engagement on 4 September 1901 that attracted a crowd of 2,000 to their Horsley Hill ground, Warrington recording a 14-7 victory.

The ground facilities were poor - their sole facility being a pavilion at the east end. Their only competitive fixture of the campaign saw them lose at home to Bradford in the Challenge Cup. But despite all the problems the end-of-season review stated that the campaign had, overall, been a success and that the club, which had fulfilled 34 fixtures in total, looked forward to taking its place in the newly formed Second Division of the Northern Union in 1902/03 as the game introduced a two-divisional system for the first time.

Wallsend, from north of the Tyne, also joined the Northern Union in November 1901 and competed in the Cumberland League, playing at the Avenue Grounds, though their membership lasted only fleetingly as the club disbanded the following season, failing to fulfil its fixtures.

But the brief existence of two clubs in the north-east allowed for the formation of a Durham & Northumberland county side that, after playing friendly games in 1901/02 then competed in the County Championship alongside Lancashire, Yorkshire, Cheshire and

Cumberland. The county side was usually composed almost entirely of South Shields players and recorded a total of two wins in eight competitive fixtures before folding after South Shields' demise.

South Shields, boosted by the formation of a local junior league (South Shields St Pauls were the most prominent junior club), won their first league game, 5-3 at Stockport but then suffered a series of setbacks on the field. By Christmas they were reported as being in a bad way financially. They eventually struggled through the season, winning a respectable ten games, and finishing 14th of out 18 clubs, but owed players' wages and back rent on the Horsley Hill ground.

With the management of the club taken over by the lessees of the ground, South Shields did survive another season but their home crowds were again very disappointing. At that time the bottom three clubs had to apply for re-election and despite finishing ahead of Morecambe and Normanton (who were both re-elected) South Shields were voted out of the Northern Union, with clubs considering the onerous travelling expenses of a trip to the north-east above other factors.

Horsley Hill, located on the north side of Horsley Hill Road in the Westoe district, lay dormant until the formation of South Shields Adelaide AFC in 1908. After dropping the Adelaide tag South Shields were accepted into membership of the Football League in 1919 and played at Horsley Hill until 1930 when they moved lock, stock and barrel to Gateshead. In their first few seasons in the League South Shields often drew crowds of 20,000 or more but by their last season the average had fallen to just over 3,000. Horsley Hill was later used as a greyhound track before being demolished in 1960 and the site is now covered by housing.

The growth of soccer at the expense of old established rugby clubs was mirrored elsewhere in the region. Tudhoe, for instance, closed down in 1904 and their Brewery Field ground was taken over by Spennymoor United AFC, while West Hartlepool folded in 1908 and became Hartlepools United AFC, playing at Victoria Park.

Despite the ending of club representation in the north-east, due largely to their own member clubs' self-interest in taking the geographical position into account at the re-election vote, the authorities still persisted with the idea of pushing the game forward in the region. In January 1909 the second Test against the first Australian tourists was staged at Newcastle United's St James' Park. The attendance of 22,000 (£568) was easily the best of the tour (the next best was 12,000). By contrast, though, just a month previously, 56,000 had seen Newcastle United sensationally lose 1-9 at home to Sunderland - their highest home defeat. St James' Park then had a capacity of around 60,000, the vast majority accommodated on vast open banked terraces on three sides of the ground, with the sole seated stand holding only 4,500. Jimmy Lomas scored a try and kicked three goals against Dally Messenger's Kangaroos in the home side's 15-5 victory. Billy Batten and Albert Rosenfeld, who would both enter RL's Hall of Fame, were in direct opposition that day.

In November 1911 the Australians returned for the first Test of their second tour, this time for a game played on a Wednesday afternoon instead of Saturday. This had a detrimental affect on the attendance - just 6,500 (£338) saw the Kangaroos record their first win over Great Britain, 19-10. The game marked the Test debut of future great Harold Wagstaff for the home side. It was not until December 1929 that the code returned when a Northern Rugby League XIII lost 22-32 to Australia before a crowd of 9,690 on a Wednesday afternoon, match reports describing the action as "spectacular."

In January 1934 the Australians were back on Tyneside for the final game of their tour, losing 14-19 to England at Redheugh Park, Gateshead thanks to a late try by Leigh centre Fred Harris. By now Redheugh Park was an established Football League ground following Gateshead taking over South Shields' name in 1930. There was an encouraging attendance of 15,576 and after the game the players linked hands and sang "Auld Lang Syne" with the spectators.

Located in the Low Team area south-west of the town centre, formerly a clay pit and in the shadow of the gas holders, Redheugh Park was developed by the local council and opened in August 1930. An oval-shaped arena, it had cover on all four sides and was sub-let to a greyhound racing company in 1937. Ironically its grandstand originated from Harraby Park, Carlisle - former home of the ill-fated Carlisle City RL side who failed to see out their fixtures in their inaugural season of 1928/29. Gateshead AFC stayed in the League until they failed to gain re-election in 1960. Despite finishing third from bottom of Third Division (North) above Oldham Athletic and Hartlepools United (who were both re-elected) and making only their second application (their first was 23 years previously) they were replaced by Peterborough United - shades of South Shields NU all those years ago. Redheugh Park was demolished in the early 1970s.

The 1930s saw a growth in greyhound racing in this country with a knock-on effect for Rugby League with syndicate owners seeing the game as an opportunity to increase usage of their facilities. The short-lived London clubs, London Highfield, Streatham & Mitcham and Acton & Willesden, all played in grounds primarily used for greyhounds, as did Liverpool Stanley at the Stanley dog track.

In December 1935 a Mr Alfred Peel attended a RL Council Meeting to outline his plans for a club in Newcastle playing at Brough Park. He must have been a persuasive man for the Council agreed to donate £100 to re-turf parts of the ground and Newcastle were later admitted into membership in time for the 1936/37 season, having agreed a rent of £10 per match. Two exhibition games, involving Broughton Rangers and Keighley and Batley and York were staged in February and March 1936.

Brough Park, situated in Byker, was built in 1910 and was originally a horse-racing course and park, later staging greyhound racing and speedway. The stadium staged a representative game in April 1937 when Wales beat a Northern Rugby League side 15-12 on a waterlogged pitch before a crowd of 3,000. However, for their second season Newcastle decided to leave Brough Park and take up residence at the new White City Stadium, built on a 12-acre site in Gateshead. This was constructed at a cost of £50,000 and was said to be able to accommodate up to 24,000 spectators. Greyhound racing, baseball, athletics and boxing were other sports to feature at the new stadium. But its location, situated in "No Man's Land" on the Durham side of Scotswood Bridge was considered to be far from ideal.

Newcastle continued to struggle to attract support, enticing only 4,000 (one of their best gates) for the biggest game in their short history against the 1937 Kangaroos, who recorded a 37-0 win. But the club was very unlucky in that it coincided with Gateshead playing Lincoln City at Redheugh Park - the only time that ground ever attracted over 20,000 (20,792 the official return) after the soccer club's unbeaten start to their league campaign.

Newcastle's two seasons in the league were disastrous in terms of playing results. They finished 29th out of 30 clubs in their first campaign, winning five of 38 games with one draw. "The Babes" as they were known did have one famous moment, however. Their first win, at the 16th attempt, was by 5-0 against the reigning champions, Hull - a result that sent shockwaves throughout the game. But they only struggled into a second season with a £500 grant from the RFL. They then recorded only two wins and four draws in 1937/38 and struggled to the end of the season with further aid in the shape of a £200 grant from the game's governing body.

At the end of the season Newcastle, willing to carry on despite heavy financial losses, had to apply for re-election at the AGM alongside Leigh and Bramley. Although the latter two clubs were re-admitted without further discussion Newcastle, whose representative did not attend, was not as fortunate. After being voted out by 15-6 senior Rugby League again disappeared from the north-east. Brough Park survives as a greyhound stadium, but the site of the White City is now covered by warehousing and light engineering works.

Rugby League returned to the north-east in the 1990s, aided by the help of Gateshead Council, eager to use the Gateshead International Stadium to its full potential. Opened in 1955 and built on reclaimed industrial land, the venue was initially known as the Gateshead Youth Stadium. The first grandstand seated a modest 170 but the impressive Tyne & Wear stand, opened in 1981, now accommodates 3,300 under cover and the stadium has a capacity of 11,750. Known throughout the world as the hometown track of 3,000m world record holder Brendan Foster the stadium has staged many high-profile athletics meetings.

The 1991 and 1992 Charity Shield games were staged at the ground and these successful occasions led to further big games being accommodated, accompanied by a long-term development programme in the local community spearheaded by Mick Hogan. The Gateshead Mets Academy side, formed in 1995, nurtured local talent with local players competing in national schools competitions from the age of eleven. Annual events included a residential junior summer camp, Finals Day, Touch RL festival, Little League festivals, Nines tournaments, Academy fun days, coaching courses and various holiday schemes. There was also the development of a north-east amateur competition that soon encompassed Gateshead Panthers, Teesside Steelers, Benfield Lions, South Shields Raiders, Sunderland City and Durham Tigers alongside a student RL competition in the five universities of Teesside, Sunderland, Newcastle, Durham and Northumbria. At long last there were the roots that the old clubs of South Shields and Newcastle were unable to grow.

Gateshead also hosted an Australian tour match against Great Britain under-21s in 1994, England-France internationals in 1995 and 1996 and a game in the Centenary World Cup when Australia defeated South Africa 86-6 before 9,191 to whet the appetite of the north-east public. The Kangaroos returned in 2000 to defeat Fiji, 66-8. In 1998 two "On the Road" Super League games were staged in Gateshead and a council-backed bid for a consortium fronted by ex-Cronulla Sharks boss Shane Richardson and Sheffield Eagles co-founder Kath Hetherington saw a Super League franchise, Gateshead Thunder, admitted for the 1999 competition.

Jeff Bowron is a freelance journalist who has enjoyed a long association with Gateshead sport. He saw soccer at Redheugh Park and still follows Gateshead's progress in the Unibond League playing at the Gateshead International Stadium and has reported on Thunder since their formation.

"The stadium was built on top of an old refuse tip and that's one of the reasons there are so many pitch problems at the moment," Bowron explains. "When it opened the stadium had an ash track and a small stand with standing in front and a hill opposite. It was really basic. But Brendan Foster's feats and the growth of the Gateshead Harriers was the catalyst for the council to develop the stadium.

"People in Gateshead shop in Newcastle over the bridge and sports-wise the region is dominated by Newcastle United," he adds. "Gateshead AFC had a purple patch when they played in the Conference but in all that time never had a four-figure attendance. Then out of the blue along came Gateshead Thunder. We'd had the big rep games there and the "On the Road" games and suddenly we had a team in Super League. It dropped in from nowhere but it was absolutely marvellous. The opening game against Leeds, at the newly-named Thunderdome, was staged in the worst weather imaginable - it was very cold and it absolutely bucketed down - but attracted almost 6,000 and it kicked on from there. There was such a feel-good factor and the game-day experience (with Hogan as the club's marketing manager) was almost as good as the game itself - it was unique and innovative.

"People used to go just for the entertainment and then got hooked on Rugby League. Captain Thunder, the team's mascot, was a huge cult figure. It built up by word of mouth that there was a great product and spectacle in Gateshead." (Hogan is now commercial director with rugby union's Newcastle Falcons).

Gateshead averaged 3,895 in their only season in the top flight and staged a successful "On the Road" game at Tynecastle Stadium in Edinburgh - when, aided by an early try from emerging Irish winger Brian Carney - they defeated reigning champions Wigan before a crowd of 4,978. Boosted by a strong Australian influence, the "Geordie Aussies", they performed with huge credit under Australian coach Shaun McRae, defeating St Helens home and away and finishing sixth in the table. Then came the bombshell news - Thunder would be no more. They would "merge" with Hull and thus accept a Super League financial incentive of £1.25m to defray accumulated debts of a reported £700,000.

Gateshead fans enjoy Super League in 1999

"We've had a huge loss," Richardson told the press conference assembled to announce their move to Hull. "The problems began when I ran out of money. We could have been in a position where we couldn't pay creditors. The gates did improve as the season went on and the fans were absolutely committed to the club. They were wonderful, but there weren't just enough of them. We were having to make financial projections for the 2000 season and we needed our gates to double to break even, and to make budget forecasts on that basis and present them to our bank wouldn't have looked realistic."

"The news came as a bolt from the blue," Bowron recalls. "There was never any inclination that the club might be in financial trouble. The Australian players were absolutely wonderful and got involved in the community and were fantastic ambassadors. The club would really have kicked on in the second year. At first we thought the club would stay in Gateshead and it would benefit from the "merger" by utilising the strong youth league set-up in Hull. They were still selling Thunder merchandise to the end. Then one night I got home to find a fax from Super League awaiting me - I couldn't believe my eyes. It was the biggest kick in the teeth I've ever felt - it was a surreal experience.

"There was a massive press conference and everyone was there. Shane Richardson got absolutely slaughtered, while Kath Hetherington stood ashen faced. Everyone was so angry and felt a massive disappointment. So much effort had gone into Thunder and so many walked away determined never to have anything more to do with Rugby League. They were so disillusioned with what had happened."

Thunder had begun life with an 18-8 friendly defeat at Castleford on a cold, wet and wintry January night and ended it - though no-one knew it at the time - with a 48-22 win at Warrington backed by several hundred Geordies who gave the game a carnival atmosphere in anticipation of a second season that was never to be.

"The news that Gateshead are to become, in effect, Hull FC is the most depressing event to have occurred in our game for a very long time," one correspondent wrote to League Express. "I attended a match at Gateshead last year and it was one of the most vibrant, positive clubs I have visited in 15 years as a spectator. If Gateshead is classed as unsuccessful then heaven help any future bids."

"Yes we had no real League heritage but the game has now lost 3,000 fans," wrote another. "The bitterest pill was telling the kids that no more rugby was to be played at Gateshead. They loved it, everything, the game, the atmosphere, the Captain. Is there a more secure and friendly sport than League to take the kids? We doubt it - we were welcomed by fans wherever we went."

Gateshead Thunder 'On The Road', Tynecastle Stadium, Edinburgh (August 1999)

Bowron helped form a supporters' group, Thunder Storm, determined to keep the Rugby League flag flying on Tyneside. "The response was phenomenal," he recalls. "We got 300 at meetings, raised money and got some impetus going. We could never save the original club - that was never on - but it helped resurrect a new one."

Rising from the ashes, Gateshead Thunder Mark II was re-formed in time to enter the Northern Ford Premiership in time for the 2000/01 season. Under new coach Andy Kelly they finished third bottom with just two league wins after attracting a promising crowd of 2,332 for their opening game against Hull KR (lost 0-18). But early in the following season spiralling debts forced the club into administration and Kelly and the Yorkshire-based squad members were jettisoned as part of the cost-cutting exercise. Thunder Mark III limped to the end of a win-less second season under Leeds-based coach Paul Fletcher. They did draw one game, against Featherstone Rovers, but finished the season with some heavy defeats, including a 0-82 thrashing by Leigh in a "home" game staged at Hilton Park that ironically attracted their best "home" gate of the season - 1,200.

Further upheaval at board level saw chairman and club owner Mike Jeffels pull out early in 2003 and a new board, including several Thunder Storm officials, took charge. A long wait for an elusive victory was ended when Thunder defeated Workington Town, 42-12, in the National League Cup in April 2003 - their first win for nearly two years. Thunder

gained three more wins to finish second bottom in NL2. But the next year, under a new coach in Seamus McCallion, Thunder managed just one league win and picked up the wooden spoon for a second time. In their first four years after reformation the future of Rugby League on Tyneside often hung by a thread.

Nothing if not resilient, Thunder entered the 2005 season with a new coach in Dean Thomas and eighteeen new signings, including three Fijian internationals, four West Indies internationals and a host of promising Australians. Off the field former Durham CCC chairman Bill Midgley fronted an eight-strong board. Though starting the season slowly Thomas was rewarded with an extension to his contract as Thunder reached the NL2 play-offs. "Organisation-wise Thunder are probably in their best shape since they were re-formed and there is greater stability," Bowron says. "The players all live on Tyneside and it is the best squad they have assembled once they are all fit and on the park.

"But it is still a huge battle - against the position of the ground, which is a bit isolated from the town centre, the lack of history for the game in the town, and the fact that the game is not really known in the area. To get the missing fans back they have to be in the top three - otherwise the effort behind the scenes counts for nothing. In 1999 they really had something - the locals were fired up and the club had a good name in the area. Now they are associated with struggle and defeat. That is an image that they need to rid themselves of as quickly as possible."

In the few years Thunder has been a groundhopper's delight, playing games at a variety of temporary venues while their notorious home pitch was being renovated. Thunder have played at local rugby union grounds at Gateshead Fell RUFC's Hedley Lawson Park, Percy Park RU, a dual complex ground next to Tynedale CC on Preston Avenue, North Shields and the Monkton Stadium in Jarrow, an athletics venue first opened in 1988 with a small playing pitch. In May 2005 they played York City Knights at Newcastle Falcons RU's Kingston Park ground, also host to Newcastle United's reserves, which represented a huge step-up in terms of profile and facilities from their other recent options.

"Ironically Thunder have reserved some of their best performances for out-grounds," Bowron says. "They beat Workington at Gateshead Fell to end that run of 47 games without a win and hammered London Skolars 50-20 at Monkton Stadium, with Andy Walker scoring five tries. In the long term they need to get the product right on the pitch and get the people back into watching Rugby League on Tyneside. But sport in Gateshead has always been a struggle."

HALIFAX

The years either side of the end of the last century will be looked back upon by future historians as the time when so many of the game's great traditional grounds disappeared.

Such was the case with Thrum Hall where senior Rugby League was played for the final time in March 1998, though in its death throes the old ground enjoyed a glorious swansong as Halifax beat Leeds 35-28 in an authentic friendly game before a crowd of 4,350. Supporters, young and old, flocked to the ground to pay their last respects and the weather was kind - the sun shone from a perfect blue sky, glistening off the surrounding hills. The views down the valleys, plunging away on all sides, were crystal clear and the shirt-sleeved crowd created a carnival atmosphere. What a contrast with fourteen months earlier when another old ground, Oldham's Watersheddings, saw its final game, a friendly against Swinton marred by murky grey drizzle as the spectators huddled on the crumbling terraces.

Todmorden Old Brass Band played at Thrum Hall's finale and the weather that day is not how people will remember the great old ground where postponements over the years through snow and ice were commonplace.

Halifax played in traditional blue and white hoped jerseys and a late try by Danny Seal ensured their win. There were mixed feelings for the old Halifax players, who got a tremendous reception when introduced to the crowd at half-time.

For the late Hubert Lockwood, then 89, who was Halifax's fullback in their Wembley triumph over Salford in 1939, it was a day that brought back happy memories. Lockwood's career spanned the war years and, in all, he made 348 appearances for Halifax.

"My first game for Halifax was at Bradford at their old Birch Lane ground," he recalled. "I played on many other old Rugby League grounds which are now no more, like Station Road, Mather Lane, Watersheddings, Fartown and the Athletic Grounds. They've all gone. Who'd have thought that Thrum Hall would follow them?

"It is a sad day for many of us. When you've had a long association with a club it becomes a big part of your life. I always enjoyed coming here and playing here. But I've been down to the Shay and I think the ground has great possibilities. It will be ideal. There's room to develop, which we haven't got at Thrum Hall. I just hope the club gets the brass together and makes a good job of it."

Johnny Freeman was one of the all-time Thrum Hall favourites, scoring 290 tries in 395 games for Halifax between 1954 and 1967. "A lot of my tries were scored in that top right-hand corner," explained Johnny, as he pointed to the spot, a tear in his eye. "I've got great memories of playing here. The atmosphere and crowds were something special."

Scrum-half Stan Kielty made more appearances for Halifax than anyone, 482 between 1946 and 1958, often in tandem with his halfback partner Ken Dean. "My biggest memory of playing at Thrum Hall was coming out of the pavilion and down on to the pitch

The Shay - still incomplete, despite it being Halifax's home since 1998

through the crowds of people," he said. "You got a slap on the back going out before the match and a slap in the mouth at the end if you'd lost. For my game the slope worked a treat and I soon got used to playing here. It's a sad day but you have to move with the times and I'm looking forward to seeing Halifax at their new ground."

Paul Rowley played with distinction for Halifax at Thrum Hall and the Shay and reflects on his time at Halifax with affection. "I loved it at Thrum Hall," he said. "I always liked to think it was our fortress. You always knew that other teams didn't relish coming there and that gave you an advantage. Attacking the Scrattin' Shed, with the crowd roaring you on, was a special feeling.

"The last day at Thrum Hall was a sad occasion, especially for the local lads in the team and for the spectators. But it was an old ground and you have to move with the times. The massive slope certainly worked to our advantage - it was a strange slope, kind of across the pitch instead of from end to end. We used to send the forwards driving down the hill and swung the ball out up the hill, letting the ball do our work for us.

"We trained on the pitch all the time so that gave us a massive advantage. We certainly used it to its full potential. We got to know every inch of the pitch. The home dressing rooms were in the pavilion and rather nice. But the away ones were horrible - split into two and damp. It was hard to stand up straight in them. When we played the Australian sides there in the World Club Championship in 1997 some of their players couldn't believe the place. One remarked to me that he could now understand what it must have been like to play rugby in the nineteenth century. But Thrum Hall wasn't there to please - it was there for the home side to play with an advantage. And for many years it served its purpose.

"A lot of people didn't want to leave Thrum Hall but it was something the club had to do. It was just an old, crumbling ground and the costs of renovation and meeting all the safety criteria got too much. It was a sad moment but Thrum Hall really was on its last legs and the last straw came when the local council were going to condemn the main stand. I actually soon got used to playing at the Shay. It was a tidy little ground and if they got around to finishing the construction of the main stand it would definitely be one of the best grounds in the Rugby League.

"The playing pitch is excellent and also very close to the spectators and there is a great atmosphere with a decent crowd on the ground. In that first season there in 1998 we finished third in Super League and had a fantastic year. But unfortunately the club wasn't able to build upon that and there were the well-documented financial problems. But Halifax remains a town where a lot of people are interested in Rugby League and hopefully they will be back in Super League one day."

One of the most famous and prominent Yorkshire rugby clubs, Halifax's formation can be traced back to December 1873, though their first competitive game was not until November 1874.

As cricket clubs were the first to establish properly enclosed grounds, rugby clubs were often indebted to them for use of their facilities. Halifax played their early games on a variety of grounds; Halifax Trinity Cricket Field in King Cross Street, briefly at Ovenden United Cricket Club and then Skircoat Moor (Savile Park) where rugby in Halifax really began to take off.

Halifax then secured an arrangement to share the Hanson Lane ground with the cricket club. Halifax Trinity CC had secured the new ground in 1876. Two open stands were erected and a crowd of over 20,000 saw a floodlit match against Birch (a Manchester club) in 1878 played under Siemens Lights.

Hanson Lane was a venue for Yorkshire county games and also staged the prestigious North v South representative fixture as well as the Yorkshire Cup Final in 1879 between Wakefield Trinity and Kirkstall. Its major drawback was that there was only one field and the cricket square went unprotected from the ravages of rugby throughout the winter months. The ground was also some distance from the town centre and a considerable trek up hill on foot.

Halifax had won the inaugural Yorkshire Cup Final, staged in December 1877, and after that success it was decided to amalgamate and form the Halifax Cricket, Football and Athletic Club.

The control of the ground and pavilion, however, remained in the hands of the cricket committee. The new organisation, though, was hampered by the short lease and a lack of space for ground improvements and so decided to purchase the farm opposite from Major Dyson - that had been let to a farmer known as Riley Whittaker - for the sum of £3,000, known as Thrum Hall and develop a vast area covering 55,000 square yards.

"Thrum" had a connection with the local woollen industry - being the name of a loose thread. The site was an "L-shaped" piece of land and was large enough to accommodate separate cricket and rugby fields as well as bowling greens. The ground was levelled and laid out at a cost of over £1,000. At the time the lay-out of the site was considered unique, with the rugby and cricket fields being diagonally opposed. The cricket club got the best part of the land, the rugby pitch being smaller and on more of a slope.

The cricket ground was officially opened in May 1886 with a game between Yorkshire and Eighteen of Halifax. Yorkshire CCC returned later in the season to play Cheshire at Thrum Hall and county games continued until 1898. The official reason that was given by the Yorkshire committee for the discontinuance of fixtures was "the chill air of the neighbourhood" caused by the ground being 800 feet above sea level. Yorkshire 2nd XI, though, played Minor Counties cricket at Thrum Hall until the 1930s.

A running track once ran around the cricket field and speedway and greyhound racing also took place. The rugby players also used the cricket field for training on occasions. In its early days the ground also staged lacrosse and cycling meetings and annual athletics festivals were also a feature - the one in 1893 attracting a crowd of 12,000.

A soccer club was also based there for a few years after interest generated from an exhibition match between Preston North End and Blackburn Rovers staged in 1895 on the cricket field that attracted a crowd of 5,000. The opening dirt track speedway meeting took place in May 1928 and was the first one in Britain to be held under artificial lighting, the last in 1930 when England defeated Australia. Greyhound racing was first held in 1931 and ceased in 1978.

As a rugby ground, Thrum Hall was officially opened on 18 September 1886 when a crowd of 8,000 saw a game against Hull. Halifax marked the occasion with a victory, forward Ernest Williamson having the distinction of scoring the first try on the new ground. It proved also to be his last for Halifax.

Yorkshire played Cheshire in the first county rugby game held there in 1887 and the Maoris visited twice during their mammoth tour of 1888/89, attracting 7,000 and 6,000.

The first New Zealanders visited in 1907/08 when 11,000 saw Halifax win, 9-4. The following season Halifax defeated the first Australians 12-8 before 6,000 to complete a hat-trick of wins against touring sides (they had also won the first game against the Maoris). In the early 1890s Halifax attracted some huge crowds, 20,000 for one game against Bradford in 1892/93 and 15,000 for a Boxing Day game against Hunslet in 1892.

On at least three occasions (in 1904 against Leigh and 1911 against Warrington and Bradford Northern) Halifax staged rugby games on the cricket oval, as the rugby field was either waterlogged or frost-bound. Halifax won the first two games, 8-5 and 44-0 but then crashed out of the Challenge Cup to Northern.

The boundary walls were built by the Halifax Corporation in exchange for land with which they widened Thrum Hall Lane, Spring Hall Lane and Gibbet Street.

From the outset Thrum Hall had its distinctive 12-foot slope from touch-line to touch-line. The ground in its early days had a 95-yard long open stand on the Thrum Hall Lane side that was transported from Hanson Lane. This lasted only a few years and was replaced by a new open wooden grandstand just before the formation of the Northern Union in 1895. The main stand was then 60-yards in length, built of brick and timber and seated 2,000 spectators on seven rows of open seats.

The only terracing was at the Gibbet Street end and the double-fronted pavilion, built at a cost of £1,900 during the winter of 1886/87, had a scoreboard in front which detailed the kick-off time and home and visitors' score. Before the covered stand was built and housing developed around the area the pavilion was even more imposing, as surviving photographs illustrate.

The concept of covered stands in the Northern Union took time to develop. It was not until 1911 that the first cover was erected at Thrum Hall in the shape of the main stand, built at a cost of £988. Until then spectators had to bear the worst of the winter weather at one of the coldest and bleakest grounds in the League.

Seating 1,800 with a further 1,000 accommodated in the standing paddock area in front, the main stand was built from brick and wood and officially opened for the game against Rochdale Hornets on 16 September 1911.

**June 1919. Local Sunday School children gather at Thrum Hall
to sing hymns and say prayers in thanks for the end of the First World War**

Dressing rooms were added later at the rear of the stand. The away dressing room continued to be used until the ground closed but by then the home players changed in the pavilion and came onto the field by a separate entrance.

As a reward for the improvements Thrum Hall was allocated some big games, including the 1912 Championship Final between Huddersfield and Wigan when rain and low cloud contributed to a disappointing crowd of 15,000 to see Huddersfield win, 13-5.

In the 1913/14 season, with war clouds looming, the ground also staged the Yorkshire Cup and Challenge Cup finals. It was during this season that a new ground record was established when 29,122 were present to see Huddersfield inflict a 39-0 defeat on the home side in a Yorkshire Cup-tie. Thrum Hall was certainly Huddersfield's lucky ground - they returned in 1929 and 1930, each time defeating Leeds in Championship Finals. The first game attracted a crowd of 25,604, the second 18,563.

Hull and Wakefield Trinity contested the 1914 Challenge Cup Final, the former winning 6-0 due to late tries by wingers Jack Harrison and Alf Francis. The Lee Mount Band played "See the Conquering Hero Comes" as Hull captain Bert Gilbert was carried to the grandstand to receive the cup from the Mayor of Halifax, Alderman WH Ingham.

After the war was over and threats to build on the land had been averted by the trustees, Halifax continued to develop the ground, spending £1,000 on essential improvements and then a further £2,000 on a roof at the Gibbet Street end.

In 1921, after a fund had been set up to purchase the estate, a deed was set up which guaranteed, or so they thought, that Thrum Hall be used for the purpose of sport for all time. Cynics would ask since when was pushing a trolley around Asda a sport, admittedly though more people do that than play or watch Rugby League in Halifax these days. The bowling club, now relocated to part of the old playing area, is the only remaining link with sport on the famous ground.

The stand roof, which gave that side of the ground the name of the "Scrattin' Shed" (then a common name for covered terraces) unfortunately served to cut out the sun from reaching part of the playing area and this led to several games being postponed as the pitch had not been able to thaw out properly.

In the late 1920s this end was terraced after donations from the supporters' club and a new scoreboard was constructed at the pavilion corner of the Hanson Lane end. The pavilion was modernised at a cost of £6,000 and opened in November 1930. The opening ceremony was conducted by Mr James Pearson, the only surviving member of the original club and chairman of the trustees that helped save the ground during the war.

In 1934 the Thrum Hall Estate Joint Committee was inaugurated, comprising members of each of the sporting bodies represented at the ground - rugby, cricket and bowling. The estate was vested to the trustees "to hold perpetuity for the purpose of sport for the benefit of the public of Halifax." One of the conditions of the trustees was that soccer could not be played for profit at Thrum Hall so long as rugby was played on the estate.

The eventual sale of Thrum Hall was after the full agreement of the trustees with the money from the sale to be used for the furtherance of sport in Halifax. A Thrum Hall "hall of fame" is now accommodated in McDonald's inside the Asda building. The cricket club recently announced plans to relocate to South Halifax High School and merge with Mytholmroyd Mills CC.

The construction of cover on the Thrum Hall Lane side in the mid-1930s, providing shelter for around 3,000, gave Thrum Hall an enclosed feel and made it one of the best appointed grounds in Yorkshire.

Unfortunately the ground improvements had taken their toll on the club's finances, however, and the rugby section took the decision to hand over most of the pavilion to the cricket club in exchange for the writing-off of a £750 debt. A boardroom, secretary's office and changing room in the end wing of the pavilion was all that remained for use by the rugby club, which became a limited liability company in 1936.

Thrum Hall then lost out to the newly-constructed Odsal as a venue for big matches, though it did host the Yorkshire Cup Finals of 1935 and 1945 and the England-France international in 1937, though this was only as an afterthought after the Odsal pitch was deemed unplayable. A crowd of 7,204 saw England win, 23-9. In the first international staged at Thrum Hall, in April 1930, there had been a crowd of only 2,300 to see England play Other Nationalities though the attendance was greatly affected by it taking place on a Monday afternoon.

As a club venue, though, Thrum Hall continued to attract huge crowds, especially in the post-war boom after 1945. A new ground record was set when 28,150 saw Halifax lose to Wigan in a Championship semi-final replay in 1950. Wigan also provided the opposition in a Challenge Cup-tie in 1959 when an all-ticket crowd of 29,153 extended the ground record as the visitors won 26-0. There were also crowds of 25,000 and 27,500 respectively for cup-ties against St Helens and Leeds in the 1950s. By this time both ends at the ground had been completely re-terraced and a new scoreboard constructed at the Hanson Lane end. By the time of Thrum Hall's closure, safety officers restricted the capacity to about 6,000.

Thrum Hall's facilities were extended further when the supporters' club bar was opened in 1961 - this was later re-named the Taverners' Bar. And Thrum Hall was lit-up, literally, in 1967 after the first floodlights were erected at the ground. The lights, though, were deemed unsuitable for a league match against Widnes during Halifax's championship-

Thrum Hall

winning season of 1985/86 and this game was switched to the Shay. A crowd of 6,368 saw Widnes win, 15-8. After this Thrum Hall's lights were upgraded. Back in February 1889 Halifax had played St Helens under Wells' Lights, which involved pumping inflammable oil under high air pressure to a burner and creating a flare. The experiment was not repeated.

One of the most memorable of all games at Thrum Hall was the final league game of the season against Featherstone Rovers on 20 April 1986 when a 13-13 draw was sufficient both to earn Halifax the title and also save Rovers from relegation.

The match, which is part of local folklore, finished in controversy with claims that the hooter was sounded with three minutes of normal time remaining. The joyous scenes that day were a far cry from those of a few years earlier. In 1977/78, for instance, Halifax's fortunes were at low ebb after they lost the opening twenty-four games of the season and were knocked-out of the John Player Trophy by an amateur side from Hull. The plaque above the dressing room door had seemed inappropriate after the ignominy brought about by that defeat against Cawoods. It read: "Let only those enter who do so with pride and a determination to uphold the fine tradition of the club."

The ramifications of new ground regulations following the Valley Parade disaster affected Halifax more than most and the main stand, with its three narrow exit ways, was the focus of most attention. Halifax had to spend thousands of pounds on work under the safety regulations, making new concrete terracing all around the ground and installing plastic seating in the main stand, a fire-proofed floor and crush barriers in the Scrattin' Shed. The ground also changed its appearance when hospitality boxes were added behind the posts at the pavilion end.

No ground has changed its appearance more in recent years, though, than the Shay. The old tale goes that one former Halifax Town manager used to sign new players at the railway station before they had chance to see the ground. The old speedway track, since removed, distanced spectators from the pitch and hardly helped the atmosphere.

Originally a council refuse tip, Halifax Town (formed in 1911 and originally playing at Sandhall Lane) moved there from Exley in 1921 in the year they joined the Football League. The old main stand, situated on the west side and knocked down soon after the rugby club moved to the ground, was actually purchased from Manchester City's old ground at Hyde Road.

Town beat Darlington 5-1 in the first Football League game held there, on 27 August 1921 before a crowd of 10,143. Their highest league attendance was 19,935 against Bradford City in 1927, the lowest 856 for a game against Colchester United in 1976. Town lost their Football League status in 1993, regained it briefly from 1998/2002 and now are back in the Conference. Their last home Football League game was a 2-4 defeat at the hands of Rushden & Diamonds on 20 April 2002.

The Shay's record attendance was established for the visit of Tottenham Hotspur in 1953 for an FA Cup fifth-round tie when 36,885 crammed inside.

Floodlights were first used in 1961 with Red Star Belgrade providing the opposition at the friendly to mark the occasion. Before its redevelopment the Shay was a wide, open ground, overlooked by hills but inadequate for the needs of spectators. The Patrons' Stand, sited on the east side of the ground, ran a third of the way along the touch-line, either side of the halfway line, and was little more than an old covered terrace with seats added. To its left stood the Tramshed End with a shallow ash bank behind the cinder track. To the right was the Trinity Garage end, the centre portion terraced, with the rest of the area being ash covered with grassed patches and weeds. At the top of this end was a small cover, a legacy of the days when the ground was also used as a golf driving range. Opposite the Patrons' Stand was the old main stand with bench seats in the centre and terraces on either side and in front.

From every vantage point the pitch looked remote and the legacy of the speedway was that everything appeared to have been caked in dust and grime.

These days, after a major overhaul during the late 1990s that included new terracing at both ends and a revamped seated stand on the west side, the Shay is a most pleasant and spectator-friendly place. Construction of a new main stand commenced on the east side in 2000 but a lack of finance has led to it remaining uncompleted.

Speedway was first held at the Shay in 1949 on a steeply-banked 402-yard circuit around the outside of the soccer pitch, attracting a crowd of 7,000 for the first meeting. The speedway team was nicknamed the "Dukes" after the Duke of Wellington's Regiment that was stationed in the town.

A record attendance of 18,000 was set at one meeting in 1949 but declining crowds led to speedway leaving to the town in 1951. The sport returned in 1965 and ceased in 1985 when the riders and management transferred to Odsal. With the new stands erected and the playing area squared off, the speedway track has disappeared and as a result the ground has a far more intimate feel. Baseball was also staged at the ground after the Second World War.

The Shay staged its first representative game in the 2000 Emerging Nations World Cup when Italy defeated USA before a crowd of 1,487.

In 2005 there was fresh hope that the east stand - one of the great white elephants - would at last be on track for completion as Calderdale Council's regeneration and scrutiny committee supported plans to give the Shay Stadium Trust a 125-year lease on the ground. The idea was that by granting the commercial lease, housing and commercial units be built around the ground with the income from that used to finish the stand.

The Council originally bought the ground in 1987 and managed it for ten years until it was rented to the soccer and rugby clubs. If the plans come to fruition the Shay will also boast five-a-side pitches, offices, corporate facilities, a creche and an IT suite, and would be a vastly different place from the dreary, ramshackle ground of yesteryear.

HUDDERSFIELD

The venerable old lady slipped out quietly and, many thought, with indecent haste. There was no lingering curtain call or fanfare, no emotional crowd to pay their last respects, no souvenir hunters to grasp a lasting memento, no ceremony to acknowledge the heroes and triumphs of the past.

After all that had passed before, a Yorkshire Cup-tie and a preliminary round one at that, against Ryedale-York, was hardly a fitting way for Fartown to stage its last professional game.

That was on 23 August 1992 when just 1,619 spectators gathered on what had long become a crumbling old ground that had plainly seen better days, but at least Huddersfield signed off in style with a 36-12 victory.

A week later they took up temporary residence with Huddersfield Town at Leeds Road, opening their league campaign with a 15-34 defeat against Featherstone Rovers in front of 3,008 fans. Planning permission for a new ground had just been granted. Two years later came their opening match at the space age Alfred McAlpine stadium, marked by a 50-12 win over Barrow before 4,300 fans. A new era in the history of the famous old club had begun.

But unlike, say, Central Park, Fartown remains. A visit there remains a poignant one and on the chill of a winter afternoon it is possible to close your eyes and imagine the ghosts of Wagstaff, Rosenfeld, Gleeson et al scoring great tries in front of a passionate and adoring crowd.

Huddersfield's links with Rugby League will remain forever enshrined in folklore after the historic meeting at the George Hotel in the town on 29 August 1895, when the decision was taken by the leading clubs of Lancashire and Yorkshire to form a Northern Rugby Football Union and split from the governing body. That meeting laid the first steps for the game of Rugby League as we know it today with Huddersfield one of the twenty-two founder members.

Long before then the Huddersfield club had become one of the leading lights in the north. Formed in 1864 as Huddersfield Athletic Club, a football section soon started and they played their first game in December 1866 at Rifle Field. They amalgamated with the Cricket Club to form Huddersfield Cricket, Athletic and Football Club in November 1875.

The Cricket Club, originally known as Huddersfield St John's, had opened their innings on 2 May 1868 on a six-acre field in the Fartown district that was owned by a Mr Rutter of the George Hotel and soon a tennis ground and bowling-green were incorporated into the complex. The ground was referred to as the St John's Ground, though soon became more generally known as Fartown.

The first rugby game at Fartown was staged on 2 November 1878 when Huddersfield entertained Manchester Rangers. By now the site had been extended to one of eleven acres and the cricket and rugby fields had a common boundary. The rugby club had its headquarters a mile away at the George Hotel and the teams travelled to the ground by horse-drawn wagonette.

In the early days the ground was better known for cricket, with the Yorkshire county side making regular visits. They played the Australians there in 1878, 1886 and 1888 and staged their first county championship game at Fartown against Nottinghamshire as early as 1873. Yorkshire continued to make an annual visit to Fartown until the final first-class game was played there in August 1955, Fred Trueman taking 7 for 30 as Gloucestershire were routed for 84 in their second innings as the home county secured a 67-run victory.

Yorkshire also staged ten Sunday League games at the venue between 1969 and 1982. The potential for a ground even clearly long past its best was shown when the county three times recorded their highest paying gate of the season at Fartown with a highest crowd of 14,000.

In 1882 Fartown staged an FA Cup semi-final with Blackburn Rovers taking on Sheffield Wednesday before a 7,000 crowd. It would be 50 years later before a similar tie was staged in the town when Newcastle United played Chelsea at Leeds Road.

In the early days there was a slight overlap between the cricket and rugby grounds and the club possessed a small stand that could be turned either way. But ground developments continued apace. The cricket pavilion, which survives to this day, was opened in 1884 and a new permanent grandstand was built in 1886. After Huddersfield won the Yorkshire Cup for the first time in 1889/90, the committee bought an extra three acres of land and invested £8,600 towards further developments that included moving the rugby field to its present position. A stand separating the two grounds was later built.

A cycle track was laid around the cricket ground, which was levelled, and terraces

were erected. On Halloween 1891 Huddersfield beat Cardiff, 14-7, before 10,000 at the impressive new Fartown. The north terrace had 15 steps in front of the embankment that ran all the way down one side of the field and the stand opposite was an imposing 70-yard long structure. A Roses match a month after the opening established a new ground record of 23,250, even though three-quarters of the ground remained undeveloped.

After the Northern Union was formed the game continued its popularity, with a derby game against Brighouse Rangers on 27 December 1897 attracting a gate of 14,500. But by contrast only a hundred or so saw Huddersfield's game against Dewsbury in December 1904. A smallpox epidemic had broken out in Dewsbury but the Northern Union insisted that their fixtures should continue. Members only were allowed inside the ground with police on foot and horseback stationed outside to prevent any other fans from getting inside.

Huddersfield enjoyed a glorious era in the years leading up to the outbreak of the First World War when their ambitious committee recruited players from far and wide and they became known as the "Empire Team of Stars" and later the "Team of all Talents" culminating in the four-cup season of 1914/15.

A crowd of 28,053 witnessed a Challenge Cup third round tie against Wigan in March 1909 and 28,606 were present for Huddersfield's Yorkshire Cup semi-final tie against Halifax the following November. By then the north terrace embankment had been extended with a stand covering the whole length of the field at its top while there was another small stand, an "open wooden affair" less than 30 yards long, to the left of the members' stand at the pavilion end.

From 1895 to 1905 an association football section had also been operated at Fartown playing in a minor league. This section was abandoned due to poor support. In 1907 Huddersfield Association Football Ground Co. was formed and a site occupied by the Leeds Road recreation fields was purchased. At that time the Northern Union specifically discouraged groundsharing with soccer teams, whereas in another era a joint venture at Fartown could well have taken place. In 1908 Huddersfield Town AFC began playing at Leeds Road in the North-Eastern League, later joining the Midland League.

In 1910 Town gained election to the Football League, replacing Grimsby Town in Division Two, as soccer began to gain a permanent foothold in a town previously dominated by the handling code. Bradford City (1903), Leeds City (1905) and Bradford (Park Avenue) in 1909 had also secured Football League membership as soccer's bid to broaden its base in West Yorkshire proved successful. The Leeds Road ground was able to house a gate of 67,037 for the visit of Arsenal in the FA Cup in 1932.

At Fartown, meanwhile, a new record was set in February 1914 when 30,125 attended for the visit of Wigan and later that year main grandstand renovations were completed at a cost of £2,600.

Quite what Huddersfield would have achieved with their wonderful array of talent can only be imagined but the onset of hostilities led to the cessation of competitive football as attentions were drawn to the horrors and carnage of the Great War.

When peace returned, Fartown remained one of the game's finest grounds and the proximity of the cricket field added to the splendour of the complex.

It also came in useful, for on three occasions, starting with a Christmas Day game in 1914 against Hull, the cricket field was used to stage games with the rugby pitch frostbound. Matches against Leeds in 1922 and Bramley in 1925 were also played on the cricket field, the game against Leeds attracting a crowd of 10,200.

The inter-war years marked a generally glorious era for sport in Huddersfield with Town surviving two financial crises to lift a hat-trick of Football League championships between 1923/24 and 1925/26 and the FA Cup in 1922 while their rugby counterparts earned successive championship wins in 1929 and 1930 to add to Challenge Cup triumphs in 1920 and 1933. Huge crowds also attended Yorkshire's annual visit to Fartown.

By 1930, when the stand had been extended towards the pavilion, the seating capacity of the ground was 3,200 and a new attendance record was set in 1932 when 32,258 saw Halifax play Leeds in the Challenge Cup semi-final.

Fartown staged its first Ashes Test match in 1937 when Australia, who had lost the first two Tests, gained some consolation with a 13-3 victory before a crowd of only 9,093. This was the first match to be broadcast from Huddersfield, with Lance Todd providing a running commentary in the second half on the BBC's North Regional programme.

Only Gus Risman of the 26 players that played that day was to feature again in an Ashes Test, as the onset of the Second World War ensured that it was nine years before the two countries could renew their sporting rivalry.

The immediate post-war years produced some glorious moments as the ground enjoyed its heyday. The ground record was extended to 35,136 when Leeds played Wakefield in another Challenge Cup semi-final in April 1947 and in that year the arrival of Australians Lionel Cooper, Johnny Hunter and Pat Devery helped Huddersfield become one of the finest sides in the game.

A club record 32,912 saw a game against Wigan in March 1950 and work on the north terrace was completed in 1951 with the aim of increasing visibility and safety. That side of the ground then had a 20,000 capacity, and the view from the top terrace step was

one of the most magnificent in the game. But Leeds Road, instead of Fartown, was chosen as the venue for the 1952 Championship Final when Wigan defeated Bradford Northern before a crowd of 48,684.

The supporters' social club was opened in 1965 and floodlights were switched on for the first time at the ground two years later, but by now the ground was slipping into general decline.

In 1976 Fartown staged its last of 23 Challenge Cup semi-finals when St Helens beat Keighley 5-4 before 9,829 spectators and staged its last final in 1979 when Leeds beat Bradford Northern 24-2 in the Premiership Trophy before 19,486.

Huddersfield had become a limited company in 1977 and six years later, with the fortunes of the club at a low ebb, the chairmanship and later sole ownership passed to a Mr John Bailey, one of whose first tasks was to rename the famous ground Arena '84 and add the moniker Barracudas to the club's name, while turning the mock Tudor pavilion into a night club. These moves brought a mixture of cynical humour from most Rugby League followers but only anger and resentment from older fans brought up on the legends of the "claret and golds".

The 1980s were barren years, with a crumbling ground and interest at an all-time low. The lowest crowd for a first-team game, apart from that unusual game against Dewsbury in 1904, was recorded in 1983 when 422 saw the visit of Whitehaven and three years later just 303 turned up for a game against Keighley. The main stand was closed after the Valley Parade fire of 1985 due to safety reasons and for a time it was standing room only at the ground.

In 1988 a new three-man consortium took over from Bailey and the Barracudas title was abandoned. Slowly but surely the great old club was dragged up from near oblivion. In 1989 the main stand was partly re-opened with the aid of a £25,000 grant from Kirklees Council and the ground renamed Fartown with further money spent on upgrading floodlights and on repairing the scoreboard, originally erected in memory of the great Dave Valentine. But in truth they were only papering over the cracks.

The cricket ground was an even sadder sight, with the facilities non-existent, the playing surface in an atrocious condition, the terraces crumbling and weed strewn and the burnt-out remains of a car on the third-man boundary adding to the pitiful atmosphere. A clock tower erected to the memory of GH Hirst, the famous Yorkshire cricketer, had been vandalised and the bowling green abandoned and overgrown. The cricket club broke up after 1985, though cricket continued at a very minor level for a while.

Kirklees Council paid the Huddersfield club £50,000 in return for them relinquishing the lease of Fartown. There was no choice but to move as they would have had to have spent up to £50,000 in safety work just to keep the ground open, while estimates ranged from £300,000 up to £2m for bringing the ground up to standards required to stage first division rugby.

Ian Laybourn cut his journalistic teeth covering Huddersfield and is now the respected Rugby League correspondent of the Press Association.

"I went to Fartown for the first time in 1976 and was immediately struck by the fantastic terracing," he says. "You could get so high up and from your vantage point you were right on top of the action. It was a fantastic place from which to watch the game. But there was a good view, too, from the other side in the main stand and the press box was centrally situated, over the players' tunnel, and so was ideal.

"The club really reached rock bottom in the '80s and several times looked on the verge of folding. I was sick of doing stories about it. There were several takeovers and we thought the good times were coming back and were temporarily filled with optimism, only for those hopes to evaporate. It was a struggle to remain positive.

"Renaming the club the Barracudas and the A team the Piranhas was revolutionary at the time and maybe could have worked if the team had been successful but, like Arena '84, Mr Bailey's ideas just didn't take off."

Laybourn feels that the move from Fartown was inevitable. "When the club moved no one was sure if it was the final game or not," he recalls. "The club couldn't get a safety

certificate but a lot of people refused to believe it and there was a lot of opposition to going to Leeds Road.

"People were always talking about Hunter, Cooper and Devery and other great players of the '50s and '60s but meanwhile the ground was steadily drifting into a state of disrepair. When the main stand was condemned and a huge section of the north terrace cordoned off it was such a sad sight and the fortunes of the team were at an all-time low. I remember going up to an away game at Carlisle when we only played with 12 men. That was the lowest point."

With Fartown and the club's financial position in a parlous state, Huddersfield Town had the good sense to realise that, by inviting their rivals to share Leeds Road it would avoid the need for costly repairs to Fartown and also open up the possibility of a groundshare at a new stadium.

With the rugby club on board, £1m was secured from the Foundation for Sport and the Arts, £2.5m from the Football Trust, while the sale of Leeds Road realised £5m.

The Council handed over, free of charge, a 51-acre wasteland site formerly earmarked for industrial development, and a further £1m was raised from the Urban Partnership Fund. The Council committed £2m to the development and the remaining money was raised from grants, catering franchises and sponsorship, with stadium developers Alfred McAlpine plc paying £2m for a ten-year consultancy deal including "naming rights."

The Huddersfield club, who added the suffix Giants for the start of the summer era, obtained a 20% share in the stadium, an excellent deal for them considering they had little to offer at the time. The McAlpine Stadium was

PAST AND PRESENT -
Huddersfield's Fartown
ground, with The Galpharm
Stadium in the distance

owned by Kirklees Stadium Development Limited, whose shareholders were forty per cent Kirklees Council, forty Huddersfield Town and twenty per cent the Giants.

"As for the McAlpine, people accepted that more readily," Laybourn adds. "It took a big effort for many to go for the first time, but most people like it even though they still chant Fartown."

Until recently, with its redevelopment plans underway, Fartown staged Huddersfield's under-21 and under-18 games and hosted Huddersfield St Joseph's amateur club. But planning wrangles stymied proposals for the development of a centre of excellence and reluctantly Huddersfield left Fartown in 2004.

After ten years the stadium's naming rights were due for renewal and the McAlpine Stadium became known as the Galpharm Stadium, named after a pharmaceutical concern. At the stadium the Lawrence Batley stand holds 3,127 in its upper tier and 4,788 in the lower with the John Smith's stand opposite holding 7,333. The Panasonic stand holds 2,720 in the upper tier and 1,944 in the lower while 4,054 are accommodated in the south stand. There are spaces for 1,100 cars and 42 hospitality boxes with lounges to fit parties from 20 to 500.

In the time since Fartown staged its final game of senior Rugby League, the changes that have taken place in the sporting face of the town since would have defied belief. Now the Giants play in summer, in a modern stadium and in Super League and maybe one day there will be new heroes to rival those of the past in a town that will forever be known as the birthplace of Rugby League.

HULL FC

On 22 October 2002 the Boulevard, another traditional old Rugby League ground, staged its final match and Hull FC embarked on a new journey at the brand-spanking, all-singing, all-dancing Kingston Communications Stadium.

With Bradford leaving Valley Parade (once home of the first Northern Union champions Manningham) to return to Odsal for 2003, of the 22 grounds that staged fixtures in the first season of the Northern Union in 1895/96, just a handful now remain for Rugby League: Headingley, Knowsley Road, Belle Vue and Mount Pleasant. In addition, the Halton Stadium is built on the site of Widnes's old ground at Lowerhouse Lane.

While the passing of many famous venues such as Thrum Hall, Fartown, Station Road, Central Park, Watersheddings and the Athletic Grounds have been met with regret it is probably fair to say that the demise of the Boulevard provoked mixed feelings from many Rugby League followers. Hardly the favourite ground for many visiting fans, the Boulevard could be an intimidating and hostile place though the passion and fervour generated by the Hull FC faithful was a sight in itself.

But at least Hull bowed out in style, playing the Kiwis in the final game at the old ground on a memorable occasion. Though Hull lost, 11-28, they at least had the consolation of scoring the last points on the ground when winger Paul Parker dived over in the corner in the closing seconds. Led by former Great Britain hooker, Lee Jackson, who was playing his final game in the black and white, Hull put on a creditable show and held a 7-6 lead at the interval. Richard Swain, Stephen Kearney and Motu Tony, later to be members of the first Hull side to win the Challenge Cup for twenty years after their 25-24 win over Leeds in Cardiff in 2005, were in the Kiwi ranks that evening. Perhaps the most memorable feature of the evening was the New Zealand Haka - not the pre-match one that was drowned out by the full-blooded rendition of "Old Faithful" from the Threepenny Stand which was

fair enough - it is used to challenge the opposition, after all; but the impromptu after-match Haka in front of the same Hull fans. The Kiwis were cheered to the rafters.

Hull moved to the Hull Athletic Ground, situated just off the Boulevard on Airlie Street, in 1895 after members of the club agreed a ten-year lease with the Hull Athletic Company, taking over the ground that had been occupied by their then junior neighbours, Hull Kingston Rovers. The Hull officials agreed to pay three times the sum Rovers were paying in rent. In 1899 the club bought the six-acre site for £6,500, renamed it the Boulevard and soon acquired the nickname of the "Airlie Birds".

Hull's opening game at the ground, against Liversedge on 21 September 1895, attracted a crowd estimated at 8,000, at the time the largest for a rugby match in Hull. In no time the ground underwent massive redevelopment with the construction of the covered Threepenny Stand making one of the game's major architectural landmarks. Seventy-five yards in length with eleven wooden terraces and a roof made from Russian pine, the stand became home to the most vociferous and passionate Hull supporters and helped give the ground a unique atmosphere, especially when the anthem of "Old Faithful" was sung.

Prior to the rugby club's tenure, the Athletic Ground incorporated a cycle track that meant spectators at either end of the ground were up to forty yards away from the field of play. The track was re-introduced for greyhound racing in 1927 and speedway was also staged at the Boulevard from 1971 onwards. The oval shape of the ground remained, making the Boulevard one of the worst viewing grounds of all, particularly the east side stand with the sunken terrace that gives a worm's eye view of play.

Hull City AFC had intended to use the Boulevard as their home ground when they joined the Football League in 1905 having staged some exhibition matches there. But the Northern Union authorities, fearful that soccer would become more popular, banned any of its member clubs from letting their grounds unless no gate was taken, and the soccer team had to play at the Circle instead.

After a while there was a re-think and Hull City used the ground for four league games before making a permanent move to Anlaby Road, adjacent to the cricket ground, in 1906. The Tigers, who played some games at the Boulevard during the Second World War, moved to Boothferry Park in 1946.

The Boulevard staged its first Test match in 1921 when Australia beat Great Britain 16-2 before 21,504 spectators. Britain, handicapped by an early injury to winger Squire Stockwell in the days long before substitutes, gallantly held the Kangaroos to 2-2 at half-time before the tourists scored four second-half tries. The game marked the last international appearances of Hull centre Billy Batten and Kangaroos forward Syd "Sandy" Pearce, who had opposed one another in the first Anglo-Australian Test in 1908. Its last international game was staged during the 2000 World Cup when Australia defeated Russia, 110-4. Ryan Girdler scored three of Australia's 19 tries and also kicked 17 goals though the biggest cheer from the 3,044 crowd was reserved for Matthew Donovan, who qualified for Russia through the grandparents' ruling, when he scored his side's only try. The ground record was established in 1936 when 28,798 saw a third round Challenge Cup-tie against Leeds. During the Second World War there was serious damage to the east stand due to German bombing and the Prime Minister, Winston Churchill, visited the area to raise morale.

The Safety of Sports Ground Act following the Valley Parade fire in 1985 led to the Threepenny Stand being closed down and ultimately demolished with a new structure, part seating and part standing, being erected in its place.

The distinguished Rugby League journalist and statistician, Raymond Fletcher, virtually grew up at the Boulevard and captured the thoughts and experiences of many Hull supporters through the generations in his wonderfully evocative history, "Boulevard Voices" as part of the splendid Tempus series. Few people are better placed than Fletcher to explain the unique history and feel of the Boulevard.

Fletcher admits that the press box protocol he has observed immaculately throughout a long career almost went out of the window when Richard Horne scored a late match-clinching try in the Saturday night thriller against Wigan in the final season at the ground.

"I must confess that I felt a bit embarrassed at the end of that game," Fletcher says. "I half stood up in my seat when Horne went in for that try and I haven't done that for years. It was a wonderful, gripping game and Hull came out on top in the end."

The Boulevard that night, even with a crowd of around 6,000, was a cauldron of noise

The final game at the Boulevard -
Hull v New Zealand, 22 October 2002

and brought back many happy memories for Hull-born Fletcher who grew up within spitting distance of the ground.

"There are many things that stay in your mind from when you were young and I was literally brought up on the Boulevard," he says. "There was always a feel about the ground and I played for Hull juniors there in curtain-raisers when there would be crowds of 15-20,000 in attendance.

"There would be so many people in the Threepenny Stand that you couldn't put your hands in your pockets for fear you couldn't get them out again, such was the crush. There was a kind of graduation you undertook as a fan, from the end that we used to call Bunker's Hill to the railings in the Threepenny Stand and then, as you got older, you moved up the steps.

"I suppose the Boulevard has never been ideal for Rugby League because of its shape at the ends meant you could never get far back to watch the game. Then there is that incredible well on the best stand side and yet the area was always packed. How people viewed the game I don't know.

"Yet there is so much nostalgia about the place. When they tore the old Threepenny Stand down I wished they would let me buy a length of the railings. They could have got a lot of money for selling off pieces of the stand."

Grounds have their own unique feel and atmosphere and the Boulevard was no exception.

"Christmas Day and Boxing Day games were always special," Fletcher recalls. "There was a smell of rum and cigar smoke from the crowd and that memory has stayed with me. At half-time people would squeeze to the back and relieve themselves at the back of the stand and I remember the steam coming up.

"Especially on a rainy day in spring or early autumn a combination of the rain and

97

A view of the Boulevard from the famous Threepenny Stand side

the steam from the crowd was incredible. I've got to say it was rough but then Hull was a fish dock and a lot of their fans were dockers. Over the years the docks have declined and I remember doing a piece for the Yorkshire Post about an old game when I said there were ten thousand dockers shouting for Hull. Someone wrote in and said he wished there were still ten thousand dockers in Hull but they had nearly all gone.

"I remember Blackpool Borough coming for a cup-tie and some of their players threw sticks of rock into the crowd. Someone remarked that if there was a replay the Hull players would throw cod heads into the crowd. It was a rough place but my sister used to go with my father and me. My father told her to keep her ears closed. There was a lot of swearing but it didn't sound vile.

"Opposing players and referees always got plenty of stick but, as a kid, I wouldn't say it ever offended me. In the '50s there used to be ringside seats round the touch-line. I remember one game against Rovers when their fans had to walk the full length of the field to those seats and they were met with a barrage of abuse, mostly humorous.

"Over the years some of the abuse got more vicious and some of the chanting got vile and obscene. It is still pretty loud. When Julian O'Neill was lining up a conversion after a Brian Carney try in that Wigan game right in front of the stand it was like a howling mob. The barrage of noise was non-stop, it was like a lynch mob but O'Neill just shut out the noise and put in a wonderful kick."

Fletcher was brought up on nearby Hessle Road at the heart of the Hull support. "In that era, because of the fishing industry, that area was regarded as the rough end of Hull," Fletcher explains. "It is more run down now but it had a certain character. It may have been a bit rough and ready but I was always proud to call myself a 'Hessle Roader'.

"In those days the men would spend three weeks at sea and then two days at home throughout the year. So although they were all Hull supporters they didn't see much of

Hull. I remember the story of a cup-tie in 1954 when Hull played Workington and drew. One man got off the ship and enquired about the score. Discovering that the replay was in Workington that very afternoon, he immediately called a taxi to take him all the way to Cumbria.

"That was the sort of thing people did then. The club used to wire the results to trawlers and, for big games, would get telegrams back from the trawlers with good luck messages.

"Many of the players worked at the docks as well and the supporters always liked cheering their own. For many people it was a case of choosing Rugby League or soccer, one or the other. Hull is definitely a traditional Rugby League town but I always say that if Hull City ever got in the Premier League they could attract 40-50,000 every week, no question.

"In effect Hull is a bit like Welsh rugby union where people regard a game almost as a religion. In the '50s it was a much more close-knit area but a lot of Hull supporters have since moved out to the estates and some of that communal thing has been lost.

"But there is still a special feel to the Boulevard and visiting supporters are aware of that for sure. A lot of them were not keen to go because of the intimidation. I know what they mean but I have always seen it from the other side and I have always loved going to the Boulevard and the smells, the atmosphere of the place and the noise will stay with me forever.

"They said that the directors could always tell the size of the crowd by looking at the urinal at the back of the stand. If it was over your ankles there would be at least fifteen thousand on and if it was up to your ankles there would be at least ten thousand. They used to say the Threepenny Stand would never burn down because it was covered with that much piss."

One memory that Fletcher cherishes concerns the Threepenny Stand. "It was the year Hull won the championship (1983) and they played Barrow in the final game before nearly 17,000," he recalls. "I went to the game as a reporter but took my son along with me and took him in the stand. It was absolutely packed and we could only get in the first few rows but at least he could say he has been in there. There was a fantastic atmosphere that day and a feeling of jollity about the occasion - it was just like the days that I remember as a kid."

So how did Fletcher and all the Hull fans react to the end of the Boulevard? "Let's wait and see," was his guarded response before the move. "If the ground is like Wigan's new ground I don't think they'll take to it. I am not against the move but these days a lot of new grounds are a bit clinical and sanitized. They might get big gates early on but if the people can't congregate they won't like that.

"At the Boulevard everyone meets up at certain areas. You see the same crowd of people around you game after game. You might never see them apart from at the games but they feel like friends for life.

"But when I was researching 'Boulevard Voices' I asked each of the contributors for their thoughts on leaving and no one was really against it. 'If it has to be, it has to be', that was the general view. It's a new era for the club and it's up to the marketing people to ensure that Hull hold on to the old fans and attract new ones. The facilities will be so much better and it's a great opportunity for the club."

Hull's opening game at the KC Stadium could hardly have been more dramatic. They lost their Australian loose forward, Jason Smith, sent-off for a high-tackle inside the opening minute of the Challenge Cup-tie with Halifax on 9 February 2003. Despite also having Richard Fletcher dismissed they won a thrilling game, 24-16, before a 15,310 crowd.

You might think that Fletcher was still full of regret for the passing of the Boulevard, since used as a greyhound stadium. You'd be wrong. He admits to falling in love with the new place on first sight. "I wrote a colour piece on the occasion and likened myself to having been faithful to the same old girl for over 40 years and then falling for the new girl in the neighbourhood," Fletcher says. "My only regret was that the Hull team wasn't wearing their irregular black and white hoops - that hurt more than leaving the Boulevard. The Boulevard is a thing of the past - the black and white hoops should be a thing of the present.

"But my first reaction to the KC Stadium was very good. People tend to think that traditionalists, like me, always live in the past. Nostalgia is in the past - you can look back but not dwell. The Boulevard had a lot to be desired as a seeing ground and the sight-lines at the new stadium are marvellous. My brother has followed Hull for a long time and goes regularly in the east stand and loves the new ground. Everything about the place is better than the Boulevard - that's the general view. If Hull were to progress and keep up with the top clubs they had to move on. The only drawback is that they need at least ten thousand in to get a good atmosphere. Yet ten thousand at the Boulevard and it was heaving.

"The surroundings are terrific, too. Walking through the entrance of the old West Park is just about the best walk to any stadium in any sport I know, especially when the blossom is on the trees. The facilities inside are very good and I've not heard anyone against it."

Named after the stadium's ten-year naming rights sponsors, Kingston Communications, the new stadium was the first in England to be built in a parkland setting. With an all-seated capacity of 25,404 and designed as a single tier, asymmetrical bowl of approximately 20,000 seats with a second upper tier to the West Stand of 5,000 seats, the stadium has a modern and eye-catching appearance. Further expansion is possible if the East Stand is made similar to the West and would raise capacity to over 30,000. This may be needed if Hull City continue their remarkable progress, having earned promotions in successive seasons in 2003/04 and 2004/05.

The KC Stadium is built partly on the site of the Circle, which had been developed as a cricket ground in the late 1890s. Situated adjacent to West Park, it staged its first county game in 1899 and regular annual first-class games continued there until 1974. Yorkshire last used the venue for one-day cricket in 1990. The northern part of the site was used by Hull & East Riding RU club and later West Hull ARL club played there. In 1904, when Hull City were elected to the Football League, they built a stadium immediately to the east of the Circle and stayed there until 1939. But before that stadium was ready Hull City used the Circle as a temporary venue, staging eleven Football League games there and

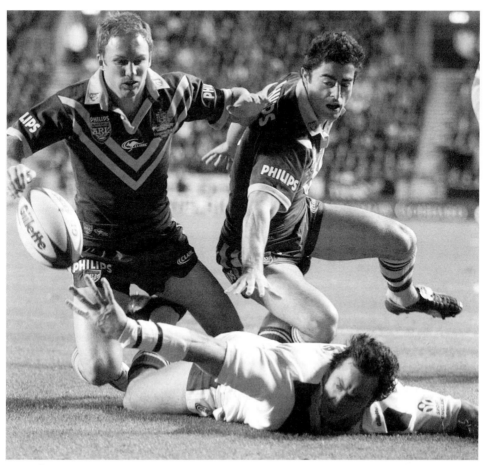

**Great Britain's Adrian Morley flicks out a pass to set up a try for Terry Newton against Australia,
as international Rugby League arrived at the Kingston Communications Stadium**

attracting a highest crowd of 10,000 for the visit of Leeds City. The Anlaby Road ground opened in March 1906 for the visit of Blackpool and staged a total of 595 Football League games. The record attendance was 32,930 for a FA Cup sixth-round replay against Newcastle United in 1930. The Circle suffered significant bomb damage during the second world war and Hull City moved to Boothferry Park for the commencement of League football in 1946. The junior sides continued to use the ground until 1965 when a railway loop line was built across the site.

The new stadium took fourteen months to complete and had an estimated cost of £44m. Hull City opened up with a friendly against Sunderland on 18 December 2002 just four days after playing at Boothferry Park for a final time. As an international Rugby League venue the stadium soon became a hit after staging Great Britain's second Test against the Australians in 2003 when a capacity crowd of 25,147 saw a thrilling game as the Kangaroos came back from 8-20 behind after 23 minutes to make sure of retaining the Ashes with a 23-20 victory. In 2004 a Tri-Nations game against New Zealand attracted a crowd of 23,377 spectators who saw the home nation triumph, 26-24. The highest crowd for a Hull FC game is 19,549 for the Super League game against Bradford Bulls in June 2003.

HULL KR

Rovers by name and rovers by nature, Hull Kingston Rovers are currently at their ninth home venue, having laid a ground-hopping trail across the East Riding city.

Rovers are now associated with the east of the city, with the River Hull the dividing line, but their origins were to the west after they were formed in the winter of 1882/83 by a group of apprentice boilermakers at Charles D Holmes and Amos and Smith in the Hessle Road area. The club was known initially as Kingston Amateurs and was one of a large number of junior clubs in the area, with the senior club in the city, Hull FC, already establishing a strong fixture list.

Kingston Amateurs first played on waste ground off the long-defunct Albert Street, sharing the site with a gypsy encampment. Fixtures commenced in 1883 but the facilities were primitive - there was no stand or enclosure and the club had to use portable goalposts. Their first ground became known as 'Flag End Touch' as the raised flagging of the adjoining streets gave an elevated view and easily ascertained touchlines. The club's second home was a field near the railway crossing on Anlaby Road, for which an annual rent was paid.

From there they moved to a site off Chalk Lane, nearer the city centre, in 1885, when the club's name was changed to Kingston Rovers.

Little more than two years later Rovers were on the move again, to Dairycoates, at that time an outlying village largely comprising dwellings of workers whose employment was with the North Eastern Railway Company. The venue was known as the Hessle Road Locomotive ground.

Hull KR in action against Halifax and Wigan *(below left)* at Craven Street

But it was not home for long as, when the rival Athletic club disbanded, Rovers moved into their ground on Hessle Road in the 1889/90 season. This was located opposite the Star and Garter.

The ground had a stand that seated 250 but its facilities were not considered good enough for an ambitious outfit and in 1892 they moved to the Hull Athletic Ground, off the Boulevard, on a three-year lease.

When this lease ran out, Rovers re-located again, moving for the first time across the River Hull to a site at Craven Street, off Holderness Road.

This was largely because Rovers' rivals, Hull FC, agreed to pay three times the rent Rovers had paid to take over the lease at the Boulevard. Craven Street had been previously home to the old Southcoates club. Outwood Church from Wakefield provided the opposition for Rovers' first game at their new home, on 28 September 1895.

In 1896/97 there was a brief ground-share as Rovers amalgamated with the Albany association football club. A number of soccer games were played at Craven Street before the soccer club moved to Dairycoates and changed their name to Hull City, before folding.

A new Hull City soccer club was formed in 1904 and reached agreement for a three-year lease of Hull FC's Boulevard ground. However, problems soon arose and City played a few games at Dairycoates before moving to share the Circle with Hull Cricket Club in time for their election to the Football League in 1905. They played four Football League fixtures at the Boulevard but concentrated their efforts on developing a new ground next to the cricket field known as Anlaby Road where they stayed from 1906-39 until Boothferry Park was opened in 1946.

By 1897 Rovers, despite winning the Yorkshire Cup and Yorkshire Senior Competition for the first time, were isolated as the only union club in a Northern Union area and the decision was taken to join the Northern Union. They played Crompton (from near Oldham) in their first game under the new code at Craven Street on 4 September 1897.

After winning the Yorkshire Second Competition in 1898/99, Rovers achieved senior status and played Hull FC for the first time on 16 September 1899. A crowd of 14,000 (£500) saw the first of many Hull derbies, Rovers winning 8-2 with tries by Starks and Kemp. A surviving photograph of the time shows that the majority of the crowd were standing and huge advertising signs for Bovril dominated one end of the ground, while the playing area looked rough and undulating.

Craven Street was a compact ground, bordered by the railway on one side. Rovers spent £1,000 on ground improvements, including building a large covered stand, though most of the rest of the ground was constructed of terracing made from wooden planks. It was here that GH (Tich) West accumulated a Rugby League record 53 points (11 tries and 10 goals) as Rovers beat Brookland Rovers, 73-5, on their way to the 1905 Challenge Cup Final. Craven Street played host to the first New Zealand and Australian touring sides during 1908 and a ground record attendance was established in 1914 when Huddersfield's visit for a Challenge Cup-tie attracted a crowd of 18,000 (£601).

Rovers' success in the immediate post-war period provided a severe test to the ground's capacity. Matters came to a head during the 1920/21 season when it was estimated that £3,000 had been lost in receipts through having to close the gates, and steps were undertaken to secure a bigger ground. After initial opposition from some quarters, Rovers purchased and developed a site adjacent to the tram and bus depot on the eastern end of Holderness Road at a total cost of over £13,000, aided by a grant from the Northern Union of £500. Craven Street was later developed as the site of an old people's home and the ground's assets were sold for £600. In the last season at Craven Street the visit of the Australians produced receipts of £1,337.

Rovers' eighth home, though still in the process of being constructed, was deemed ready for the visit of Wakefield Trinity on 2 September 1922, with their legendary

Australian wingman Albert Rosenfeld scoring the only try in a 3-0 win before a crowd of 15,000.

Prior to the game the opposing sides had taken part in a procession from Hull Paragon station to the ground and the Lord Mayor, Cllr GF Wokes, was given the honour of making the kick-off.

The main grandstand at Craven Park, as the new ground became known, was designed by a local firm of architects and was built from steel and concrete. Its construction took only three months, though it was only partly roofed for the opening game. Housing the dressing rooms, with seating for 2,750 on wooden seats and a paddock for a further 1,500 standing spectators, it was a fine construction, deemed worthy of its £8,000 cost. The terraces at Craven Park were constructed from ash that was donated by a local company, the British Oil and Cake Mills, and the playing area was then the maximum parameters allowed, 110x75 yards.

In the first season at Craven Park the derby game with Hull, on 7 October 1922, attracted a record crowd of 22,282. Hull won, 10-7, but Rovers went on to lift the Championship that season, beating Huddersfield at Headingley with a team containing eleven local players. Craven Park also hosted the Yorkshire-Lancashire county game in December 1922 when 8,000 witnessed an 11-11 draw on a Thursday afternoon.

On New Year's Day 1927 Rovers, with twelve local players, beat the Kiwis, 20-15, and during that season the Prince of Wales was entertained at the ground when 10,000 local schoolchildren sung to him during his visit to Hull.

In 1929 the ground staged its one and only Test as Australia beat Great Britain, 31-8, before a crowd of 20,000 (£2,065). Loose forward Jack Feetham became the first Rovers player to take part in a Test against Australia and scored a try. But the Australians, despite being starved of possession, ran in seven tries in total, thrilling an appreciative home crowd with the quality of their back play with centre Tom Gorman, their captain, in outstanding form.

In February 1936 Craven Park staged another international, when Wales, by virtue of a 17-14 victory over England on a mud-bath of a pitch, clinched the European Championship before a crowd of 17,000 (£880) despite there being no Hull KR players on view.

It was to be another 44 years before another full international was held there and this time it was a more low-key occasion on a Wednesday evening in February 1980. England,

The Roger Millward Stand, from outside and inside *(right)* New Craven Park

including Rovers players Mike Smith, Roy Holdstock and Len Casey, beat Wales 26-9 before a crowd of 7,557 (£7,950). The following season England, with the same three Rovers players on duty opposing their teammate, Colin Dixon, beat Wales 17-4 before a crowd of only 4,786 (£5,386) on a Wednesday evening in March 1981.

Craven Park also hosted two Great Britain under-24s internationals against France in 1976 and Australia in 1978.

It was something of a lucky ground for the Yorkshire county side. Yorkshire beat Lancashire there in 1958 and 1968, the Kiwis in 1961 and the Kangaroos in 1963, losing only against the Kiwis in 1955.

As well as greyhound racing, first staged there in 1928, Craven Park also staged baseball matches in 1937, often before 10,000-plus crowds.

But the late 1930s proved a difficult time for Rovers and they sold Craven Park to the Greyhound Racing Company for £10,750 in 1938, securing a 21-year lease to continue

playing there. A huge totaliser was constructed at the Holderness Road end in 1939 and this served to reduce the capacity of the ground. After closing down during the war from the end of the 1939/40 season, Rovers returned to Craven Park when hostilities were over.

They suffered a major blow when the ground's east stand, financed by the Supporters' Club, was razed to the ground by a fire in the summer of 1946. The stadium club and lounge and the totaliser offices of the greyhound company were also destroyed. In its place a new stand, with a double-pitched roof, was constructed that uniquely included three former railway carriages at the rear. In 1951/52 a Ground Fund was set up and a working party of four directors and two Supporters' Club members began to look for a new site for a ground.

Hull City AFC kindly lent Rovers the use of their Boothferry Park ground for the derby with Hull on 3 April 1953 when a crowd of 27,670 paid £3,280, receipts that went a long way towards alleviating Rovers' financial problems.

By way of comparison, it was stated that the average receipts for a game at Craven Park were £256. A further six Rovers 'home' derby games were staged at Boothferry Park in subsequent years, attracting average crowds of around 18,500, but the derby game returned to Craven Park in 1959/60 when the soccer authorities temporarily banned RL games on their grounds.

Rovers secured a new three-year lease in 1959/60 but several new sites for a new ground were under consideration. Rovers purchased an eleven-acre site at Winchester Avenue for £1,500, used initially as a training ground, with the aim of building a new stadium there. The site was later levelled and fenced off at a further cost of £2,495. Those plans, however, never reached fruition and in 1971 the site was sold to private developer and the funds used to help buy back Craven Park for £65,000 and run greyhound racing as a subsidiary concern.

Stars of the past - the Hull Kingston Rovers side of 1900

With the boom in the game on Humberside in full swing in the late 1970s and early 1980s, Craven Park hosted its biggest post-war crowd in 1981 - 14,315 for the game against Salford. This was surpassed when 15,574 attended the derby game against Hull FC in March 1982 and a new record was set when 16,081 saw another derby game in April 1984. The diamond jubilee anniversary of the opening match at Craven Park was held against St Helens in September 1982 with Joe McGlone, the only surviving member of the Rovers side against Wakefield, the guest of honour.

Improved floodlights (first installed in 1967) were added and a new Supporters' Club building opened and a new office block built. But the implications of the Valley Parade fire of 1985 proved serious for Rovers, amongst many other clubs, and the ground capacity was restricted to 7,227 despite the club having spent over £100,000 on essential safety work.

With Rovers said to be £500,000 in debt the ground was finally sold to the Wright Group of Companies for £4m and a new Craven Park was developed at Preston Road for £3m.

The last game at the old Craven Park was against Widnes on 9 April 1989 when a capacity crowd of 7,844 saw the champions inflict a 16-13 win on their hosts. The last derby game, in January 1989, had attracted a crowd of 8,837. The site, first covered by a Co-operative Retail Services superstore, is now covered by a Morrison's supermarket. Unlike a similar development at Rochdale, where there is a display of memorabilia in the foyer of the supermarket covering the old Athletic Grounds, there is no mention of the historical importance of the site that was once a Mecca for generations of Rovers fans.

The new Craven Park was built on the playground of the former Shakespeare Hall High school. Another site had been earmarked, at the junction of Sutton Road and Leads Road, but a proposal to re-locate here was rejected by the planning committee after complaints from local residents. The first sod was cut in December 1988 and the opening match, a second division encounter against Trafford Borough, took place on 24 September 1989 when Rovers romped to a 48-8 victory before an all-ticket crowd of 8,095.

The new ground was essentially two-sided with a main grandstand, of propped cantilever design with screen ends, seating 1,992 in 19 rows with the letters HKR spelt out in the central bays of red and white plastic seats. Opposite was a covered terrace holding 3,500 spectators on 41 terraces. At the docks end of the ground there was an arc of eighteen concrete terraces and an electronic scoreboard and totaliser, costing £80,000, with the opposite end grass banked. For all but the big games the two ends are scarcely populated. The four corner floodlight pylons were transported from the old ground. From the outset there were problems with the drainage of the pitch due largely to the clay soil. The greyhound and speedway track made the pitch seem remote

A Rovers fixture card, from the 1890/91 season

from the terraces and there was not the same intimacy as at the old Craven Park.

The greyhounds have recently moved to the Boulevard but speedway, introduced to the venue in 1995, remains. Average attendances in the first season were 4,851, compared to 5,298 for the last campaign at the old Craven Park - respectable enough considering Rovers had been relegated. A ground record crowd was set in February 1993 when the visit of Wigan for a league game attracted a crowd of 8,660 but the average crowd in recent years has been around the 2,000 mark, not helped by Rovers being out of the top-flight since 1994. The New Craven Park staged an international game during the 2000 Emerging Nations World Cup tournament when Morocco beat Japan 12-8 before a crowd of 1,488.

HUNSLET

Each year, on the first Sunday in June, a nostalgic reunion takes place at a plush city centre hotel in the centre of Leeds. The numbers at the reunion will never grow, only diminish over time, and the youngest attendee this year will be around the age of 50.

The only criterion for entry is that you had to be associated with the Hunslet club at Parkside, either as a player or a member of the backroom staff. Few Rugby League grounds awake the nostalgic feelings that are attributed to a ground that staged its final game in 1973, and the affection that people feel for the place hardly seems to diminish with time.

Harry Jepson first got involved with Hunslet in the 1930s - the start of a distinguished career as a Rugby League administrator in the game he still follows with a boyish enthusiasm - and he organises the Parkside reunion.

"Parkside was a very well appointed ground, a relic of the past in many ways and its passing was extremely sad," he says. "The reunion is still as popular as it ever was. We get old players coming from all over the globe to attend and I often get asked for an invitation. But if you didn't play at Parkside, the answer, sadly, is "no."

"At our luncheon there is a remarkable atmosphere. We are all getting older, a lot of us in our 70s and 80s, but Alan Snowden (a former Hunslet player) summed it up at last year's reunion. "If you could bottle and encapsulate the spirit in this room, you'd make a fortune," he said.

Harry's uncle first took him to Parkside in 1927. By chance a young player making his Hunslet debut that day went on to become a club legend.

Jack Walkington went on to make 572 appearances for Hunslet and captained them to Challenge Cup and Championship triumphs in the 1930s.

"Parkside was not just a rugby ground but the centre of sporting action," says Harry. "It also had a cricket ground, like those at Huddersfield, Halifax, Batley and Leeds, and a bowling-green.

"Everyone talked about "going to Parkside" not "watching Hunslet". And as well as the rugby, Hunslet had a good cricket side then. Four-figure crowds were commonplace and when Learie Constantine (the famous West Indian cricketer) played there in the mid-1930s there were 8,000 to watch him play.

"As a schoolboy I played at Parkside and all the local schoolboy finals were staged at the ground. I played in the under-11s final in 1930. For me and many of my school pals Parkside soon became a place of pilgrimage."

Harry's life changed forever when he completed his teacher training. "A clerk in the education department sent me to a school in Hunslet for my first teaching post," he recalls. "The headmaster at the school was Edgar Meeks, who was also the chairman of Hunslet. After a while, knowing of my interest in Rugby League, he asked me to give him a hand and I became the assistant secretary. My direct involvement in the game had begun."

The South Leeds Stadium

Parkside's glory years were those immediately before and after the second world war. In 1938, with war clouds looming, Hunslet was involved in one of the most famous of all Rugby League finals, defeating Leeds, 8-2, in the Championship Final at Elland Road.

The game had been scheduled for Wakefield but after a clamour from officials, spectators and the press the venue was switched. The result was a remarkable crowd - 54,112 - at the time the highest ever for a Rugby League game in this country.

"Hunslet beat Barrow, 13-7, in the semi-final and then had to wait two days to find out their opponents," Harry recalls. "Leeds played Swinton on the Monday night and were losing until Eric Harris scored an interception try on the South Stand side and they won, 5-2, to set up the All Leeds Final.

"Parkside was a grand ground," Harry says with obvious affection. "It had cover on three sides and a really good playing surface - the best in the game at that time. There was also a massive car park at the ground. As an example of how times have changed I remember a game at Parkside, against Leeds, in 1949. There was a crowd of 19,000 but on the car park we had only seven cars. Everyone either walked to the ground or went by tram."

Harry got to know Albert Goldthorpe, one of the Hunslet legends of the "All Four Cups" side of 1907/08. Like the long-serving trainer, Billy Hannah, and club chairman, Mr Joe Lewthwaite, Albert had a huge affection for Hunslet and long after his playing days were over he retained his links with the club.

"Albert was a true gentleman and was teetotal." Harry says. "In the late 1980s an Australian company produced a film on the First Kangaroos (the first Australian tourists) and Albert, one of the game's leading players, was portrayed very wrongly in that film. It amounted to nothing more than a character assassination.

"He used to tell me how Parkside had been constructed out of a rubble heap in 1888 and a pitch laid and a stand built," Harry recalls. "There were lots of people around then who'd been concerned with the "split" from rugby union in 1895 and my uncle used to regale me with tales of the great team of the 1900s with Billy Batten and the pack, known as "The Terrible Six." One of that pack, Harry Wilson, kept the local pub, the Anchor, where Hunslet used to change.

"There was no electricity at the ground until after the war and we had to use paraffin lamps. The cricket team dressed in the football dressing rooms and the clubs shared the same perimeter fence. It was possible to stand at the top of the terrace and watch cricket and rugby games taking place at the same time."

Harry was immersed in the character of Parkside and enjoyed the competition with Leeds. "A small group of wealthier, small businessmen watched both Hunslet and Leeds but I only went to Headingley to watch Leeds get beaten," he says. "The two clubs weren't daggers drawn and the officials were very friendly with one another, but there was a tremendous rivalry.

"The gate for the Leeds game paid for the running of the club. It financed us for the year. It was a remarkable era. Hunslet was a financially sound club in a small way and so many people helped out at the ground on a voluntary basis. I remember supporters extending the terracing and building the Spion Kop at the end where Mother Benson's cottage used to be.

"But the club declined after getting to Wembley in 1965. Players were sold, such as Ken Eyre and Bill Ramsey to Leeds and Geoff Shelton to Oldham and Billy Langton and Brian Gabbitas retired. After being secretary, I left the club in 1969/70 as life had become so unpleasant. The directors were not prepared to hand over control and for some reason decided to sell the ground. I didn't go to the last match, it was too sad. But those that went, and a sizeable contingent of past players were there, were disappointed that the club made no special provision for them."

Hunslet's roots pre-date Parkside. They were originally formed in 1883 when Hunslet Cricket Club made a grant to two local sides, Albion and Excelsior, to merge and share their Woodhouse Hill ground. The ground's boundaries were the Cemetery Tavern (now re-named the Parnaby) to the north, Middleton Road to the west and Hunslet cemetery to the south, with open fields to the east. The M1 motorway now covers much of the site. At that time Hunslet was still a separate village but rapid urbanisation in the late 19th century soon saw it engulfed by the growth of Leeds.

The cricket ground, first used around the late 1840s, had staged some famous matches, hosting the Australian Aborigines and Australian touring sides and staged a Yorkshire first-class game in 1869. The ground was given up in 1888 and the club, taking their grandstand with them, moved to Parkside. The cricket club at Parkside folded after the 1959 season.

The ground at Parkside comprised a ten-acre site that was transformed from wasteland, owned by the Low Moor Iron and Coal Company, and 2,000 tons of rubble was used in the laying-out of the ground.

The first rugby game staged there was on 11 February 1888 against Mirfield. When Hunslet became founder members of the Northern Union in 1895 the ground was under suspension by the rugby union authorities. This followed a stormy match against Brighouse Rangers when the referee and visiting players had to be rescued from an angry mob of home spectators by a force of 21 policemen. The club used the Anchor and Engine public houses as headquarters prior to the building of a pavilion in 1901.

Hunslet line up at Parkside for the final time in 1973

Hunslet formed a limited liability company in 1911 in a bid to raise capital for ground improvements and a new wooden stand, seating 1,600, on the Parkside Lane side was built in 1914. This survived until being burnt down by vandals in 1971, shortly after a local fire officer had insisted on its closure.

The Supporters' Club succeeded in covering the original old grandstand on the pavilion side and they also built a new pavilion behind it on the cricket ground.

The Parkside site was finally purchased by the club for the sum of £6,500 in 1949. The contract gave the club a strip of land at the Middleton Colliery end, the colliery workings providing a dramatic backdrop to the ground. This end was later developed into a Kop. In 1959 the supporters concreted the Dewsbury Road end, built a bar underneath and covered it two years later.

Ironically Hunslet's record home attendance was established before most of the ground improvements had taken place when 24,700 saw a third-round Challenge Cup-tie against Wigan in 1924, the visitors running out 13-8 winners.

The huge car park, covering two-and-a-half acres, referred to earlier by Harry Jepson, was sold for £10,250 in 1963/64.

In 1971 a move to sell Parkside for £300,000 was rejected by the shareholders but in the autumn of the following year a faction on the board forced through its sale for industrial development to a property company based in Huddersfield and the club closed down in July 1973.

The rapid decline of the club's playing fortunes was mirrored in the local community, with the Hunslet district undergoing great changes around that time. The wholesale clearance of the old housing around the ground and the closure of many local mines and factories were important factors for a club that had prided itself on its links with local schools and workshops.

But the Hunslet spirit lived on and Geoff Gunney, awarded an MBE in 1970, refused to accept the inevitable. He was instrumental in reviving the club, which entered the Rugby League in the 1973/74 season, re-titled New Hunslet and playing at the Elland Road Greyhound Stadium, opposite the Elland Road ground.

Gunney, a member of the '65 Wembley side, played 625 games for Hunslet between 1951-73, ignoring the chance to move on to bigger and more fashionable clubs, and fittingly was the last to leave the pitch at Parkside after that final game against York on 21 April 1973.

In their first home game New Hunslet beat Huyton, 23-0, before a crowd of 4,000 and in October 1974 inaugurated their floodlights with a 12-5 win over Widnes in the popular BBC2 Floodlit Trophy.

A ground record attendance was set when 5,859 saw Warrington win a third-round Challenge Cup-tie, 23-3, in March 1975.

Once the initial enthusiasm wore off the reality set in. The Greyhound Stadium had the narrowest pitch in the League and moreover was very uneven. Apart from a few rows of seating on the Elland Road side and a bank of terracing in front of the social club, the ground had few facilities for spectators keen to get a close view of the action. The best view was perhaps to be found in the bars and restaurant but, as this was behind glass, there was no atmosphere.

The current Hunslet coach, Roy Sampson, is a club stalwart, his loyalty rewarded by a testimonial at the club. "The Greyhound Stadium was a really strange place to play Rugby League, very unusual," he recalls. "You could walk around and around the ground and not find the best place to watch. The field was very small and they had those unusual tuning fork posts, like the ones in American Football. I never played there but I watched Hunslet there. It reminded me of a club that was really struggling and they didn't have a great deal of support at that time."

The club was re-titled Hunslet in 1979/80, their last season at the Greyhound Stadium, which was later demolished by its owners, Ladbrokes.

Hunslet then played at Mount Pleasant, Batley for two seasons, also staging one "home" game at Dewsbury. Then they took up residence at Elland Road for the 1982/83

Viewing the old Parkside site from South Leeds Stadium

season after reaching a ground-sharing agreement with Leeds United, then owners of the ground. A crowd of 2,000 saw Hunslet open their new home against Salford in August 1982. History had indeed come full circle as the ground had originally been home to Holbeck Northern Union club, whose closure in 1904 opened the door for the soccer code to take root in Leeds.

Leeds City AFC took over the lease of the ground from Holbeck and, with the Football League authorities keen to establish a foothold in Northern Union strongholds, were effectively "fast-tracked" into the League in 1905 after playing their first season in the West Yorkshire League.

Like Woodhouse Hill, Holbeck's original home, the Recreation Ground, off Top Moor Side and Brown Lane, was also a major cricket venue, staging the Roses Match in 1868 when Lancashire were routed by an innings and 186 runs, mustering a total of only 68 runs in their two innings.

Two further Yorkshire first-class fixtures were staged there, the home county maintaining their winning record, but the venue was considered less than ideal and the development of Headingley, opened in 1890, proved a major blow to the Holbeck club. They eventually left the Recreation Ground in 1897 after their first season as a senior club and the site was developed for housing. The present day road names bear witness to the old ground, being named Recreation View, Place, Row and Street respectively.

Holbeck moved half-a-mile down Elland Road to take over the cricket and rugby grounds of the "Old Peacock" public house, purchasing the site for £1,100. They built a 70-yard long stand on Elland Road but the stand on the opposite side, behind which was located the disused Beeston pit, was much smaller. Originally the ground of the old Leeds (Athletic) club from 1878, the land, though flat, had been extensively mined and colliery waste was used for embankments around the playing area.

Though the rugby section did not last long, resigning from the Northern Union after losing to St Helens in the Second Division Play-Off game in 1904, the cricket club, to the east of the rugby field, survived until the 1960s. The cricket ground is now covered by road developments.

During Holbeck's years at Elland Road the rugby pitch ran from east to west. But Leeds City made numerous ground improvements, re-draining and re-turfing the pitch and then, in 1906, turning it at right angles so it ran from north to south. The grandstand at Elland Road then became the popular stand behind the goal.

Soccer's growing popularity in a previously rugby stronghold was demonstrated when 22,000 saw a league game against Bradford City in December 1905, with 35,000 attending the corresponding fixture in 1908.

City stayed in the League until 1919 when they were sensationally thrown out after playing eight league games after a furore over alleged illegal payments to players. Port Vale took their place and inherited their record and fixtures. This draconian act could have spelt the end of soccer in Leeds, but Leeds United was formed almost immediately and took their place in the Football League in 1920.

Elland Road had been used for occasional Rugby League games, the 1938 Championship Final the highlight and 20 years on from that Hunslet played Leeds there in the first game to be played under modern floodlights in the city, running out 15-8 winners.

But it then became a regular "big match" venue for the game, hosting cup finals, semi-finals and Test matches, due largely to the extra seating capacity available. For the 1982 Challenge Cup Final replay between Hull and Widnes, for instance, 19,626 of the

115

41,171 crowd were seated, five times the number any traditional RL ground could seat. Capacity crowds of 32,500 and then 39,468 saw the third and decisive Tests against Australia in 1990 and 1994.

Roy Sampson loved playing at Elland Road. "As a kid I had the chance to sign for Featherstone and Bradford but Paul Daley, then the Hunslet coach, took me to Elland Road and I was really impressed," he recalls. "That swung it for me. It was obviously a massive stadium, covered on all four sides and capable of holding 40,000 people. Even for rugby games, when only the West Stand and the Kop were open, the crowd could generate some noise. We also used the training field next to the ground and the facilities were fantastic. It was a big pull for players to play at Elland Road and when I meet up with old teammates now we all say what a fantastic place it was to play."

One memorable occasion was when Hunslet played Castleford at Elland Road in the Challenge Cup quarter-final in 1983, losing 8-13 but recording a crowd of 14,004. "I was a spectator that day and remember thinking that it would be seemingly impossible to get another 20,000 in. It was a massive crowd," Sampson says.

"We had two seasons in the old first division and the derby matches against Leeds really stick out in the memory. In years gone by it had been a great derby game, one to be part of with an amazing feeling of rivalry, and we re-created that atmosphere. The pitch wasn't the best at Elland Road then and the soccer lot used to give us a lot of stick about churning it up. But the groundsman told me that was rubbish - it was down to the really bad drainage. "

Hunslet played at Bramley's McLaren Field ground for most of the 1994/95 season, though they did play three further fixtures in that campaign at Elland Road. They began the Centenary season at Bramley before playing their first match at the council-run South Leeds Stadium on 19 November 1995. Hunslet celebrated with a 37-10 win over Leigh before a crowd of 2,350.

It was an emotional day. Twenty-two years and seven months on from leaving Parkside Gunney led a parade of proud ex-players before the game.

"Parkside was a wonderful place," Gunney recalled. "It was a broken-down ground, but it was friendly with a tremendous atmosphere and we had the best team spirit in the Rugby League. The ground was the life and soul of the community but it needed repairing when I started, never mind when I finished. Back in 1973 the old directors gave the new club six months. Well we're still here. We've not done badly."

Mooted plans to develop the other three sides to make a 12,000 all-seater multi-purpose arena have not reached fruition and Hunslet were denied promotion after winning the Grand Final against Dewsbury in 1999.

Hunslet's new home has covered seating for 2,471 on four floors and has hospitality accommodation and a banqueting suite. It is part of a magnificent sporting complex, incorporating an eight-lane all-weather athletics track, ten all-weather five-a-side pitches, a full-size all-weather hockey and football pitch, a tennis centre and gym with several bars. A £4.5m indoor athletics and bowls complex was built alongside the stadium in 2002.

Sampson initially had mixed views on the South Leeds Stadium. "I'm a traditionalist and I didn't know what to think," he admits. "Now, a decade in, I think it's one of the best stadiums about. It's just a shame it only holds about 2,600 people. The playing surface is second to none and the ground has grown on me. It's the best place to play.

"People think of an athletics stadium and think of places like Sheffield and York. But it's nothing like those and there is a genuine atmosphere. We train there, have our own floodlit training ground, gym, bars, boardroom, club shop and offices.

Hunslet celebrate winning the 1999 Northern Ford Premiership grand final

"We owe everything to Grahame Liles, our former chairman, now president. Without him there wouldn't be a club. We had the lease at Elland Road. Leeds United wanted to buy back the ground and the move to the South Leeds Stadium came about because of him. We are now moving forward at a rapid pace, setting down roots in the community and we are involved in the schools, have four scholarship age groups and are starting an Academy. Grahame was the best chairman in the Rugby League and devoted all his time to Hunslet.

"The name Hunslet still means a lot to a lot of people. When we played Bradford in the Cup in 1997 we took the game to Headingley and the Hunslet fans outnumbered Bradford in a crowd of 6,000. Parkside was undoubtedly a tremendous place but this can be a massive team in its own right. We don't want to lose that tradition that Hunslet built up and we are determined to survive and prosper."

The last words go to Harry Jepson. "The South Leeds Stadium is very different to Parkside," Harry says. "I was there for the Lazenby Cup game in January (2004), sitting in the stand looking across to where the old Parkside ground used to be. All that remains are twelve or thirteen poplar trees that we planted in 1948 on the far side of the cricket field to give it a screen. If you are going down the motorway look across to your left and you will see them. I'm glad Hunslet have gone back in sight of the old ground."

117

KEIGHLEY

The beginning of the tenth year of Super League had an added poignancy for supporters of Keighley, reminding them of an anniversary of what they believed to be one of the biggest betrayals in sporting history.

In the early 1990s the team, ground and town had been transformed in a quite revolutionary way, and a small Rugby League club situated between the metropolis of Bradford and the scenic beauty of the Dales became the focus of an entire community.

At the start of the revolution Lawkholme Lane was near-derelict and the club seemed on the brink of oblivion. But along came two men, in the shape of Mike Smith and Mick O'Neill, who had a vision and drive to push through so many changes that a few years later the club and town was barely recognisable.

Adopting the nickname of the Cougars, a member of the cat family and the largest and most powerful Canadian predator, and changing the name of the ground to Cougar Park, they made unbelievable progress, on and off the field. Lawkholme Lane was transformed into a colourful and vibrant place, rocking to music and with a buzz and contagious sense of fun and enjoyment on match days. They set up community schemes to help combat drugs and crime, introduced a classroom at the ground for local schoolchildren and encouraged all the local schools to play the greatest game of all. They organised huge convoys of coachloads of chattering kids to go to big games at Wembley.

And on the field the Cougars were transformed, too, as they attracted a top British coach and signed star players from around the globe.

It all ended in triumph in the 1994/95 season. The Cougars won the second division, seemingly qualifying for the top flight, and lifted the Second Division Premiership Trophy at Old Trafford.

But along came the bombshell news that Keighley were to be denied their hard-won place among the elite. The Super League revolution, the plans for which were outlined in the first days of April 1995 just as the Cougars' triumphant season was nearing its climax, had no place for Keighley.

The Cougars served a writ on the RFL, claiming their omission cost them hundreds of thousands of pounds in lost sponsorship. But the dream effectively had ended.

Ten years on all the fans can do is reflect on what might have been.

Rugby was first played on the Lawkholme Lane ground on 3 October 1885 after Keighley Cricket Club bought land from the Duke of Devonshire to make a sporting club encompassing a cricket and rugby field, a common feature of the time. Keighley played Liversedge in the first rugby game held there.

Keighley Rugby Club had been formed in 1876, playing their early games on a field in the Lawkholme Lane area and then off Dalton Lane. The rugby club continued to be tenants of the cricketers until 1933 when they bought the leasehold.

The Keighley club was a latecomer to the Northern Union, finally transferring allegiances in June 1900, nearly five years after the 'great split'. Sowerby Bridge provided the first league opposition as Keighley won 5-0 before a crowd of 2,000.

Though a scenic ground with magnificent views, Lawkholme Lane was open to the elements and spectator facilities were rudimentary. Keighley were often said to have the worst ground in the League in the early decades of the twentieth century.

A surviving photograph of the ground from a game against Broughton Rangers in 1902 shows an open, uncovered ground with some spectators accommodated in a large uncovered stand, reserved for members and known as the 'hen pen'.

One of the best crowds in the early days was in November 1907 when the first New Zealand tourists attracted 8,000. Australia made their first visit in January 1909.

Dressing rooms were only constructed at the ground in the mid-1920s; before then the teams and officials had to change in often primitive conditions in a variety of public houses. For a long time they used a building behind the King's Arms on Church Green and made their way to and from the ground in horse-drawn charabancs.

The club became a limited liability company in 1929 and the ground underwent great changes in the early 1930s driven by the ambitions of chairman JW Booth and secretary Norman Harrison. The club was granted a long lease on the ground and this added security gave them the impetus to increase capacity to around 15,000.

A new covered grandstand was built on the side adjoining the cricket field and the playing area, one of the narrowest in the game, was widened. Cover was then built on the side opposite the main stand which became known as the 'Scrattin' Shed' and terracing was built at the town end of the ground.

A club record crowd was set in February 1934 when 14,245 saw Warrington's visit in a Challenge Cup-tie; this was extended in March 1951 when 14,500 (£1,645) saw Keighley go down 6-7 to Halifax in the same competition.

In 1957 the club agreed to purchase the 13-acre site from the Duke of Devonshire's estate, including the cricket field and a training pitch. The transaction was completed in 1961. Floodlights were installed in 1967.

By the 1980s Keighley was in decline and the ground looked in a state of bad neglect. In the aftermath of the Valley Parade fire the main stand was declared unfit by safety officers and the floodlights condemned as dangerous. At one point the ground's capacity was reduced to 1,200.

In November 1986, faced with mounting debts and with no money in the kitty to finance essential ground improvements and maintenance, the directors took the drastic step of selling the ground. After long negotiations with interested parties, the club finally agreed a deal with the West Yorkshire Motor Group (Co-operative Society). Under the terms of the deal the club leased back the ground for 25 years.

Terry Hollindrake, Keighley's only Great Britain representative, is credited with bringing Messrs Smith and O'Neill together.

A strong and speedy winger and excellent goal-kicker, Terry played for Keighley from 1951-60 (when he was transferred to Hull for a then club record £6,000 fee) and returned to the club for a brief spell nearly a decade later. A Keighley Albion product, Terry became the first player to score over 1,000 points for the club. His Great Britain debut came in 1955 when he played against New Zealand at Headingley.

O'Neill first got involved with the club as a sponsor before joining the board alongside Smith.

The Cougar revolution officially began at the start of the 1991/92 season when former player Peter Roe replaced Tony Fisher as head coach, and gathered momentum the following season when the Cougars won the third division, bolstered by key signings Joe Grima and Ian Gately. In 1993 the Cougars began their far-reaching community initiatives, headed by Mary Calvert.

Smith takes up the story. "I had watched Keighley all my life and Mick O'Neill was very much the same frame of mind as me as to what needed doing.

"It was our aim to create a modern-day Rugby League club. We realised that Keighley RL as a brand had no worth and we went in to transform the club. The team had been on its heels for so long Keighley RL did not mean anything in the town.

Lawkholme Lane, circa 1902

"We immediately went for a nickname to create a brand and playing music, which we did before, during and after the game, was something that worked really well. We gave individual players a snatch of music that was specific to themselves (for example, "The Pink Panther" theme tune when Nick Pinkney scored a try). By doing that we branded the players and even average players turned into crowd favourites.

"Both Mick and I had entrepreneurial backgrounds and we went on to tear up a lot of the traditions. We had to create an entertainment out of the game instead of the dour image that was being presented. We set out deliberately to create a family sport with razzmatazz.

"We deliberately targeted women to become fans, as more often than not they control the family purse strings and we gave away thousands of tickets to children.

"We started in late 1990 and were killed off in '95. In just over four years what had been a washed-up, broken-down shambles of a ground was a vibrant place. We rebuilt the ground, making conference facilities and bars, got the stand fully opened again and worked hard on the terracing. We signed players from all over the world and had Phil Larder as coach.

"What happened to us was a disgrace after all the work we had done to put the team together, rebuild the stadium and after all our work in the community."

The onset of Cougarmania initially found many detractors. "A lot of visiting teams didn't like it and I remember an official from Bradford calling the place a mad-house and like Fred Karnos," Smith says. "Yet look at Odsal now.

"The people of Keighley embraced the new culture virtually straight away. Overnight we completely changed the environment and it is interesting to see clubs like Castleford, with the way they changed Wheldon Road into the Jungle later, going down the same path as we did, with such great success. The Cougar legacy lives on."

Smith's business background was fundamental to putting the ideas into practice. "I was involved in corporate communications and was fascinated by the psychology of how to encourage and develop businesses on the back of enjoyment. We created first-class facilities and had a business club that met regularly at the ground. Many of the local businesses in the area helped us and I remember one Sunday afternoon when we raised £15,000 in the bar.

"We were in our pomp in '95 when we won at Old Trafford. The people were so proud and there was a smile on everyone's face. Our game was played before the Premiership Final and after our game a third of the crowd departed. I think we got up a lot of people's noses - what people perceived as a 'rubbin' rag club' challenging the elite. The game of Rugby League was like a gentleman's club where everyone had to fit in. But we couldn't give a monkey's about that. I think that people were frightened of us and if we had continued for another three years we would have been the leading light in the game. Everyone knew us, we had internationals playing at Keighley and the whole thing was just unbelievable."

The nickname came about almost by accident. "We ran a competition and someone chose the name Cougars," Smith recalls. "I thought right away about renaming the ground Cougar Park and everyone was up for it.

"We were the first football and Rugby League club to

Mick O'Neill jumps for joy as the Cougars secure the 1995 Second Division Premiership at Old Trafford

have a community scheme and a classroom for local school children. The Sports Minister came up from London and I feel that from that visit derived many of the community initiatives that you see clubs running these days. Joe Grima was fantastic. I remember when he organised to take a thousand local kids to a Wembley Cup Final.

"The police gave them a convoy all the way to the motorway. We gave local kids a purpose and many people who had never taken an interest in the game before appreciated what we were trying to do. At one time we were taking over £20,000 a week in merchandise at the shop. It was an incredible time and so you can imagine that when the dream ended so abruptly it was also the biggest disappointment I've had in my life."

Just prior to the bombshell news about the formation of Super League, a competition from which they would be excluded, Keighley signed Daryl Powell. At the time he was a Great Britain international and one of the game's leading players. It was a clear signal that Keighley meant business for their intended step-up to the top flight.

"I remember sitting round a hotel table discussing the transfer with Daryl," Smith recalls. "I thought that sooner or later we were going to have to do some serious negotiating about money and yet all Daryl seemed bothered about was the theme music that would be played for him when he scored a try. To me, that summed up the whole of the Cougar philosophy."

The news that Keighley would be denied their deserved promotion came as a bombshell to Smith and O'Neill, and the former still recalls the events clearly.

"Prior to that I had been commissioned by the RFL to prepare a report on the game through my company, Global Sports Marketing," Smith says. "The report spoke about embracing satellite television and the switch to summer with a complete re-brand of Rugby League. All the concepts that were later adopted were in there.

"One day Mick O'Neill rushed to a hastily-convened meeting four weeks before the end of the season," Smith says. "I remember that it was a lovely day and I suddenly heard on the radio about the £87m deal with Sky. At first I was really excited by the news, but as more details came out, including the talk of mergers, things changed. I realised straight away that mergers were something you couldn't force - you have to change culture over a period of time.

"At the time we were one of the best-supported teams in the Rugby League and we were going to be sacked off for a £100,000 pay-off. Yet we had spent £130,000 on Daryl Powell three weeks earlier. We immediately took out an injunction and fought the decision. We were fighting for all the clubs, not just ours. We had risen from nothing and that had created a lot of resentment and jealousy from the top end and we weren't very popular. Eventually we got an agreement that more money would be shared between clubs and that the winners of division two would be promoted to Super League. But as far as we were concerned I knew the Keighley dream was finished.

"We had turned fully professional before all this, and had all our funding in place on the basis of being a top-flight club. We had sponsors ready to put in £400,000. They all pulled out. It was a very difficult period.

"For the first time in a hundred years Keighley had a chance to dominate the Rugby League. That was not just the club, but Keighley people as a whole. We had encouraged the fans to be involved and everyone had some ownership of the club. So many people were hands on and in touch.

"I look back and think that what happened to us was the start of a new era in British sport. We were the first casualty of the way that money had started to dominate sport. You

Glory days - Keighley celebrate winning the second division title in 1995

can see how it has affected soccer in the last ten years, and clubs with money are desperate not to lose it."

Smith still goes down to Cougar Park, though O'Neill is now living in Australia. "I still watch the team but it is so difficult at times when you see what it is like now to the way it could have been," Smith says. "What was different about us was that it was not just a Keighley thing. People would travel from all over the country to Cougar Park and got caught up in the whole ethos. If the match was in doubt due to the weather we'd get calls from the south west and London, for example, checking if the game would take place because they were travelling such a long way. It was very humbling.

"So many people had put their total trust in us and in our vision. I'd had my own heroes, people like Terry Hollindrake and Brian Jefferson. Brian was a wonderful player, the most talented I'd ever seen. He had a very rare individual flair, was a very balanced runner and a clever thinker.

"Yet over the five years we were in charge, a whole new range of heroes emerged like Grima, who was a massive influence - a man mountain who also did so much work in the community. All our players performed really well, but Pinkney and Andy Eyres were two that typified the professionalism of the club. They would be there on the pitch on their nights off practising and as young players they felt they could come to Keighley and achieve all their dreams. They knew that they need not go anywhere else to fulfil those ambitions. Another player that really stands out was Steve Hall, who was absolutely superb for us.

"Peter Roe was our first coach and then Larder took over. I had a policy of changing the coach every two or three years as I felt the players would give their best if they were not complacent. It worked really well and brought in a lot of fresh ideas. In some respects we were ruthless and success orientated, but we were loyal to players that got injured and everyone played their role.

"Mick was the figurehead and a very good front-man, and my role was to bring the

123

cash in. It was marvellous when we had a big game at Cougar Park to see the ground packed and queues of people stretching a quarter-of-a-mile down the road waiting to get in. Yet when we had taken over, the ground was waiting to be condemned and the local authority was threatening to reduce the capacity to 300.

"After the rejection it was hard to bounce back and in many ways it was like a slow death. I was one of the last to go. It all ended so sadly, yet if you speak to players who played during that time they will tell you it was the pinnacle of their careers."

Terry Hollindrake is still an avid supporter of Rugby League and maintains: "Keighley is a Rugby League town and definitely always has been. In the days when I played and before they had some big gates but a big factor was the ending of the one league system in the early 1970s. After that the standard of play dropped and Keighley didn't get to play Leeds, Bradford and the other big teams on a regular basis. In my playing days we used to compete both home and away against the big clubs and it gave our players the chance to enjoy playing at grounds like Headingley and Odsal. In the 1950s there were much more even standards throughout the Rugby League."

Hollindrake watched all his early rugby at Lawkholme Lane. "My hero was the winger Len Ward who I half styled myself on," he says. "I was spotted playing for Keighley Albion and then played in the under-18s and the A team before getting my chance. Second-team games would have 2-3,000 crowds on a regular basis and you learnt quickly playing against a lot of older, more experienced professionals.

"Bert Cook, the New Zealander, was my first coach and had a big influence on me. He had his own ideas and he really helped me. It did seem strange playing alongside players that I had regarded as heroes when I watched them from the terraces.

"It had always been my ambition to play for my hometown club and I was just happy to be there. I didn't really feel any pressure and just really enjoyed the experience. One of my first big games was a friendly against Bradford in 1952. It was a charity game and we got a crowd of around 10,000 - so Lawkholme Lane was absolutely packed and there was a tremendous atmosphere that day.

"Keighley has always had a narrow field and many opposing sides have found it difficult to play on. We used to train on the pitch even when the ground was a quagmire. We'd have lights on the stand and run up and down one side of the field. During the winter months we would be ankle deep in mud. We did have moves, but not the same as they do today and there was nothing like sliding defences. We just defended - things are far more technical today. In general the coaches were far more concerned with fitness training than developing the players' skills, but it was always difficult to do that with the restricted facilities that we had."

Recently non-league football has been staged at Cougar Park following Silsden's election to the North West Counties League. Silsden attracted their record crowd when a gate of 763 saw their West Riding County Cup tie against Halifax Town on 2 February 2005. "I have been impressed by the league and it is a good standard of football," Hollindrake says. "If they can progress up the leagues it can only be good for both clubs and will open up the possibility of getting more funding for ground developments. Though Keighley is an RL town there is still a place for football and Silsden do seem to have become accepted."

Hollindrake doesn't fall into the trap of saying that things were far better in his day. "Overall the game and the skills of the players are far superior today, though a lot of the players that I played with would have been terrific in today's game," he says. "When I first started I had a fine centre in Alan Taylor. We developed a good understanding and he was a brilliant tackler who really looked after his wing man and gave him plenty of ball.

1995 World Cup - Fiji perform the haka at Cougar Park

"But the make-up of the team changed so much. We'd have a mix of about 50-50 with local lads and those from further afield. Keighley Albion and the Keighley RU team provided a lot of our players and all the time I played there, there was a good team spirit. There always seemed to be a really good atmosphere and the crowds were good in the '50s. The ground was alive and Keighley people are very knowledgeable about the game and as partisan as they come.

Keighley stake their claim for a Super League place

"But in the depths of winter it was also one of the coldest places to play - though Batley also takes some beating. It really is an idyllic location at times in summer with the open and picturesque countryside around the ground."

Hollindrake looks back with affection on the early days of Cougarmania. "It was a superb time and the ground really came alive again. Peter Roe really started it off and then Phil Larder carried on the success. Lots of new people got involved with the club and some of the things they did were revolutionary. Mick O'Neill on the microphone was quite something and though a lot of visiting teams didn't like his antics at first, a lot of the things he did were copied by them. The Cougars didn't get everything right straight away, but they did a fantastic job in building up a tremendous level of interest in the town.

"The fact that they did not get promoted to the top division when they had earned it was the turning point. The directors had done a great job but they had a team of full-time players that needed funding and they also then lost so much of the sponsorship they had built up."

But Hollindrake still feels that Keighley is a true Rugby League town. "There is still a strong level of feeling for the game and they are not badly supported for the position they are in," he says. "The aim must be to get back to NL1 and hopefully build up the crowds again.

"Keighley certainly respect their old players and the history of the club and we have a lot of reunions and inductions into the club's Hall of Fame. The ground is still a lovely little place and when it is filled up there is a tremendous atmosphere." Cougar Park looked at its best on a glorious autumnal afternoon when it staged the Fiji-South Africa game on the opening weekend of the 1995 World Cup.

Hollindrake has gone down in history as the only Keighley player to play for Great Britain, but his Test debut at Headingley was something of a disappointment. "I was in the shadow squad but then the team got a few injuries and I got called in at the last minute," he says. "I turned up for the game but the gateman wouldn't let me in because he didn't recognise me. So I had to pay at the turnstile for the honour of playing for Great Britain. It was all a bit of an anticlimax, but it was still a huge honour."

LEEDS

Few districts of a city are as famous as Headingley, known the world over as a venue for Rugby League and test match cricket.

What visions are conjured by a mere mention of the name: for veteran supporters, Eric Harris running down the south stand side or Arthur Clues bossing things in the pack.

Those timeless skills of John Holmes or the majestic wingers John Atkinson and Alan Smith; Garry Schofield or Ellery Hanley in their pomp perhaps or, to the current generation the thrill and excitement of seeing modern-day heroes like Danny McGuire and Kevin Sinfield lift the Super League trophy.

Or as summer turned to mellow fruitfulness and the latest cricket season was consigned to the pages of Wisden you could look across Headingley's green sward and imagine Rhodes, Verity and Hutton plying their trade or the brilliant Don Bradman in his baggy green Australian cap effortlessly stroking another boundary. Or recall the incredible events of Botham's Ashes test in 1981 and the epitome of Yorkshireness himself, Geoff Boycott, playing Greg Chappell to long-on during an Ashes test of 1977 to record his 100th first-class century.

Wherever you go in the sporting world Headingley will mean something to somebody. Tony Currie, for example, had never left Brisbane before he joined Leeds; he had not even been to Sydney but he had heard of Headingley. For the great John Arlott, cricket writer and broadcaster supreme, it was a wonderful place and a trip to Bryan's, the famous fish and chip emporium a Botham six-hit away, replete with a few bottles of red, was the perfect end to a perfect day.

Yet for all the deeds of the past there has rarely been a better time to be a Leeds supporter, only their fourth league title in 109 years in the bag and a stream of exciting, talented players emerging through the ranks. Ten of the seventeen players in the Grand Final came through the Leeds Academy ranks - home-town pride personified. Home league attendances averaged 16,028 - the best for around 50 years.

Headingley could have been made for summer rugby but of all clubs Leeds were perhaps the tardiest to embrace the wind of change. Perhaps it stemmed back to a statement made by their chairman, Jack Myerscough, before the 1969 Championship Final, in response to a St Helens proposal to examine changing the timing of the season.

"Summer rugby would be the death-knell of the game," was the gist. That attitude prevailed and so Leeds, still smarting from the financial ramifications of the early 1990s when they tried and failed to keep pace with Wigan, entered Super League cast as the sulky, reluctant bride.

Burdened by a reported £5m overdraft, Leeds struggled through the 1996 season and a host of unlikely players wore the famous blue and amber with many high-profile stars leaving or having left the club. Dean Bell came over from Auckland, ended up as coach and

had to lace his boots again for a late-season match against Paris to earn the win that secured their survival. Only Paris and Workington's inadequacies lightened the load - in other years, Leeds' points-tally of 12 might have spelled relegation.

The board of Leeds Cricket, Football and Athletic Club Limited (Leeds CF&A) had long been regarded as a closed shop, presided over by a board of private individuals and effectively controlled by two families - the Greenwoods of the menswear chain and the Stockdales, of Asda stores.

In the first summer season attendances slumped to an average of 8,581 (a massive fall of over 3,000 on the Centenary season). With no apparent hope in sight of reducing the debt burden, many observers thought the only option available to the board was to sell Headingley - perhaps for a supermarket development in what was a heavily residential area, and move in with Leeds United at Elland Road.

Alf Davies was the chief executive at the time and it is thought that, largely through his instigation, word got around that Leeds, for the first time in living memory, was up for sale. There were two main interested parties - Gary Hetherington, a former Leeds player who had founded the Sheffield Eagles, and Paul Caddick, a successful businessman in building and construction whose first love was rugby union.

Davies is credited with bringing the two parties together - Hetherington for his Rugby League knowledge, Caddick for his business acumen and financial clout. It was an unlikely marriage but it worked and Leeds emerged from the precipice, though many would say at a price.

Hetherington swiftly turned around the fortunes on the rugby side, developing youth systems for players and community programmes that bore such rich fruit in 2004. Caddick, who had expressed from the start of his involvement that he was concerned Headingley might disappear, was able to find a home for the embryonic Leeds Tykes, born out of a

127

merger between the Headingley and Roundhay clubs, at a time of rapid change in rugby union. That was the price Leeds RL fans had to pay - rah-rah on their beloved turf.

The Tykes won promotion to the top division of the union game, even though their games appeared to attract little if no interest from the League fans and Headingley staged an A international between England and Scotland in 1999.

Leeds became the Rhinos, after Hetherington quickly changed the mindset around the place - by 1998, under the coaching of Graham Murray, they were good enough to reach the inaugural Super League Grand Final.

In 1999 they marked the occasion of the last Wembley Challenge Cup final with an emphatic victory over London Broncos. Ronnie the Rhino was an instantly recognisable mascot and even stood for Parliament in the 1997 general election.

The visionaries who set about creating the huge Headingley complex in the last years of the Victorian era would be no doubt delighted if they could be transplanted in time to cast a look now at one of the world's most famous and evocative sporting arenas.

Under the chairmanship of the future Lord Hawke, then the Yorkshire cricket captain, the Leeds CF&A was incorporated on 21 February 1889 and Lot 17A of the Cardigan Estate (a 22-acre site) was purchased for £25,000.

As well as the cricket and rugby pitches Headingley also housed eleven tennis courts and a bowling green in its early days and a cycling and athletics track around the cricket field. There was also a brief flirtation with association football with some exhibition games and a couple of amateur cup finals staged there.

Hawke was keen to challenge the dominance of Sheffield as home to Yorkshire cricket - their Bramall Lane ground had already staged many major games since 1855 - and was mindful that Bradford's Park Avenue ground was also rapidly developing. The deputy chairman was Mr CF Tetley, of the famous brewing family, while the city's MP, Mr WL

Jackson, father of FS, another famous cricketer, was also on the board.

Prior to the purchase, the site had been used as playing fields; a Headingley Cricket Club played nearby and, from 1872 a Leeds Athletic Club played rugby - in 1885 they were succeeded by Headingley.

During 1889 the ground was prepared and a double-fronted grandstand to accommodate both rugby and cricket and a pavilion were constructed. The Leeds CF&A persuaded two clubs, Leeds Clarendon CC and Leeds St John's FC (formed in 1870) to drop their suffixes and re-locate to Headingley. The latter club had first played at the Militia Barracks ground before moving to Cardigan Fields.

Leeds CC survived until their demise in 1983. As for the rugby club, few would deny that they are doing alright, though quite what Lord Hawke would have thought of the branding of Leeds Rhinos, not to mention coloured clothing for one-day cricket matches does not bear thinking about.

And Headingley has far outlived the famous dual sports grounds of Bramall Lane and Park Avenue. The former staged its last first-class cricket game in 1973 before a new stand for the Sheffield United soccer club was built over the hallowed turf. Park Avenue, once a venue for Northern Union and home to Bradford Park Avenue in their Football League career (which ended in 1970) is now a pale shadow of its former self. A similar depressing tale is told at Fartown in Huddersfield, another ground once famous as home to Rugby League and cricket.

The cricket ground was officially opened in May 1890 and later that year the touring Australians played The North in the inaugural first-class game at Headingley. Yorkshire played their first game at the ground in 1891 and the venue was an almost instant hit with spectators. When Yorkshire played Surrey in 1897 the attendance on the second day was estimated at 30,000. In 1899 Headingley staged its first cricket test match when England played Australia.

Leeds played Manningham in the first rugby game there on 20 September 1890 and staged an England v Scotland international three years later. The biggest attendance for a rugby union game was 27,654 when Leeds played Halifax in the Yorkshire Cup in 1892. When Leeds became inaugural members of the Northern Union in 1895 they averaged around 4,000 in their first season.

Headingley was recognised as a premier sporting arena, staging the first Challenge Cup Final in 1897 when Batley defeated St Helens before a crowd of 13,492. It was certainly Batley's lucky ground - the Gallant Youths won two further finals there in 1898 and 1901.

In all Headingley has staged 13 Challenge Cup Finals, the last in 1943, seven Championship Finals, no less than 46 Yorkshire Cup Finals (plus another four under the union code before the 1895 split) and 29 Test matches, 12 against Australia, eight against New Zealand and nine against France, Great Britain winning 23 of them.

It also staged a further seven World Cup games, including the 1970 final when Australia defeated Great Britain 12-7 in a game that became notorious for its brutality and was dubbed "the battle of Leeds," plus a dozen other internationals, the last in 2003 when England A defeated Wales in the European Championship.

Its next biggest challenge is to get Rugby League Test matches back at the ground - the lack of seating and capacity restraints meaning that the last Test against Australia was way back in 1982.

Then a crowd of 17,318 saw the invincible Kangaroos run out 32-8 winners in the third game of that memorable series to complete their first clean sweep in this country. The crowd was hugely disappointing considering that the final Test of the 1978 series (admittedly after GB had won the previous game at Odsal to set up a series decider) attracted 29,627.

Headingley has staged so many famous games, Leeds' first games against the tourists from New Zealand in 1907 and Australia in 1908 and their 102-0 win against Coventry in 1913 to name but three. It staged rugby union games during both world wars and was the scene of devastation on the occasion of the Leeds-Halifax game on Good Friday, 25 March 1932 when fire destroyed the north stand. The grandstand was packed but a tragedy was mercifully avoided as a safe evacuation took place, even though the structure was completely destroyed.

Later that year, with the stand resembling a building site, Hedley Verity returned an analysis of 10 wickets for 10 runs, still a record in first-class cricket, in a county game against Nottinghamshire.

The new grandstand was ready by May 1933; built at a cost of £20,000 by the construction company of the Leeds CF&A chairman, Sir Edwin Airey, it remains the dominant structure, on both the cricket and rugby sides, of Headingley.

The original seating capacity of this stand was 3,668 and this was extended during the 1990/91 season when a further 1,670 seats were installed in the paddock. The current ground capacity is 21,225, including 5,200 seats.

The south stand had undergone a major refurbishment in 1931 when the present 128-yard long structure was constructed to replace the barrel-roofed stand that held 4,700. When the new stand was ready for the York game in August 1931, its capacity was said to be 13,000. The second pitched roof was constructed in the late 1950s.

Always near the forefront of new ideas, Headingley installed undersoil heating in 1963, three years after Murrayfield became the first stadium in this country to boast the facility, while floodlights were constructed in 1966 and switched on for a Yorkshire-Lancashire encounter in September of that year.

In the early 1990s the facilities were extensively renovated, including new changing rooms and banqueting suites in the refurbished pavilion, as Leeds successfully chased the corporate dollar, while the south stand, home to Leeds' most vociferous supporters, underwent a £750,000 renovation in 2000. A seven million pound development of the eastern terrace was due to be completed in 2006.

Billy Watts is one of the unsung long-serving employees without whom Rugby League clubs would simply not function.

Now in his seventies he helps out at training every day, sells club lottery tickets and is the club's timekeeper. He is steeped in the folklore of Headingley and saw his first matches there in 1938.

That was the year that a game, played on Christmas Eve, was switched to the cricket ground, Leeds running out 5-0 winners over Salford with the great Australian Vic Hey scoring the game's only try.

"The rugby pitch was frozen but the committee had a good look at the cricket ground, found it well grassed and decided to stage the game," Billy recalls. "One touch-line was parallel to the west stand, the other was kept well away from the test wicket (where Bradman had scored his third test century in three visits - the previous two were triple centuries - just a few months before. He concluded with 173 on the 1948 tour. On the latter occasion a total of 158,000 witnessed the five days and on the Saturday it was reckoned that as many were locked out as were inside the ground.

"Ironically, in the stand watching on was the Salford manager, Lance Todd, who was way ahead of his time in leading the cry for summer rugby," Watts says. "I remember Hey's try - he received a reverse ball from Dai Jenkins and bounced off two Salford forwards before slamming the ball over the line. There was a great atmosphere that day." The crowd was estimated at between 12,000 and 15,000.

1938 was also the year of the All-Leeds Championship Final with Hunslet earning a famous victory at Elland Road. To make sure of their final place Leeds had beaten Swinton in the semi-final at Headingley when the Toowoomba Ghost, Eric Harris, scored a memorable try. "We were so close to the final and to play Hunslet meant so much to everyone in the city," Billy recalls. "Harris scored after a scissor move, running down the south stand side, for the try that decided a very tight and tension-packed game that ended 5-2. I remember catching the tramcar back into Leeds after the game. The streets were packed with people and I stood on the bumper bar of the tram all the way down into the centre.

"I remember the game against Bradford on 1947 when Headingley had its biggest ever attendance (40,175). They had beaten us in the Challenge Cup Final (eighteen) days before and this game ended in a 2-2 draw. It wasn't the most exciting of games but the atmosphere was absolutely marvellous that day. I stood in the south stand, behind a crush barrier, and couldn't move because of the density of the crowd packed into the ground.

"Also that same year I remember there was a strike in Leeds City Transport. Virtually everyone either walked or used public transport to get to games in those days. That day there was no choice - everyone had to walk, but they still got a crowd of 30,000."

Billy counts himself lucky to have seen the last matches of the great Eric Harris, whose talents are still recalled by veteran Leeds supporters today.

Another Australian, Clues, was a big hero, too. "I would have loved to have seen him

Headingley is also a world famous venue for test match cricket

pack down alongside Adrian Morley in the second row," Bills says, whimsically. "What a sight that would have been. As a second row Arthur was out of this world. Drew Turnbull was another favourite of mine - he had a lovely body-swerve and great pace and Ike Owens, a Welsh international, was a terrific player. He could play it hard or play football, just as the occasion demanded.

"The 1960s were another wonderful era with a lot of locally-produced players, and Smith and Atkinson on the wings were wonderful to watch. They were completely different types of players. John was the flamboyant type with a great swerve and sidestep. He could move in and out and scored some marvellous tries. Alan was very under-rated, a real workhorse who would come in and make superb cover-tackles and was a great ambassador for the club. Then there was John Holmes. He started as a 16-year-old and went on to have two benefits for Leeds. He was a great footballer, a wonderful halfback, deft with all the skills.

"Lewis Jones was the complete footballer - he could play anywhere and Mick Shoebottom was another. I can see him now in his pomp. He was a lion-hearted player and a great man to talk to. It was a tragedy when he was badly injured in a match against Salford at Headingley - his whole life changed after that and he was never the same again."

Many Leeds fans, Billy maintains, have watched soccer as well over the years though Leeds United were largely in the shadow until the Don Revie era.

"Prior to the war and just after it Rugby League certainly had it," Billy says. "Crowds of 25-30,000 were commonplace and the football generally used to average less than that. Then Rugby League dipped in the late 1960s and early 1970s but that was a really grey era for the game, just as Revie was building up his side at Elland Road." In Leeds' last championship season of 1971/72 average gates at Headingley were around the 8,000 mark and they attracted only two home league gates higher than 10,000; United in the same season averaged 35,637. Between 1964/65 to 1976/77 United's average never fell below 30,000.

Billy's enthusiasm for Leeds and Headingley shows no sign of waning despite his advancing years. He has been the timekeeper since 1975 and has missed only two games since then, ironically both at Wigan in deepest winter when he was ill.

He reports for training every morning at 7am sharp at the Kirkstall training ground, preparing everything for the players' arrival an hour later. "If there's no rugby union or cricket on, our final session of the week is at Headingley," Billy explains. "When training is over I'll often have a cup of tea and sit and gaze over the ground. Your mind goes back to great games and players of the past.

"The atmosphere at Headingley is still incredible for the top games, even though crowds are only half what they were due to the safety constraints in operation these days.

An example of that was the recent play-off game against Bradford when, just before the kick-off, you could have cut the atmosphere with a knife. It was just like before some of the games we had against Castleford in the 1960s and '70s. They were always fighting matches and punch-ups were guaranteed. The game is much cleaner these days and the players are wonderful athletes.

"The south stand is where the most voluble Leeds fans go and you get generations of Leeds fans standing together, often grandfather, father and son. Leeds did great work after the war building up their support in the community. Nearly every one of the workingmen's clubs in all the outlying and city areas would run coaches to away games in those days and they have really built up their support in recent seasons."

It has not always been a success story. Bramley played out their existence at Headingley between 1997 and '99 in a forerunner to Leeds' current link-up with York after briefly finding a home at Clarence Field following the tragic loss of their McLaren Field ground in 1995. They lost 10-23 to York in their final "home" game before 300 people on 22 August 1999.

As for the other sports at Headingley Billy is less enthusiastic. "I'm not a cricket person," he says. "But I don't think that cricket, apart from international games, gets the support it did by a long way. I know Yorkshire are in the second division of the championship at the moment but a lot of their games are watched by the proverbial man and his dog. That's very sad considering the tradition Yorkshire has got.

"When Leeds Tykes first played at Headingley there was a bit of interest in the novelty of it but 4,000 is a good crowd for them these days. Rugby League people just won't watch union - they are so used to seeing open play and there are too many rules that they don't understand. I watch them occasionally but, to me, it's just not taking."

LEIGH

Hilton Park was once again the stage for some of world's finest players after Leigh's elevation to Super League in 2005 saw them end a barren decade out of the top flight.

No one was more delighted than club legend Tommy Sale, whose association with the club now extends to three-quarters of a century - player, captain, director, secretary, groundsman, timekeeper, supporters' club official, voluntary worker - he's done the lot.

Tommy began his association with Leigh as a ten-year-old, operating the scoreboard at the old Mather Lane ground in 1928. "The joke was that they would only let me put up the Leigh score as I could only count to ten," he smiles. Rugby League soon became his way of life and he befriended Leigh's star second row forward, Billy Wood.

"Billy had a job on the ground and every chance I got I'd go along and help him and Joe Briscoe, the groundsman," Tommy recalls. "One of my jobs every dinner time was to go and get Billy two meat-and-potato pies from Waterfield's and after every training session and game I'd sweep out the dressing rooms. Billy was later sold to Wigan - all Leigh's best players ended up being transferred in those days as money was tight. But he was badly injured in a game against Swinton early in his Wigan career and never played again. He is the only player to receive a tour cap without going on tour - he would have done, undoubtedly, but for that injury.

"Mather Lane was once a marvellous ground, very atmospheric with a decent crowd on, but by the late 1930s the club was in a poor way and there was no money for upkeep," Tommy says. "The playing pitch was still very good but the stands and terraces were falling into disrepair."

Leigh had moved to Mather Lane in 1889 after first playing at Buck's Farm, in the Pennington area of the town, and then on a field behind the Three Crowns public house in Bedford.

It was while they were based at the latter ground that Leigh first made their mark in rugby circles, increasing their crowds from a few score to a few thousand during the course of a decade. Rather rudimentary, with one main grandstand and a post and rail fence around the playing area, the ground saw its greatest day in February 1889 when Leigh played the New Zealand Maoris in what proved to be their final season there; a crowd of 6,000 saw the locals record a famous win.

Matches against local rivals such as Tyldesley, Wigan and Warrington regularly attracted gates of around four to five thousand around this time.

The Mather Lane ground was part of the Frog Hall Estate on the south side of the canal. Not for the only time in the club's history local townsfolk rallied around to help construct a grandstand on the north side of the field, able to accommodate 500 spectators, a ten-foot hoarding around the ground and six large entrances and two exits, all for a total cost of £250. The ground was drained and levelled and looked in fine condition ready for

the opening game, against Aspull on 7 September 1889.

In those days the players changed at the club's headquarters, the Railway Hotel, and travelled to the ground by wagonette. As Leigh became one of the most respected sides in the Northern Union, ground improvements continued and another seated stand was constructed down one side and terracing built.

Old players that the writer met when researching his books on Leigh in the early 1990s always recalled Mather Lane with affection.

Jack Kenny, a winger in the pre-war period, remembered that the dressing room had a large sunken bath, quite a rarity in those days. That always helped guarantee a good turn-out at training.

The former Oldham and GB centre Alan Davies recalled that his father, Harry, played for Leigh in the depression-ridden '30s. "At that time a committee used to pick the team and one of them was a timber merchant and joiner, who had the job of repairing the ground," Alan said. "My father was a scrum-half who would always try blind-side runs in the days when there were often up to 80 scrums in a game. He was often tackled into the wooden fence surrounding the pitch which would then need repairing. The committee man later told my dad that he kept on selecting him because the repair bill helped keep his firm afloat!"

In March 1909, the touring Australians defeated Lancashire in the first representative game to be staged at a Leigh ground and in the 1920s the ground enjoyed its heyday as crowds flocked to see a successful Leigh side that lifted the Challenge Cup for the first time in 1921.

Fine locally-produced players such as Joe Cartwright, Joe Darwell and Walter Mooney all won Great Britain honours during this period.

A Lancashire Cup-tie against Rochdale Hornets on a Wednesday afternoon in November 1920 attracted a crowd of 21,500 to see Leigh win, 9-7, the highest crowd for a game involving Leigh at the ground. In the same season a Challenge Cup-tie against Warrington attracted 21,000 and the Christmas Day derby against Wigan 19,000.

Two Challenge Cup semi-finals were staged at Mather Lane. In April 1929 the Wigan-St Helens Recs tie attracted 21,940 and this was surpassed the following season when 25,000 saw the Wigan-St Helens clash.

However, as Leigh's playing fortunes declined Mather Lane never again saw crowds anywhere approaching that mark. A nadir was reached in November 1937 when Leigh's home game against Dewsbury attracted a crowd of only 200, though most matches in the 1930s saw crowds of around two to three thousand, with higher gates for local derbies and cup-ties.

In 1940 the Callender's Cable and Construction Company of London and Leigh acquired the five-acre site from the previous owners, Messrs George Shaw and Company Ltd, of the Leigh Brewery. The company needed the ground for storage of steel drums and cases and they advised the club that they were unable to let them have a lease of the ground, though the main grandstand stayed in place.

Leigh's last game at Mather Lane was a War Emergency League fixture with St Helens on 27 April 1940 when a crowd of only 300 saw the visitors win, 16-5.

After a season of playing all their games away from home, Leigh then folded for the duration of the hostilities.

After playing for the Leigh supporters' club team and then for Callender's Cables Works junior club, whose pitch was next to Mather Lane ground, Tommy was drafted into the Leigh A team as an emergency and signed as a professional after the game.

"The club was that short of money the secretary used to come around the dressing room after home games and pay the players straight out of the gate money," Tommy recalls. "As a junior I was always last in the queue. One day he came up to me and said: 'Sorry, Tommy lad, we've run out of cash. Will you take 30 shillings in draw tickets?' I agreed to, but there wasn't a winner among them. When I told my mates they just laughed at me and said: 'Well, that's all you are worth, any road'. I didn't get any sympathy at all." Tommy was just making his way in the first team when war intervened and served in the forces in the Middle East, Italy and Germany. When the war was over and he returned home Tommy found Leigh in a dreadful state.

"They had no ground and no team and, tragically, a number of lads had died in the war," he says. "Fortunately, a few stalwarts like Jack Harding (later Leigh chairman and a future GB tour manager) and Fred Palmer kept up Leigh's registration with the Rugby League and when the war was over a committee, led by James Hilton, was formed with the aim of getting going again. The committee secured temporary use of the athletics ground on Charles Street and purchased some land, formerly used as allotments, where the current ground stands, for £2,500."

In 1946/47 Leigh re-entered the Rugby League and the enthusiasm generated by the townsfolk was heart-warming. "They were hard times, rationing was still in place and there was a huge shortage of building materials but there was a wonderful spirit," Tommy recalls. "Supporters banded together, gave their time voluntarily and set about the task in hand."

Tommy had it all to do - not only was he the club's first post-war skipper but he had trained in the parks department at the council and his first-hand knowledge of horticulture came in very useful. He had two main projects which, in retrospect, look quite daunting.

He had to ensure the Charles Street ground was able to stage fixtures and also set about the planning and construction of the new ground.

The Leigh Harriers and Athletic Club ground was one of the unlikeliest of venues for top-class Rugby League, but such was the enthusiasm for "live" sport after the dark days of war there was a sudden upsurge in interest for the game in the town again. The first match to be staged at the ground was a Lancashire Cup-tie against St Helens on 14 September 1946 when 9,300 paid £650 and saw Leigh win, 17-4. The ground record was set when 13,000 saw a league game against Warrington in April 1947.

"Charles Street was a major problem," Tommy says. "It was situated close to the town centre but it was very rudimentary. We got some huge crowds considering the state of the ground - 10,000 gates were commonplace. But the biggest problem was the state of the pitch - it was nearly always flooded. A brook ran close by and that was always overflowing. One day we got a horse along to help roll the ground but the poor animal got stuck in the mud and had to be helped out by the fire brigade. After a game against Barrow in mid-February the pitch was covered in sand but thereafter resembled Blackpool beach with the tide in.

"Many times the opposing team would arrive and their players would say: 'Tommy, we can't play on that'. I'd reply: 'Why not? We play on it every week', and the game would go ahead." Paying a visit to the site today it seems incredible to think that nearly sixty years ago it housed five-figure crowds.

Meanwhile the construction of the new ground began to gather pace. "The reason this ground belongs to Leigh people is that Leigh people built it," Tommy says. "During the day-time I had about ten people working full-time under my supervision, but come tea-time the ground was flooded with volunteers of all ages. When we first bought the ground there was a lot of work to do. We had to clear the greenhouses and huts before we could start levelling the ground and we only had six months in which to do this.

"We dismantled the old main stand at Mather Lane, brick by brick, and the framework was used together with new bricks to erect a stand at the new ground. Then we set about laying the pitch. John Sumner had a haulage company in Leigh and used to bring the cotton bails from the docks in Liverpool to the mills in Leigh. He had three big wagons and after they had finished for the day the drivers used to turn up and set off, with six or seven volunteers, to Hale in Cheshire, from where we got the turf. When the wagons came back there was a chain of people passing the turf along and the laying it down.

"We had a lovely summer that year - perfect for working on the ground, but it had a disastrous effect on the turf. So I approached the fire station and asked if we could use their hoses to water the ground. People were a lot more co-operative than they are now because everybody was enthusiastic about the club. They said 'no problem' and we had three or four hoses watering through the night. Before that we had to lay the drainage - remember, at that time materials were not easy to get and everything was still on ration after the war. You couldn't just go to a builders' yard and order cement, bricks or tiles or whatever. You had to compromise and use a bit of intuition.

"The drains were put in herring-bone style, which is every four yards apart. We had a drain running down the centre and one on either side leading to manholes at the bottom corner. These led to a centre one in the middle of the posts, against the fence at the Chadwick Street end and then out into the main drains in the streets. It has been one of the best draining grounds in the League.

"The club held an auction for the right to lay the last ten pieces of turf. Jack Harding's father made the highest bid for the final piece and very kindly passed on the honour to me. I have a photograph of me laying the last piece of turf which I treasure to this day. An old lady gave me a silver horseshoe to lay under it and said that it would bring us good luck. There have been many times when I wished I had dug up the horseshoe - you wouldn't believe the number of people who have asked me to find it and sling it. But it's now buried under the floodlight pylon near the Mick Martyn Bar.

"We got all the banking from the Parsonage tip and for a while had only railway sleepers as terracing because we couldn't get concrete. We had wooden fencing all around the pitch, not the concrete we have now. We had a vast number of tradesmen who all gave their time for nothing. Anything we wanted doing they'd do it or know someone who could. They didn't expect to be paid - they just wanted to help the club and get the game going. What a difference to today. A few years ago I remember one of our home games was doubtful because of snow on the pitch so we 'phoned up some stewards on the Sunday morning to ask them to help clear the pitch and surrounds. The first question some of them asked was: 'How much do we get paid?'

"The walls around the ground were made from old air-raid shelters, scrapped from the war. The Leigh chairman was James Hilton and we were very fortunate to have someone as progressive as him at the helm at such a difficult time. The stress was incredible at times, given the time constraints we were operating under and the way we had to scrounge materials. But everyone pulled together and we got the job done. Mr Hilton did so much for this club and when he died, tragically at quite a young age in 1959, it was decided we name the ground "Hilton Park", instead of Kirkhall Lane, as a mark of respect."

Tommy was Leigh's first post-war captain and the side in that first season, 1946/47, more than held their own. "We did better than anyone could have expected given we didn't spend much money," Tommy says. "When we moved grounds it was then we started to buy players - great ones like Billy Kindon, Charlie Pawsey and Jimmy Ledgard and the Australian, Trevor Allan, the best overseas signing this club ever made. When we signed Jimmy from Dewsbury in 1948 the fee was a world record at the time, £2,650.

"The crowds came flocking to watch Leigh. The crowds at Charles Street were pretty good and at the new ground it was commonplace to have 20,000 crowds and even more when the likes of Wigan were the visitors. They used to cram into the ground and the authorities were pretty casual about the safety aspects - it is all so different today, of course."

Leigh's first game at Kirkhall Lane was a Lancashire Cup-tie against St Helens on 30 August 1947 when a crowd of 17,000 (receipts £1,500) saw Saints win, 15-0. The average home crowd in that season was 11,500 and in the post-war boom period Leigh attracted some massive crowds, the highest 31,326 for a Challenge Cup-tie against Saints on 14 March 1953. Two Challenge Cup-ties against Wigan attracted 28,000 and 29,500 respectively in 1949 and a crowd of 28,000 saw Wigan's visit for a league game in 1951, with 26,262 present for a Challenge Cup-tie against Leeds a year later.

After three years at Widnes that included captaining them in the 1950 Challenge Cup Final at Wembley, Tommy returned to Leigh, working on the supporters' club and then the board. "When I first got involved with the supporters' club one of our first tasks was the construction of the supporters' club stand," Tommy recalls. "I will never forget that I was there when the builder put in the first girder. There was an old man who shouted across to the builder: 'That's no use at all, it's completely at the wrong angle'. The builder just looked across and in not so many words said: 'Get lost, don't be so stupid'. Well, of course, the old man was right because when they put in the sixth and seventh row of seating in the stand, when you sat down you couldn't see the nearside touchline.

"It is a great pity, really, because other than that it is a well-built stand, but it was very badly designed. As well as the angle it also has a tremendous amount of girders holding it up. I never understood why they used that many. In many ways the stand turned out to be a white elephant."

The stand, which now looks extremely well appointed and maintained, with rows of shining red seats in place, has since been renamed the Tommy Sale Stand and bars underneath pay tribute to two of Leigh's other favourite sons, Mick Martyn and the incomparable stand-off genius John Woods, who Tommy rates as simply: "the greatest locally-produced player and the best stand-off ever to play for the club."

Tommy adds: "John Woods had it all - he could score wonderful tries, kick goals from the touchline and tackle with the best of them. He was the complete all-rounder and above all a gentleman - he kept his feet on the ground and people respected him for that."

Woods and Jamaican born winger Des Drummond were stars of the Leigh side that upset all the odds by lifting the Championship in 1981/82.

The title was secured in the last game of the season, on a Wednesday night in Whitehaven that has gone down in Leigh folklore, as Leigh's 13-4 victory saw them emulate the side of 1905/06 in lifting the Championship. The coach in 1982 was Alex Murphy, who had returned for a second spell following his successful initial stint that ended abruptly after Leigh's 1971 Wembley triumph over Leeds when he upped and joined Warrington.

As a board member Tommy had been instrumental in initially securing Murphy's services from St Helens for his first coaching role. "You either love Alex or hate him," Tommy laughs, "and I love him. The effect he had on the club was simply amazing. The players had great respect for him and he was a great leader on and off the pitch with a terrific personality. He was very assertive and a great motivator and that day at Wembley was the proudest of all our lives for anyone associated with the club. With Murphy at the helm we achieved our finest hour. The town was decked out in red and white - I've never seen anything like it and the welcome we got when we got home was simply tremendous. There must have been 50,000 people lining the route through Boothstown and Tyldesley into Leigh and the town hall square was absolutely packed. It was absolutely unbelievable."

Hilton Park has staged a number of representative fixtures, including county games and one Test Match when Great Britain defeated France 39-0 before 4,750 in 1964.

Leigh were also one of the first clubs to erect floodlights and a crowd of 13,000 saw Lancashire beat Yorkshire, 18-10, in the first floodlit game at the ground in October 1953. New modern and distinctive floodlights were erected in 1998.

The ground has changed little in character since its construction, though there are now plush social facilities and the main stand, dating back over a century to its origination at Mather Lane, has new plastic red and white seats.

Much of the surroundings have changed dramatically, though, and a fan from 50 years ago would have trouble placing the ground today. The old training pitch was sold to a DIY supermarket chain in the 1980s, Leigh East ARL have built an impressive adjoining complex incorporating a clubhouse, floodlit all-weather training pitch and first-team pitch and the landmarks of Victoria Mill and Parsonage pit have gone, to be replaced by another supermarket.

Famously, television commentator Eddie Warring used to refer to this end as the "Satanic Mills End", later the title of a distinctive and ground-breaking fanzine on the club. Many of Leigh's players worked at a pit and the writer remembers interviewing one of the '71 Wembley heroes, Jimmy Fiddler, after a training session at Hilton Park just before he began a shift underground.

A busy by-pass road now passes the ground at this end, built on what was originally a railway line connecting Bolton and Newton-le-Willows that opened in 1828. The famous railway engineer, George Stephenson, constructed the steam locomotive Lancashire Witch to commemorate the opening of the line.

Less than a decade on from their second championship success Leigh faced a crucial battle for survival and the early 1990s were marred by constant money problems. "We had become a yo-yo club between the divisions," Tommy says. "Towards the end of the 1980s the directors made the mistake of paying out extraordinary contracts to ordinary players, some of whom were coming to the end of their careers. The club was simply paying out far more than it could afford and it went into liquidation and the club was hours away from extinction at one stage."

Eventual salvation for Hilton Park came from an unlikely source. Horwich RMI soccer club decided to sell their Grundy Hill home, with its famous sloping pitch that would render it impossible for them to maintain senior non-league status due to new regulations. The owners of the ground, Grundy Hill Estates Limited, then bought Hilton Park and re-located the soccer club, ensuring not only that the Rugby League club would survive but that RMI could have a new home.

Horwich RMI's first game at Hilton Park was against Boston United on 4 March 1995 when they lost 0-4 before 481 spectators. They soon changed their name to Leigh RMI and reached Conference status in 2000. They played Fulham in a famous FA Cup-tie in November 1998, losing 0-2 before a crowd of 7,125 after earning a draw at Craven Cottage. But they have continually struggled to attract support in what remains a true Rugby League hotbed and many of their games are watched by paltry crowds of 200-300.

Come the onset of summer rugby Leigh caught on with the nickname craze but the origins of the Centurions are more complicated than first appears. There was a mini contest run by the club in 1995, asking fans to come up with a nickname. Several were suggested but the CenturiAns one was accepted as it tied in with the 100-year celebration of Leigh being founder members of the Northern Union in 1895. Initial artwork for the new logo had Centurians, not Centurions, despite the logo depicting a Roman soldier, complete with the big brush in his helmet. When this was pointed out to the commercial manager the spelling was changed from CenturiAns to CenturiOns to tie in with the new artwork.

As a consequence of that Australian coach Paul Terzis came up with the idea to rename Hilton Park 'The Coliseum', though this found little favour with die-hard fans for whom the ground will always be Hilton Park.

Sadly, though, the ground's days are numbered, with the Leigh Sports Village, a John Woods punt or two down the by-pass, planned for the town. Work on the vast project will start soon and Leigh hope to take up residence in a new 10,000-seat stadium, to be shared with Leigh RMI, around mid-2007. Their former temporary home at the athletic track, now known as Madely Park, is still in use by Leigh Harriers but will become housing when Leigh Sports Village is built. The Harriers are to use the new track at LSV.

You might think that Tommy Sale, steeped in the folklore of Hilton Park, would, like many people of his age, be against change. You'd be wrong. Instead, he is full of enthusiasm for the project which will transform the leisure and community facilities of Leigh, just as the current ground did all those years ago.

"I shall be upset when the final game is played at Hilton Park, there's no doubt about that," he says. "There are so many good memories attached to the place. But you have to move with the times and the advantages far outweigh the disadvantages. It's very difficult to get to Hilton Park, landlocked as it is with houses, the by-pass and supermarket. Car parking is chaotic on a match-day. The new ground will have better car parking, access and facilities and hopefully will enable Leigh to establish themselves in the top flight for years to come.

"I keep asking the people involved will I be still around by the time Leigh move and they assure me I will. I have just one other wish - that they transfer the name of the old ground to the new one. James Hilton was simply the best chairman this club ever had."

LIVERPOOL

They might have had an identity crisis, changing names and grounds with almost monotonous regularity, but until 1997 they seemed to be always there, usually propping up the rest of the Rugby League.

But after a RL Council meeting on December 3 1997 they were no more, as Prescot Panthers chairman Geoff Fletcher threw in the towel, receiving a one-off payment, believed to be £30,000, for agreeing to withdraw from all Rugby League competitions.

So ended a rich rugby lineage dating back over a century.

It all started in the Highfield area of Wigan where a rugby club was operating by the late 1870s.

After a seven-year gap, another victim of the carnage surrounding the formation of the Northern Union in 1895, Wigan Highfield was re-formed in 1902 and went on to forge a reputation as one of the game's leading junior clubs before being accepted for membership of the League in 1922.

Highfield played at a field off Tunstall Lane and used the nearby Hare and Hounds public house as their headquarters. They were often referred to as 'Mrs Walker's Boys' after the landlady. A deputation from the League visited the ground in the summer of 1922 and was said to be well satisfied with the arrangements made for a ground thought able to accommodate 25,000 people.

Highfield erected dressing rooms and baths at the ground, then built a covered stand for 2,000 people at the Queen Street (west) end by mid-1923, and a new seated stand for 500 spectators along the north side a year later.

Relying on a core of staunch followers, Highfield struggled for support from the outset and had only around 250 members during their time as a senior club.

But derby days with Wigan were a site to behold. A crowd estimated at 15,000 saw their opening game, on 2 September 1922, when Highfield held a 10-2 lead before going down 10-25 to their illustrious neighbours, the peerless Jim Sullivan landing eight goals, despite the inconvenience of the long grass on the playing area. "The phenomenal rise of the Highfield club was nothing compared to the phenomenal rise of the grass on the field," noted one reporter.

Under the watchful eye of director Jimmy Green, who was renowned as a talent spotter, Highfield developed many locally-produced players, most of them being sold on to richer clubs to help make ends meet. "Highfield is the football factory where they hew the rough material from the coal face and mill it into gems," wrote one critic in 1925.

Highfield had their record crowd when an estimated 16,000 paid £502 into the coffers for Wigan's visit in September 1924.

In 1926 a crowd of 13,350 produced receipts of £729 as Highfield beat Leeds in a third round Challenge Cup-tie, only to lose to Oldham at Salford in the semi-final.

But the nadir was a gate of only 2 pounds 19 shillings (£2.95) for a home game with Bramley in 1931, while the 1926 All Blacks drew a mere 2,000 for a midweek game in November of a year marked by trade depression and industrial unrest.

In 1926 the club took ownership of the ground from Colonel Blundell, a local colliery owner, but then took out a mortgage of £450, secured on the ground, with a club director, Harry Swift, to provide some working capital. It was the failure to pay due interest on the debt that led to Swift issuing a winding-up notice that brought the club's financial battles to a head.

In May 1930 club members voted unanimously to reject a bid from a Liverpool-based consortium to relocate.

But in the summer of 1933, with what the Wigan Examiner termed "dramatic suddenness", Highfield was taken over by the White City (Greyhound) Stadium Company and re-christened London Highfield.

The new owners bought Tunstall Lane and retained it for training purposes and reserve games, with the players travelling down to the capital for "home" games played on Wednesday evenings under floodlights.

The site of Highfield's ground is now covered by housing, though the gap between the houses on Tunstall Lane, through which led a path to the turnstiles, is still there, as is the Hare and Hounds pub, on the corner of Tunstall Lane and Billinge Road.

White City, located in the Shepherd's Bush area of London, was originally built to stage the 1908 Olympic Games, its name deriving from the brilliant whiteness of its ferro-concrete buildings.

The stadium then lay derelict until it was bought by Brigadier-General AC Critchley to stage greyhound racing in 1927, with speedway following a year later.

Critchley, a Canadian by birth, who later became an MP, had first introduced greyhound racing into this country in Manchester a year previously.

April 1966 - Liverpool City play St Helens at Knotty Ash. *(Above)* the view from the Prescot End, showing the main seating stand. The building in the distance is the convent that owned the land on which the ground stood. *(Facing page)* The view from the open banking at the Liverpool end. The covered stand on the left was donated by St Helens RLFC and erected in the early part of the 1961/62 season.

The British Empire Games were staged at White City in 1934 and AAA annual championships from 1932-70.

Rugby League returned to the White City when it staged the second Test between Great Britain and Australia in November 1967 when the tourists' 17-11 win, before 17,445 spectators, levelled the series at 1-1.

The final speedway meeting took place in 1983, the final greyhound meeting in 1984 and the BBC's new headquarters now cover the stadium site.

Queens Park Rangers left the nearby Loftus Road ground and played at White City in 1931/32.

After a Rugby League exhibition match between Wigan and Leeds under floodlights in December 1932 attracted a curious crowd of 10,000, QPR tried and failed to persuade the football authorities to stage league games under lights (they did not relent until 1950) before returning to their previous home.

Floodlit Rugby League was a bold experiment, years ahead of its time, and survived only one season. Average crowds were around the 6,000-mark, about half the number required for break-even, with a top gate of 14,500 for the Australian tourists of 1933/34, who won 20-5.

Many years later, Highfield forward Harry Woods recalled how he would work in the foundry until 2pm, then catch the afternoon train down to Euston with his teammates, returning overnight to start work again early the following morning.

One highlight was a 30-12 win over Wigan. "They blamed it on the lights, but that

was nonsense," Harry recalled. "We were simply the better team."

The venture cost its owners an estimated £8,000 in losses and in the summer of 1934 the club was on the move again, to Liverpool.

Their new home was the Stanley Greyhound Stadium on Prescot Road, with Liverpool Stanley the new name. The owner of the Electric Hare Greyhound Racing Ltd company, John Bilsland, agreed to accommodate them.

Liverpool City had endured one ill-starred season in 1906/07, losing all of its 30 league games, scoring 76 points and conceding 1,398. City did manage a draw, 3-3 at home to Bramley in November, but this was scratched from the records when the return fixture went unfulfilled.

City played at Stanley Athletic Grounds, Fairfield Street, now the Merseyside Police Sports & Social Association Ground, over the railway line from the Stanley Stadium. City's opening fixture saw a 8-41 home defeat against Wigan but after playing Leigh in mid-December the club's final 16 games were all played away.

Stanley Stadium, first used for greyhound racing in 1927, was built on the site previously occupied by a brickworks and had a stand capable of seating 2,500 with covered standing for 10,000 on the opposite side.

Some of the players worked on the maintenance of the stadium. It was used for speedway between 1928 and 1960 and greyhound racing was held there until 1961. A fruit and vegetable market, located off Church Road, now covers the site. "Despite its grandiose name, the ground was a tip," recalls veteran journalist, Denis Whittle.

To help the new venture the RL staged an international at the ground, England (with Stanley players Woods and Billy Belshaw in their ranks) defeating Wales, 24-11, before 7,100 spectators (£462).

The site of Alt Park...   **and Wigan Highfield...**   **and the original Liverpool City**

Stanley's second season was easily their most successful; they won the Lancashire League and finished second in the league table, losing 9-10 at home to Widnes in the Championship Play-off semi-final before a ground record crowd of 14,000.

At the end of that season Woods and Belshaw were selected for the Great Britain tour, emulating Nat Bentham in 1928. Another club stalwart, Jack Maloney (413 appearances from 1926 to 1945) just missed out on selection.

That season was League's highest point in Liverpool. They finished fourth in the following season but lost at Salford in the Championship semi-final and then lost direction after the death of Jimmy Green.

They offered their resignation to the RFL in 1937 having lost £15,000 on average home gates of 2,500, being saved by the backing of the Supporters' Club.

Soon the war clouds loomed and the RAF requisitioned the ground as the site for a barrage balloon, in order to dissuade any low-flying German bombers. After playing some home games at Prescot, Stanley closed for the duration of the hostilities.

When peacetime football resumed in 1945, Stanley faced a constant battle for survival, being subsidised by the RFL on more than one occasion, and began a search to leave behind the eerie, vast emptiness of the Stanley Stadium.

In 1950 they moved to a new ground at Knotty Ash, rented by the RFL from St Francis Xavier's Church, and situated at Mill Yard, off East Prescot Road.

New green and white hooped jerseys replaced the traditional yellow and blue ones.

"The ground was primitive," Whittle recalls. "There were large cinder bankings but they provided no cover for the spectators and the pitch was enclosed by a rickety wooden fence."

A large tent was used for the first dressing rooms as the club fought against the odds, with a shortage of materials and labour and other restrictions in the immediate post war years.

In 1951 the club became Liverpool City and the following year the first cover on the ground (with dressing rooms underneath) was constructed. But in six successive seasons up until 1954 they finished bottom of the League. One rare highlight was being chosen as the first opposition for the 1956 Australians. An attendance of 4,712 saw the tourists run in ten tries in a 40-12 win on an autumnal Wednesday afternoon. The occasion gave club stalwarts like Jack Wood, Wilf Hunt and Ray Ashby (who, in 1964, became club's only post-war GB representative) a rare taste of the limelight.

"In the true spirit of Rugby League," as Whittle terms it, St Helens donated their old popular-side grandstand to the City club and a RFL loan of £1,600 enabled it to be re-erected at Knotty Ash.

"I still remember the wagons taking the construction away, brick by brick, and down the road to Liverpool," Whittle adds. "It was always a struggle for the club and they seemed to be full of players who had previously played for Saints, Warrington, Widnes, Wigan or Leigh."

In 1968 the club finally quit Liverpool, after they had become aware that the lease at Knotty Ash was not to be renewed. The council had earmarked the site for the building of the Catholic Blind Institute.

Steps had been taken to secure a new ground at Huyton, though £4,000 was spent on releasing the site, at Endmoor Road, from covenants. During 1968 the club secured a 21-year lease and, for 1968/69, was re-titled as Huyton, playing at a variety of venues before their Alt Park home was given the green light to open by the local council after problems with the foundations under the main grandstand.

Huyton-with-Roby RLFC (known as 'Huyton') first played at Alt Park against Swinton in March 1969 and Lord Derby officially opened the ground before a game against Salford in August 1969, the visitors running out 60-5 winners.

Huyton built a clubhouse behind one set of goalposts, with a small covered stand down one side, but the conditions for spectators were rather rudimentary. Under coaches Terry Gorman and Geoff Fletcher, Huyton began to hold their own in the mid-to late 1970s, with a best place of seventh in the second division in 1974/75. Fletcher was player-coach, fundraiser, groundsman and general factotum and kept the club going on a shoestring, earning the respect and admiration of the RL community.

But dreadful crowds and recurring problems with vandals dragged the club down time and again and the final straw came when the stand was decreed unsafe following persistent attacks.

Huyton's final home game at Alt Park was on 26 April 1984 when a crowd of 200 saw them beat Rochdale Hornets 14-12. Their average home league attendance in their final season there was 172. Knowsley United AFC, formerly Kirkby Town, moved into a revamped Alt Park in 1988 and soon attained Northern Premier League status but folded in 1997 after also struggling for support.

The old ground remains, but now fenced off and left to ruin, and the site of the old clubhouse is now occupied by the Alt Park Resource Centre.

1984 brought with it new hopes for one of the game's perennial strugglers - a move to Canal Street, Runcorn and a new title as Runcorn Highfield, as tenants of the soccer club.

Canal Street, which sadly has recently been demolished for housing, was one of the venues that hosted the first season of Northern Union football in 1895 with Runcorn (known as the Linnets) playing there from 1879 until 1916.

Around 15,000 crammed in to watch Runcorn play Oldham in 1900, but the club's fortunes declined and they ceased membership of the Northern Union during the First World War.

The former HQ of "Mrs Walker's Boys"

After the ground was sold, the new owner would only allow association football to be played, bringing about the formation of Runcorn FC (who, ironically, shared Widnes Vikings' Halton Stadium across the Mersey until 2005).

Canal Street was an atmospheric ground (that once held 10,111 for a 1939 FA Cup-tie against Preston North End) with

147

stunning views of the River Mersey, though very cold at times when the battering winds, that often caused damage to several generations of stand roofs, howled across the estuary.

It also provided a relief for long-suffering players, officials and fans alike after the tribulations of Alt Park and visiting supporters found it an altogether more pleasant experience.

With the pitch at right angles to that used by the Northern Unionists, fullback Peter Wood revelled in the new surroundings.

He joined the select band of players to play and score in each of his side's games throughout a season as Highfield, in 1984/85, finished 14th out of 20 clubs in the second division, having begun with a 1,750 gate for a friendly against Widnes. Two years later they attained 11th place, with teams such as Fulham, Huddersfield, Workington and Keighley below them.

But a strike by the club's players prior to a John Player Trophy tie at Wigan in 1988 heralded another decline. A makeshift Highfield side, after conceding ground advantage, was hammered 2-92 at Central Park- a savage blow from which the club never really seemed to recover.

By 1989/90 Runcorn Highfield was a laughing stock, ending the season by losing all 28 of their league games.

At the end of that disastrous campaign the club was on the move again, leaving Runcorn behind to share another non-league soccer club's home, this time St Helens Town FC's Hoghton Road ground in the Sutton area of the town. This venue, like Canal Street, has been recently demolished and covered by housing and Town now play at St Helens' Knowsley Road ground in the North-West Counties League.

The Hoghton Road site had been purchased by a group of businessmen after the Second World War and converted from allotments. A small 250-seat stand, still in use for Highfield's tenure there, was built in 1949 and soon afterwards a crowd of 5,000 saw a friendly against Manchester City to mark the transfer of the famous German goalkeeper Bert Trautmann to Maine Road. The former Warrington international forward, Jack

Canal Street,
Runcorn

Arkwright, kept the nearby Boilermakers Arms for many years.

In 1991 the club became known as, simply, Highfield and in 1992/93 enjoyed an escape act of which Houdini would have been proud. They won their final league games against Barrow and Nottingham City (both away) to preserve their league status, while the bottom three clubs (Chorley, Blackpool and Nottingham) dropped into the Conference.

It was to be a temporary respite for, in each of their final five seasons as a senior club the club finished bottom of the pile, winning just six and drawing two of 122 league games. In the Centenary season, 1995/96, they garnered just a single point.

In 1994 came the final move, to the Hope Street ground at which they played briefly in the war years. But this move and another name change, to Prescot Panthers, again failed to herald a change in fortunes.

Hope Street was opened in 1906, originally laid out for soccer, cycling and athletics before becoming the sole home of the town's soccer club, who even made an application (unsuccessful) for Football League status in 1930. A new stand was built in 1960, with a social club underneath, after a fire destroyed the old one, but for much of the Panthers' tenure was unusable due to fire regulations imposed by the local council.

The Panthers' end came after a 10-72 thrashing at Carlisle in July 1997, ironically against another club that was to be in its final season. In their last campaign the Panthers used 58 players, including former Great Britain internationals Des Drummond, Paul Groves and Barry Ledger. Northern Premier League outfit Prescot Cables FC still play at Hope Street, now re-named Valerie Park. From 2005/06 Runcorn FC agreed a ground-share with them after being unable to afford the rent at Widnes.

From Tunstall Lane, where it all started, to Hope Street is a journey of about 12 miles but there were many more covered in-between. In a constant struggle against adversity, the good times were heavily outnumbered by the bad.

But a small band of stalwarts kept the faith and the Rugby League flag flying in some unlikely venues, often against incredible odds, creating a rich seam of Rugby League folklore along the way and a trail to test the most ardent of groundhoppers.

Hope Street,
Prescot

LONDON

Peter Lush and Dave Farrar have done much to replenish Rugby League bookshelves with their publications these last few years. The title of one of their books, "Touch and Go", admirably serves to sum up just how close we have been to losing the game in the capital since Fulham's formation in 1980.

It seems hard to believe that it is 25 years since Fulham burst onto the scene, defeating then fallen giants Wigan, 24-5, in their first match, in a blaze of publicity.

Welsh flyer Adrian Cambriani and Neil Tuffs each scored two tries that day and the crowd of 9,552 was way beyond anyone's expectations. At long last it appeared that Rugby League's battle to establish a base outside its northern heartland had been won.

The brainchild of the new club was Harold Genders, then a Warrington director who approached Ernie Clay, a Huddersfield-based businessman who was then chairman of third division Fulham FC. Former Widnes star Reg Bowden was made captain-coach and succeeded with Genders in the aim of building a team from scratch.

Fulham's first season went like a dream with some huge attendances –12,583 game against Leeds in the John Player Trophy and 15,013 for the visit of Wakefield in the Challenge Cup. Bowden's team of northern-based players won promotion at the first attempt, with the average league attendance at Craven Cottage a healthy 6,096.

But the next three years were turbulent ones, as Fulham became one of the yo-yo clubs so prevalent at the time. Relegation followed, then promotion again the following season but, by the time the club were relegated again, average seasonal attendances had slipped steadily from 4,321 to 2,688 and 2,238 and, in August 1984, the rugby club was put into liquidation after what was termed "a four-year trial period".

"As the club's original home, Craven Cottage was very special," Lush says. "The layer of Fulham support had come from football supporters curious to see this strange northern game. Even though many of them had supported other football teams and been to the ground as away supporters, they soon felt at home.

"The setting was unique with the cottage in the corner and the park and river nearby in a nice friendly area. Lots of supporters have great memories of games played there. I remember one game, against Leigh, in '81/82. They won the championship that year but we beat them, 11-10. I remember the ball boys time-wasting and our relief at the end."

Defeat was a bitter blow to a visiting journalist who had his headline ready after Leigh's Steve Donlan dislodged the letter "L" out of Fulham on the riverside stand roof with a penalty kick to touch. "Donlan knocks the L out of Fulham," was one headline that never saw the light of day after Fulham spoilt the script.

"Then the Australian tourists came later that year," Lush continues. "We had over 10,000 on a day that bucketed down with rain. We were a second division team then but gave a good account of ourselves, losing only 5-22, and one of the crowd favourites,

Euphoria after Fulham's first game in 1980, a 24-5 victory over Wigan

Hussein M'Barki, scored our try.

"But the abiding memory was Ian Van Bellen. He was a huge bloke with a big beer gut and balding hair but no one could get the ball off him. Players like John Crossley and Steve Diamond achieved so many scoring feats, but Van Bellen was the ultimate Fulham hero."

Fulham played one game at Chelsea FC's Stamford Bridge on the eve of the 1983 Challenge Cup Final when a crowd of 3,321 saw Cardiff City run out 20-14 victors of an often violent, bad-tempered clash. Craven Cottage was unavailable due to pitch repairs.

In April 1983 Fulham also played two midweek games, against Swinton and Huddersfield, at Widnes, also due to pitch repairs at Craven Cottage, and the end came in April 1984 when a crowd of just 1,146 saw a relegated Fulham sign off with a 23-13 win over Widnes.

Fulham's rescue from oblivion was down to Roy and Barbara Close who bought, so they thought, a Rugby League club complete with playing staff. However, following a ruling in the High Court, Fulham's players were declared free agents and all the Closes owned were "two bags of second hand kit and a set of goal posts".

But the Closes were made of stern stuff and, undaunted, Fulham began the next season at the National Sports Centre at Crystal Palace. After switching their home Lancashire Cup-tie against Swinton to Station Road the new-look Fulham, now under a new coach in Roy Lester, began life in their new home with an 18-47 defeat against Carlisle before 2,300 fans in October 1984.

"What can you say about Crystal Palace?" asks Lush. "It was far too big. There were nice seats but even with a good crowd the fans were lost in the ground. The floodlights were not too good and it took an age to get there. It simply didn't work. I remember talking to a Wigan fan, used to the "river caves" (as the toilets at Central Park were known). He remarked how good the facilities were. I replied: "I would swap the toilets for a good pack of forwards any day."

"I remember the ground for another reason: a game against Hull played on a frozen pitch. It was the coldest I have ever been at a rugby match."

Towards the end of that season Fulham played one game at the Polytechnic of Central London Stadium, Chiswick. They beat Runcorn, 17-16, before 650 spectators. They also staged three games, against Whitehaven, Bramley and Swinton at Lower Mead in Harrow, the home of Wealdstone FC where none other than Vinnie, then Vince, Jones first made his name before moving on to Wimbledon FC.

"Wealdstone was a nice ground and fitted our crowds," Lush says. "But the ground was up for sale and is now a supermarket, so it was only ever going to be temporary. After being at Crystal Palace it was terrific to be so close to the pitch and you could hear every word said by the players and referee."

For the start of the 1985/86 season, Fulham moved permanently to Chiswick and, though crowds continued to decline, the place was popular amongst the hard-core supporters.

Fulham stayed there until 1990 when 717 saw their final hurrah with M'Barki scoring three tries in a convincing win against Chorley.

Ironically, that final season was the first time since the club's formation that the average attendance did anything other than decline. Seasonal averages fell from 817 to 684, 615 and 588 before Fulham averaged 841 in their last season at Chiswick.

"It was the only Rugby League ground with a model railway behind the stand and a yachting marina nearby," Lush says, almost misty eyed by now.

"Fulham was a real community club at Chiswick and a lot of people got involved to help rebuild the club, especially in the dark days in 1986 when it looked again as though the club was going to fold. With the groundsman's co-operation I remember fans getting back into Craven Cottage to rescue the original posts and triumphantly marching down the riverside to Chiswick with them.

"I've been back to Chiswick recently to do some photographs and the supporters' club caravan is still there. There was a huge bar where everyone used to congregate and many stood on the grass banking opposite the small cantilever stand. We didn't have a great team there but the players tried hard and for the first time, apart from Martin Herdman, we started seeing southern-based players in the side and the beginnings of a colts development. Richard Lawton and Tim Lamb held it together though the Closes continued to provide financial support. One highlight was the tour game against the tourists from Papua New Guinea in 1987."

With no floodlights at Chiswick, Fulham staged a midweek Lancashire Cup-tie in September 1989 against Wigan at Hendon FC's Claremont Road ground, losing 4-34 before a healthy 3,204 attendance. Highlights of the game were later shown on BBC's "Sportsnight" programme.

The Polytechnic authorities were unwilling to give Fulham the long term lease necessary to develop the ground and maintain minimum standards and, for the 1990/91 season the club, then under the control of the Australian coach Ross Strudwick, controversially returned to Crystal Palace.

But the fans voted with their feet and the average attendances went down to a miserly 557. The following season, when the club's name was changed to London Crusaders, was slightly better, with four 1,000-plus attendances at the start of the campaign. But generally the move back to South London was hardly a success. A nadir was reached for a replayed Challenge Cup-tie against Highfield, played on a Tuesday evening in February 1992, when a crowd of 245 was recorded.

The New Zealand coach, Tony Gordon, replaced Strudwick in February 1993 and that summer the Crusaders were on the move again, this time to another frustratingly inaccessible athletics stadium, Barnet Copthall Stadium in North London.

"Even though it was an athletics stadium again, it was actually a much nicer atmosphere than at Palace and, under Gordon, we developed a fantastic team with some real crowd pleasers," says Lush.

"We had players like John Gallagher, Scott Roskell, Mark Johnson and Sam Stewart. The team just seemed to gel and played some great rugby and yet, despite this, the club was in disarray. I remember a Regal Trophy tie when Bradford brought 900 fans with them and a great game against Workington. It was the first second division game to be shown live on Sky and it finished 20-20, with Gallagher just missing a drop goal in the last seconds. We got to Old Trafford that year for the Premiership final but sadly that was Gordon's last game in charge."

In 1994/95 London became the Broncos and, returned to the Hendon FC ground for five games, with the rest at Copthall. "I grew up on Hendon FC's ground so for me it was a dream to see Rugby League there," Lush says. "The ground was about the right size, but again it was never going to be our permanent home."

In their centenary season, 1995/96, with the Broncos controversially moved up into the top division despite only finishing fourth in the previous campaign, the club prepared for the onset of Super League. Of their twelve home games, two were played at Copthall, two at Brentford FC's Griffin Park with four apiece at the Valley, home of Charlton Athletic FC, and the Stoop Memorial Ground, home of Harlequins RU club.

The Broncos made the Valley their permanent home in 1996, recording a crowd of 9,638 for their opening home Super League game against Paris (won 38-22) on the Thursday evening before Easter and 10,014 for Wigan's visit in August of that year. The seasonal average was 5,699, 400 or so short of Fulham's inaugural campaign.

But then, with Sir Richard Branson's Virgin Group taking control, the Broncos spent three seasons at the Stoop. Average attendances declined from 5,125 in 1997 to 3,575 and then 2,935.

Back to the Valley they went in 2000 but gates were well below the levels achieved in Super League I: 3,419 in 2000 and 3,177 the following year. A move to Brentford was made for 2002 when attendances rose slightly, to 3,760.

"The Paris game produced so many great memories," Lush says. "The Sun had given out vouchers for the game and there were people queuing all around the ground. Quite how many of the crowd got in cheaply or for free I'm not sure, but the atmosphere was fantastic. After all the years of struggle the hard core fans had to pinch themselves to see London playing Paris before 9,000 people in a decent ground. Then after the game Tony Currie put a real dampener on it, ignoring the positives and, instead, complaining how bad our defence had been in typical Australian coach's fashion.

"Barry Maranta, our Australian chairman, was great for the club, but the one mistake he made, I feel, was not persevering with Charlton after that first season. If we'd stuck there I'm sure we'd have laid down roots."

The Broncos' first season at the Stoop saw them enjoy a memorable hat-trick of games in the World Club Championship when the visits of Canberra, Brisbane and Canterbury pulled in a total of 24,588 fans. But as often in a story of Rugby League in the capital, it proved a false dawn, despite the Broncos' tremendous feat in reaching Wembley for the 1999 Challenge Cup Final.

"The first season there was brilliant and, as in 1993/94, we played some really good rugby and had a good team," Lush says. "The highlight was the Canberra game. All the British teams were getting smashed in that competition but we bucked the trend and beat them, 38-18.

"I remembered that we played Bradford on the day that Princess Diana died and Richard Branson made a speech that was really emotional.

"But no one really felt at home at the Stoop. After all it was a rugby union ground and the residents around the ground made life difficult for the club, especially for evening games under floodlights. We had some great players and it was tremendous to see legends like Shaun Edwards and Martin Offiah playing for London, especially after some of the "bits and pieces" players that coach Gary Greinke had brought over in the first year of the Broncos. It gave us so much credibility that, but again we didn't keep the team together."

"Never go back" the saying goes and the Broncos' return to Charlton was proof of that old adage. "The ground was now bigger and there were loads of empty seats," Lush says. "We didn't have a winning team and, though the relationship with Charlton was good, it didn't work second time around."

So the Broncos moved back west to Brentford, though the tenure there was uncertain from the start, with boardroom turmoil at the soccer club and rumours afoot of the possible sale of Griffin Park and a move to a new ground.

"David Hughes completed the take over from the Virgin Group and the move back to Brentford coincided with us becoming a community club once again," Lush said at the time. "Griffin Park is a nice size and it worked in a way. We hadn't got the corporate facilities of the Stoop or Charlton but we had got our community spirit back. When Branson took over, a lot of the volunteers were not needed any more, but Mr Hughes and Nic Cartwright, the Chief Executive, have got everyone involved again."

So 23 years on and the club had almost come full circle, playing in West London at a soccer ground. But so many things have happened in the intervening years and, after a dependence on northern-based players in the early years and then a whole string of Australians, the Broncos are now setting up roots and developing more English players who live in the capital. In 2003 Griffin Park staged a representative game when a crowd of 6,817 saw England A put up a terrific fight against the Australians before going down to a 22-26 defeat.

In recent years, the Broncos have also staged "home" games at Leicester RU's Welford Road ground, against Bradford Bulls in 1999 and 2001, at Newport RU's historic Rodney Parade ground, against Warrington in 2000 and at Stade Albert Domec, Carcassonne, against Warrington in 2002. The Broncos' first game at Welford Road attracted their best attendance of the 1999 season, 8,233 on a beautiful summer's evening, but for the return the "gate" was down to 5,259.

In 2003 the Broncos played at Aberavon against Widnes, winning 40-18 before 3,128, returned to Welford Road for the Hull game in 2004 (when the crowd was 3,589) and in 2005 took their "home" game with Hull to Brewery Field, Bridgend, attracting a crowd of 3,775 for a 24-24 draw. More spectacularly, they then played Leeds at Stade Aime Giral, Perpignan, defeating the reigning champions 32-24 before 7,000.

When visits to Kingstonian FC's Kingsmeadow Ground at Kingston-upon-Thames, for a cup-tie against the Cumbrian amateurs, Wath Brow, in February 2000 and Crawley Town FC's Broadfield Stadium in 2001 for a cup-tie against Batley, are thrown in, anyone following the Broncos, as Peter Lush has done for a generation, has become a groundhopper in the finest tradition.

Then the staggering development, even for those seemingly immune to shocks. Early in the 2005 season the Broncos went into liquidation with reported £3m debts and a new company was allowed to form and continue to play in Super League. In July 2005 it was announced that the Broncos had entered into the first joint union/ League brand and that the top-flight team representing London in Super League in 2006 will be called Harlequins Rugby League Club, playing its home games at the re-named Twickenham Stoop. The logo will be Harlequins' Jester and the kit will comprise the four-quartered shirt known throughout the union world. Wigan-born Ian Lenagan, the new Broncos chairman, explained: "Compared to others, our club's 25-year history is relatively short, but what an eventful journey it's been. Stability has been the major obstacle. This partnership gives us every opportunity to finally have a permanent base." Time will tell.

Stability has been the key ingredient missing from the development of League in London. From the early days of the Northern Union, when Test Matches were played at Stamford Bridge and Park Royal, the game has struggled to hold down a permanent base in the capital.

Stamford Bridge, home to Chelsea FC since 1905, was the second largest ground in England (behind Crystal Palace) when it staged the second Test between Great Britain and New Zealand in February 1908. With one main grandstand, capable of holding 5,000, the rest of the ground had steep bankings around an oval shaped running track and could accommodate 70,000. A crowd of 14,000 witnessed the tourists' 18-6 victory. The Park Royal Stadium lay between Park Royal Station and Coronation Road. On the south, railway side of the ground was a 4,000-seat barrel-roofed stand and the remaining three sides were open terraces. Opened in 1907 when Queens Park Rangers entertained Millwall in a Southern League game, Park Royal was chosen to host the first-ever Great Britain-Australia Test Match in December 1908. But the ground's estimated 60,000 capacity was never tested as only 2,014 saw an exciting game that ended in a 22-22 draw, producing receipts of only £70. Rangers left the ground when it was taken over by the Army in February 1915 and two years later moved to Shepherd's Bush. In 2004 their Loftus Road Stadium hosted the New Zealand-Australia Tri-Nations international. Either side of the first world war the Australians played two more internationals against England at London soccer grounds, at Craven Cottage in 1911 and Arsenal FC's Highbury Stadium in 1921.

Another, more substantial Park Royal Stadium was built in the 1930s as the London adventure continued. London Highfield's one season in the RFL in 1933/34 (see Liverpool

London's 2000 squad display many of the kits that have been worn in the capital

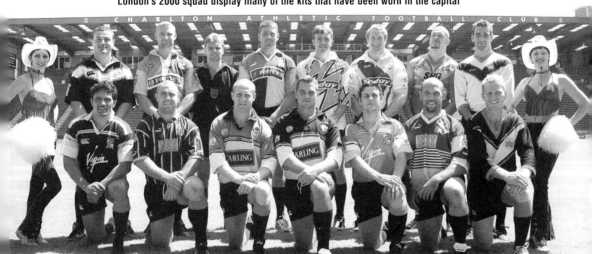

Craven Cottage, Fulham

National Sports Centre, Crystal Palace

The Valley, Charlton

The Stoop, Twickenham

Griffin Park, Brentford

section) failed to dampen the enthusiasm of greyhound racing entrepreneur, Sydney E Parkes. He built two new venues, one the Acton Stadium situated 500 yards north of Coronation Road and near the site of the old Park Royal ground. Acton & Willesden played just one season in the RFL, in 1935/36, before folding.

Streatham & Mitcham played at the Mitcham Stadium, built on waste ground between Eastfields Road and Sandy Lane. The players for both clubs were engaged in working on the construction of both grounds, earning a weekly wage of between £2 and £3 per week. Both venues were virtually identical with a grandstand seating 10,000 spectators and another smaller one accommodating 5,000. Acton, known as "The Royals" drew 17-17 against York in their opening game, attracting a crowd of 5,000. But by Christmas their crowds had fallen to low levels and they switched most of their remaining games to Mitcham Stadium after Parkes was successfully granted a licence to operate greyhound racing.

Streatham, known as "The Hams" lost 5-10 against Oldham in their opening home game before around 15,000 spectators but their initial expectations were not realised. After finishing 24th in the League in their first season, three places below their London rivals, the club did carry on for another year but sold many of their best players before playing their final game against Swinton on 20 February 1937.

Rugby League in London's biggest success has been in making Wembley Stadium synonymous with the Challenge Cup Final. The Wembley area was selected in 1921 for the British Empire Exhibition, staged at a cost of £12m on a site covering 220 acres. Wembley Stadium opened on 28 April 1923 when Bolton Wanderers defeated West Ham United 2-0 in the FA Cup Final. On that famous occasion the nominal ground capacity of 126,500 was vastly exceeded as an estimated 200,000 gained access to the stadium. This final became known as the "White Horse Final" after a police horse, named Billy, was used to clear the playing area.

At the time the stadium was oval in shape and the pitch was surrounded by a running track. Covered seated stands were located on the north and south sides with open terracing covering the remainder of the ground. The central feature of the stadium, the 126 feet high twin towers, became the trademark of a 75-acre complex that later housed the Wembley Arena, conference centre and New Exhibition Hall. After the exhibition closed in October 1925 the whole site was in danger of being demolished until the Wembley Stadium and Greyhound Racecourse Company Limited took

The famous Wembley twin towers, before the 1999 Leeds v London Challenge Cup Final

control. Greyhound racing was introduced in December 1927 and speedway was also staged there from 1929. The decision by the RFL to take the Challenge Cup final to Wembley in 1929 was one of the most momentous in the game's history. Not that the RFL minutes give any clue to the significance of the decision. The Marine Hotel in Llandudno was the venue for the 1928 annual conference and there, it is recorded: "Mr John Leake moved that it be a recommendation to the Council that the Final tie for the Challenge Cup be played each year in London. Mr Walter Waide seconded and after a number of members had spoken for and against, the recommendation was carried 13 votes to 10."

Various London venues were considered, including Crystal Palace and the White City before the unanimous decision was made to play the final at Wembley. Wigan defeated Dewsbury 13-2 in the first final there, staged on Saturday 4 May 1929 before a crowd of 41,500 (£5,614). Apart from 1932, the war years between 1940 and 1945 and the replayed finals of 1954 and 1982, Wembley staged every Challenge Cup final until 1999. On that occasion, when Leeds defeated London Broncos 52-16, Leroy Rivett famously set a new final record with his four tries.

Although Wembley is inextricably linked to the Challenge Cup it has also staged several internationals of note, beginning with Australia's defeat of Wales before a 16,000 crowd in 1930. In 1963, Australia defeated Great Britain 28-2 in the game's first ever floodlit Test, played on a wet Wednesday October evening, but the attendance was a disappointing 13,946. By then the covering had been extended around the stadium at a cost of £500,000 to make Wembley the only all-covered 100,000–capacity stadium in the world. At that time there were seats for 44,803 spectators. Great Britain had more success when they defeated Australia 21-12 in the first Test of the 1973 series marked by a magnificent two-try display by Hull KR forward Phil Lowe. Again, though, the attendance was hugely disappointing, being recorded at only 9,874 and the RFL lost £500 on the venture. But by the 1990s attendances for Test matches had improved markedly and 54,569 saw Great Britain defeat Australia 19-12 in the first Test of 1990. Four years later 57,037 set a new record for a test in this country when Great Britain, despite the early dismissal of Shaun Edwards beat Australia 8-4.

The stadium was finally made all-seated in 1990 with a capacity of 80,000. Wembley staged the 1992 World Cup final when Australia beat Great Britain 10-6 before 73,631 – a world record for an international match. The 1995 Centenary World Cup final attracted 66,540 when Australia beat England 16-8.

Also used for the athletics events in the 1948 Olympics, Wembley Stadium closed in 2000. Though it had staged many of the most famous games in Rugby League history its poor infrastructure and location within a residential area meant there was popular support for a new national stadium to be located at a more accessible site. However, the Football Association decided they would be able to earn a greater income from corporate clients and despite considerable obstacles, not least the estimated £700m cost of redevelopment, the project to re-build Wembley Stadium was given the go-ahead in 2002. After a gap of seven years the Challenge Cup final should resume at Wembley in 2006.

The introduction of another London team into the professional ranks for the 2003 season certainly gave the game in the capital a massive boost. The London Skolars club was founded in 1995 by the Student Rugby League Alumni principally for all students that had graduated and were living in London. They have since widened their source of players to include anyone from the university of life. Committed to junior development, Skolars were one of the few amateur clubs to have their own development officer.

Originally playing in the London League, the Skolars became a founder member of the Southern Conference in 1997 and also entered the BARLA National Conference League. Playing in both competitions meant they played Rugby League all the year round until they resigned from the latter competition in 2001. The progress and ambition of the club was such that the Skolars entered the National League Two competition and played their opening game as a professional club in a National League Cup-tie against Dewsbury Rams on 19 January 2003, attracting a crowd of 820 to see them go down to a creditable 10-22 defeat. Mark Croston and Hector McNeil were the two men credited with bringing the Skolars from a park pitch where they had to mark out the lines before a game to the professional ranks. "Today was the culmination of many years' hard work by a lot of people at the club," Croston said after the Dewsbury game. "It is a new start and we are determined to move on and improve each week."

Skolars play at the New River Sports Stadium on White Hart Lane, Wood Green. Opened in November 1973 the stadium is home to the famous Enfield & Haringey Athletic Club and has seating for approximately 1,000 spectators. The bulk of the crowd tends to gather in the main grandstand, with its excellent sight-lines, but there is accommodation on the terracing and banking on the opposite side. With good bar and catering facilities it is a friendly and

New River Stadium, the home of London Skolars

pleasant place to visit and is a worthy addition to the groundhoppers' list. Skolars had an average crowd of 430 in their first season, achieving their first win as a senior club against Gateshead in August 2003, falling to 407 in 2004 when Skolars achieved a highly creditable six league wins.

MANCHESTER & SALFORD

Thousands of people travel along the A6 on a daily basis, in and out of the twin cities of Salford and Manchester, but quite how many of those realise, as they pass the familiar sight of Salford University, that behind it in the Irwell Valley once was situated a veritable cornucopia of sporting venues?

That is just one of the fascinating facts unearthed in two recently published books, Graham Morris's "Rugby League in Manchester" (Tempus Publishing) and Simon Inglis's "Played in Manchester" (English Heritage) which have highlighted the rich sporting heritage of the Salford and Manchester area and reiterated, for Rugby League followers at least, the opportunities lost.

Inglis takes us on a journey, with the focus in particular on three clusters - the Irwell Valley that once housed, amongst many others, Broughton Rangers rugby team and the Castle Irwell racecourse, that staged its last meeting in 1963; the Trafford Park area - now home to Old Trafford cricket and football grounds; and Belle Vue.

Morris, while acknowledging that the title of his work does much to perpetuate the myth that Salford is part of Manchester, dispels the popularly-held notion that the round-ball game has been the only version of football played around Manchester, noting that within a four-mile radius of the city centre eleven venues have staged Rugby League at a senior level. That figure has since increased after Swinton took up residence at Sedgley Park RUFC and the City of Manchester Stadium housed the Great Britain-Australia Tri-Nations international last autumn, after his book was published.

As the Salford and Swinton clubs is covered later in this book the focus of this chapter is on Broughton/Belle Vue Rangers and the venues for representative matches in the area.

Formed 1877 and founder members of the Lancashire County RU, Rangers were one of the most prominent clubs in the early years of the Northern Union and have left sufficient remaining traces to satisfy the groundhopper's thirst.

Rangers' original ground was in the shadow of the Walness Bridge on the banks of the Irwell, where the river bends in a sharp U turn. It was here that they played host to the touring New Zealand Maoris in December 1888, attracting a crowd of 4,000.

In 1892 they moved to Wheater's Field, located off Lower Broughton Road, and the venue for their first game after the 1895 breakaway when Wigan provided the first opposition under the Northern Union code.

A crowd of 3,000 saw Wigan secure a victory by 9-0 on Saturday 7 September 1895 after a tightly-contested game. Yates scored the opening try, converted by Webster, just before half-time for the visitors and Walkden added a late drop goal (then worth four points). As Broughton Rangers were then the only Manchester club to "go over" to the new code (Salford and Swinton following in 1896) there was considerable interest in their progress throughout the season, even though Rangers finished a disappointing second bottom of the 22-team competition. They recovered in style, however, winning the Lancashire Senior Competition in 1896/97 and 1898/99.

The land on which Rangers made home was owned by the Deane family, with one of the family members, Tom Deane, being a former Broughton and Lancashire county player. The playing area was hurriedly converted from a cinder bed to a grassy surface, but from the outset Rangers had problems with their pitch. Even in early season the pitch was almost devoid of grass and invariably rock-hard, and its poor standard was often criticised by opposing teams.

Wheater's Field was located in a densely-populated area and was hemmed in on all sides, making it very difficult for Rangers to develop their facilities. The ground's main facility was a large grandstand at the Lower Broughton Road end that comprised long wooden seats, but open standing areas and terraces provided the majority of the viewing areas. The ground was enclosed by large and ramshackle hoardings. Despite its less than pretty appearance and location Wheater's Field was a regular venue for Lancashire Cup Finals, including the first such occasion, between Leigh and Wigan, in 1905.

Rangers had provided a host of county players and three internationals before the split and one of their most prominent players, Bob Seddon, was one of the club's original members. Seddon was captain of the first touring team to Australia in 1888, only to meet a tragic end when he drowned on a boating expedition in New South Wales. Their status increased after a neighbouring club, Broughton, folded after the 1897/98 season. Regarded as the region's 'elite' club, Broughton, who had also provided three England RU internationals, would have nothing to do with the breakaway.

The Cliff, the former home of Broughton Rangers

Rangers made history in the 1901/02 season, becoming the first club to 'do the double' as they lifted the Championship and Challenge Cup. Their cup final victory was one to savour, as they defeated neighbours Salford, 25-0 in the final. Rangers' captain, Bob Wilson, scored a hat-trick in the game - a feat equalled but never bettered in a final until Leroy Rivett scored four tries at Wembley in 1999.

Wheater's Field staged Rangers' historic first meetings with the New Zealanders in 1907 (when the reported attendance of 24,000 was the second highest of the tour as the visitors won 20-14) and the Australians in 1909 when 12,000 saw Rangers beat the Kangaroos 14-12. It also hosted an international in December 1908 when England played Wales. In a game marred by the frosty weather, England recorded a 31-7 victory before 4,000 people. Rangers' ground was also chosen to stage the Championship Finals of 1910 and 1911 (Oldham being victorious on both occasions), the Challenge Cup final of 1907 (when Warrington defeated Oldham, 17-3 before 18,500) and several county games. Wheater's Field's highest non-tour attendance, though, was recorded for a club game - 23,000 against Swinton in January 1898.

Despite its popularity amongst the authorities as a big match choice the ground had its detractors who pointed to the unpleasant crowded surroundings in a densely-populated and heavily-industrialised area, with smoke from neighbouring chimneys often hanging over the pitch, the battered and scarred-looking facilities and the poor playing pitch.

Rangers played their last match there on 9 April 1913, defeating St Helens 22-11, before refusing to yield to demands for a higher rent and instead moving along Lower Broughton Road to a new home at The Cliff. Wheater's Field was subsequently developed for housing, though lasting memories of the location of one of the foremost grounds of the Northern Union's early days are provided by the street signs of Wheater's Crescent, Street and Terrace. A visit to the site today reveals a densely-populated and run-down urban area vastly in need of the type of re-generation that has been seen elsewhere in the city.

The Northern Union authorities were eager to promote their game in the city of Manchester but until the construction of Station Road, Swinton in 1929 there was no stand-out venue. Another early big-match location was the Fallowfield Stadium, near Old Hall Lane. Built for the Manchester Athletic Club, who transferred from their base in Old Trafford due to the development of the Manchester Ship Canal, it was also home for a local cycling club.

Fallowfield had briefly been chosen by the Football Association to stage some important games but the venture was not repeated after two disastrous experiences. The first was the FA Cup Final of 1893 between Wolverhampton and Everton when the reported crowd, 45,000, set a new record for the final. But the game was marred by crowd violence and regular skirmishes with police. The venue was also heavily criticised for its lack of spectator facilities.

Despite that the FA went to Fallowfield again six years later for a replayed FA Cup semi-final tie, between Sheffield United and Liverpool, played on a Monday afternoon. Before an estimated 30,000 crowd the ground failed to cope with the crowds and congestion at the entrances spilled over onto the terraces. The game had to be abandoned at half-time with crowds lining the touch-lines.

Fallowfield, also the venue for an England-Scotland rugby union international in 1897, was chosen to host the 1899 Challenge Cup Final between Oldham and Hunslet, just a month after the unruly scenes at the FA Cup semi-final. A crowd of 15,762 saw the Roughyeds victorious 19-9, winger Sam Williams scoring two tries.

In 1900 the final, a local affair between Salford and Swinton, was again staged at Fallowfield after a late switch from the first choice, Broughton, when Wheater's Field was deemed inadequate following an inspection. The "accommodation and conveniences were not up to standard" according to officials. Swinton lifted the cup for the first time with a 16-8 victory before an official crowd of 17,864, though contemporary reports estimated the crowd at anything between 25 and 30,000.

"The Fallowfield Ground was a capital place for the match," wrote the correspondent of the Swinton Journal. "The level sward, with its fresh green of spring, looked in perfect condition, and the deep crowd of spectators, brightened up here and there by the gay attire of lady enthusiasts, combined to make an exhilarating picture of life and colour."

However, that was the last major Rugby League game staged at Fallowfield, poor spectator facilities and the expense of ground hire and erecting temporary stands counting against the venue. After the ground's demolition in 1994 (it is now the site of the Vice-Chancellor's Court for Manchester University) the Willows (opened 1901) is the oldest senior sports venue in the Manchester and Salford area.

Broughton Rangers' new ground at The Cliff immediately found favour with spectators and officials alike. Situated in the Higher Broughton area, an altogether pleasanter location than Wheater's Field, it was a former cricket and tennis field across the Irwell from the Manchester Racecourse and had a six-acre site for the club to develop (compared to just over three at Wheater's Field). The ground took three months to prepare and 5,000 loads of materials were transported from the old ground and two stands erected in time for the start of the 1913/14 season.

A reporter from the Wigan Examiner got an early chance to see The Cliff and reported in favourable terms: "The new enclosure of the Broughton Rangers club is in a rough state at the present moment," he wrote, "but there are already two fine stands erected, one being a close facsimile of that at Central Park on the members' side. The playing portion appears on the small side, but upon inquiry the information was vouchsafed that it was larger than the one recently vacated at Wheater's Field, being from one goal post to the other exactly one hundred yards in extent, with a breadth of seventy-five yards between the touch lines.

"The ground is situated amongst the pleasantest of surroundings in close proximity to the Castle Irwell Racecourse. In fact a stone could be thrown from the ground to alight on the course itself. There was a splendid view of the big race that was decided prior to the commencement of the match."

The main grandstand, on the Lower Broughton Road side, accommodated 2,000 spectators with seating for 250. On the opposite side, next to the river, was the popular side shelter for 1,000. For the first time Rangers' players, and their opponents, were able to use dressing rooms at the ground instead of at a local hostelry.

For Rangers, though, there was disappointment in that many of their supporters failed to make the move with them, despite the relatively short distance along Lower Broughton Road. Rangers' first home match at their new home saw them defeated 0-14 by Swinton after a scoreless first half on 13 September 1913.

Though the demographics of the area have changed from a once middle class enclave with a significant Jewish settlement, The Cliff exists today as a training ground for the junior sides of Manchester United. Walking around the site, it is easy to imagine it as a venue for top rugby games. An administration building occupies the site of the old grandstand on the Lower Broughton Road side but the popular side shelter remains as a reminder of the ground's former glories and the playing pitch is in immaculate condition. A large building at the entrance housing an indoor training pitch now dominates the site which was used by United's first team until their training operations were transferred to Carrington in the late 1990s, much to the relief of local residents who on occasions had to contend with the streets packed by autograph seekers and journalists.

With the Northern Union authorities keen to promote the game in the city, The Cliff was regularly chosen as a host to big games in its early years.

The early 1920s saw The Cliff share in something of the post war boom, attracting 25,000 for Rangers' second-round Challenge Cup-tie against Rochdale Hornets in March 1921. The following month Leigh defeated Halifax, 13-0, in the final, again before a crowd of 25,000. Due to a stoppage in the local coal industry many Leigh supporters walked or cycled to the game and the scenes before the game were described as "absolute chaos" as people tried to gain entrance. Two gates were crashed open, hundreds getting in without paying as mounted police tried to restore order outside the ground.

In May 1922 the Championship Final between Oldham and Wigan attracted 26,000, Welshman Jerry Shea scoring the only try in Wigan's 13-2 victory. The 1924 Championship Final was also staged there when Batley defeated Wigan 13-7 before 13,729, as well as several Lancashire Cup Finals and county games. England defeated Wales 11-8 before 6,500 in April 1927, when Alf Ellaby scored the game's decisive late try.

The clash of neighbours Swinton and Salford in the 1931 Lancashire Cup Final drew 26,471 to the ground (setting what was then a new record for the Final) with Salford prevailing 10-8 thanks to a last-minute penalty goal by Fergie Southward.

But Rangers' home attendances were generally considered poor, averaging only a few thousand for most games. Rangers had enjoyed their second Lancashire Cup Final triumph in 1920, their forwards outstanding in a 6-3 victory over Leigh, but by the late 1920s they were generally languishing in the lower half of the table.

In 1933 the club was approached out of the blue by the management of the Belle Vue Zoological Gardens in Gorton with a view to moving their operations. It was an invitation that was to prove too good to refuse. Rangers' last game at The Cliff was on 14 April 1933 when they defeated Dewsbury 10-5. At that stage the club had 30 schoolboy teams under its wing.

The Cliff lay vacant until Manchester United approached the Clowes Estate and leased the ground for training purposes in 1938, later purchasing the site outright in 1952. It was in this latter year that Rugby League briefly returned to The Cliff when England played France in an amateur international.

Rangers transferred their operations lock, stock and barrel to Belle Vue on a 21-year lease though they retained their old name until 1946 when they were re-named Belle Vue Rangers. The Belle Vue stadium was highly impressive, with a capacity of 40,000 (including 25,000 under cover) and the playing pitch was rated as the best in the league. But as a downside Rangers shared their facilities with speedway, meaning a remoteness of the playing action from the spectators.

The massive complex at Belle Vue was first opened in 1830s. Soon it boasted a maze, lake, natural history museum, ballroom, bear pits and polar bear cage among other attractions. Elephants were introduced to the zoo in 1873. In the early 1900s a helter skelter and 'figure 8' toboggan ride were built and a scenic railway was constructed in 1926. The appointment of John Henry Isles as general manager coincided with the site's activities being expanded. Speedway was introduced in 1929 when the athletics and cycling track, first used by Salford Harriers in the late 1880s, was taken over.

A soccer club, Manchester Central, was formed, playing in the Cheshire League but when the club folded Isles turned his attention to Rugby League. The Belle Vue company took over the management of the Rangers club and spent £10,000 on players in the first two seasons.

Initially the venture attracted a great deal of interest, 12,793 turning up for the opening game, against Warrington, on 2 September 1933, and 25,000 attending the Salford game later that month.

The game's ruling body staged the first Test against the Australians at Belle Vue in October 1933 in a further bid to promote the game and were rewarded by an attendance of 34,000 - the highest of the tour. Heavy rain ruined the game as a spectacle with Great Britain running out winners by 4-0, captain Jim Sullivan capping a magnificent display of fullback play with two late penalty goals. But spectators encroached onto the speedway track surrounding the playing area, being dispersed by mounted police. This counted against the venue and no further Tests were allocated to Belle Vue.

In October 1934 the Duke of York (the future King George VI) paid a visit to the ground, arriving just before a game against Leigh, having earlier called in for a soccer match at Maine Road. He was introduced to the muddied players at the half-time interval. Rangers were duly inspired to post a 27-7 victory before 6,000 spectators.

In 1935/36 Rangers finished sixth, their highest position for 21 years, but despite this fact, attendances did not improve on those at The Cliff. On Christmas Day 1937 the Australians returned, for a club match against Rangers but the attendance was only 3,000. Rangers recorded a 13-0 win, only their second over the Kangaroos. A Challenge Cup semi-final between those old rivals Swinton and Salford was staged at Belle Vue in 1938, attracting a crowd of 31,664, to see Salford win 6-0. But the occasion was again marred by crowd trouble with many climbing over the wall after the gates had closed and thousands lining the speedway track around the pitch.

By the 1938/39 season, by which time Rangers had swapped their traditional blue and white hooped jerseys for a distinctive design of blue and white quarters, the club was down to 20th in the league and as war clouds gathered there were rumours that they would fold.

Rangers were forced to vacate their ground during the war and played several games at Edgeley Park, the home of Stockport County AFC but a former venue of the Stockport side that had been founder members of the Northern Union in 1895. Rangers' first match at Stockport was for a Lancashire Cup-tie against St Helens in March 1940 and attracted a gate of 4,000. But attendances dropped to the hundreds and in October 1941 Rangers suspended their activities until the cessation of hostilities.

Confounding rumours of their demise by resuming activities in the 1945/46 season, the club finally shed its Broughton tag the following year and became Belle Vue Rangers. Tom Spedding, who acted as director, secretary and team manager, was a stalwart official. In 1949 Rangers sold their star winger, Stan McCormick, to St Helens for £4,000 to help stay afloat. The tale goes that McCormick, who did not initially want to leave the club, was told by Spedding that either he or Lennie the Lion had to be sold but that the lion was staying as more people came to watch him.

After further struggle (Rangers finished 30th out of 31 in 1954/55) the Belle Vue company refused further use of the stadium after that season over issues of unpaid rent. The club requested to the RFL that it revert to their old Broughton Rangers name and play at the Fallowfield Stadium, home to those cup finals of over 50 years previously, but the ground was unable to meet the criteria laid down by the League and the club's great tradition counted for nothing. Rangers sadly died at that point.

Their last home game was on 18 April 1955 when their 13-7 victory over Salford ended a run of ten successive home defeats. In the club's last game they lost 0-43 at Workington. The Belle Vue complex was taken over by Charles Forte in 1963. To great sadness the zoo ceased in 1977 and Belle Vue Stadium closed in November 1987 and a car auctions operation now occupies the site.

Rugby League's link with the city of Manchester had been further strengthened either side of the war when Maine Road was a regular venue for Championship Finals. After moving there from their old Hyde Road ground (situated about a mile from Belle Vue and their home since 1887) in 1923, City attracted huge crowds around this time, the highest 84,569 for an FA Cup-tie against Stoke City in 1934. Their new ground had one of the biggest capacities in England, around 90,000.

Using posts borrowed from Belle Vue, the Castleford-Salford Championship Final of 1939 became the first Rugby League game to be held at Maine Road.

At that time Maine Road had a 10,000 seat main stand but the rest of the stadium consisted of steep terraced embankments. Salford won 8-6 before a crowd of 69,504 - then the highest for a Rugby League game in this country. Excepting the 1952 final (held at Leeds Road, Huddersfield) Maine Road was then used between 1946 and 1956. The venue of the Championship Final was then switched to Odsal.

The 1949 final, between Huddersfield and Warrington, attracted a record Championship Final crowd of 75,194 (subsequently bettered by the 83,190 who attended the 1960 final at Odsal).

Perhaps the most famous Maine Road final was in 1950 when Wigan, despite lacking the services of eight players who had departed on the Australian tour, defeated Dewsbury, 20-2. The last final at Maine Road was in 1956 when 36,675 saw the game between Halifax and Hull.

Rugby League briefly returned to Maine Road when Oldham and Warrington staged 'home' games there during January 1987 to take advantage of the under-soil heating, but the combined attendances for the two games were less than 5,000.

In 1989 Wigan beat Warrington in an epic Challenge Cup semi-final, the game made famous by Joe Lydon's monster 61-yard drop goal as the scores were locked at 6-6 late in the game. Wigan went on to win, 13-6, before a crowd of 26,529. Maine Road also staged the Wigan-Bath cross-code game in 1996.

Manchester City's move to the 48,000 capacity City of Manchester Stadium in 2003 opened up fresh possibilities for the 13-a-side code and after intense negotiations the magnificent venue, originally built to host the 2002 Commonwealth Games and then re-fitted out as a football stadium at a cost of £20m, became a notable new addition to the big-match panel. A crowd of 38,572 saw Australia defeat Great Britain 12-8 in a dramatic Tri-Nations game on 30 October 2004, Luke Rooney scoring a last-minute winning try for the Kangaroos.

The White City Stadium on Chester Road, midway between the Old Trafford cricket and football grounds and technically located in Trafford, staged one game of Rugby League in September 1961. A RLXIII, including the likes of Brian Bevan and Tom Van Vollenhoven, defeated the New Zealand tourists 22-20. The attendance of 5,271 for the midweek game under floodlights was extremely disappointing and was the second lowest of the tour.

Originally opened as a botanical gardens and zoo in 1827, White City re-opened as an amusement park with a lake in 1907. A 40,000-capacity greyhound stadium was opened in 1928 on the site and the stadium later staged speedway, stock car racing and athletics, with many of the world's finest athletes appearing there following the construction of a six-lane cinder running track in 1953.

The City of Manchester Stadium hosted its first Rugby League game during the 2004 Tri-Nations

Old Trafford, home of the Super League grand final

White City closed in 1981 and remained derelict for a decade until being re-developed as a retail park. The location of the site is marked by a surviving and distinctive archway.

Old Trafford, perhaps the world's most famous soccer ground, was a relatively late addition to the Rugby League roster.

United's home since 1910 when they moved from Bank Street, Old Trafford staged Salford's game against Leeds under floodlights in November 1958 and the code returned in the 1986/87 season for the first Ashes Test when Australia's 38-16 victory before 50,583 featured hat-tricks from the left-wing pair of Gene Miles and Michael O'Connor, the latter also kicking five goals. The Australians returned to win the second Tests of 1990 (when Mal Meninga's dramatic late breakaway try broke British hearts after the scores were tied at 10-10) and 1994 (when the Kangaroos triumphed, 38-8). Great Britain lost 16-24 to the Kiwis in 1989 but finally recorded a victory at the fifth attempt, defeating the 1997 Super League Australians 20-12.

At the end of the 1986/87 campaign the double-header of the Premiership and Second Division Premiership Finals was staged for the first time at Old Trafford, Wigan defeating Warrington 8-0 in the main event before 38,756.

The success of the venue made Old Trafford a regular host of the end-of-season extravaganza. Since 1998 the ground has been the stage for the Super League Grand Final. After 43,553 saw the inaugural Grand Final between Leeds and Wigan the attendance surpassed the 65,000 mark in each of the last two years - proof of the growing popularity and acceptance of the play-off concept as a method of deciding the champions. Other significant games staged there include the Widnes-Canberra World Club Challenge in 1989, the St Helens-Wigan Challenge Cup semi-final in March 1990, and the England-Wales World Cup semi-final in 1995.

In 2000 the World Cup Final between Australia and New Zealand was held at Old Trafford, Australia winning 40-12 before a crowd of 44,329.

Historians can only ponder quite what progress the game may have made had Belle Vue Rangers in the post Second World War boom not played in such a remote and relatively inaccessible stadium or had a name change that incorporated the title Manchester. Maybe soccer had taken too firm a hold anyway but the demise of Rangers represented a huge body blow for Rugby League in the city and its greatest lost opportunity.

OLDHAM

The old curmudgeon still had one last act of defiance as people gathered to pay their last respects. Watersheddings was due to stage its final game against Swinton - fittingly the opponents for the first game there in 1889 - on Sunday 29 December 1996. But the game was called off because of frost. Another failed attempt was made before the final curtain came down on Sunday 19 January 1997 when 4,717 hardy souls - you had to be hardy to gather at Watersheddings in mid-winter - saw the final act played out.

A brass band played "Auld Lang Syne", a low cloud cover shrouded the crumbling ground and, to their enormous credit, the two teams played out an authentic match, unlike so many friendlies of recent times. Oldham edged home, 20-16, and many a tear was shed.

Like so many things in life, Watersheddings was never fully appreciated until it had gone. Its loss still has vast ramifications for Rugby League in Oldham. Many supporters, it is thought, have not been regulars at the game since.

Brian Walker is president of the Oldham RL Heritage Trust, a wonderful body that aims to seek out, preserve for posterity and display historical items such as medals, jerseys, photographs and other memorabilia. Their recently published book, "Roughyeds" is a monumental effort - 472 packed pages full of text, photographs and images that brings the past to life and shows what a rich heritage exists in the old cotton-spinning town. As a sister book to Michael Turner's mammoth "Oldham RLFC - The Complete History" published in 1997 it gives Oldham the best historical references in the game.

"No one was chaining themselves to the gates when the bulldozers moved in," Walker says. "Maybe if they had, the ground might have been saved. Watersheddings should have been the subject of a preservation order and rebuilt to be made available for future generations of Oldhamers.

"It was an absolute disgrace that the ground was allowed to become so dilapidated and eventually demolished. But I also believe that the blame sits fairly and squarely on the shoulders of us all. It's far too easy to blame this or that former club management or to point the finger at the council. At the end of the day everyone associated with the club - supporters, officials and council alike must carry a share of the blame."

The erection of the Watersheddings end stand and scoreboard in the late 1950s was the last major project carried out on the ground. From then on club officials fought a losing battle maintaining the rapidly ageing, weather-lashed ground - the problems accentuated after the implementation of new ground safety regulations in the wake of the Valley Parade fire tragedy in 1985.

At a stroke the popular Herbert Street side-stand, a mostly wooden structure, was ordered to be demolished, leaving just an uncovered terrace and ending Watersheddings' proud boast of having cover on all four sides. The capacity of the main stand was severely reduced with just the middle section staying open. A ground that had once housed crowds of well over 20,000 in comfort saw its capacity reduced to 9,315 for example for the 1989/90 season, just 685 of them seated.

Oldham battled on but the debts mounted and an ambitious plan to end the old members' club structure and form a plc in 1990 saw only a-third of the £750,000 authorised shares actually subscribed. The end came with the formation of Super League. Although inaugural members, Oldham lasted just two years before finishing bottom in 1997, and the plc went into voluntary liquidation.

"Watersheddings had served the rugby fraternity of Oldham for all those years and deserved saving," Walker maintains. "It was one of the oldest and most famous rugby grounds in the world and in a facility-starved town like Oldham there was no excuse for not taking up this option. There was a new ground on the horizon but it proved to be pie in the sky. And most of Oldham's rugby fraternity would have preferred staying at a rejuvenated Watersheddings on the east side of town.

"The club deserted Watersheddings with indecent haste - it seemed the ground was there one minute and houses the next."

Walker was heavily involved with the formation of a new club that took its place in the Northern Ford Premiership for the 1998 season. Since then the club has battled with the ground question that still remains unresolved.

At first they shared Boundary Park, home of soccer neighbours Oldham Athletic, but a move unpopular with many League fans in the town for whom never the twain shall meet. In mid-summer of 1998 three "home" games were staged at the joint Spotland home of Rochdale AFC and Hornets while Boundary Park was re-seeded. In 1999 all but one home game was staged at Spotland, the one game at Boundary Park (against Hornets) attracting a crowd of 3,023 as part of the Charter Day celebrations marking the 150th anniversary of

The scene inside and outside *(right)* **Watersheddings for the ground's final game, 19 January 1997**

Oldham Borough's municipal status.

In 2000 Oldham played entirely at Spotland and then returned to Boundary Park for the following season, attracting 4,747 against Leigh and eventually reaching the 2001 grand final before losing to Widnes. But then they were forced off Boundary Park and moved to Hurst Cross, home of Unibond League soccer side Ashton United.

They are now back at Boundary Park though problems of having to vacate the ground in mid-summer for pitch renovations meant them having to find temporary refuge at Blackpool AFC's Bloomfield Road ground and Chorley's Victory Park for three games in 2004. In 2005 Oldham staged three "home" games at the Sedgley Park RUFC ground that is now shared by Swinton.

"Playing at Ashton was the one thing that drove away more people than anything else," Walker adds. "People thought it was a second rate ground and wouldn't go. The contrast between the 2002 season and that of 2001 was very notable." League average attendances fell 691 to 1,150.

"When the new club was formed it showed what a small group of dedicated and committed people working together could achieve." he continues. "At first the crowds were good, 3-4,000 for some games. But people will only put up with mediocrity for so long.

"I wouldn't say Oldham is a sleeping giant but it hosts three Conference amateur sides and a strong schoolboy game. There are a lot of people involved in the amateur game that are not involved with the professional club. If you look at our average attendances now they are around the 1,200 mark. If Oldham had a reasonably successful Super League side they'd average 5-6,000. The supporters are still there but a lot won't go to the other side of town to watch at a soccer ground.

"But a problem the club faced is shown by that first season of Super League. Average attendances actually dropped from 3,889 in the last full winter season to 3,629 in the first full summer one. In '97 we beat North Queensland Cowboys in the World Club Championship and attracted only 2,961 people. The following week we played Adelaide Rams but the attendance was only 3,513. That showed what a hard battle it was."

John Blair watched Oldham from an early age and played for the club throughout the 1970s. He still goes to nearly every game, working for hospital radio.

"Watersheddings had its own unique atmosphere, especially in midweek under floodlights," he recalls. "I remember one cup-tie replay in particular, against Bradford Northern in 1968 when we won 12-2 after an unbelievable game before more than 18,000. There was a tremendous game against the '86 Australians when we gave them perhaps the hardest game of that tour.

"The ground had cover on all four sides and the crowd was very close to the pitch.

"The terracing was deep and Watersheddings was one of the best of all viewing grounds. One of the best views was in the top tier of the Hutchins Stand, behind the posts at the Waterhead end. Underneath was the old "Penny Rush" stand - that got very claustrophobic.

"You didn't notice the slope on the pitch too much until you played on it. You could pen opposing sides in at the Waterhead/Herbert Street corner and it was hard for them to get out - a bit like Dewsbury and Batley."

Another unusual feature was the way the players changed in the old pavilion and then made their way through the crowds to the tunnel under the main stand. "We changed upstairs, level with the bar and then later in the '70s underneath. It was a bit dank, like being in the cellars of the pavilion," Blair explains. "Going to the pitch was OK - everyone was up for the game and there'd be a lot of good luck shouts and backslapping.

"Going back to the pavilion was alright if you'd won. We never needed any protection but if you'd lost the Oldham fans would let you know what they thought in no uncertain terms. But they'd all be back again for the next game. Opposing teams found it all very intimidating."

Winters at Watersheddings are the stuff of legend. Take the 1962/63 season as an extreme example - after playing at home on 15 December the next home game was played on 9 March. "In the depths of winter Watersheddings was a bit frightening - it was worth ten points start to us," Blair maintains. "It was very cold, wet and miserable and that was when it wasn't snowing."

Blair grew up on the great Oldham team of the mid to late 1950s and would regularly go and watch his heroes, like Alan Davies and Ike Southward, train on the three-quarter pitch at the back of the pavilion. When this was sold off later Oldham teams trained in the middle of the dog track at the ground.

"But from the '70s the club was on a downward spiral," Blair says. "Crowds dwindled and there were so many other options for people to do in their leisure time. The change to Sunday wasn't universally popular - a lot of people would work on a Saturday morning and then go to the rugby. The club always seemed skint. At the start of each season a committee-man would address the players and say: "Here are the terms - like it or lump it."

"They'd had the great team of the '50s and the big crowds but where did the money go? It certainly didn't go on the ground and the players would say it didn't go to them. That's why players like Davies left. But the loss of Watersheddings was tragic and a sad indictment. Even if we had only the use of one stand we could still be playing there. Look at other clubs, like Wigan, Huddersfield and Warrington. They didn't move away from their old ground until they had somewhere to go to.

"There is still a fair amount of support for the game but Oldham is essentially split into two with the southern part Latics territory and the top end Rugby League. A lot of people I know will watch Oldham away but won't go to Boundary Park. They say that end of town is the soccer end of town. The best thing the club could do is get a ground on this side of town where Watersheddings was - the town centre is still the dividing line between the two sports and sets of supporters.

"It is very difficult when you are nomads. This year, playing a third of our home league programme on neutral grounds is not the best for anyone. It gets the supporters down and it must get the players down. There is nothing like home advantage. It counts for a lot. Watersheddings was a big advantage with the cold, the wind, the rain and the slope. The crowd was on top of the pitch and it was an intimidating place for opposing teams and for the officials. People still talk about Rugby League in Oldham but a lot of the talk is subdued. What's happened over the last 10-15 years has been like a kick in the teeth for a lot of people. A lot of people are fed up and can't see an end goal."

It was all so different when Watersheddings opened in 1889 - a magnificent sporting complex, especially for its day, sited next to the hamlet of Knuckett.

After their formation in 1876 Oldham first played on a field to the rear of Glodwick Spinning Mill before, in 1878, they moved in with the cricket club at Clarksfield, just south of the Huddersfield Road below Watersheddings, sited south-west of the Greenacres cemetery. Housing off Clarksfield Road now covers the site with the road-name providing a lasting reminder of the ground's name.

The enclosed ground at Clarksfield, home of the Oldham Cricket, Bowling and Tennis Club, enabled the rugby club to take a gate for the first time and it was here that one of the most famous games in the club's early history was played in 1889 when Oldham beat the touring New Zealand Maoris.

The growing popularity of rugby meant Clarksfield was soon inadequate for the club's needs and a solution was found in a move to the nine-acre site which became known as Watersheddings. Initially, the rugby club was a sub-tenant of the cricket club but then bought the grounds outright and appointed trustees with the aim of the ground to "remain an open space for sport for all time."

A fine £2,000 pavilion - where the town's MP, Winston Churchill (later the famous wartime prime minister) was said to have taken tea - overlooked a magnificent cricket ground, with the rugby ground boasting a small main stand with terracing in front and terracing on the opposite Herbert Street side. The two ends were uncovered with only a grassy bank at the Waterhead end.

Behind the Watersheddings end, tennis courts were sited and a bowling green, adjacent to the pavilion, was also part of the complex. Until the Watersheddings end was covered in the late 1950s a good view of the pitch could be found from standing on what was known as Minder's Hill, overlooking the ground at this end. During the general strike in the 1920s many striking cotton operatives took advantage of this, as they were unable to afford the admission charge.

The Watersheddings skyline was dominated by the Ruby Mill, constructed in 1889, the same year as the ground. The pitch drained into the mill reservoir. The mill chimney had "Ruby 1889" engrained on its brickwork and its demolition in 1935 was said by those of a superstitious nature to have brought the rugby club bad luck. Eventually Watersheddings, like the local cotton industry, would fall into terminal decline.

The cricket club stayed until the early 1930s when they left to take up the offer of a new ground off Huddersfield Road. The town's ex-mayor, Mr Pollard, gave the land to the cricket club and the ground was named The Pollards in his honour. The rugby club then leased the site of the cricket ground to a greyhound racing company. Baseball was also staged on the former cricket field. The greyhound stadium was sold in the early 1990s as the club, then seemingly haemorrhaging money, seemed to dispose of its assets piecemeal before the ground closure itself.

For that opening game in 1889 the Watersheddings ground was still six years off being fully completed. The great Jim Valentine of Swinton had the honour of scoring the first try on the new ground before a 7,000 crowd. The Oldham Chronicle remarked: "The ground is well set out and there will be every chance of witnessing brilliant play, when the weather permits."

The occasion was also noteworthy for Oldham switching from black and amber jerseys to the red and white hooped variety that became their hallmark. Two of the Oldham players in that match, Bill McCutcheon and Jack Armstrong, took part in a brief ceremony to mark the ground's 50th anniversary in September 1939.

Watersheddings staged the first Roses county game in the Northern Union, Yorkshire defeating Lancashire 8-0 before 9,059 on 7 December 1895 and would have staged the first-ever international, between England and Other Nationalities, on New Year's Day 1904. But the game had to be postponed due to frost and was later switched to Wigan's Central Park.

But Watersheddings also staged four Challenge Cup semi-finals between 1898-1913 and in 1915, the last year before competitive football was stopped for the duration of the First World War, the "Team of All Talents", Huddersfield, defeated St Helens 37-3 before 8,000, the joint lowest crowd ever (alongside the 1911 final at Broughton) for a Challenge Cup Final.

Bad weather, then, was nothing new for Watersheddings, hewn into the Pennine hills and sited 860 feet above sea level. Fans of a more recent vintage will remember turning up for a Lancashire game against the touring New Zealanders in 1985 on what seemed a balmy November evening in most parts of the county only to find Watersheddings frost-bound and the game postponed.

Watersheddings was capable of hosting big crowds, first seriously tested when 20,000 turned up for the game with Salford in 1897. Ground improvements continued

Boundary Park

apace to accommodate them. The main stand, constructed in three sections with a curved front to allow for a better view, was completed by 1909. On the opposite side an open stand, 120-yards long, was constructed with wooden planking. This was also covered in three stages and became known as E stand. The original double-decker stand at the Waterhead end, known as the "Penny Rush" was built in 1896 and covered 80 yards.

A ground record was established when 28,000 saw the league game against Huddersfield in February 1912. The following month 25,000 paid receipts of £824 for a third-round Challenge Cup-tie against the same opponents, Oldham running out narrow victors on both occasions. Despite these crowds the club was in debt by the time competitive football was suspended and so sold off a wooden stand that had been erected at the Watersheddings end in order to clear its debts.

Watersheddings also staged the 1928 Championship Final when Swinton defeated Featherstone Rovers, 11-0, before a crowd of 15,583.

During the Second World War Watersheddings hosted its only major international game when England defeated Wales, 8-5, before 5,000 on Saturday 9 November 1940. Oldham hooker Edgar Brooks was in the England side that afternoon. During the First World War, though, it had hosted a rugby union match between two teams of New Zealand servicemen stationed at nearby Chadderton that attracted a 12,000 crowd that contributed £400 to the funds of Oldham Royal Infirmary.

Watersheddings also staged a spiteful game against Leigh in January 1984 that lingers in the memory - with the visitors leading 26-14 referee John Mean saw fit to abandon the game after 56 minutes because of brawling and the match was replayed.

In 1901/02 Oldham used Sheepfoot Lane, home to junior rivals Werneth, for reserve games. Werneth had moved there from Block Lane when Oldham County AFC, the town's first professional soccer club, became defunct. A new club, Pine Villa, became the club's most prominent soccer outfit, playing at Hudson Fold from 1900/06 until soccer returned to the ground. Renamed Oldham Athletic, playing at the renamed Boundary Park, they earned Football League status in 1907.

Oldham used Boundary Park for a number of games in the 1980s to take advantage of the under-soil heating prior to the temporary installation of a plastic pitch in 1986. The first game staged there was against Batley in January 1982 when 2,743 saw a 17-9 "home" win. In January 1987 Oldham staged one game at Manchester City's Maine Road ground, due to their under-pitch heating, a crowd of 2,719 witnessing the fixture against Featherstone Rovers.

Oldham shared in the post-war prosperity after 1945 and ground improvements continued. The "Penny Rush" stand was refurbished and renamed the GF Hutchins Stand in honour of George Hutchins, a long-serving Oldham official and one of the original trustees. A pitched roof stand with 50 terraces was also built at the Watersheddings end after Oldham won the championship in 1957, paid for by the club pools. It was then estimated that Watersheddings could accommodate 16,000 under cover.

The 1960s and '70s, though, witnessed a gradual decline in attendances. For example, the tour game against the 1967 Kangaroos attracted only 3,329 on a Saturday

afternoon. A nadir was reached in April 1979 when only 659 attended a home game against Whitehaven.

Floodlights were switched on for the first time for an under-24s international against France in 1965 and a £30,000 social club was opened two years later. The pavilion housed the club offices and social lounges, dressing and medical rooms. Little was then done to the ground, other than maintenance or repair, until its closure.

The last "big" crowd at Watersheddings was the 11,906 that assembled on a Wednesday evening on 4 February 1987 when Paddy Kirwan's late try, converted by Mick Burke, helped the Roughyeds defeat then mighty Wigan, 10-8, in a first round Challenge Cup-tie that has gone down in Oldham folklore.

In the first Super League season Oldham staged three games at Boundary Park, including the opener against Wigan that attracted a gate of 7,709 and eight at Watersheddings. In the last competitive game at the old ground Oldham defeated Sheffield Eagles 34-25 on 25 August 1996, Scott Ranson marking the occasion with a hat-trick. Just 2,515 were in attendance. But the lack of a firm announcement from the club that this would be the last game at Watersheddings prompted supporters to press for another game to properly mark the significance of the occasion - hence the friendly against Swinton.

During the 1997 season, the club, then briefly re-titled Oldham Bears, staged one game at Hyde United FC's Ewen Fields ground when Boundary Park was unavailable because of re-seeding. Oldham lost 20-21 to Sheffield Eagles, before a season's worst crowd of 2,168, a defeat Walker claims above all others contributed to them finishing bottom of the table.

Hurst Cross

The Roughyeds have also played one "home" match at Stalybridge Celtic FC's Bower Fold, a Football League ground in the early 1920s. The visit of Challenge Cup-holders St Helens for a fourth-round tie in 2002 attracted a season's best crowd of 4,089.

From leaving Watersheddings in 1997 it has been a trial to test the most loyal of supporters and fervent of groundhoppers and would never had been necessary but for the loss of one of Rugby League's most idiosyncratic grounds.

"Let's face it," says Walker. "By the end Watersheddings was a dump. But at least it was our dump."

ROCHDALE

The best ground outside Super League? Few would argue with that assessment of Spotland, the stadium shared by Rochdale Hornets and their soccer counterparts. Home for the Hornets since leaving the Athletic Grounds in 1988, Spotland has undergone a remarkable transformation. All four sides have been fully redeveloped during the last ten years and many people regard the ground as a model for others to seek to emulate.

Not long ago Rochdale AFC had fewer seats than any club in the Football League, a paltry 730, to go along with their unwanted tag of having earned only one promotion (in 1968/69) since entering the Football League in 1921 and having been rooted in the lowest division since 1974. But the current ground capacity of 10,208 includes a total of 8,310 seats with just one standing end, at the Sandy Lane side, that holds 1,898.

Spotland's roots as a sporting arena derived from the nearby parish church with Rochdale St Clement's rugby section, formed in 1878, the original occupants, alongside a cricket club. The ground was initially known as St Clement's playing field. At one time a huge rival to the Hornets, St Clement's folded in September 1897, shortly after the start of the Northern Union.

Spotland was then taken over by Rochdale AFC in 1900 and by Rochdale Town AFC in 1903, both teams lasting less than one year at their new ground after leaving other homes before disbanding.

The present Rochdale AFC took up residence from their formation in 1907, after a meeting convened by Harvey Rigg, a local businessman who had been the secretary of the St Clement's rugby team and who held the lease at the ground. At that time cricket was still played there and a cricket pavilion occupied the current site of the main stand. Rochdale AFC bought the ground for £1,700 in 1914 and joined the Football League seven years later as founder members of Division Three (North).

Until 1948 Spotland had a notorious five-foot slope from the Pearl Street end to the Sandy Lane end but this was rectified when the pitch was levelled and the excess earth dumped onto a corner of terracing to form a miniature Spion Kop.

Financial problems forced the club to secretly sell Spotland for £175,000 in 1980 to a company owned by the then chairman and then lease it back. But less than three years later, with the aid of a £60,000 Council loan, the club bought back the ground from the Official Receiver. But the ground, with its small main stand, situated well back from the pitch behind a wide track and a flat path that ran round three sides, its flat terracing and views of distant hills was often the butt of cruel jokes. The locally-produced Hilton's meat pies, though, won national acclaim.

In March 1990 came the signing of a three-way partnership deal, with Hornets contributing £500,000 from the sale of the Athletic Grounds, the soccer club throwing in Spotland (valued at £500,000) and the Council injecting £100,000 into a £1.1m company,

Denehurst Park (Rochdale) Limited, responsible for the development of Spotland. At the time it was a groundbreaking partnership between the two codes and a local Council. Though a minority shareholder the Council has equal voting rights.

Hornets, formed in 1871 from the amalgamation of two junior sides, staged most of their early Northern Union games at the Dane Street cricket ground, home of Rochdale CC, little more than a stone's throw from the Town Hall. The cricket club stayed there until 1994 when the site was taken over for retail development, and dug up the square and re-laid it at their new home at Redbrook, down the road from Spotland.

Hornets had initially played at the Old Athletic Grounds, occupying the same site on Milnrow Road as their later home. They had two other temporary homes, at the old Rochdale CC ground at Vavasour Street and at Roach Mills. Hornets then entered into an agreement to rent part of the Dane Street cricket field in 1878, broken only by one season when they played at a field off Bury Road in 1879.

Hornets played Halifax at Dane Street under electric lights in November 1878, attracting a crowd of 5,000 and a similar attendance witnessed the tour game against the Maoris the following March.

The Athletic Grounds were re-constructed in 1894, with eight of the 40 acres leased by Rochdale Athletic Club. The remainder of the site was used for farming and gardening purposes. There were two tracks, an outer banked 502-yard long cycling circuit with a quarter-mile ash track on its inside, good enough for the Northern Counties AAA to hold their 1924 Olympic trials there. On the railway side of the ground was an uncovered structure accommodating 2,500 spectators that had been used for the 1894 England-Wales rugby union international at Birkenhead. Opposite was a long, covered stand, seating 1,200 incorporating a temperance bar and dressing rooms. A bowling green was later built behind the latter stand.

Hornets took up permanent tenancy at the Athletic Grounds in season 1900/01, having used the ground occasionally beforehand. Their first game there was against Crompton in September 1894 and their first game under the auspices of the Northern Union was on Wednesday 22 April 1896 when they lost 0-23 to Runcorn. Rochdale AFC had played there from 1896-1900. In 1913 Hornets completed the purchase of the site.

The Athletic Grounds soon received an early taste of big games. A crowd of 18,000 witnessed the Roses match in November 1900 and Hornets' home was also allocated the 1902 Challenge Cup Final. Broughton Rangers ran out convincing winners, 25-0, over neighbours Salford, whose late arrival, due to problems on the railway, caused the kick-off to be delayed for 25 minutes.

Rangers' captain Bob Wilson scored three tries that day before a crowd of 15,006. The railway side stand was boarded up for this game due to fears of overcrowding

following the Ibrox disaster in Glasgow and was later demolished, being replaced by a new covered stand, 35 yards long, in 1911. At this time the main stand was extended to 100-yards in length.

Hornets lifted the Challenge Cup in 1922 and their third-round tie against neighbours Oldham saw a new ground record established of 26,664 (£1,823). Many spectators found a vantage point on the un-terraced mound of ashes at the scoreboard end of the ground.

In 1924 Wigan lifted the Challenge Cup for the first time, after defeating Oldham, 21-4, at the Athletic Grounds.

"This final will go down in the annals of Rugby League competitions as the most memorable ever decided," reported the Wigan Examiner. "To begin with, the attendance was a record for any game played under that code in this country, there being over 40,000 people present, and the receipts were also considerably higher than on any previous occasion, while it is stated that several thousand were unable to gain admission. The scenes at Rochdale, where the game took place, were unprecedented. The crowd invaded the field long before the start and there was the amazing spectacle of a player (Wigan's South African winger, Attie Van Heerden) running around a mounted policeman to score a try, while another Wigan player (Bert Webster) grounded the ball between the hoofs of a horse."

The official attendance was returned at 41,831 (£3,611) and despite the chaotic scenes, with the crowds lining the touch-lines, the Athletic Grounds was allocated another cup final two years later when Swinton beat Oldham, 9-3, before 27,000 spectators (£2,551) who braved high winds and continuous rain. This was the first time the final had been broadcast live by BBC Radio.

Speedway was first staged there in 1928 and a 25-year-old rider, Cliff Mawson, died after crashing at the track in October of that year. Speedway gave way to greyhound racing, first held in 1932 and continuing until 1969 when stock-car racing was introduced. Speedway briefly returned for two years from 1970 but the narrow square-shaped track was unpopular with devotees of that sport. Stock-car racing ceased in 1987, after complaints from local residents about noise were upheld.

Perhaps the most famous match ever staged at the ground was the 1930 Ashes Test match. With the three-match series tied at 1-1, after a score-less draw in the third Test at Swinton, pressure largely from the Australian party brought about a fourth and deciding game, on the basis it would be "good business," for the first and only time in Anglo-Australian Test history. The match, played on Wednesday 15 January, was decided when the Leeds winger, Stan Smith, scored the only try of the game with six minutes remaining before a crowd of 16,743 (£2,056).

Hornets faced severe financial problems in the 1930s, especially following the 1935 fire that gutted the main stand. Happily, they survived and a new stand built on the ashes

of the old one by Fletcher Bolton of Rochdale, seating 1,300 and costing £4,725, was opened in 1936.

The railway stand roof was blown off in 1936 and three years later its replacement collapsed at the Challenge Cup semi-final between Wigan and Salford, killing two spectators, a 43 year old Rochdale man and a 51 year old woman from Eccles, and injuring 15 others.

The official crowd was returned at 31,212, though a further 5,000 people were estimated to have gained free admittance. After two minutes' play, as the Wigan Examiner reported: "A good many spectators, unable to gain a decent view, had climbed on the roof of shelters on the popular side. The spectators on the stand side were horrified to see the roof of one of the shelters collapse with an ominous crack. Men were flung onto the crowd densely packed in front and many of those underneath crushed by falling timber. The crowd was so tightly packed it would have been impossible to get clear." This proved to be the last major game to be staged there.

Ray Myers, the long-standing Hornets time-keeper, first went to the Athletic Grounds in the late 1940s and, like visitors before him and since, was unimpressed. "I was eight-years-old and my father took me along," he recalls. "I thought what kind of a ground and game is this?"

But those perceptions all changed when Hornets recruited an Aboriginal winger, Wally McArthur, in 1953. "He could catch pigeons and was brilliant to watch," Ray says. "Wally had recorded a time of 9.7 seconds for the 100 yards and when he got the ball with an open space there was no stopping him. Thanks to him I got the bug."

Many others did too as Hornets briefly averaged 10,000 for home games in a season for the first time in their history. A few years later, in 1961, after Hornets took out an advertisement in the Fiji Times, a number of Fijians arrived with Orisi Dawai and Joe Levula the trailblazers. "They created tremendous interest, they were like the Harlem

Globetrotters," Ray recalls. "They all had hands like shovels and could kick for goal in bare feet. They were all laid-back men and in a way were too popular. They had a South Sea island band that went around the local pubs and maybe they were offered too much hospitality."

Hornets suffered a blow in 1964 when, after attracting a brewery loan of £25,000, they were refused planning permission to build a new social club on the Kingsway car park. "There were a lot of objections, particularly from local licensees and the plan was scrapped," Ray says. "That might have put Hornets on a much better financial footing had it gone through."

Floodlights were opened at the ground in 1966 when Hornets beat Huddersfield, 9-4, before 3,912. "Lights came a bit late in the day but they were a big thing for Rochdale," Ray says, as the club soon entered into better times.

"In the early '70s, with Frank Myler as coach, we had a great era," Ray says. "In a three-year spell we could play anyone, no matter who, and be in with a chance. We played some great rugby."

One game that has gone down in Hornets' folklore was the John Player Trophy quarter-final tie against Leeds in December 1973 when a last-second Bill Holliday drop goal earned Hornets a 7-5 win on their way to the final. "The Leeds fans were making plans for the replay just as the kick went over," Ray says. To make matters worse the bench seating the Leeds coaching staff collapsed, dumping its occupants into the mud surrounding the pitch. But then life at the Athletic Grounds was never glamorous.

But by the mid-1980s Hornets were in dire financial straits occupying a semi-derelict and vandalised ground, unloved by many Rugby League followers primarily because of the distance of the playing area from the terraces. Many of the Hornets faithful gathered in the paddock under the main stand, with the railway stand opposite sparsely populated. Behind

179

the posts to the left was the hill and the Tote board dominated the other end. The "Hornets Nest" was a long, low wooden building that housed the supporters' club with a Vice-Presidents lounge under the main stand.

In 1987, with debts of £350,000, Hornets entered into negotiations with the Council to turn the Athletic Grounds into a new £3m athletics stadium. These plans never came to fruition and Hornets accepted a £2.4m bid for the building of a Morrisons supermarket and petrol garage on the site and in the summer of 1988 entered into a ground-sharing agreement with Rochdale FC, at an initial rent of £11,000 per annum.

Hornets' last game at their old home was a dismal affair; they were hammered 6-58 by neighbours Oldham before 3,260 spectators, who came to pay their last respects on Good Friday 1988. This was a far cry from the crowd of 19,654 for a league match between the old rivals in October 1954.

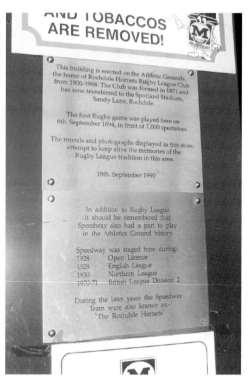

Hornets had played a midweek game against Keighley at Spotland in March 1954 under floodlights, drawing 13-13 before 10,682 spectators but their first game as permanent residents was marked by a 36-26 win over Barrow in August 1988 before a crowd of 1,088.

"It was a very sad day when we played Oldham," Ray recalls. "But the general feeling was that the club had to move or die. The Athletic Grounds were badly vandalised and I remember turning up for one game and finding the safe from the social club on the 25-yard line.

"There was lot of trepidation when we first went to Spotland. Would the ground-share work, how would we be received? A lot of people thought the clubs should have jointly developed the Athletic Grounds site where there was more room. They were fraught times but now we have moved up to a different level. You look around Spotland today and it is a superb ground. Some of the clubs that come here think they are in Paradise."

SALFORD

Relegation from Super League was a rotten way to close the centenary season of Rugby League at the Willows.

Ironically, on the day when Castleford's hard fought victory sealed Salford's fate in 2002, the Willows looked at its best. The Castleford fans packed the north stand end to provide a noisy and colourful backdrop while the Reds supporters on the popular side gave unceasing support. Long after the end of the game, fans mingled on the terraces at the clubhouse end, drowned their sorrows in the bars and kids played improvised games of rugby on the beautifully manicured Willows turf.

It was a particularly sad day for Graham Morris, a lifelong Salford supporter and erstwhile club secretary, whose splendid book, "Salford City Reds: A Willows Century" captures the highs and lows of one of the game's traditional clubs.

Morris was brought up in the shadow of the Willows and has spent countless hours piecing together the threads that make up the rich tapestry of Salford's history.

Before moving to the Willows, Salford had played since 1878 at New Barnes, often described as a "classical ground" as it had the Manchester racecourse as its backdrop. It was here that Salford played their first games in the Northern Union after becoming members for the 1896/97 season. In their first home game they were defeated 0-9 by Oldham and only recorded their first win of the campaign at the tenth attempt, defeating Wigan, 16-3. During 1900, however, the club received notice to quit, as the Manchester Ship Canal company had bought the land, including the adjoining racecourse, with plans to build the new number nine dock, which became the terminus for timber imports. The racecourse was moved back to its original location at Castle Irwell, ironically close to another Northern Union ground, that of Broughton Rangers, while Salford took on a new home venue that, in 2005, was the oldest surviving senior sports stadium in the Manchester and Salford area.

Salford agreed a 14-year lease on five acres of land belonging to the Willows Estate Company, the company being so named due to the large number of willow trees covering the area. A limited company was set up to help raise the necessary capital involved and the ground was opened on 21 December 1901 when Jimmy Lomas's drop goal gave Salford a 2-0 win over local rivals Swinton before 16,981 spectators.

The ground adjoined Weaste Cricket Club, who only recently vacated their home due to repeated vandalism. Originally, a stand covering 97 yards, 22 steps deep, with seating in the central area was constructed on the west (Kennedy Street) side and the popular side, next to Weaste Lane, had two other adjoining enclosures, one with bench seats, the other standing, that extended the length of the touchline. After strenuous fund raising and additional contributions from the directors, a two-storey pavilion was built on the Kennedy Road and cricket ground corner with changing facilities, a boardroom and offices. A cycling track was laid that ran down both sides of the playing area. Its steeped banking

behind the goalposts created an oval shape. The track, constructed of black cinders, was also used for athletics and provided standing space for spectators.

Salford won their first major trophy under Northern Union rules in 1914, defeating Huddersfield 5-3 in the Championship final. At that time, however, the club was in the hands of an Official Receiver and four months later the original Salford Football Club was wound up. A new company, Salford Football Club (1914) Limited was then formed. This company is still in existence today.

"The ground remained the same until the 1930s," Morris explains, "when major changes took place. In 1933 the club purchased the ground from the brewers, Groves and Whitnall Limited, and this gave them the security they needed to develop the ground that was not possible when they were tenants.

"Lance Todd, the former Wigan and New Zealand international, had been appointed secretary-coach and he helped lift the club from obscurity to the golden era of the Red Devils that lasted until the outbreak of the Second World War in 1939."

Nicknamed the "Red Devils" in the 1930s by the French because of their turkey-red jerseys, Salford's greatest day came in May 1938 when they lifted the Challenge Cup for the only time in their history after beating Barrow 7-4 at Wembley.

"By the '30s cycling and athletics were no longer thought to be the thing," Morris adds. "The track, which had also been used for motor cycling time trials, was replaced and the oval was filled in by terraces. Under the chairmanship of Charles B Riley, the club pushed forward with major ground improvements. More terracing was installed and the current popular side stand was built. The main grandstand had been replaced by the current main stand in the 1920s."

The Willows staged its first international fixture in January 1922 when the ground was a controversial choice to host the third and deciding Test against Australia. Critics pointed out that the Willows ground was not big enough to stage a game of this importance.

The match had originally been scheduled somewhat vaguely "in Manchester" with Old Trafford and the Cliff also mooted. To accommodate the anticipated crowd a total of 2,000 tons of cinders had to be laid for banking around the ground.

The game only went ahead after ten tons of straw protected the pitch from snow and frost and the home side were at an advantage with only one member of the Australian side having previously seen snow. On a treacherous surface Britain scored tries by forwards Herman Hilton and Frank Gallagher to record a 6-0 win before 21,000 (£2,450). The Kangaroos did not regain the Ashes until 1950. Australia became the first team in Test history to be "nilled" and it was the first Test without a goal being kicked. It proved to be the final Test for Britain captain Harold Wagstaff together with his Huddersfield teammates Johnny Rogers and Gwyn Thomas.

After staging the England-Wales international in 1932, when 8,000 saw England win 19-2, the Willows briefly became an international venue again from the late 1960s. A total of five internationals were played there, including the first Test of the 1971 Great Britain-New Zealand series. A crowd of only 3,764 saw the Kiwis win, 18-13, at a time when the game was going through a particularly bad patch crowds-wise. The Willows staged its last international in November 1975 when Wales' 23-2 victory over France in the final game of the elongated World Cup (strictly speaking christened the World Championship that began in March 1975) was watched by only 2,247 spectators. Salford scrum-half Peter Banner scored one of Wales' five tries and David Watkins kicked four goals.

Morris made his Willows bow in the 1950s, inevitable considering that his bedroom window overlooked the ground. "One of my earliest memories is looking out and seeing the supporters' hut at the top of the north terrace, which remained until the north stand was built, and the pavilion in the corner with the flag flying," he recalls.

"In the 1950s the Willows was a typical Rugby League ground of its day, with an open terrace at both its ends, a small main stand and the popular stand as it is now. A lot of

the players lived in the area and many, particularly the younger players and those that came up from Wales, stayed in boarding houses. The atmosphere at the ground was more robust then because of the terracing. There were more people on the terraces and they were very vociferous. The supporters were mainly working class and they were good, decent people.

"Games were played on Saturday afternoons, of course, and Salford were not normally at home at the same time as Manchester United. When the A team were at home you could hear the roars from the football ground at Old Trafford and, at half-time and full-time, the result of Salford's game away from home would be passed over the tannoy system. Before the tannoy was introduced a boy used to come round the ground with a board, holding up the team changes and then the latest scores."

The next major change in Salford's history came after Brian Snape was elected chairman in 1963. "Mr Snape had joined the board in 1960 and his entrepreneurial skills brought about the club's most exciting period since the 1930s," says Morris. "In addition to many major signings, his period in charge saw the Willows being completely transformed."

The creation of the Salford Football and Social Club (later named the Willows Variety Centre) which was completed in 1966, led to the end of the open terracing at the south side of the ground and five years later the imposing propped cantilever north stand was erected. When the wooden main grandstand was partly gutted by a fire, the cause of which was thought to be a discarded cigarette end following a game against Workington Town in 1972, the stand was rebuilt and modernised with a top tier inserted in the centre part.

"Floodlights were added in 1966 and the club made the bold move of playing home games on a Friday evening," Morris adds. "Brian Snape's vision heralded a new era for the club, not just on the field but in the facilities for spectators.

"His ideas were well received and Salford, which as a team had been in the doldrums, was suddenly flourishing. Floodlit games, the social club opening and players brought to the club of a far higher standard than at any time since the 1930s made it a very exciting place to be. In the five seasons from 1967/68 home crowds averaged 7,500, more than double those of the mid-sixties."

Mr Snape's biggest signing was David Watkins, the British Lions and Wales RU international, persuaded to switch codes in a £16,000 deal in October 1967. But many other great players went on to grace the Willows turf in the Salford jersey in the late '60s and early '70s. These included former union international wingers Keith Fielding and Maurice Richards, Cumbrian fullback Paul Charlton, centre Chris Hesketh, halfbacks Ken Gill and Steve Nash and forwards Colin Dixon and Mike Coulman.

"The enthusiasm the signings created was tremendous and hadn't been seen since the '30s," Morris says. "The fans would have turned up at midnight if necessary to see the players on view. The Willows became the only place to be on a Friday night. People could

come and see the game and have dinner and see cabaret if they liked. The Salford support widened. A lot of university students came along and many others were swallowed up in the excitement. The Salford side of that era didn't win a lot of trophies but it was a very exciting team to watch."

In January 1982 John Wilkinson joined the board and immediately took over as chairman. Mr Wilkinson, who received the OBE in 2001, is the longest current chairman in Rugby League and the longest in the history of the Salford club.

"Mr Wilkinson took over at a difficult time," Morris recalls. "What happened to Salford happens to so many - players get older and are not replaced, maybe the support falls away a little bit and the structure that was built is more difficult to maintain. The club had sustained some serious losses, it was a great period but the success was not built on.

"You have seen it with so many other clubs, Leigh and Swinton to name just two. They had short periods of great success but an inability to maintain those. Very few clubs, apart from St Helens, Leeds and Wigan, have been able to sustain that kind of momentum."

Salford, under Andy Gregory's coaching, did reach Super League in 1997 but their six-year stint ended in 2002. After one year in the National League, Salford regained their Super League status but despite that the club faces huge challenges.

On the field, the Reds want to maintain their hard-won place in the top flight. Off it, the club intends to move to Barton and the second purpose-built Rugby League stadium of the new century, following Warrington's occupancy of the Halliwell Jones. It is intended that the Willows remains to hold reserve games and as a community asset.

Like so many, Morris accepts the need for change but would be sad to see the demise of Salford's traditional home. "We have yet to see a situation where a Rugby League club has moved grounds and it has been a success," he asserts. "In Salford much of the support is in the immediate vicinity. A high proportion of the club's supporters live there and walk to the game.

"It was the same at Swinton and since they left Station Road they have lost a lot of supporters. But Salford have recognised that they need more fans. You are increasingly aware of that on match days, playing one of the top sides when the north stand terrace is dominated by away support.

"The level of finance afforded today dictates what progress can be achieved, more than in any other era," Morris adds. "It is only through strong sponsorship and increased spectator support that the club can prosper.

"Just like the visionaries who took that leap forward in acquiring the Willows Estate in 1901, it is now time for the present administration to secure the future for the next one hundred years," Morris concludes.

"But when that hooter sounds at the end of the final match at the Willows, I know I will not be alone in pausing for a tearful farewell."

SHEFFIELD

Sheffield is a city known mainly for two things - its steel industry and its famous soccer tradition.

Sheffield AFC (not to be confused with Wednesday, founded 1867 or United, founded 1889), founded in 1857, is the oldest football club in the world.

In the Victorian era, Sheffield enjoyed a reputation as one of the pioneering centres of a winter sport that enjoyed such a dramatic increase in popularity to forge an integral role in the sporting fabric of the nation.

Despite being situated only 30 miles or so from one of the game's main heartlands, in West Yorkshire, Sheffield was alien and indifferent territory for Rugby League until the determination and drive of a husband and wife team, Gary and Kath Hetherington, set up the Eagles in 1984.

It was a time of expansion for the game. Fulham had been launched four years previously, Cardiff/Bridgend Blue Dragons, Kent/Southend Invicta and, later, Scarborough Pirates, followed.

The Eagles grew from the ground upwards, building a strong band of volunteer enthusiasts and developing a family feel that the club has never lost.

The Hetheringtons initially thought they had agreed a deal to ground-share United's Bramall Lane ground only for the football club to cancel this option. Instead, the Eagles took up residence in the far less grandiose surroundings of Owlerton Sports Stadium, situated just a few hundred yards from Wednesday's Hillsborough ground.

Owlerton Stadium began life as a speedway stadium in the late 1920s after Provincial Dirt-Tracks Ltd purchased some open land at Owlerton Meadows and began the construction of a track. The first speedway meeting was held there in March 1929 in front of a crowd of 15,000 spectators. However, the early momentum was not maintained and the promotion went bankrupt just over two years later.

The stadium was bought off the official receiver for £1,000 and the new owners shortened the dirt-track from 442 to 400 yards and installed a greyhound circuit. Again the new venture soon failed and the stadium lay dormant for four years before being re-opened in 1938 with the track changed to a 'D' shape, also staging stock car racing.

The stadium continued a fluctuating existence, several new owners trying and failing to establish speedway in the city, closing down for five years during the war and for another eight between 1952 and 1960.

Sheffield Eagles entered into an agreement to stage games at the then council-owned Owlerton after being admitted to the RFL. Due to the speedway track the corner of the pitch and the in-goal areas had to be laid on rubber mats. After running continuously from 1960, the Sheffield Tigers speedway side closed at the end of the 1988 season, and the Eagles tenure was not much longer lived.

The Eagles' first home game was against Rochdale Hornets on 2 September 1984 when Paul McDermott scored a hat-trick of tries in a heartening 29-10 victory before 1,425 spectators, Hetherington registering a field goal.

John Cornwell has been involved with the Eagles since the early days. "In the first season the club was incredibly small," he recalls. "Everyone knew everyone else and that was the case with the fans, too. When the cameras rolled round the Eagles fans at the play-off final at Widnes in 2003, I recognised all the faces and knew most of the names and many of those had followed the club since day one or thereabouts.

"The first match against Rochdale coincided with the Sheffield Show and, on my way to the ground, it looked as though there was a vast crowd converging. By the end we'd get 500 from Sheffield for a big match at Owlerton. We started with a hard core of about 250.

"The pitch was dreadful and soon turned to mud and a lot of the conditions for spectators were primitive. But there was a superb glass-fronted bar that was used for dog racing with a panoramic view of the pitch. That was a good facility for sponsors and, for the rest of us, somewhere warm and pleasant before the game.

"There were six or seven rows of wooden seats - you might call them bleachers - where the majority of the fans watched the game. You knew virtually all the spectators. That bred a very strong sense of loyalty. Eagles were a peculiar club, essentially a family club, and Gary (Hetherington) had been everything. The sense of family was very strong, just as it is today with the Aston family."

A home Challenge Cup-tie against Warrington the following February realised a crowd of 1,479 but the Eagles' average home league crowds were recorded at 885, falling to 698 in their second season, though raising the attendance record to 1,658 for Rochdale's visit.

The Eagles, in the first of a number of ground-sharing ventures, played Swinton at

Rotherham United's Millmoor ground in March 1985, attracting a crowd of 1,146 for the Friday evening fixture. In May 1986 they attracted 500 for a "home" game against Workington Town at Doncaster's Tattersfield ground and in January 1987 had 709 when they played Bramley at Headingley.

Local derby games against Doncaster saw the Eagles record some of their biggest gates at Owlerton - 1,922 in the last home game of the 1986/87 season and 2,254 in March 1989. But Oldham, who had a terrific travelling support in the late '80s twice set new attendance records at Owlerton, the highest 3,636 for a Challenge Cup-tie in February 1989.

The Eagles' last game at Owlerton was against Doncaster in their promotion year of 1988/89 when 1,725 saw the home side run out 28-10 winners, nearly double the average home league gate.

"In a short space of time we'd worked up a reasonable head of steam," Cornwell adds. "But Sheffield was a soccer city and we didn't realise what a hard nut to crack soccer would be. There was no hostility to Rugby League and little union around as competition. But though there seemed to be goodwill towards the Eagles, and Gary certainly made an impact on the city with his personal efforts to promote Rugby League, not many came to watch."

Eagles stalwart Mark Aston's abiding memory of Owlerton was the game against Chorley where promotion was clinched. "The photographs taken after the game show the players freezing, covered from top to toe in mud, clutching bottles of champagne," he says.

"Owlerton's facilities were never the best, and were definitely run down at that stage, even though the stadium has since been done up impressively. Other teams didn't fancy playing there. The changing rooms were small, cold and dingy, and the showers were always on the blink.

"We used it to our advantage and the pitch was always in such a bad state it brought players back to my pace. That suited me - in the mud I was as fast as anyone."

In the wake of the Hillsborough disaster, all sports grounds faced stringent new safety measures, and Owlerton was closed to all sports on 14 September 1989. It was subsequently re-opened with a capacity of 2,400, speedway eventually returning in 1991, but by this time the Eagles had exciting new plans.

It was the Eagles' misfortune that their entry into the elite of British RL, after five years in division two, coincided with Owlerton's closure. But they made a terrific fist of a

Don Valley Stadium

bad job, staging home games at no less than seven venues in their first season in the top flight and raising their attendance average to 4,038, a figure only bettered in the first year of Super League (4,613 in 1996).

Despite their nomadic existence the Eagles consolidated their hard-won place in the top league. Their opening home game saw a crowd of 6,200 for St Helens' visit to Hillsborough, bettered when 7,642 saw the game against Wigan. They also played two games at Bramall Lane, including a famous 31-6 win over newly-crowned world champions Widnes, watched by 8,636.

The Eagles also staged five home games at Doncaster and three at Chesterfield FC's Saltergate ground, and one apiece at Halifax's Thrum Hall, Wakefield's Belle Vue and Barnsley FC's Oakwell ground.

Meanwhile, completely by accident, a new home for the Eagles was fast taking shape. Specifically built for the 1991 World Student Games, the 25,000 all-seater Don Valley Stadium, costing £25 million, was a vast, ambitious project, officially completed in August 1990. Built on a derelict site, formerly occupied by Brown Bayley Steelworks, the stadium had three major features. The main stand roof comprised distinctive steel arches and yellow ladder beams, incorporating eleven translucent roof canopies. Illumination was provided by five masts accommodating 108 floodlights (for Eagles games only a third of the lighting capacity is required for optimum effect) while a £300,000 Omega scoreboard put many others in the RL world to shame.

"Originally the plan was to develop the track at Woodbourn for the games, with the Don Valley site being redeveloped as a boating lake as part of an east-end park," Cornwell explains. "But the plans changed when it became clear Woodbourn was too small.

"The games are part of the folklore of the city and Don Valley was the great flagship project to regenerate the Attercliffe Valley after the collapse of the steel industry. It also served as a rapprochement between Tory industry and the Labour council. It was a great event and served to bring everyone together and made people aware of the city."

For the Eagles' second season in the Stones Bitter Championship the magnificent Don Valley Stadium was ready. The stadium was officially opened when a crowd of 22,000 saw an athletics meeting that included Steve Cram and Peter Elliott. A crowd of 7,984 watched the Eagles christen their new home with a 34-6 win over Wakefield Trinity on Wednesday 26 September 1990 despite the fixture having been put back three days due to their neighbours' involvement in the Yorkshire Cup Final.

Rugby League comes to Bramall Lane

By the end of a season that ended in relegation the crowds fell to 2,578 for the last game against Widnes, with the average 4,031.

Don Valley recorded its highest crowd for a Rugby League game on a perfect summer Saturday evening, 16 August 1997, when Bradford Bulls secured the Super League title with a 32-12 victory before 10,603 spectators. "With fans seated behind the posts at the scoreboard end and on the far side, suddenly the remoteness of the stadium was forgotten," Cornwell recalls. "It was a wonderful atmosphere that night and the stadium, with a good crowd, looked a terrific sight."

It was a night when Don Valley, so often labelled an expensive white elephant, came alive as the thousands of Bulls fans, bedecked in replica shirts and waving flags and scarves provided the perfect backdrop to a memorable sporting experience.

Another Eagles stalwart, their long-serving prop Paul Broadbent, said at the time: "A few years ago, Odsal was a cold, unwelcoming place, with no atmosphere and crowds of a few thousand. Now the place has come alive, it's an intimidating place to go, and every game is an occasion.

"They say that Don Valley is no good for Rugby League. But it was a great setting tonight, with all those people in, the colour and the noise and the great atmosphere. Bradford have turned a real dead hole completely around and at Sheffield we've got to set out to do what they've done."

Sadly, that evening was to prove a tantalising glimpse of what might have been. After their momentous Cup Final victory over Wigan in 1998, the Eagles returned to Don Valley the following week, ironically playing Wigan and attracted a crowd of 7,365. But the success of Wembley did not signal a glorious new era and little more than a year later came

Oakwell, Barnsley

Saltergate, Chesterfield

Sheffield's finest hour - celebrating the 1998 Challenge Cup Final win over Wigan

news of the controversial "merger" with Huddersfield Giants. Ironically, the Eagles last home game before the merger became known was a 47-32 win over the Giants before 3,500 spectators.

"I felt that up until the Cup Final the Eagles had an incremental success," Cornwell adds. "It was very sad when the news came out. Mark (Aston) reacted by saying he'd form a club of his own to keep RL in the city, that was picked up by the press and we had meetings with a thousand people present."

The re-formed Eagles attracted 1,612 for their first home game, against Batley, on 16 January 2000 and have averaged around the thousand mark ever since. The fans that have stuck by the club are incredibly loyal and fervent in their support of the side and those converts from soccer view their newly-discovered game with an almost evangelical zeal.

But Don Valley is the club's biggest draw and also its biggest drawback. "Don Valley has a playing surface and training and corporate facilities as good as anywhere," Aston says. "The biggest drawback has always been the distance of the pitch from the spectators. With the eight running track lanes, sandpit and everything else it is too far away and the stadium has always struggled for atmosphere as a result. To become a pure rugby stadium it would need developing."

Whether that will ever happen remains to be seen. One of Britain's most attractive stadiums is still recognised as being under-used. But only if the Eagles were to regain their Super League status and start to attract big crowds on a regular basis, would the transformation of the Don Valley into a League-friendly stadium ever happen.

In 2005 the Eagles added two more grounds to their list. On Good Friday, 22 March 2005 they played Doncaster Dragons at Rotherham RUFC's Clifton Lane ground. A crowd of 1,003 saw the Dragons win the Northern Rail Cup-tie 38-20. With Don Valley unavailable due to track repairs Eagles played Workington Town in a league game at Woodbourn Athletic Stadium on Saturday 11 June 2005, recording an exciting 31-28 win before a reported 650 attendance.

ST HELENS

One day someone might put up a blue plaque at Knowsley Road, marking a site of great historical interest. For now there are only five remaining grounds that staged the first season of Northern Union football in 1895/96 with Batley, Leeds, Wakefield and Widnes the others.

For a time it looked as though that number might be reduced by one but Saints have abandoned plans to re-locate, at least for the time being.

That news brought a deep sigh of relief from one of their most ardent supporters, Denis Whittle, who has followed the club's fortunes for sixty years, many of them as a distinguished local newspaper reporter.

"People might call me an old stick-in-the-mud, but as a member of the older age group I was relieved at the decision to stay," Denis says. "I first went on the ground with my father as a ten-year-old in 1942 and, apart from three years away in the forces in the Middle East, I have been going ever since. Knowsley Road has been an integral part of my life, just as it has been for many people in the town. I recently asked Eric Ashton if I could have my ashes scattered on the ground and he replied, tongue in cheek: 'We'll have to think about that.' That is how much the place means to me."

A chemist of German descent, William Douglas Herman, who worked at the glassworks, is credited with being the club's founder. "He became known as "Herman the German," and advertised for players," Denis explains. "The response was heartening and the club began to grow. Their first ground was at the Recreation Ground at Boundary Road. In the late 1870s they moved to a new ground at Queen's Park, just off Prescot Road between West Park Road and Boundary Road. Then they played on a farmer's field off Boundary Road and at Windle, between the vicarage and cemetery. Their last ground, before moving to Knowsley Road, was shared with St Helens Cricket Club, off Bishop Road in Dentons Green." It was at this latter ground that Saints played Wigan in a floodlit match on 24 January 1889. A crowd of 7,000 gathered to see the game, the pitch lit by Wells Patent Electric Lamps. In March 1889 Saints lost to the touring Maoris there before a crowd of 5,000.

Knowsley Road today is far different than when it opened for business in 1890 as little more than an open field, with spectators paying their entrance fees through holes in the fence at the town end.

Manchester Rangers provided the first opposition at the ground the St Helens club rented from the glass manufacturers, Pilkington Brothers. Later that season a small open stand was opened and turnstiles appeared by 1893. On 7 September 1895 Saints beat

St Helens Recs as it stands today

Rochdale Hornets, 8-3, before 3,000 in their inaugural Northern Union fixture. Saints' headquarters were at the Duke of Cambridge, later transferred along Duke Street to the Talbot Hotel.

In 1903 a wooden main stand, seating around 1,000 on the Knowsley Road side, was built by public subscription. It remained there until 1958, but, with 29 Y-shaped roof supports, viewing was difficult. Behind it ran the LMSR Eccleston Branch railway line and for some time there was talk of making a halt there. The line disappeared after the Second World War.

Between the wars there were two professional teams in St Helens with the Recs, a works team for Pilkingtons, playing at City Road. The derby matches started in 1919 and ended in 1939, Saints winning 21 and Recs 20, with six draws.

The most famous clash of the rivals came in the Lancashire Cup Final of 1926 when a crowd of 19,430 saw Saints win their first major trophy, beating Recs 10-2 at Warrington.

Recs had their revenge five months later, defeating Saints, 33-0, in the Championship semi-final tie at City Road before 19,000.

"That was THE derby and matches were played at Christmas and Easter," Denis says. "Many people would only watch the Recs - they didn't want to know the team from the other side of town. Both clubs had a cloth cap image. I have an old photograph of the stand at City Road and all the spectators, bar none, were wearing cloth caps. The rivalry matched anything between, say, Liverpool or Everton or Hull KR and Hull.

"The Recs folded because Pilkingtons refused to foot the bill any more. Some people say it was because of the war but that wasn't the reason. It was a cost thing, pure and simple. When the war was over a lot of spectators who'd watched Recs turned their attentions to Saints and the Saints/Wigan derby games took over as the highlights of the season."

St Helens

Pilkington Brothers had taken the enlightened step of introducing a works recreational club as far back as 1847 and the Recs rugby section was formed in 1879. They played initially at Boundary Park, produced an England RU international in Jimmy Pyke in 1892 and withdrew from the Northern Union in 1898. Re-formed in June 1913 and accepted into the Lancashire Combination playing at City Road, Recs were accepted into the senior ranks after the end of the first world war.

For ten successive seasons Recs finished above Saints in the league table and in 1929 went desperately close to playing in the first Wembley Challenge Cup Final, losing 12-13 to Wigan in a semi-final replay at Leigh after a 7-7 draw at Swinton. But that season saw the eighth successive year in which the club had made a financial loss with the main benefactor, Pilkington Brothers, footing the bill. In 1923 they beat Swinton in the Lancashire Cup Final at Wigan. In 1928 a total of seven players from St Helens, including Oliver Dolan, Frank Bowen and Albert Fildes from Recs, were selected for the tour. In 1930, when Recs lost 3-18 to Wigan in the Lancashire Cup Final home "gates" for all but the local derbies had fallen to around the 2,000 mark. Their last hope of major honours ended in 1933 when they lost to Oldham in the Lancashire Cup Final after beating Saints, 9-2, in the semi-final. The demise of Rugby League in the town was such that, for the 1937 tour game against the Australians, the RFL granted a fixture only to a combined selection from the two clubs. This game attracted a crowd of only 2,000 at Knowsley Road to see the Kangaroos run out 15-7 winners.

City Road, a compact ground with one main stand, remained in use for amateur Rugby League before gradually falling into a growing state of disrepair. It staged one representative match when Lancashire defeated Yorkshire, 26-10, before 13,000 in December 1925. Recs' last home game, on 22 April 1939, saw them beat York, 17-10 before losing their final game, 12-25 at Hull KR a week later. Honours were shared in the last St Helens derbies, Recs winning 5-4 at Knowsley Road on Christmas Day, 1938 before losing 3-5 at City Road on 2 January 1939

The Knowsley Road ground, meanwhile, staged its first international as war clouds loomed in 1939 when France defeated England, 12-9 before 10,000 spectators. It later

staged five Great Britain-France Tests between 1957 and 1971 and last staged an international when England played Russia in the 2000 World Cup. The ground was requisitioned by the Ministry of Defence and used as an air-raid warning post in 1940 and for fire watching. But Rugby League carried on with cattle from Cook's Farm allowed to graze on the pitch to keep the grass under control.

Denis got involved at Saints taking a blackboard around the ground to inform spectators of team changes and hanging up numbers on the scoreboard that was situated in the boys' pen.

"Fixtures in the war years were hit and miss," he recalls. "You would see a notice in the chip shop: 'Saints will play Dewsbury on Saturday'. Players would be unable to play at short notice and appeals would be made on a loudhailer to ask if there were any players in the crowd home on leave."

A new clubhouse was opened by Lord Derby on Boxing Day 1920 when Saints wore his racing colours, white jerseys and black shorts, for the occasion. The popular side stand was built, at a cost of £1,000, in 1925 after an appeal fund initiated by the newly set-up Supporters' Club. Within two years the structure had been extended to one of 70 yards in length, covering 16 terraces. In 1925 the club also bought the ground and pavilion from Pilkington Brothers with the assistance of a £2,500 mortgage advanced from Mr Sam Robinson of Greenalls Brewery. The loan was paid off in 1948. In 1930 Saints also bought the adjoining allotments, on which the car park and training pitch are built, for £1,000.

In 1926 Alf Ellaby scored two tries on his debut against Keighley. "He was a former soccer player who turned to Rugby League," Denis says. "He remains one of the all-time Saints greats. There was a wonderful story about Ellaby. One day a father took his son to see the stained glass windows at Low House Church. 'They are dedicated to saints,' the father explained. 'Which one is Ellaby?' the son replied. "When Alf died his ashes were scattered along the touch-line down the popular side in the corner where he scored many of his tries."

Work on the Kop at the Eccleston end commenced when post-war building restrictions were lifted and a terrace, with cover for 8,000, was constructed.

"Previously that end had been like a glorified slag-heap," Denis recalls. "But it could accommodate thousands of spectators who were seemingly banked up to the heavens." The Supporters' Club raised £6,000 for the project and the end was re-named the Edington Stand, in memory of George Edington, a former Supporters' Club official. Saints' record crowd was posted in 1949 when 35,695 saw them defeat Wigan, 15-8, on Boxing Day.

Alex Murphy made his St Helens debut against Whitehaven in 1956, the year in which Saints enjoyed a record 44-2 win over Australia.

A year later Tom Van Vollenhoven scored on his debut against Leeds. Denis's biggest hero remains the magical Murphy: "If you asked anyone over the age of fifty who's the greatest player to play for Saints the majority would say Alex. He was a magnificent player, absolutely sensational in his time."

But the South African wingman Tom Van Vollenhoven is not far behind. "He is still regarded in revered terms in this town," Denis says. "People say he is the greatest winger who ever lived. Whenever he comes back to St Helens people still flock to see him."

The ground took on more of its current-day appearance after the new main stand was erected in 1958 at a cost of £32,000. The rear of the stand overhangs the car park due to restrictions caused by the old railway branch line. Two club directors, Frank Yearsley and Jim Todd, who ran a building and steel company respectively, were heavily involved in the project. The new stand had only four steel supports, instead of the twenty-nine previously, and so spectators were happy. The seating capacity was 2,372. The seats of the old stand were given to Rochdale Hornets.

The new popular side, built at a cost of £15,000, opened in 1962 and the old

construction was dismantled, piece by piece, and transferred by road to Liverpool City's ground at Knotty Ash.

Floodlights were inaugurated in January 1965 when Saints played Other Nationalities before a 15,000 crowd.

The present offices and club shop were opened in 1972 and the restaurant complex a year later when singer Kathy Kirby topped the entertainment bill. In 1997 the dressing rooms were moved from the clubhouse to beneath the main stand.

In 1996 Liverpool Reserves began playing at Knowsley Road and in 2000 NWCL side St Helens Town left their Hoghton Road ground (a former home of Highfield) to move in as part of a grandiose plan called 'Sporting Club St Helens', that also incorporated Liverpool-St Helens RU club.

"But St Helens will never be anything other than a Rugby League town," Denis says. "The game is part and parcel of the town's fabric and the place is steeped in Rugby League football. Rugby League is a religion here and remains the major talking-point among the people."

Eric Ashton MBE grew up in Mulberry Avenue and the ground, just 50 yards away, had a magnetic appeal for him. "As a kid, I used to climb over the wall to watch the players train and get into matches as best I could," he recalls. "The gates always opened anyway five minutes into the second half.

"In the '40s Saints were just a run of the mill team and had no real stand-out stars. They never won any trophies and the ground was nothing spectacular. You could watch the game over the old main stand and the Edington end was just shale with the odd wooden sleeper for terrace."

Eric's glorious playing career was spent with Wigan but since retiring as a player, apart from one season as Leeds coach, he has served Saints as coach, director and chairman, and celebrated 50 years in continuous service to Rugby League in June 2005.

"Although I never played for Saints I was lucky to play in the golden era for

The great Alex Murphy

St Helens (shown celebrating their 2002 Super League Grand Final win) have enjoyed great success in the summer era

Rugby League when the crowds were huge," he says. "I was talking to Paul Sculthorpe recently and explained that we'd have loved the money some of today's top players are on but that they couldn't take away the times we had.

"Many of my greatest memories concern derby games at Knowsley Road. The pitch was always one of the best playing areas in the game - flat and well grassed and I loved playing on it. As a local lad there was always a lot of banter in the week leading up to a derby game. It was horrendous the week after if Wigan had lost. There is nothing in the game to match the atmosphere of a Saints-Wigan derby, that crackle and tension in the air just before kick-off is something else.

"St Helens people have no other distraction than Rugby League. Even Wigan has Wigan Athletic. Our soccer side never mounted a challenge to Rugby League and the town has always been dominated by the game. Knowsley Road has a tremendous atmosphere with 12,000 on and the summer era has been marvellous. But then Saints have always been an entertaining side to watch, playing expansive football."

Since the plans were hatched for Saints' new stadium, the club has gone through two chief executives, and the new ground scheme has been turned down by central government. But that doesn't displease Eric Ashton too much.

"It would be great if the club could stay at Knowsley Road and develop the facilities," he says. "It has always been a "walked-to" ground - even now, though the roads are full of cars, I think there are more walk than drive. There is a feeling we may have been left behind with other clubs getting new grounds.

"But the tradition of Knowsley Road is unbelievable."

SWINTON

Of all the great Rugby League venues that have disappeared over the last few years, Station Road was one of the most lamented.

Not least because there was no real way to say goodbye and a rich rugby tradition in Swinton stretching back over 120 years was lost virtually overnight.

The Lions closed their disastrous 1991/92 season (a campaign that realised just three league wins) with an 18-26 defeat against arch-rivals Salford before 3,487 spectators on 20 April 1992, and have never played in Swinton and Pendlebury, or in the top flight, since.

A month later came the devastating news for Swinton supporters that the ground had been sold to a housing company and Station Road, once a magnificent, atmospheric ground, was soon no more, replaced by yet another unremarkable housing estate.

The Lions opened up their next season eight miles away in Bury, in a ground-sharing arrangement with the Shakers that was never going to work, and overnight had seemingly lost over half their support.

Recent moves to share Salford City FC's ground in Kersal and the 2004 move to Sedgley Park RUFC's Park Lane ground, situated in the leafy suburb of Whitefield, have been more palatable to the Lions' long suffering fans, but the feeling persists that until the club returns to its roots, it will forever have a shiftless and nomadic feel. Park Lane has a capacity of about 2,500 with 312 seats in the main grandstand. But with its excellent social facilities and fine playing surface it has proved a popular short-term venue.

Steve Wild's magnificent history 'The Lions of Swinton' is one of the most comprehensive tomes ever written on any sporting club, all 644 pages of it, with detailed text laced with some superb atmospheric photographs. His chapter 'End of an Era' is compulsory reading for anyone wishing to get an understanding on just how much clubs like Swinton meant to the local people.

Thirteen years on, the open wounds from the move from Station Road still fester for the author, just as they do for legions of proud Swintonians.

"More than anything Station Road was part and parcel of the community," says Wild. "The club and the ground put Swinton on the map. Without it, it would be considered just another suburb of Manchester. There was an incredible sense of belonging, standing on the terraces at Station Road, and now that has been taken away I'll never feel that way again.

"That has been reflected in the crowds since Swinton's move. It is hard work to convince the Swinton public that the club represents them. There are still the four or five hundred die-hards that follow the club through thick and thin, but we have lost those casual spectators that maybe wandered to the ground after a few pints on a Sunday afternoon."

Wild's incredibly detailed researches keep alive the rich traditions of the Lions, one of the oldest rugby clubs in the country, formed in a schoolroom of St Peter's church in 1866, in what was then little more than a village of colliery and mill-workers' dwellings.

He traces the glory years of the 1880s when Swinton became one of the strongest teams in the country, their move to the Northern Union, made one year later than many in 1896 and their magnificent Challenge Cup Final win over Salford in 1900 at Fallowfield.

In the 1920s Swinton enjoyed perhaps their most glorious era, capped by the four-cups season of 1927/28, and crowds of 20,000 flocked to Chorley Road at a time when the population of Swinton was only 30,000.

In the early 'sixties the Lions enjoyed another brief spell of dominance, capped by two successive title wins in 1962/63 and 1963/64.

The deeds of great names of the past like Joe Mills, Jim Valentine, Bryn Evans, Jack Evans, Martin Hodgson, Albert Blan, George Parkinson, Alan Buckley and Ken Gowers and many more are recorded for posterity.

Ironically, Wild knew only struggle following the Lions, save for brief glimpses of glory like the 1987 Second Division Premiership Trophy win at Old Trafford. He first stepped into Station Road for the visit of the '71 Kiwis and was captivated.

"Swinton's troubles can be traced back to them not consolidating after the successes of the '60s," Wild maintains. "There was a legacy of mismanagement and the ground was allowed to go to rack and ruin. The opportunity was there - Station Road was a massive site, covering nearly eight acres, but from being built in 1929 never had a new structure."

Station Road was considered to be one of the finest venues in the game when it opened for business for Wigan's visit on 2 March 1929. Prior to that the Lions had played on the Chorley Road ground but had seemingly endless problems in agreeing security of tenure from the landowner, Tom "Totty" White.

The successes of the '20s persuaded the directors to look elsewhere after the landlord demanded another increase in rent and in 1928 work began on developing a site, that had been partly covered by allotments, next to the railway line. The total cost of the project was

ABOVE and RIGHT: Views of Park Lane, Sedgley Park

£11,665, over £5,000 above budget, including £2,000 for the land purchase, with the ground having a capacity of 45,000, twice that of the old enclosure. White had demanded £9,000 for the Chorley Road freehold.

Ironically, just as Station Road was to stage its last match without fanfare over 60 year later, Chorley Road staged its last game unheralded. Swinton defeated Leigh, 5-2, before 10,000 in a Challenge Cup-tie and when the next scheduled game, against Broughton Rangers, was frosted off, this proved to be the last game staged at Chorley Road.

Mr JC Robertson of J Gerard & Sons, a director of the club, supervised the new ground's construction and the 1,750-seater main stand from the Chorley Road ground on the New Cross Street side, was moved to the new ground, becoming the Townsend Road stand. Banking in front of this stand, later terraced, held up to 10,000 spectators. The popular side stand from Chorley Road, with cover for 1,800, was re-erected behind the posts at the Wolseley Street end and a new structure, adjoining the railway line, was built in the form of a 60-yard main stand, seating 2,000 with a paddock for 7,000.

Underneath the stand were the dressing rooms and offices and an assembly room that could hold up to 600 people. It was felt that there was sufficient scope to build up the bankings around the sides and extend the capacity to 60,000.

A crowd of 22,000 (producing receipts of £1,600) saw the opening game as Swinton defeated Wigan, 9-3, and Station Road immediately became the home for many big games in the Rugby League calendar, whereas Chorley Road had been restricted to just five

county games, two under rugby union rules.

Wigan soon returned to play St Helens Recs in a Challenge Cup semi-final tie that produced a crowd of 31,000. The game was drawn, 7-7. A year later a crowd of 37,169 saw them play St Helens in the second of thirty semi-finals staged there and the tie again finished level, 5-5.

Within ten months of its opening, Station Road staged the first of its nine Ashes Tests as Great Britain and Australia played out the only 0-0 draw in Test history. The crowd of 34,709 (£4,186) was the highest for a Test in Britain up until that point. Swinton loose forward Fred Butters made one of the most famous tackles in the history of Ashes tests to deny "Chimpy" Busch, the Kangaroos scrum-half, by the corner flag in the dying minutes of a grim struggle.

During the Second World War Station Road was requisitioned by the home guard and Swinton staged some home games at Salford, and the Ministry of Works had possession of the ground until November 1945.

In November 1951 Station Road staged the second Test against New Zealand, the first to be televised by the BBC, when 29,938 spectators witnessed Great Britain win, 20-19. Station Road staged 15 Tests in all, the last in 1967, and four other internationals, as well as 17 Lancashire Cup Finals.

The post war period was a boom time for crowds and a ground record was set when a crowd of 44,621 saw Wigan defeat Warrington, 3-2, in another Challenge Cup semi-final in April 1951.

Station Road staged the first of five Championship finals in 1965 and also was the venue for four Premiership Trophy Finals, the last in 1980.

A ground record for a Swinton game was set on a Wednesday afternoon in February 1964 when 26,891 spectators saw the Lions play Wigan in a Challenge Cup first round replay and triumph, 13-8.

Floodlights were inaugurated in 1964, fittingly against Rochdale Hornets, one of their longest-standing opponents dating back to the early rugby union days.

The last major game to be held there was the 1984 Challenge Cup semi-final between Leeds and Widnes.

With its full-size pitch and the tallest posts in the League, Station Road was a magnificent sight on a big match day with the expectant crowds surging up Station Road to the ground. The most famous, or infamous in Oldham eyes, semi-final was in 1964 when, with the Roughyeds winning 17-14 against Hull KR after eleven minutes of extra-time the game was abandoned due to the failing light. Rovers won the replay and Oldham were never to reach Wembley.

The Popplewell Report following the Bradford City fire of 1985 spelt the beginning of the end for Station Road. The capacity of the main stand was drastically reduced and the Townsend Road stand demolished on the insistence of the fire authorities. Initially a ground that had held eleven times that amount saw its capacity reduced to 4,000, later revised to 11,000.

Lifelong Swinton supporter Ian Jackson, a university lecturer, felt that the demolition of that stand was crucial. "Without it we lost that sense of enclosure," he says. "The view from there was one of the best in the Rugby League. And one of the biggest follies was building the squash courts at the Wolseley Street end. Piecemeal the ground seemed to disintegrate before your eyes. I remember taking my girlfriend, now my wife, to the ground and she refused to ever go in the toilets - they were just not suitable. The significance of the ground as a major venue disguised the level of decay going on around, year after year.

"I remember Widnes winning that 1982 semi-final. Keiron O'Loughlin scored a freak try in the last minute, when Mick Adams' kick rebounded off the bar, just as the Leeds fans were making plans for Wembley. The Leeds players all froze, they were wrong-footed and their fans around us were distraught. I remember thinking that I hoped Swinton never get that close.

"At Station Road, even towards the end, there were die-hards on the terraces that had supported the club in the glory days of the early '60s and their families had links with the great teams of the '20s. Every so often a great player of the past would present trophies to schoolboys on the pitch or such-like and maintain those links with the past, names like Blan, Johnny Stopford, Hodgson, Buckley and so on.

"Now those links to the past are not as strong. I always stood on the terrace in front of the main stand. It had the players' tunnel dividing the two sides. On one side you'd have the fans that entered from the Station Road side, at the other those from the Pendlebury and Agecroft areas. It was like the Berlin Wall - two sides of the borough and never the twain shall meet. There was one fan, wearing a flat cap and a raincoat - we called him "Mad Eric". He used to be vitriolic in his criticism of the team. One day the coach, Frank Barrow, was getting a load of grief and he had a go back at him. We never saw "Mad Eric" again.

"When the news came through that the ground was sold I was stunned. I didn't think it would ever happen but it had. And the money it was sold for - said to be £1m - never seemed to be enough for a site that size. I'm sure that was just the opening bid. I kept going

Swinton fans get behind the Lions at Sedgley Park

back to the ground until it was finally demolished. It was very sad as the ground was eventually left to the vandals. My only regret was that I never went into the changing rooms - they were sacred. When I decided to go it was too late."

Swinton switched their league game against Sheffield Eagles to Bolton Wanderers' Burnden Park ground during a particularly bad winter, in January 1985, taking advantage of their under-pitch heating. Only those present in the 1,438 crowd would remember the numbing cold that snowy evening.

Swinton later played St Helens and Wigan at Burnden during the 1985/86 season, sparking rumours of a possible full-time move to the ground. In February 1991 the Lions staged their Challenge Cup-tie against St Helens at Manchester City's Maine Road ground, again taking advantage of under-pitch heating, but the crowd of 2,922 seemed lost in the vastness of the stadium. A little more than a decade later it now seems inconceivable that a Rugby League game would be staged at a Premiership ground in such circumstances.

Quite what those early pioneers would have made of Swinton playing eight miles away in Bury is hard to imagine, but many were doubtless turning in their graves.

Some of the landmarks of Swinton's early history remain - their original headquarters at the Bull's Head and the White Lion, where they moved by 1873. That was how the nickname of "the Lions" was born and though the club moved back to the Bull's Head in 1898, it stuck.

Swinton initially played at a field off Burying Lane, just over the other side of the road from where Station Road was constructed and then at a meadow adjoining the now Pendlebury Road called Stoneacre, where they enjoyed a run of 63 games undefeated. But this site was too restrictive for developing and not properly enclosed.

To accommodate the growing crowds Swinton moved a stone's throw away to a three-and-a-half acre site adjacent to Cheetham Lane and New Cross Street, but known as Chorley Road after the main thoroughfare.

The ground was opened in 1886 with a 50-yard main stand, made of brick and wood and seating 1,000 and costing £600, built on the New Cross Street side.

When Swinton hosted the touring Maoris in 1888, a crowd of 7,500 paid receipts of £183.

In November 1901 the stand was destroyed by a fire, caused by the Wells Light used on training nights, and only the brick supports were left standing. This was replaced by a 75-yard long structure that later was moved to become the Townsend Road stand at Station Road. The ground then held 15,000, with cover for 3,500 and was considered to be one of the best equipped in Lancashire though the problems of the yearly tenancy were never far away. Chorley Road had its highest attendance on Good Friday 1925, when 22,000 spectators were present for the visit of Oldham.

In 1920 the first dressing rooms and directors room were built at a cost of £740 and the Chorley Road ground was one of the first in the League to be equipped with hot baths.

The site is now covered by housing. "I've often wondered what would have happened had Swinton remained at Chorley Road," Wild says. "Would we still be playing there? It was there that the club first achieved national fame, with Lancashire county players from 1878 and England rugby union internationals from 1882 onwards. It was a wonderful achievement for a small colliery town and a club of that size.

"Chorley Road was certainly more homely and very intimidating for the opposition. But the move to Station Road was a necessity for the club to develop. They were being held to ransom by the landowner at Chorley Road and were a victim of their own success. Station Road was a big stadium and we stayed within the confines of the town.

"Leaving Station Road was a stick-up - the supporters had no opportunity to do anything about it. Around the same time Leigh looked in danger of losing their ground but the fans got together and Hilton Park was saved. You've got to ask the question: 'Why?' Station Road was sold from underneath our feet and I'll never forgive the people that allowed that to happen.

"I, like many others, didn't want to go to Bury but we went with the dream that one day we would return to Swinton. I

Moor Lane

thought that if I, or the other loyal fans, gave up, that dream would be gone forever. But Bury was an apathetic soccer town and no one wanted to know. Swinton tried everything but there was nothing that worked.

"At Salford City we were fighting a constant battle against the soccer club. Even though the ground was council-owned they never intervened and the soccer people never made us welcome. At least the people at Sedgley Park are rugby people and we have been very much welcomed and it's nice to see, but a move back to Swinton remains the priority."

Gigg Lane, Bury

Gigg Lane, Bury FC's home since their formation in 1885, staged its first RL game on 30 August 1992 when Rochdale Hornets beat Swinton, 14-10, before 1,803 spectators.

In the fourth match to be held there Wigan legend Shaun Edwards scored ten tries in his side's 78-0 Lancashire Cup-tie win over the Lions.

Gigg Lane staged the Emerging Nations World Cup Final in 1995, when 4,147 saw the Cook Islands defeat Ireland, and hosted the 2000 NFP Grand Final when 8,487 saw Dewsbury defeat Leigh.

It staged its final game of RL on 14 April 2002 when just 428 saw Chorley defeat the Lions, 28-22.

Swinton had staged one home game, against Hunslet, at the Willows the previous season and before Moor Lane was ready played four "home" games at Leigh and another at Chorley. The former home of Manchester RUFC and then used by Langworthy ARLFC, Moor Lane has been home to Salford City FC since 1979.

Jackson differs slightly in his views but his general tenet remains the same. "I actually liked Gigg Lane but it was too far away from Swinton," he says. "Supporting Swinton since 1992 has been like a lingering death. I remember going to a fixture away to Bramley at Headingley and there was a stench of death in the air. It was actually Bramley that died soon afterwards, when I thought it would be Swinton. That day I felt there was no hope for the future of Rugby League - it was an incredibly depressing occasion.

"Since then we've had a few false dawns, like taking over a thousand fans for a Challenge Cup-tie at Wigan in 2003. I saw people I'd never seen for ages and that was a brief glimpse of how it used to be.

"I still feel there is hope. There have been some grim times but the club is still going and that is a miracle in itself."

WAKEFIELD

The number of existing grounds that staged Northern Union football in that momentous first breakaway season of 1895/96 is fast diminishing and now numbers just five.

Of those, Wakefield Trinity's Belle Vue ground is the oldest, staging its first match in 1879, followed by Batley (1880), Widnes (1884) and Leeds and St Helens (both 1890).

But newcomers to Rugby League visiting Belle Vue for the first time would hardly realise the ground's vast historical importance, nor perhaps be able to imagine the days when 30,000 crowds were commonplace for big games either side of the Second World War. Survived Belle Vue has, at times only just, but the ground bears little resemblance to the magnificent, atmospheric arena of its heyday.

Formed as part of the Holy Trinity Church Young Men's' Society in 1873, Trinity played at a number of different grounds, before taking up residence at Belle Vue. Their first ground was on Heath Common, still an oasis of calm and situated a short walk from the present ground, but the exact location has been lost in the mists of time.

They then moved to Manor Field, adjacent to the market area and a few hundred yards from the cathedral and then to Elm Tree Street, across the Doncaster Road from the present ground, near the Alexandra Hotel.

The year 1879 was a highly significant one for the fledgling club.

Trinity won the highly-prestigious Yorkshire Cup for the first time and went on to appear in nine finals over the course of thirteen years, winning on four occasions. Several sources confirm that they also marked the opening of the Belle Vue ground by taking on Birch, from Manchester, in what was an annual charity game between the two clubs on Easter Monday, 14 April 1879.

Gradually the primitive facilities were transformed. Hoardings made of canvas were erected along the Doncaster Road side to prevent non-payers from viewing the action and turnstiles installed in 1883, with the original small stand greatly enlarged. The field was then T-shaped, the first team playing on the present pitch with the second and third teams using a pitch that ran at right-angles to the main pitch, at the Agbrigg Road end. This field, known as Heathfield, was fenced off in 1887.

By the time Trinity became inaugural members of the Northern Union they had survived a potential threat of losing their ground due to the building of St Catherine's Road, which stopped at the turnstiles at the North End of the ground.

The club was run as a members' club until Wakefield Trinity Rugby League Football Club Limited was formed in 1991. But a separate company, Wakefield Trinity Athletic Company Limited, was incorporated in 1897 (and existed until it was dissolved in 1993) with the aim of raising the necessary capital to improve the ground.

This proved to be a successful venture. Extra land was purchased from St Catherine's School and a cycle track was laid around the perimeter of the field with cycling, athletics

and lacrosse staged in the summer months at Belle Vue.

At each end of the ground the standing area was moved back to accommodate the curved sweep of the cycle track but this was removed when the club officials realised that the income from occasional cycle meetings was nothing like that lost from spectators at rugby matches.

The re-constituted Belle Vue, incorporating an improved West Stand, behind which stood a new pavilion, was officially opened by the MP for Wakefield, Lord Milton, on 24 September 1898 for a game against Halifax. A crowd of 10,000 marked the occasion, most of the spectators standing on wooden footboards around the rest of the playing area, which was enclosed by strong wooden fencing.

In 1901 Wakefield attracted a crowd of 20,195 for a Challenge Cup-tie against Bradford and, to many observers' surprise, Belle Vue was chosen to host the 1902 Challenge Cup semi-final tie between Broughton Rangers and Hunslet.

By this time the accommodation for spectators had been extended by the banking-up of parts of the ground but the cramped entrances and exits were a source of concern. Belle Vue went on to stage a further eight such occasions, the last in 1964 when a post-war ground record crowd of 28,739 saw Widnes beat Castleford, 7-5, in a replay staged on a Wednesday afternoon.

There was a further accolade for Belle Vue when it hosted the replayed Championship Final of 1908 when Hunslet defeated Oldham, 12-2, before 14,054, after a 7-7 draw at Salford the previous Saturday.

Belle Vue staged its only international on Saturday 4 December 1909 when England defeated Wales, 19-13, before a disappointing crowd of only 4,000 (£90). Halfback Tommy Newbould, the only Trinity player on show, scored one of England's five tries. The game had begun in farcical manner with the Welsh fullback, Frank Young, wearing an England jersey. He later switched attire and wore a Trinity top.

Belle Vue also hosted the 1913 and 1915 Championship Finals, both won convincingly by Huddersfield.

In Trinity's jubilee year of 1923 Belle Vue staged its only Challenge Cup Final when Leeds scored six tries to one in defeating Hull, 28-3, before 29,335. In 1930 Belle Vue hosted another Championship Final when Leeds and Huddersfield played out a 2-2 draw in front of 32,095.

It staged its last Championship Final in 1932 when St Helens beat Huddersfield, 9-5, before 19,386.

Belle Vue has also hosted nine Yorkshire Cup Finals, the first in 1906 when Bradford's 8-5 defeat of Hull KR was watched by 10,500 spectators, the last in 1971 when Hull KR defeated Castleford, 11-7, before 5,536.

Trinity could also rely on pulling in big crowds for important club games, setting a new club record of 21,000 for Huddersfield's visit in a Challenge Cup-tie in 1920. This was easily surpassed a year later when the sides again faced one another in the competition before 30,676.

The great popularity of the game in the years after the ending of the First World War made further ground improvements essential if Trinity was to keep pace with rival clubs.

In 1924 the East Stand, now the present day Main Stand, was officially opened by the RFL chairman, Mr R Gale (Leigh). Built at a cost of nearly £4,000 it incorporated a full-length terrace with covered standing room for 5,800 and space for a further 2,750 on the present uncovered sunken paddock that was laid on the original cycle track. In 1952 bench seats replaced the covered standing part of this stand and consequently the capacity of the ground was substantially reduced.

The former West Stand, which had seating for 900, was officially opened in 1932 by Mr W Popplewell (Bramley), the RFL chairman, prior to a county game between Yorkshire and Lancashire.

It was a magnificently ornate structure, much loved by Trinity fans. Approximately 30 yards in length, the stand had a tiled pitched roof and an ornate roof fascia with four rear chimneys and housed the dressing rooms until they were converted to a refreshment room in 1964. Crowds passed through the stand by way of a small tunnel at the rear.

A new ground record for Belle Vue was set in 1933 when the Leeds-Huddersfield Challenge Cup semi-final attracted a crowd of 36,359. The two sides met at the same stage of the competition three years later when the record was extended to 37,906.

An aerial photograph of the ground taken at the latter game shows the crowd tightly packed on all four sides and confirms, amazingly, that there was just one narrow stairway at the South End of the ground for spectators to exit.

Ground improvements, aided by the contributions from an enthusiastic Supporters' Club, continued apace after the Second World War when concrete slab terracing at the Doncaster Road (North) Kop end was partially completed in time for the visit of the 1948 Australians. Terracing was then constructed at the opposite end and in 1958 this received some much-needed cover. The Mayor of Wakefield, Cllr M Fitzpatrick, officially opened the South Stand before a game against St Helens on 1 February 1958.

In 1962, when Belle Vue was used as the backdrop to the filming of "This Sporting Life", based on the novel by David Storey, the ground looked at its best and its magnificence was recorded for posterity.

It is still possible to obtain a video of the film, which starred Richard Harris as loose forward Frank Machin, and the contrast between Belle Vue of over 40 years ago and nowadays is a stark one. Some of the scenes were filmed prior to and during Trinity's Challenge Cup-tie against Wigan on 24 March 1962 when an all-ticket crowd of 28,254 was in attendance, just surpassing the turn-out of 27,614 between the two sides one month earlier.

In 1964, helped by a donation of £14,000 from the supporters, a new clubhouse with dressing rooms was built and St Catherine's School (demolished finally in 1983) was purchased to make extra room in the car-park.

The new £30,000 social club was opened in 1966 but this was soon wound up and two years later was taken over by a private concern and developed into Wakefield Theatre Club. It is now a ten-pin bowling alley and remains privately owned.

The present social club, known for many years as the Coach House, was built in 1983 and now, re-named CATS, is back in the club's ownership after a spell in private hands.

In the late 1970s the appearance of Belle Vue changed forever. The South Stand was dismantled and the banking at the Agbrigg Road end was levelled.

The stand, only 20-years old, was sold to a farmer for use as a Dutch barn.

At this stage it was widely expected that all or part of the ground would be sold for development as a superstore and there was the assumption that the local authority intended building a sports centre on the site.

That never happened, though with the club's debts mounting, the ground was sold to Wakefield District Council in 1986. It was a happy day for Trinity followers when the ground was sold back to the club in 1998.

The South End of the ground became eerily empty until 2000 when the Hospitality Stand was built there, at a reported cost of £750,000, as part of the short-lived reign of chief executive John Pearman. This Stand is now fully owned by the club, after reaching an agreement with the contractors following a long-running dispute over payments.

The 70-year-old West Stand was sadly demolished in 1986 as a result of new ground safety requirements in the aftermath of the Valley Parade disaster and replaced by a row of elevated executive boxes, topped by television scaffolding. The only seated accommodation is now in the East Stand, which has ten rows of seats for 1,700 spectators.

Norman Hazell, a former Mayor of Wakefield, remembers distinctly his first visit to Belle Vue.

"It was on 12 September 1945, and Trinity beat Leeds, 71-0," he says. "That game has always stuck in my mind." Norman lived nearby to Trinity star Ron Rylance, father of Mike, one of the founders of League Publications. "Ron scored two tries and kicked nine goals that day and then handed over the goal-kicking to someone else," he adds. "When he got home his mother played pop and said he'd wasted the chance to set a new club points record!

"Having been a regular at Belle Vue in the '40s and '50s it saddens me to see the ground now. The end where the Hospitality Suite stands was the end that we supporters clubbed together to provide cover and it had a great view of the pitch. I always stood at the other end with my family. You would meet so many people there and I've never seen trouble, even with crowds of 26-28,000. Those days there was a wonderful atmosphere, the spectators standing shoulder to shoulder on the banking."

Norman remembers the day he first set eyes on probably Trinity's most famous player, Neil Fox.

RECORD ATTENDANCE - 37,906 watch the 1936 Challenge Cup semi-final between Huddersfield and Leeds

"I saw him play as a schoolboy and you could see at 16 that he was going to be a Superman," he recalls. "But Fox never let it go to his head and remains to this day a lovely, modest man.

"Before Neil, we had a fantastic trio, Ron Rylance, Herbert Goodfellow and Len Marson, the hooker. Joe Egan, the famous Wigan hooker, always used to say he never enjoyed playing against Len because he could never get the better of him in the scrum.

"I have such happy memories of watching Trinity. When I was Mayor I organised a reunion of the early '60s team that won the Challenge Cup three times in four years and that was a special day. Wakefield remains a Rugby League town.

"Belle Vue was a green oasis with a wonderful, homely feel and an atmosphere all of its own. A lot of the older spectators don't go nowadays - they don't like the way Belle Vue or the game has changed. Professionalism has spoiled the game and players today don't have the same loyalty.

"But I love the thought of Wakefield continuing to play at Belle Vue and they deserve every encouragement. I'd love to see the support improving from the 3-4,000 crowds of today. It's a lovely city is Wakefield and it would be great to see Wakefield Trinity get the gates again."

Mike Rylance is currently researching a book on the history of Trinity, with his late father sure to feature strongly. "Bear in mind there is no other sport of any significance in Wakefield and in Wakefield Metropolitan District there is a population of about 300,000 with no other professional sport," he says. "Football is played, but at a lower level and Wakefield is still dominated by Rugby League. The club remains part of the fabric of the city.

"I met up with a few ex-players the other day and they were explaining that everybody talked Rugby League from Saturday night to Wednesday about the match just played and then from Thursday onwards about the game to come. But then there was a growing disaffection with the club, not the fault of the present administration, but an accumulation of problems from the late '70s and early '80s.

"Probably the greatest glory years of Wakefield were in the immediate post-war period and the early '60s when all sections of Wakefield society wanted to be part of the club. But then Belle Vue changed drastically. The covered end where the Hospitality Suite now stands provided a wonderful view. The West Stand was superb but the authorities were very nervous after the Bradford City fire and it was demolished. Belle Vue looked a picture when "This Sporting Life" was filmed. That big crowd against Wigan created a good impression. Richard Harris looked the part - he was a tall, rangy sort of bloke - and players and supporters were used as extras.

"With 20,000 on, Belle Vue had a great atmosphere and before the match there would be a huge throng of people going from the middle of town, over the bridge and along Doncaster Road, spilling into the road, and then going back again afterwards. It seemed as though the whole town was going to Belle Vue.

"One bad decision seemed to follow another with the ground, though at least that Hospitality Suite now fills that end and makes it look a bit better. The best thing Belle Vue still has going for it is the pitch - it is completely flat, drains well and copes well with a lot of hammer."

Belle Vue now stages soccer on a regular basis, with Leeds United playing their reserve fixtures at the ground. In 2000 Emley AFC, with new ground regulations from the Northern Premier League looming, were faced with spending vast, unwarranted amounts upgrading their three-sided Welfare Ground that had been perfectly adequate for their needs for a hundred years. They took the decision to re-locate at Belle Vue and the club is now known as Wakefield-Emley AFC. In their first full season at Belle Vue, in 2000/01, average gates went up from 289 to 536 and 3,708 saw a title decider against Stalybridge Celtic.

As for the future, Rylance concludes: "Trinity face a huge headache, trying to attract people back in a disaffected Rugby League town. There has been no end of plans to move to a new ground but they have all fallen through due to the withdrawal of business partners. The people at the club are working hard to stabilise matters and things on the pitch are looking better. But clearly Belle Vue can't stay as it is. It's sad to see the ground now. A lot of people are put off by the state it's in. They see the likes of Warrington's new ground, and Hull's and then they don't like going to a run-down old stadium."

Belle Vue has undoubtedly seen better days, but over the years the game's most famous players have graced its well-manicured turf and Trinity legends like Jonty Parkin, Neil Fox and Derek "Rocky" Turner have worn the Trinity colours with huge distinction.

The Maoris played there in 1888, the New Zealand All Golds in 1907 and the first Kangaroos a year later. Floodlights were switched on for the first time in 1967 when the Yorkshire county side hosted the Australians.

It has staged cup finals and club games that attracted huge crowds, five Roses Matches and as Rylance rightly points out: "It is a place of huge historical significance and resonance."

WALES

The history of Rugby League is littered with missed opportunities. But rarely can there have been a greater chance to establish the game outside its traditional boundaries than in South Wales nearly a century ago.

A decade or so after its formation, the Northern Union was facing huge problems in its hinterland, with many junior clubs struggling or having gone to the wall, unable to meet the costs of the new professional game. Of those clubs that survived there was another major worry, the increasing popularity of association football, whose spread was rapid, particularly in areas that were traditionally strongholds of the oval ball game.

Against this background the Northern Union sought to spread its boundaries, and South Wales was identified as an area ripe for expansion.

On the face of it, Welsh rugby union was in a good state, buoyed by the success of its international team, among whose notable scalps were the 1905 New Zealanders.

But behind the scenes there was considerable turmoil with underhand payments and veiled professionalism apparently as rife as they had been in Lancashire and Yorkshire prior to the 1895 split. The Valley clubs also found it well nigh impossible to arrange fixtures against the fashionable coastal clubs such as Cardiff, Swansea and Llanelli.

That part of Wales had much in common with the industrial regions of Lancashire and Yorkshire that spawned great rugby sides. Ebbw Vale, for example, was a heavily - industrialised town, the first coal-mining centre in South Wales, that later became known throughout the world for its iron and steel production. By 1900 a total of 154,571 men were employed in coalmines in South Wales and rugby was a sport that brought much-needed recreation from the rigours, hardships and drudgery of daily life.

Another factor behind the growing enthusiasm and support for entering the Northern Union came from the inducement of a fixture with Baskiville's professional New Zealand "All Golds" team that visited these shores in 1907/08.

At first it looked as though Aberdare would be the first club to enter, but that honour fell to Merthyr Tydfil, with Ebbw Vale following suit. The Ebbw Vale club turned professional with enthusiasm, adopted by a vote of 63-20 following a historic meeting. A limited company was formed and the club managed to secure the use of the Bridge End Field on favourable terms.

The players and officials were all suspended for life by the WRU, an action that caused a great deal of amusement, as the previous union club had not been in any way affiliated with the governing body.

Down the road at Merthyr the AGM of the rugby union club, know as Merthyr Alexandra, rejected professionalism, but a group of supporters, players and officials then decided to break away and set up their own professional club. Within a matter of days a ground had been found and many of the best players of the area had been persuaded to take part in the venture.

Cardiff's Millennium Stadium was a fitting venue for
the Challenge Cup Final in 2003, 2004 and 2005

To their dismay, Merthyr were unable
to secure a lease at the town's prime sports
ground, Penydarren Park, a cycling and
athletics ground and former home of the
union club, on the site of an old Roman fort.
In 1908 Merthyr Town AFC played there,
gaining admittance to the Southern League, as association football began to spread its
tentacles into South Wales.

Instead, Merthyr based themselves at a ground known as College Field, adjacent to
Penydarren Park. It was here that Merthyr staged the first Northern Union fixture in Wales,
on 7 September 1907, when 4,000 saw them defeated 6-25 by Oldham. College Field was
on the site of the present West End Bowls Club. One Northern Union game was staged at
Penydarren Park when the Welsh League beat the Australians, 14-13, before a crowd of
6,000 in January 1909. Later the ground staged Football League matches for Merthyr
Town, who were founder members of the Third Division in 1920 before failing to gain re-
election in 1930.

The fixtures had been arranged so that Merthyr and Ebbw Vale's home games did not
clash and the following week Salford were the visitors when the Bridge End Field staged
its first Northern Union fixture, running out 29-0 victors before another crowd of around
4,000.

The Bridge End Field was leased on an annual basis by the club and so the incentive
to spend large sums on ground improvements was reduced. There was a small wooden
stand and fencing around the ground was completed by November 1907. The changing

215

rooms were in the Bridge End Inn. In July 1908 a professional sports meeting was held to raise funds for a new stand and the levelling of the playing area.

The difficulties of trying to establish the game in those far-flung outposts were considerable.

The Northern Union had adopted the 13-man game and introduced many other rules that sought to make the game more attractive in the face of the increasing competition from soccer. It must have been a huge challenge for players who had learnt their skills in the Welsh rugby union to adapt to a completely new set of rules in double-quick time, particularly against some of the crack sides they encountered.

In addition to that, the travelling difficulties were huge. For away games in the north of England the sides had to set off by railway on the Friday afternoon, returning the following Sunday. The Northern Union granted the two clubs £10 for each away trip as a subsidy, but this barely covered the expenses of the trip. In no time some of the northern clubs were complaining about the costs and inconvenience of travelling to South Wales, even though they had only to make the journey once or twice a season.

Merthyr drew the better attendances but, after trouble on the terraces, some games had to be transferred to the Athletic Ground at Aberdare, where the visit of Wigan attracted a crowd of 6,000. This game was played immediately following the Wales-Ireland soccer international at the ground.

Baskiville's 'All Golds' attracted a crowd of 7,000 to Merthyr and 8,000 to Ebbw Vale, while the first full international played by Wales was a momentous occasion.

On 1 January 1908 Wales defeated the New Zealanders 9-8 before a 15,000 crowd at Aberdare. The success of this international persuaded the authorities to set up a first meeting with England, and 12,000 saw Wales victorious by 35-18 in a game staged at Pen-y-graig in Tonypandy on 20 April 1908.

At this stage the enthusiasm for the game was such that four new Welsh clubs joined the Northern Union during the summer of 1908.

Of these, the Aberdare club was thought to have the best prospects, having already staged some games in the town. Aberdare played at the Ynys Field ground, also known as the Athletic Ground, which they shared with Aberdare Athletic AFC. Their headquarters were at the nearby Locomotive Inn. A large complex, situated to the south-east of the town, the ground covered nearly six acres and had a cycle track around the playing area.

Aberdare drew 3,000 to their opening game against Wigan and, despite suffering a chastening 53-0 defeat, maintained decent crowds in their early months, the highest being 5,000 for the visit of Wakefield Trinity.

But the team won only one game during the season and failed to fulfil their final fixture, the return game at Wakefield, by which time home crowds were numbered in hundreds. Part of the banking of the ground, which once attracted a crowd of 22,584 for a schoolboys' soccer international in 1921, still exists, adjacent to the Aberaman RUFC (now known as Aberdare) ground and the town's leisure centre. Aberdare Athletic FC played in the Football League at the Athletic Ground between 1921 and 1927 before failing to gain re-election. Their highest gate was 16,350 against Bristol City in 1923.

The Mid-Rhondda club, whose official title was Mid-Rhondda Social and Athletic Club, played at the Athletic Ground, Pen-y-graig with their headquarters at the Cross Keys Hotel. With cycling and running tracks around the playing area, the site covered a full seven acres. But the club also folded after only one season, switching to professional soccer in time for the 1909/10 season and later joining the Southern League. An open space still

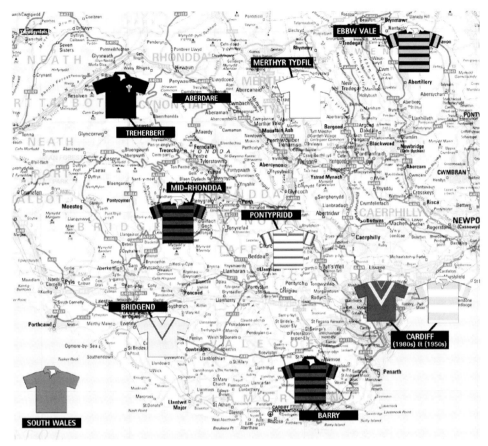

The Welsh clubs that have graced Rugby League

occupies the site, along Primrose Street.

Treherbert, an untouched idyll until the discovery of the black gold, coal, in the mid-nineteenth century, was another major coal-mining area. But although the town was again a major rugby area it could never really support a professional team. The club played its games at the Athletic Ground, near to the railway, that had been used previously by the local rugby union team, with their headquarters at the Dunraven Hotel.

Treherbert struggled on for two seasons, playing only 12 games in 1909/10 before resigning from the league. Their biggest attendance was one of 4,000 for the visit of the Australians in November 1908. The ground was later built upon for light industry.

The building of Barry docks at the end of the nineteenth century saw that town grow enormously and by 1913 it was the largest coal exporting port in the world, with a population of around 40,000. But again, the town was too small to support a professional team for long.

Barry were hit from the start when the local council refused them permission to play a professional sport at the Butterills ground that had been home to the rugby union team.

Instead they took a ground at Trinity Street, but this was thought to be a far from ideal location. Situated at the top of a hill overlooking the Bristol Channel, the ground was cold and windswept and there was also a pronounced slope from one touchline to the other.

217

Barry's highest crowd was only 2,000 for their game against Leeds and they managed only one season before folding. The ground is now partly covered by housing.

Merthyr, meanwhile, moved to a new ground on Rhydycar Road in time for the 1909/10 season. The ground was also used for cricket, tennis and athletics and was described as having a much flatter and better-maintained playing surface than that of the former enclosure, which was "a veritable terror for opponents." The club built a grandstand there but the crowds continued to decline, and the club resigned from the League on 2 January 1911 after being unable to pay the rent.

That left Ebbw Vale as the only surviving team in Wales and their resignation from the League, on 3 September 1912, spelt the end of the Welsh adventure. Ebbw Vale had staged three internationals, two against England and the other against the Australians in 1911 that attracted a gate of 7,000. Their final club game was against York on 20 April 1912.

After the end of the First World War the Ebbw Vale club was revived and joined the WRU. The ground, renamed the Ebbw Vale Welfare Association Sports Ground in 1923, later staged a number of Rugby League games, notably in October 1984 when England beat Wales 28-9 before a crowd of only 2,111. The attendance was affected by the game being televised across Wales. By this time the ground was council owned and renamed Eugene Cross Park, in honour of the long-serving chairman of the welfare trustees. Over 900 feet above sea level and incorporating six acres of fields, the site became a regular home for Glamorgan in county cricket, and was also home for the town's soccer club, who staged a European Intertoto Cup-tie there in June 1997.

A bid to revive the game in Wales came in 1926 when Pontypridd were admitted to the League - alongside Castleford. Their home games were staged at Taff Vale Park, Treforest, previously home to the town's rugby union club and later to the Pontypridd soccer club, who had played in the Southern League.

The Taff Vale Park Company bought the ground, initially for the promotion of professional athletics and cycling. Said to be capable of holding 30,000 to 40,000 people in comfort, the ground had a stand that seated 2,850. Situated twelve miles north of Cardiff at the junction of the Cardiff to Rhondda and Merthyr railway lines, the town had excellent communications, but any hope of the game being established were ended by the savage economic decline experienced by Pontypridd and the Valley towns at that time.

With the soccer club having folded and the union club in a poor financial state, portents had been good, especially after the Rugby League purchased the ground from the Taff Vale Park Company and agreed a short-term lease with the club. Taff Vale Park had staged the Wales-Australia game in December 1921, when there was a crowd of 11,000. In April 1926 Wales played England before 23,000 spectators. Pontypridd attracted a crowd of 10,000 for their opening game against Oldham. There was a crowd of 18,000 for the international between Wales and New Zealand in December 1926, but as the season wore on the club's attendances declined and it became increasingly difficult to fund expensive away trips north.

Pontypridd resigned from the League early in their second season after playing only eight games and the demise of the club also killed off a lot of the interest in local amateur leagues, particularly when the WRU gave a full pardon for all concerned in the ventures.

Pontypridd's final home game, against Oldham, on 22 October 1927, realised a gate of only £24. The ground was sold to the Greyhound Racing Association in September 1927 and later also staged speedway, trotting and boxing. Taff Vale Park did stage one further

Rugby League game when Wales beat England, 3-2, before 12,000, in 1936, but the site is now used as a school rugby ground.

Between 1935-38 Wales played three internationals at Stebonheath Park, Llanelli, the former home of the defunct Llanelli AFC. The first game, against France, attracted a crowd of 25,000. The ground also staged greyhound racing and, in 1951, an exhibition RL game was played as part of the Festival of Britain celebrations. Llanelli AFC reformed in the late 1950s and still play at the ground in the Welsh Premier League.

In the immediate aftermath of the Second World War, in November 1945, a record 30,000 crowd saw Wales beat England 11-3 at the St Helen's ground in Swansea, home of Swansea RU and one of Glamorgan CCC's venues.

A year later the fixture attracted a gate of 25,000. The Swansea club had closed down during the war and surrendered their lease to the local council. This gave the RFL the opportunity to hire a ground that from 1882 to 1954 was an international venue for the WRU. But by 1951 the gate for the Wales-Other Nationalities international was down to 5,000.

Wales returned to St Helen's in 1975 when a crowd of 15,000 saw the first ever Sunday Rugby League game in the Principality and the first international in the country for 24 years. Wales marked the occasion by defeating France, 21-8, but the last of 15 internationals at the ground came in 1978 when only 4,250 saw the Australians given one of the hardest games of their tour before running out 8-3 victors.

Post-war interest in the game was such that a Welsh Rugby League was developed in 1949, inspired by the success of a promotional tour by the Huddersfield and St Helens clubs, whose exhibition game at the council-owned Park ground in Abertillery had attracted a crowd of 29,000. Other exhibition games were played at Pontardulais and Bridgend.

Wales played three internationals at Abertillery between 1949-51, attracting 8,000 for the visit of England in 1950 and the venue remains the local rugby union club's ground.

One of the clubs in the Welsh League was based in Cardiff, and the success of the venture led to their application to join the Rugby League in April 1951.

Cardiff played at the Penarth Road Stadium, which they leased from Speedway Racing (Cardiff) Limited. There were 2,000 seats in a ground that could hold 30,000 and the playing area was thought to be equal of anything in the Rugby League.

Rugby League had previously been staged in the Welsh capital on 14 November 1928 when Wales entertained England at the Sloper Road Greyhound Stadium, Grangetown. A crowd of 15,000 saw England win 39-15. The venue was also known as the White City Stadium and also staged speedway between 1928-37. Covered on three sides, the ground was situated a few hundred yards on the opposite side of the road from Cardiff City AFC's Ninian Park and became Guest Keen's Sports Ground before being eventually demolished in 1984 for housing.

Cardiff's opening home game against Widnes on 22 August 1951 attracted a crowd of 2,500 at the Penarth Road Stadium, but attendances soon dropped markedly and the visit of Workington Town saw just 199 paying spectators.

Cardiff's first season was also their last. And after losing 59-14 to Wigan in their final home game - watched by a crowd of 1,450, in a match played at Mainde Stadium, which staged events for the 1958 Commonwealth Games - Cardiff were effectively thrown out of the League as the management committee did not consider them a sound proposition.

Speedway meetings were held at Penarth Road from 1951-53 but failed to attract decent crowds and the stadium was left in a derelict state until it was built upon in 1969.

Talbot Athletic Ground, Aberavon

Morfa Stadium, Swansea

One of the roads on the new site was named Stadium Close, the only lasting reminder of another failed attempt to establish Rugby League in Wales.

Cardiff's failure eventually led to the Welsh League losing its purpose, and it was finally abandoned in 1955.

The next venture was also in the capital a generation later at a time when football clubs were seeking to maximise their income. In 1981, a year after Fulham's entry, a bid to launch the Cardiff Blue Dragons at Ninian Park was accepted. Cardiff attracted a crowd of 9,247 for their opening game against Salford, but in no time at all home games were watched by a small hardcore of fans, falling from an average of 2,008 in their first season to 581 by their third. Those fans looked lost in a ground capable of holding 46,000 people. In April 1984 a home game against Huyton was switched to Ebbw Vale where the gate of 1,400 represented the club's highest of the season. Rugby League returned to Ninian Park for the 1995 World Cup when 10,250 saw Wales beat France.

After three seasons Cardiff City quit Rugby League. A group of businessmen bought the club and moved it to Bridgend where they played at Coychurch Road, the local soccer club ground. After attracting a crowd of 1,983 for their opening game against Swinton, gates fell dramatically and each of the last seven home games failed to attract a gate of over 200. Bridgend lasted only one season, attracting only 148 for their final home game against Doncaster on 21 April 1985.

Another bid to establish a club side in Wales came in the first summer season of 1996 when the South Wales club was set up by Mike Nicholas and Clive Griffiths. South Wales staged home fixtures at the Talbot Athletic Ground, Aberavon, Cardiff Arms Park and had one game at the Morfa Stadium in Swansea, and enjoyed a respectable playing record in the second division.

But with little prospect of securing a franchise bid for Super League, the club folded after only one season, the Welsh public clearly reluctant to watch anything other than top-class Rugby League. South Wales' highest gate was 1,876 against Hull KR, at Aberavon, but they did play Carlisle as a curtain raiser to the Sheffield-St Helens Super League game in Cardiff with the main event attracting 6,708. South Wales' final home game, against York, saw 400 attend the fixture at Cardiff Arms Park.

Attempts were still being made to nurture Rugby League in the Principality, with varying degrees of success. Cardiff RU's ground, then in the shadow of the development that became the magnificent Millennium Stadium, also staged the 'On the Road' fixture between Warrington and Castleford in 1998, before a crowd of 4,437. The following day,

Brewery Field, Bridgend

Vetch Field, Swansea

Swansea City's Vetch Field ground had 8,572 for the Wigan-Saints game.

That ground earned its place in folklore in the 1995 World Cup when Wales's memorable victory over Western Samoa attracted a crowd of 15,385. But four years later there were only 812 for the European Championship encounter against Ireland.

Newport RU's historic Rodney Parade ground staged the London-Warrington game in 2000 with 4,174 in attendance and there were fewer than that when London "entertained" Widnes at Aberavon in 2003.

In North Wales, Wrexham's Racecourse Ground staged the Wales-Cook Islands game in the 2000 World Cup before 5,017 on a dismally wet Sunday evening, and attracted 6,373 for the England international in July 2001.

Rugby League returned to Llanelli for the 2000 World Cup but only 1,497 turned up at the rugby union club's Stradey Park - on one of the most depressing evenings of the tournament - as Wales met Lebanon.

Finally, the Millennium Stadium became the latest Rugby League venue, staging the double header in the 2000 World Cup with Wales against New Zealand preceded by the Cook Islands-Lebanon encounter. The 17,612 crowd was a decent turn-out but with only 8,746 present for the international against the Kiwis in 2002 the magnificent stadium was eerily empty.

The successful staging of the 2003 Challenge Cup Final between Bradford and Leeds, however, showed the full potential of the stadium being realised. A crowd of 71,212 saw the Bulls edge home, 22-20. The 2004 (when St Helens defeated Wigan, 32-16 before 73,734 spectators) and 2005 finals followed.

In 2003 the Wales-Australia international was staged at the Brewery Field, Bridgend, Australia running out 76-4 winners before 3,112 spectators. The ground was originally leased by RL's Welsh Commission in 1949. The local rugby union club were briefly turfed out but later returned in 1957 after the Welsh League collapsed. The venue staged an international exhibition game in 1950 when a South Wales XIII defeated the Italian tourists 29-11 before 2,500.

And that sums up Rugby League in Wales - potential without realisation after nearly a century of trying with great successes outnumbered by heartbreaking failures.

In 2005 a new club, Celtic Crusaders, was admitted to the RFL for the 2006 season. Based at Bridgend's Brewery Field they brought the RFL's member clubs up to 34 and a new chapter in the history of Welsh Rugby League awaits writing.

WARRINGTON

Wilderspool was home to Warrington for over a hundred years but, sadly, its days are now coming to a close. The old ground may be tired, showing its age and, for the last thirty years, effectively three-sided, but it has an atmosphere and a feel all of its own.

Warrington moved to Wilderspool in 1898 for their fourth season in the Northern Union. After a nomadic existence following their formation in 1879, Warrington had settled, from 1883 onwards, a stone's throw from the present ground in Wilderspool Road, where Fletcher Street stands today. A ground record attendance of 10,000 was established for a game against Widnes and Warrington was also chosen by the Lancashire RFU to stage a county game in 1889. But the ground struggled to accommodate crowds of around half that number in comfort and a move became inevitable.

When a section of the ground was needed for the houses that currently stand on Fletcher Street, it appeared as though the club might have to leave the Wilderspool area for pastures new. But, happily, agreement was reached on a ten-year lease with the brewers, Greenall Whitley & Co, for an adjacent patch of land that had formerly been used as a rugby pitch by an amateur club, Latchford Rovers.

So began a long relationship between the club and the famous company, whose main brewery building had long been established on Wilderspool Causeway, and the development of the Wilderspool ground could begin.

The first year's rent was £48 and the club spent £251 removing the Fletcher Street fencing and establishing the boundaries of the new ground. A new grandstand quickly sprung up on the side where the current cantilever stand is built and the grandstand was moved from the old ground to the opposite side off Priory Street and turnstiles placed at the entrances.

Many Warrington spectators found it hard to adjust to the new location, as the main approach down Fletcher Street, as it does today, involved walking through part of the old ground. But Wilderspool soon became a home from home. A further ten-year lease was granted in 1908 and six years later Warrington purchased the freehold. The ground was held in trust for members of the club until a limited company was formed in 1941.

Warrington fans soon had a hero in winger Jack Fish, reckoned to be the greatest Warrington player until the sudden emergence of the brilliant Australian winger Brian Bevan, whose phenomenal try-scoring achievements, including 740 for the Wire between 1945 and 1962, are detailed in Robert Gate's superbly-crafted biography, recently published.

The distinguished Warrington historian, Ernie Day, lives just a short walk from Wilderspool and his memories of the famous old ground go back eighty years. Like so many people who went on to become ardent fans, Ernie's introduction to the game of Rugby League was courtesy of his father.

Wilderspool

"Wilderspool has always been like a magnet for me," he recalls. "I was eight-years-old when my father took me to my first match. Warrington played St Helens Recs and it was winter-time. Straw had been used to protect the pitch and this was piled around the perimeter. My mother was adamant that I was not big enough to go but my father persisted. There was a wooden fence around the pitch and, as kick-off time approached, the crowds got thicker and thicker.

"Standing next to us was a chap with one leg, he'd lost the other in the First World War. He decided to get over the fence and sit on the straw and he got my father to pass me over to sit next to him. As time went on, I could feel the water seeping through the straw into my trousers and I complained to my father. But the chap simply spread out his wooden leg and told me to sit on that. So I watched my first game at Wilderspool sat on a wooden leg."

So began a love affair with Wilderspool that Ernie keeps to this day. He went on to play for Halifax until, like so many of his contemporaries, his career was interrupted, and effectively ended, by the Second World War.

"I played on Wilderspool as a schoolboy, it was a dream come true," Ernie recalls. But he never realised his ambition of playing at Wilderspool in the professional game. "I was down to play for Halifax there after the war but I was nowhere near fit," he recalls. Years as a prisoner of war had left their mark. "My shoulders, knees and arms were going," Ernie adds.

Instead, Ernie settled to researching Warrington's history and keeping immaculate records on the club's fortunes. "Jack Fish was my dad's hero," he recalls. "My dad was a wire-drawer and he used to earn a few bob on the quiet making fish-shaped brooches out of wire and selling them before the games. Fish must have been a marvellous player and it took my father a while to accept that Bevan was the better of the two."

Warrington drew 3-3 with Swinton in the first game staged on the Wilderspool ground before 7,000 spectators on 3 September 1898. In 1906 Wilderspool staged the first of four Challenge Cup semi-finals and the ground began to take shape after the first stage of a new main stand was opened before a game against Leigh in 1911. Originally erected at a cost of £1,500 and seating 900 (increased to 1,500 in the mid-1920s) it was a distinctive structure, with its pedimented gable and flagpole. A month later Wilderspool staged its first representative game as Lancashire lost 7-28 to Cumberland before 4,000 spectators.

The players entered the pitch from the Fletcher Street end from a dressing room hut that doubled up as a refreshment kiosk. "There was a drop-down shelf and they served bottles of beer and stout to the spectators," Day explains. "The railway end was merely an ash bank before terracing was built that went back considerably higher than today." New dressing rooms were opened under the main stand in 1934.

The 1926/27 season was notable as Wilderspool staged the Lancashire Cup Final as St Helens beat St Helens Recs, 10-2 before 19,439 spectators and the Championship Final, as Swinton beat St Helens Recs, 13-8, before 24,432. A new ground record was established at the 1934 Championship Final when 31,565 saw Wigan beat Salford, 15-3, and the ground staged a number of other big games before the commencement of hostilities in 1939. Wilderspool was commandeered and the main stand was used as a storeroom.

The boom post-war years, with Bevan the idol of the town, saw the ground's largest crowds gather at Wilderspool. A record crowd of 34,304 saw the league game against Wigan in 1949 and over 33,000 saw the Lancashire Cup Final between Leigh and Wigan later that year, though 35,000 tickets had been sold.

"Bevan was just unbelievable, a one-off," Ernie explains. "You just can't compare him to any other player. He was so unlike an athlete and yet he was a phenomenon. I remember one match when the Leigh winger, Nebby Cleworth, was given the task of marking Bevan. When the teams came out after half-time he had a string, six-feet long, tied

to his wrist and he tried to tie the other end to Bevan's wrist.

"My wife, who stayed at home on match days, used to say she could tell how many tries Bevan had scored that afternoon by the noise of the crowd. It reached a crescendo when Bevan went over the line."

In the late 1950s the cover on the Priory Road stand was extended along the full length of the touchline and later the Fletcher Street end was covered.

But Wilderspool's appearance was changed out of all recognition when a £300,000 leisure centre was built on the Priory Road side in 1972.

Wilderspool had become a three-sided ground, apart from a small number of seats for vice-presidents and life members but the edifice, constructed under the watchful eye of directors Ossie (later Sir) Davies and Brian Pitchford heralded a new era for the club.

Under player-coach Alex Murphy, Warrington emerged from a period in the doldrums to become one of the game's dominant forces.

Kevin Ashcroft was an integral member of the side that reached Wembley twice in the mid-1970s and later returned to coach the club for six seasons.

"Sir Ossie, God rest his soul, was a gentleman and he and Brian had a vision for the club," Ashcroft says. "There was a concert hall, bars, saunas and squash courts, just like Salford had done at the Willows under Brian Snape. The spectators could watch the match and then stay on and have a meal and watch the cabaret. People like Sir Ossie were entrepreneurs but they were in the game for what they could contribute, not what they could take out."

Warrington became a team once more feared throughout Rugby League. "Opposing teams just hated coming to Wilderspool," Ashcroft adds. "There was an incredible atmosphere at the ground. Warrington spectators have always been the same - they work hard and they play hard and they love their Rugby League. That was proven a few years ago when the team served up rubbish week after week but the fans still kept turning up.

"It's a great ground, Wilderspool, and it holds nothing but good memories. Murphy always played behind a gigantic pack and opposing teams were intimidated. No one wanted to come to Warrington.

"Murphy also built a lovely, family atmosphere. We played on Saturdays in those days but never got home till Sunday afternoon at the earliest. The players played together and socialised together. My wife, Janet, and me have been married 40 years and it's only recently that she realised that Workington, Barrow and Whitehaven are in England - when we played there we were away that long she thought they were in Ireland."

Bob Eccles, the club's highest try-scoring forward, still goes down regularly to Warrington. "My era as a player was 1977-87 and they were fantastic times," he recalls. "We had some great players. I caught the tail end of Tommy Martyn and there was Ken Kelly, Mike Nicholas and the greatest goal-kicker I ever saw, Steve Hesford. The crowd was that used to him kicking goals they used to boo if he missed one from the touch-line.

"The crowd was great and I had a good relationship with them. At Wilderspool the crowd got behind the side through thick and thin. I was at the Boulevard for the last match there and was speaking to Len Casey. Even he admitted he would go anywhere but Wilderspool as a player - and he was a fearless competitor."

"It will be sad when Wilderspool is no more," Eccles said before Warrington finally left the old ground. "But I'm sure the people designing the new ground won't let that Warrington atmosphere slip away. There will be something in the new ground to refresh the old supporters and encourage the new ones."

In 1973 Wilderspool staged its one and only Test match as Australia clinched the Ashes with a 15-5 victory on a frost-bound surface before 10,019 spectators. Eighteen tons of straw had been laid to protect the pitch and there was a suggestion that the Australians' convincing win was largely due to their unfamiliarity with the alien conditions. Many of the British players, by comparison, looked tentative on the frozen surface. Second row Ken Maddison scored two of the Australians' five tries.

One of the most famous international games staged at Wilderspool was during the 1995 World Cup when New Zealand defeated Tonga, 25-24, in a match that captivated the crowd of 8,083. Tonga threatened one of the all-time upsets as they led 24-12 with ten minutes to go before the Kiwis staged a late revival, capped by skipper Matthew Ridge's injury-time winning field goal. In the Emerging Nations World Cup of the same year there was the 'Battle of the Super-Powers' as Russia defeated USA, 28-26, before 1,950 spectators.

Warrington's main stand, where Bevan had taken his farewell salute to his legions of admirers in 1962, was burnt down in 1982, shortly after Ashcroft's appointment as coach. Not that the two events were connected.

"When I was appointed, Brian Pitchford told me he wanted me to set the club alight and rebuild the club," Ashcroft laughs. "But I didn't think he meant it literally.

"All the players were real characters but some were thicker than submarine rivets. I remember Chissy (prop Dave Chisnall) picking an argument with the trainer, an ex-boxer in his 70s, who lined up Queensbury Rules style and laid him out with a single punch."

The new stand was opened in February 1983 with seating for just over 2,000 and, with covered ends, Wilderspool was one of Rugby League's most compact and intimidating arenas. Later the stand was renamed the Brian Bevan Stand. But the fourth side, with the club selling the leisure centre some years ago stripped the ground of much of its charm. Originally completed for £300,000 in 1972 on the Priory Street side of the ground when the old stand roof was transferred to the railway end, the complex was designed to help Warrington compete with clubs such as Salford who transformed their social facilities.

"The building of the club changed the whole character of the ground and, in recent years, became a bit of an eyesore," Ernie Day says. "It rapidly deteriorated and took the heart out of the ground."

But Wilderspool remained one of Rugby League's traditional homes and more than a few paused for silent reflection when it staged its final Warrington game. The home of Fish, Brian and John Bevan, Parry Gordon, Harry Bath, George Thomas, Albert Naughton, Cod Miller, Gerry Helme, Murphy and so many other Warrington legends will pass into folklore.

How will Ashcroft remember Wilderspool? "Above all for its atmosphere, something that was unique," he says. "The atmosphere was incredible, always has been. As a player, standing behind the posts at the Fletcher Street end, you could be feeling really down after conceding a try.

The great Brian Bevan

"But the Warrington fans have such a joviality and comradeship about them, they would start shouting and singing. They are tremendous people. From standing there, head bowed and feeling down at heel, thirty seconds later they would buck you up that much you were ready to take on the world. You felt like King Kong."

Warrington brought the curtain down on Wilderspool in fitting style, defeating Wakefield in the final league game, 52-12, on 21 September 2003, to qualify for the play-offs for the first time in the summer era. A crowd of 9,261 saw Australian Sid Domic score the final try that ensured rapturous scenes after the final whistle. Domic's fellow-countryman, Graham Appo, was the star of the day with a hat-trick of tries. "I am delighted with the way the players have performed today," said the Warrington coach, Paul Cullen. "Today's atmosphere was unique and went beyond everything we have witnessed before. It was very emotional and personal and the players handled it well."

Wilderspool was given a fitting send-off with a rendition of 'Abide With Me'. Cullen added: "It was a performance that does justice to the great players who have honoured this club throughout its entire history. I have to thank them publicly for doing so."

Wilderspool remains, at least for the moment, as a community stadium and a training venue. The Wolves under 18s and 21s teams play there, as do the service area teams and Warrington Wizards, who compete in National League 3. It had a rather prolonged send-off with a number of first-class games staged after the Wakefield 'finale' including a low-key tour game when a Warrington team largely made up of youngsters beat the New Zealand A tourists, 28-26. The final of the European Championship, between England and France, on

Nathan Wood celebrates scoring the first try at Warrington's new home with Brent Grose and Jon Clarke

16 November 2003 attracted a crowd of only 2,536 to witness a one-sided game won 68-6 by England. In February 2004 Crosfields hosted Workington Town in a Challenge Cup-tie at Wilderspool, losing 14-46 before a crowd of 768.

A change was first mooted in 2000 when Warrington announced they would be moving into a new 12,000 capacity stadium (the capacity was subsequently revised slightly upwards) in a joint scheme with Tesco, with the joint planning application finally given approval after a protracted series of meetings and inquiries. The final site lay-out was agreed in May 2002 and the stadium was officially handed over to Warrington Wolves from Barr Construction in October 2003.

Built on the former site of the old Carlsberg-Tetley Brewery off the A49 leading northwards from the town, the Halliwell Jones Stadium (named after a car dealership on a ten-years naming rights' agreement) is a state-of-the-art purpose built venue. One of its notable and most popular features is the way that two sides have included standing areas rather than it being an all-seated stadium. It also has enormous pitch dimensions of 120m x 74m.

The official capacity is 14,206 and that was reached exactly as Wakefield Trinity Wildcats provided the opposition on a Saturday evening, 21 February 2004 - Warrington's highest home gate since 1973. "In my time here, since 1980, I've never been past a 'sold-out' sign," Cullen remarked. "Hopefully, that's the sign of things to come. The biggest job now is maintaining that momentum. I honestly don't think we've lost any of that Wilderspool spirit by moving across town."

Warrington's Australian halfback, Nathan Wood, had the honour of scoring the first try after five minutes with captain Lee Briers going on to enjoy an outstanding individual game in the Wolves' 34-20 victory.

Already the stadium has staged other major fixtures, including the 2004 Challenge

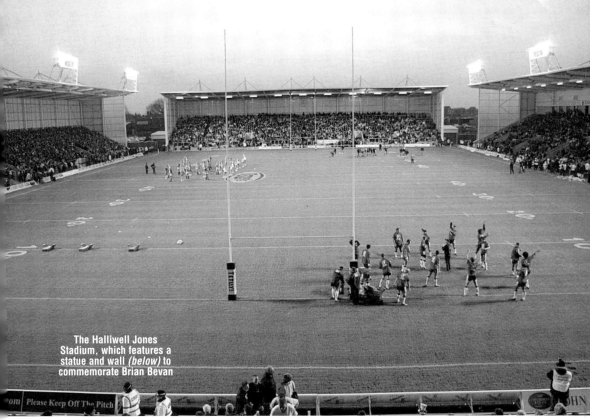

The Halliwell Jones Stadium, which features a statue and wall *(below)* to commemorate Brian Bevan

Cup semi-final between St Helens and Huddersfield (when a crowd of 13,134 saw Saints triumph, 46-6) and the 2004 European Nations Final when England defeated Ireland before 3,582. In 2005 it was also a venue for the Women's Euro 2005 soccer tournament.

In a poignant act, a statue to commemorate Brian Bevan, erected in 1993 and which stood on the 'Brian Bevan island' on Wilderspool Causeway was moved by popular local consent and re-erected at the Halliwell Jones Stadium.

Jon Clarke, the Warrington hooker, is delighted with the new stadium. "Wilderspool was a compact ground with the crowd tightly packed around three sides," he said. "It was a great place to play and the opposition often found it very intimidating, which was to our advantage. The Halliwell Jones Stadium has managed to take the best parts of Wilderspool but has also moved on a million miles. The crowd is again right on top of the action and the atmosphere is fantastic. The decision to keep two sides of the stadium for standing has been a big success. The playing pitch is superb and the facilities are terrific. It felt like home as soon as we played our first match there."

WHITEHAVEN

The game of Rugby League has long been part of the culture for many people in the seaboard town of Whitehaven, once the second leading port in the country for its trade with the Americas and latterly a leading centre of the coal-mining industry.

A senior club was formed in 1948, three years following Workington Town's admission to the Rugby League but the Recreation Ground, known locally as the Recre', had already forged its reputation in the game's folklore.

The decision to apply for membership was taken following the meeting at Kells community centre in February 1948 and, three months later, the club was admitted, albeit with a far from enthusiastic vote of 14-11 from member clubs with three clubs failing to register a vote. Workington, with an example of the kind of blinkered approach that has often blighted our great game, were leading the opposition.

Whitehaven's first game as a senior club came in August of that year when Hull's visit, on a day of unceasing rain, attracted a crowd of 8,982, the dreadful weather accounting for the shortfall from the anticipated 15,000 turn-out.

Formerly marshlands, the Recre' had been home to the Whitehaven Colliery Recreation FC, or the 'Recs' as they were known, from 1895 until 1936 when the club folded. The Recs soon went over to the Northern Union game and their greatest achievement came in 1908 when, as a junior club, they beat St Helens, 13-8, in the first round of the Challenge Cup before a crowd of 2,000.

Conditions at the ground in those days were primitive with a 50-foot long structure on the site of the present main stand providing the only cover. The Victorian pavilion and dressing rooms were situated outside the main gates, a situation that remained until 1986.

The Recre', though, soon became a regular venue for Cumberland county games, alongside Lonsdale Park, Workington, Salthouse Road, Millom and the Athletic Ground at Maryport. The Recre' staged its first representative fixture on Saturday 30 September 1899 when Cumberland, with a try from Jimmy Lomas, beat Cheshire, 3-0. In December 1901 Cheshire beat a Cumberland side containing two Recs players, 14-0. In January 1905 Cumberland beat Lancashire, 11-0, before a crowd of 1,500 and a year later defeated Yorkshire, 5-0, before 3,000.

In Oct 1908 the Recre' was allocated as the venue for the Cumberland League's tour game against the first Australians. A crowd of 4,000 saw the tourists win, 58-10, with memorable performances from the legendary Dally Messenger and Jim Devereux, who between them scored five tries.

The Recre' had a real red letter day when, on a Thursday afternoon, 4 February 1926 it staged its first and last international fixture. England beat Other Nationalities, 37-11, before a crowd of 7,000 with the occasion marked by the opening of a new 750-seater grandstand. Jim Brough, at the start of a distinguished international career and who later went on to coach Whitehaven, and the immortal Jim Sullivan were the opposing fullbacks.

Brough was the central figure seven years later when a 10,000 crowd at the Recre' witnessed a wonderful game against the Australians. Brough's 40-yard drop goal, in the fourth minute of injury time, gave the county a memorable 17-16 victory with the last act of the game. The ball was never recovered from the celebrating crowds.

Sullivan returned to the Recre' on two occasions for county games with Glamorgan & Monmouthshire, and Yorkshire and Lancashire continued to be regular visitors as the ground regularly staged county fixtures in the inter-war period. However, in 1924 and 1925 Cumberland staged two fixtures, against Yorkshire and Lancashire, on the nearby cricket field.

The Whitehaven Miners' Welfare, who remain as the present landlords of the ground but under another name, acquired the ground from the Earl of Lonsdale in 1944 and entered into a 30-year lease with the newly formed Whitehaven board in March 1948.

When Whitehaven took over the ground it was in a state of some disrepair, not having been used regularly since the Recs' demise, even though several senior clubs, including Barrow, Halifax, Wigan and Bradford Northern had featured in West Cumberland Hospital charity games inaugurated in 1937. Turnstiles were installed, the pitch re-laid and moved several feet away from the main stand and thousands of tons of waste pit slag from the seashore were used to increase the bankings prior to the first season.

The ground today retains much of its original character though the construction of new dressing rooms and sponsors' buildings in one corner, opened in 1986, meant that the players no longer had to walk the gauntlet from the old dressing rooms through the crowds before and after games. The new 500-seat main stand, built in 1995, is another fine structure with a close-up view of the game.

The banking at the Kells End, covered during the 1960/61 season, has long been the vantage point for generations for Whitehaven's keenest fans but the other two sides of the ground are uncovered, though there are plans to re-erect a cover on the popular side, opposite the main stand.

Alan Galloway was present at the Recre' for Whitehaven's opening game and has followed their fortunes ever since. "Sitting in the main stand you can feel every knock and bump and hear the smacks of the collisions," Alan says. "It all adds up to make the Recre' my favourite Rugby League ground."

Alan's first memory of a big game at the Recre' was 'Haven's first against a touring side, the 1952 Australians. Four years earlier, the Australians had been defeated, 4-5, by Cumberland at the Recre' with Workington's Billy Ivison scoring the only try before 8,818 spectators and they approached their return to Whitehaven with due caution.

"Tommy Keen, our scrum-half, became the first man to score a try against the Australians in the fourth game of their tour and that was a big thrill," Alan says, "even though the tourists prevailed, 15-5.

"Four years later we played the Australians again and beat them. There was such a big buzz around the town. Big games were played on Wednesday afternoons, when it was half day closing and there was a real sense of expectancy whenever the tourists came to the area.

"At that time there was no shed on the Kells end but there was a covered enclosure either side of the grandstand to shelter from the elements. I remember standing on old sleepers brought from the railways and when the Kells End was covered the ground was very enclosed and created a tremendous atmosphere for big games."

Whitehaven

Tries by John Tembey and Bill Smith and four goals from John McKeown gave 'Haven that historic win before 10,840 spectators.

Despite that they have never played the Kangaroos since, the tourists returning just once to the Recre' to defeat Cumbria, 28-2, in front of 3,666 spectators in 1973. There was a memorable county game, though, in 2003 when Cumbria drew 24-24 with New Zealand 'A' at the ground.

Three other games that Alan recalls vividly are also part of Whitehaven folklore. The heartbreaking Cup semi-final defeat, 9-10 at Odsal before a crowd of over 49,000 against Leeds in 1957, saw Whitehaven's hopes of a first Wembley final disappear. "That was such a traumatic experience," he says. "The lead-up to the game had been tremendous and so many people went to Bradford on special trains and, as a youngster, it was a bit bemusing watching grown men crying all the way back home, though beer might have played a part in that. I remember crates and crates of brown ale being loaded up onto the trains.

"Three years later against Wakefield in the third round of the cup we had our biggest-ever attendance. It was said to be 18,500 but many people who were there that day estimated it was much more than that. The ground was absolutely jam-packed and in various parts of the ground it was impossible to move. I remember that Wakefield were just too good for us on the day."

Wakefield's 21-10 victory attracted an official attendance of 18,650 (£2,362) and was the first all-ticket game at the Recre'. With the current capacity only 5,000 that figure will never be beaten.

Another memory was playing the Kiwis in 1965. "It was the first time that we had beaten them, 12-7 the score was," John says. "Our prop forward Les Moore played them on his own that day – what a game he had." The attendance for that match, with Whitehaven struggling fifth-bottom of the league, was only 3,218 (£406). Whitehaven have since

played the Kiwis just one more time, losing 8-21 on the 1971 tour.

The Kiwis also featured in another memorable game on their 1980 tour when Whitehaven scrum-half 'Boxer' Walker scored Cumbria's clinching try in a 9-3 success before a crowd of 4,070.

At other times Alan has held his breath when the very future of the club was threatened. "On various occasions fighting funds have been set up but there have been times when we looked in real danger of going out of the league, especially recently when there was all that talk of a merger with Workington," Alan says.

"But the people of Whitehaven didn't want that and they fought tooth and nail to retain their identity. It means a hell of a lot to a lot of people."

At the present time Alan feels that Whitehaven are in good hands. "It is a community club and all the directors and players are virtually locals, approachable and everyone knows them," he says. "All that would have been lost if we'd gone out a few years ago but all credit to the new board of directors, they've had the courage to take the club on and have done a tremendous job. Paul Cullen was a first-class coach and did so much to build up the club again and now Steve McCormack is showing that he is equally good in this regard. He is held in the same respect as Paul was and all the players are responding to him."

Alan's greatest memories, though, are derby games against Workington, even though attendances now are far less than the 18,464 that saw the September 1948 clash. "At times the tension in those games can be unbearable, they are something special," Alan says. "Anyone who has played in them will tell you that. To be beaten by Workington is very hard to swallow and they feel exactly the same way about us. Those games are very important to us and any one who comes into the team is told in no uncertain fashion that they must beat Workington come what may."

The current Whitehaven centre, David Seeds, Alan feels is fit to rank amongst the

finest of all Whitehaven players. Seeds became the first Whitehaven player to score 200 tries for the club in the home game against Featherstone Rovers in July 2005.

"Without a doubt he is one of the all-time greats and in a few years people will speak of him in the same vein as they do about Bill McAlone, Tembey, Dick Huddart and John McKeown," Alan adds. "I would say that for an all-round centre there is no one better – his defence is tremendous and he has got pace with the ability to score tries. Eppie Gibson was an excellent player and so too were Tony Colloby and Vince Gribbin but Seeds ranks alongside them and in my opinion has the edge."

Alan Galloway feels that Whitehaven will remain a town where Rugby League is the life and soul. "It is very much the case and the amateur game is also very strong with Kells, Hensingham, Wath Brow and Egremont all having tremendous amateur set-ups," he says. "Whitehaven are now doing some excellent work in the schools and that is where you get your supporters of tomorrow. In recent years there has been a lack of young ones to support the team and as the old supporters die off they haven't been replaced by the same amount but at long last the club is doing something about that. There should be no shortage of players – there is plenty of talent for Whitehaven and Workington to pick from."

John Cox has been watching Whitehaven for over half a century and for more years than he cares to remember has been following the club's fortunes for BBC Radio Cumbria. John retains a boyish enthusiasm for his home town club and takes pride in the fact that many players have gone on to wear the chocolate, blue and gold strip having first learnt the rudiments of the game at the primary school from which he recently retired as headmaster.

One of his fondest memories is the cup-tie against St Helens in 2001 when

**Whitehaven celebrate winning the 2005 National League One League Leaders trophy,
the first piece of silverware in the club's history**

Whitehaven went down to an heroic 22-34 defeat. "There were 5,000 present that day and place was bouncing when Aaron Lester went in for an early try," he said.

"There we were, beating the world champions and the noise from the Kells End was incredible, resonating off the back of the stand. I went a bit over the top in my commentary and it has been replayed many times as an advert for manic local commentators. But how many days do you get to play the world champions?

"Not long before, the club had been in serious difficulties and then there was all that hoohah over the merger with Town. Those like me that didn't like that at all were delighted with that St Helens game because it showed just what fervour there is in the town for the club.

"Whitehaven remains a Rugby League town as opposed to a soccer one whereas Workington is a bit of both. All the local primary schools play the game, the supporters are reasonably loyal and the club is running on average crowds of around a thousand but many more people do come when the team is winning.

"The directors are very careful with the purse strings and are building locally. There are a lot of local lads and even the Kiwis like Aaron Lester and Leroy Joe are regarded as Marras. That is very important as all Rugby League people want to identify with the players out there on the field. There is such a good, vibrant amateur scene and seeing lads like Mark Cox and Rob Purdham move on and play in Super League gives everyone that extra incentive."

Alan Galloway has the last word: "No matter how the club has been going I have always been confident that, whoever we play at the Recreation Ground, we can give them a good game."

WIDNES

The founders of Farnworth and Appleton Cricket and Football Club could hardly have known what they started in 1873.

Over a century and a quarter later the results of their enterprise are there for all to see. From little acorns grew a Rugby League club, known the world over, playing in the top flight at an impressive new stadium and, to the horror of many cricketers everywhere, in the summer months.

The name was changed to Widnes in 1875 and, in its first few years, the club had a variety of grounds. They played at a fenced enclosure off Peel House Lane, another unfenced ground at Simms Cross and at the Widnes cricket ground off Lowerhouse Lane (which was situated just a few yards from their present ground).

In 1884 Widnes moved to their current site and opened with a game against Liversedge. The players changed at the Central Hotel and journeyed to the ground by horse-drawn wagonettes. Dressing rooms were finally built at the ground in 1902.

One of the biggest days in the fledgling club's history took place on 9 March 1889 when they hosted the touring Maori side in the 65th match of their mammoth tour of the British Isles. A crowd of 5,000 saw the tourists win but the Maoris said they were "never more cordially received" than at Widnes. Arriving from Manchester by train at Widnes Central Station the tourists changed at Widnes's new headquarters, the Railway Hotel, before both sides made their way to the ground.

Afterwards Widnes put on 'a knife and fork tea' before the teams 'adjourned to another room where some convivialities were indulged in'. The teams were then entertained by a pantomime at the Alexandra Theatre. The Maoris formed 'a great opinion of the chemical metropolis', so much so they returned for another game sixteen days later (which they again won) just before leaving for home.

The town's close links with the chemical industry provided the nickname of the 'Chemicals', which later became the 'Chemics'.

The ground had few facilities with a small stand at the current scoreboard end and a small stand on the present site of the main (south) stand. Athletic and cycling meetings were also held regularly at the ground during the summer months. Widnes rose steadily through the Lancashire rugby union ranks and, in 1895, found themselves embroiled in the turmoil of the game, becoming one of the twenty-two founder members of the Northern Union. Widnes's first home game under the new organisation saw them defeat Leeds, 11-8, after an opening day 4-15 defeat at Runcorn.

The next tourists to visit Widnes were the New Zealanders, for the third match of their tour in 1907/08 and the tradition of tourist games was maintained until 1993 when the Kiwis beat Widnes, 18-10.

236

One of the most famous of all games was in 1978 when Widnes beat Australia, 11-10, courtesy of a Stuart Wright try and four Mick Burke goals. A crowd of 12,202 saw the game and Widnes remain the last British club side to defeat the Kangaroos.

Widnes maintained a policy of nurturing and fostering local players with the area a rich breeding ground for talent. Across the river, Runcorn played in the Northern Union from their Canal Street ground until folding in 1916 and derby games between the 'Chemicals' and the 'Linnets' were closely fought and produced bitter rivalries.

In 1911 the main stand was extended to a length of 200 feet and its wooden roof, with fifteen stanchions, survived until 1959. On the popular side a wooden flat-roofed stand with Y-shaped supports sported an advertisement for the local picturedome and cinema.

But the future of the Widnes club was plunged into crisis after the First World War when the ground was compulsorily purchased by the council and then earmarked for housing as part of the 'Housing fit for Heroes' scheme.

In 1926 the Widnes club was granted an extension to their lease of the ground but it was thought that when this was up, five years later, the ground would become part of the huge Kingsway council estate then under construction.

After a series of delicate negotiations the Ministry of Housing and Local Government finally sold the ground to the club for £3,250 with a range of supporters' club initiatives, together with some financial assistance from the Rugby League, finally raising enough money. One of the fund-raising efforts saw the FA Cup holders, West Bromwich Albion, play a Mersey-Widnes select side in a soccer game at the ground that attracted a crowd of 5,000 and raised £200.

The ground purchase was completed in September 1932 but, as part of the sale, the council insisted on the right to purchase the ground back for the same price. This factor, together with the Widnes club being structured as a members' club, hindered major ground improvements in following years, for fear of running up debts and hence losing the ground.

Widnes

In 1928 the position of the club had been described as 'calamitous', with a cash balance of only £8 to start the new season. But, two years later, Widnes had recovered and lifted the Challenge Cup for the first time, beating St Helens at Wembley with a side comprising a dozen local players and the veteran South African forward, George Van Rooyen.

In 1932 the ground was re-named Naughton Park as a tribute to the club secretary, Tom Naughton, who had died in a motor accident. The official ceremony to mark the event was performed on 27 August 1932 when 7,500 saw a 12-10 win over St Helens. A year later the pavilion on the Lowerhouse Lane end was built at a cost of £1,479 and officially opened on Boxing Day of that year before the game against St Helens Recs. This end was later banked and terraced while a players' tunnel was constructed.

In 1934 Widnes returned to Wembley, losing to Hunslet, having posted a new ground record with a first round win over Leeds that attracted 14,337 (£789). Not one of their locally-produced side had cost a penny in transfer fees. Two years later the club reached its first Championship Final, losing to Hull at Fartown, but in 1937 Widnes beat Keighley in the Wembley final with twelve Widnes-born players in their ranks, the other one coming from Runcorn.

During the austere war years of 1939-45 the ground fell into disuse but, upon the cessation of hostilities, work was carried out to make extra terracing and construct walls and crush barriers. Widnes shared in the thirst for live sport of the late 1940s and early '50s and the ground record was regularly surpassed. A record 17,446 gate was posted for Wigan's visit in January 1948, then 20,286 for the Good Friday game with Warrington two months later. In April 1950, 22,729 were present for the derby game with Warrington.

In the mid-1950s the roof on the popular side was rebuilt and shelters constructed at either end of the main stand, whose roof was then re-built. A new ground record was set on 16 February 1961 when 24,205, on a Thursday afternoon, saw St Helens beat Widnes, 29-10, in a Challenge Cup first-round replay.

Widnes beat the 'big freeze' of the winter of 1962/63 through their connections with the local chemical industry, using the defrosting agent, GL5, on the pitch. Floodlights were built at the ground in 1965 and switched on for the first time on 27 September of that year when St Helens won 9-4 before a crowd of 17,319.

In a major development, the local council finally released the "buy-back" clause for a sum of £1,000 in 1971, enabling the club to develop its facilities. As part of that a social club was opened in 1977.

The 1970s and '80s were a glorious era for Widnes as they became known as the 'cup kings', making seven trips to Wembley inside ten years and lifting a great deal of

silverware. Eric Hughes was one of the mainstays of the Chemics sides of the time, and made nearly 500 appearances for the club in all.

"The ground went with the image of Widnes as an industrial town," Hughes recalls. "Even by Rugby League standards of the time the ground was old-fashioned and the club relied on volunteers for a lot of the maintenance.

"But when you played there the spectators were virtually amongst you and very much part of the things that went on out on the pitch. There are not many grounds like that now, though Knowsley Road is one. A lot of opposing players just didn't fancy it.

"The dressing rooms, by the standards of the time, were OK and certainly much bigger than those at Salford and Castleford today. There was an unwritten law that there was one dressing room for the first team and one for the A team. As a young player you had to wait for the nod from the coach before changing with the first team. That was the target of any lad that signed on as a junior.

"The ground was always tidy and well maintained and the playing surface was good. It was a huge thrill for me, brought up five minutes from the ground, to walk to training and mix with my heroes. As a teenager I went down to the Wembley win of 1964 but after that the club didn't have much success for a few years and top players, such as Frank Myler, were sold.

"My brother, Arthur, also played for the club and there was a large dependence upon local players. The Wembley side of 1975 was made up of all local players, apart from Jim Mills and Chris Anderson. A lot of us signed as youngsters together and came up through the ranks together. Later, we all seemed to have testimonials, one after another.

"The big catalyst in changing Widnes's fortunes was getting Vince Karalius as coach. He was a local legend and we hung on his every word. He brought professionalism to the club and was one of those coaches smart enough to realise that, if things were going well, he didn't have to change too much."

Hughes felt that the 1975 win was a big turning point for Widnes. "It was the first Wembley for eleven years and was a new experience to a lot of people in the town," he recalls. "For the first couple of Wembleys the town went down 'en bloc' but towards the end it was taken for granted a little bit. We won a lot of trophies and it was a boom time for the club.

"Widnes also did it right with overseas players. The ones they brought in improved the side and mixed in really well. Anderson and John Peek were the first and players such as Kevin Tamati and Kurt Sorensen followed. Then the lads they brought from rugby union came in and did a job. Martin Offiah was after my time but he had a tremendous impact."

Despite their successes on the field, culminating in the 1989 World Club Challenge

win over Canberra at Old Trafford, Widnes, now a cosmopolitan side with stars drawn from all around the globe, failed to keep pace off the field with ground improvements. With its piecemeal developments the ground looked a hotchpotch of design and the club faced huge obstacles in the wake of ground safety measures introduced after the Valley Parade and Hillsborough disasters.

A sum of £100,000 was spent concreting the main stand and replacing the wooden seats with those of a plastic tip-up variety after two separate small fires. But, with only 1,043 seats, Widnes had plainly not got the facilities to match their talent on the park.

But the crowds flocked in. The debut of union convert Jonathan Davies in January 1989 attracted huge media interest and a crowd of 11,871 while three months later a crowd of 17,323, Widnes's biggest home gate of the modern era, saw the game against Wigan, just a day after the Hillsborough tragedy.

The journalist and broadcaster, Graham Lovett, has covered Widnes for many years and has many memories, good and bad, of the ground.

"In the late '80s journalists had the run of the ground. There were no 'jobsworths' (stewards) in those days," he recalls. "The downside to that was that you couldn't leave anything behind in the press box. Once, coming back after interviewing some players in the dressing room, there were three or four kids rifling through my case. It may be dangerous outside the ground at times now, walking to your car with a load of recording equipment when all the crowds have gone but in those days it was dangerous sometimes inside the ground. You were always watching over your shoulder.

"The dressing rooms were like dungeons and the away one was particularly dingy. The officials changed upstairs in a room near to the committee room, which doubled up as a sponsors' room on match-day. That was the limit of corporate hospitality in those days.

"There was a door out of the dressing room that went straight out onto the pavement of Lowerhouse Lane. I soon got to know the players, the big stars. They were all brought quickly down to earth and with people like the Hulme brothers (David and Paul) around they couldn't afford to be anything else. The Hulmes, 'Old and Young Yommer' they were called, 'Dazzler' (Darren Wright) and 'Jiffy' (Davies) were all terrific and the I've lost count of the times I interviewed Offiah in a smoky room under the main stand with other players outside taking the mickey. But they soon cottoned on that he was a very fast rugby player who would win them games and earn them lots of winning money.

"Sorensen was always last out of the changing room. He'd sit there for ages, covered in mud with tapes all over his fingers and thumbs. My glasses used to steam up as soon as I went in, the atmosphere was like a foggy day.

"There were no press conferences after games and I used to interview the coach, Doug Laughton, while he was walking across to the social club for a pint and a fag. They were great days and nobody ever refused me an interview. The groundsman had a sign on the grass: 'No running on the pitch' it said. We used to joke that some players took it literally. The scoreboard doesn't work now and it never worked in those days.

"There was a great sense of humour about the place. I remember when Burke played and one day a fan turned up with a banner that read: 'We've got one Burke, you've got 13'.

"When I think of Naughton Park I think of winter rugby, muck and bullets. It's nice to have the memories but you have to move on and the Halton Stadium is a world away from that."

Widnes's exclusion from Super League, coupled with a precarious financial position, threatened the very existence of the club, playing outside the top flight for the first time.

But a far-sighted Council initiative came to Widnes's rescue, with the opportunity to develop a new stadium with conference, catering and function facilities and a social club. The redevelopment of the famous Naughton Park site began, substantially supported and managed by the Council, who formed a joint-venture company with the re-named Widnes Vikings, now set up as a limited company.

Phase one of the new development began in earnest in August 1996. Consisting of two stands, north and south (the main stand), with seating, banqueting and conference facilities, twenty-six executive boxes and a social club, it was officially opened on 2 November 1997. The total cost was £4.5 million, none of which was grant funded. The north stand has a capacity of 4,199 while the south holds 3,665.

While part of the work was being completed, Widnes staged four home games, in July and August 1997, at Canal Street, Runcorn, attracting the largest crowd, 1,800, for the visit of Leigh.

In January 1999 Halton Borough Council took over responsibility for the entire stadium and the second phase was completed in August of that year, when the west stand development was finished, funded in part by a Lottery grant of £2.3 million. Within the structure is a table tennis centre to regional standard, a health and fitness facility, a creche and an injury clinic. This stand has a capacity of 3,019, taking the ground capacity to around the 11,000 mark.

Briefly renamed in 1998 the Auto Quest Stadium, after a short-lived sponsorship agreement with a local car dealership, the Halton Stadium also staged home reserve games for Everton FC. Their first match at the ground, on 11 November 1997, saw the kick-off delayed for 30 minutes to accommodate the 5,000 crowd to see them lose 1-0 to Leeds United Reserves. Since Runcorn FC sold their historic Canal Street home (one of the last-surviving venues of the first season of the Northern Union) in 2001, that soccer club, re-named Runcorn FC Halton, also ground-shared with Widnes. Their first game as permanent residents saw them beat Emley, 2-0, before a crowd of 468 on 23 August 2001. But late in the 2004/05 season Runcorn moved out, unable to afford the match rental charge and took up a ground-sharing at Prescot for the 2005/06 campaign. They hope to re-locate back to a new stadium in Runcorn within the next few years.

The new-look Widnes ground staged the Wales-PNG 2000 World Cup quarter-final and the 2002 NFP Grand Final, as well as Emerging England against Wales in 1998. Previously, the ground's lack of seating accommodation ruled it out of contention for many representative games. But the old ground had been the venue for a couple of Wales' European Championship internationals (against France in 1978 and England in 1979) and a number of county games, the first a Lancashire-Yorkshire clash in October 1935.

But the greatest day in Widnes's recent history was their victory over Oldham in the NFP Grand Final at Spotland in 2001, ensuring top-flight Rugby League's return to a ground, now with facilities to match the team's status.

"Naughton Park may have disappeared, apart from the terrace that remains at the east-side, and there's a twinge of sadness attached to that," Eric Hughes added. "But the new ground is on the same site, so in many ways it hasn't disappeared and that's important. It's great to see Widnes in the top flight after they were cast out at the start."

Sadly, after escaping relegation on the last day of the 2004 season the Vikings faced another relegation struggle in 2005, ironically as the construction of the east stand was nearing completion to make the Halton Stadium a superbly well-appointed, all-seated, four-sided ground. Not long ago they had a magnificent team and a poor ground - what those heroes of the 'cup kings' era would have given to play at the new stadium.

WIGAN

In the 1890s Wigan was a bustling, fast-growing town strategically situated on the south Lancashire coalfield.

It had good railway connections and had increased in size and importance over the previous 20 years. The population had enjoyed improved living standards and households typically had two sources of income from local coalmines, textile mills, engineering works and myriad other small industries. This was the era of the house-proud Lancastrian with the clean front step and the aspidistra in the front room. The potential support for a sporting club was considerable.

Many of the upper class of Wigan, who referred to themselves as the gentry, took a great interest in sport, particularly cricket. The Wigan rugby club was formed in the early 1870s as a pastime for the cricketers to pursue in the winter months and it grew to become one of the foremost organisations in the north by the late 1880s. Ned Bullough became the club's first international player at this time. Other famous players such as Jim Slevin and Billy Atkinson went close to emulating Bullough's selection for England and Wigan enjoyed a strong fixture list, one which featured many of the country's leading clubs.

The rugby club shared the cricket field at Prescott Street, off Frog Lane, situated to the west of the town, and crowds approaching ten thousand were not uncommon. Association football, fast growing in popularity in neighbouring towns such as Bolton, Blackburn and Preston made little headway in Wigan.

When the Northern Union (NU) was formed in 1895, Wigan become one of the 22 founder members. Though formed on the principle of paying players broken-time (compensation for wages lost while playing the game), the move towards unrestricted professionalism was not far away. This development caused a number of problems and many clubs, unable to cope with the financial realities, fell by the wayside.

By contrast association football was spreading its roots and by 1897 the Football League comprised two divisions each containing 18 clubs. In the early years of the NU the fortunes of Wigan declined and on more than one occasion the club's future was imperilled. Many of the local junior sides had folded following the miners' strike of 1893 and without the supply of local talent the senior club increasingly looked outside the area for its players. A number of major blows almost brought about the demise of the senior rugby club in the town.

The rugby club was a sub-tenant of the cricket club and the latter organisation was looking elsewhere for a ground. Prescott Street was surrounded by local industry and was not in the best area. Many cricket matches were played while smoke from the local factories swirled around with the result that the cricketers' whites soon became discoloured. The turf was poor, the facilities spartan and the ground was in a relatively inaccessible location. The cricket club decided to purchase a new site which became known as Bull Hey

and Lancashire captain AN Hornby brought along the county side for the inaugural fixture in April 1898.

The rugby club, though, had to stay at Prescott Street as by this time it had lost many of its previous benefactors. The new era of professional rugby did not meet with universal approval and, with vital league points at stake, many matches were dull, uninspiring affairs, dominated by forward play.

Many of the rules were inherited from rugby union, as games were played 15-a-side, with incessant scrums and kicking. Wigan scored only 119 points in 36 games in the 1896/97 season and in the following two seasons combined scored 89 tries in a total of 57 games.

A successful side had been allowed to grow old together and players nearing the end of their careers were not adequately replaced. Many of the outsiders failed to settle in the town or behave properly. Two Wigan players were jailed following an incident arising from Wigan's game at Morecambe in October 1896 on charges of assaulting a station master and there were many instances of players being hauled up before the local magistrates on charges of drunkenness. As a result most of the gentry of the town withdrew their support and playing fortunes declined as Wigan languished near the bottom of the Lancashire Senior Competition.

Into this environment came the idea of an association football club. Springfield Park was acquired in 1896 for the sum of £2,750 by a new organisation, the Wigan Trotting and Athletic Grounds Company. Located to the north-west of Wigan, about a mile from the town centre, Springfield Park was an ambitious project. Five directors, all local businessmen, subscribed an initial share capital of £4,500. The first sod was cut in January 1897 with the intention of opening the ground on 12 May 1897. On the 16-acre site was a horse-trotting track, considered to be one of the best in the country, a cement cycle track and a pedestrian and running track while inside those tracks was a football ground.

Wigan County AFC were immediately elected to the prestigious Lancashire League, regarded as a stepping-stone to the Football League, and there were high hopes that, with the rugby club's fortunes so low, soccer would become the foremost spectator sport in Wigan. The directors splashed out huge wages at the time - a reported £40 a week when the rugby club's annual wage-bill was around £130. But the gamble of recruiting many Football League players in a bid to earn instant success failed to pay off.

The site also contained two pavilions, a boating lake, two bowling greens and three lawn tennis courts along with stands and some stables. But from the outset the new company hit problems as the construction of the complex took longer than expected. The opening was put back to August and as a consequence the company had a cash flow hit with lost revenue from athletic competitions, cycling races and trotting meetings.

After high initial hopes the fortunes of County also declined and early enthusiasm was not maintained. Springfield Park's lack of spectator facilities hardly helped as the main grandstand was not completed by the start of the season, there was no cover and with the tracks the game was remote from the spectators. The ground was known locally as 'Pneumonia Park'. Finally, in September 1899 the complex was sold at auction for £6,000 and County's affairs were wound up in March 1900. Two further attempts were made to establish soccer in the town, Wigan United FC folding after three years and Wigan Town FC closing down in 1908.

By this time the rugby club was enjoying a revival. In 1901 they vacated Prescott Street when the ground was taken over for railway extension purposes by the landlord, the Lancashire and Yorkshire Railway Company. Wigan played one season at Springfield Park, ground-sharing with United, before moving to Central Park in 1902. The move to Central Park heralded a surge in the club's fortunes and by 1910 the ground was frequently staging games with twenty to thirty thousand people in attendance. Wigan recruited players from all around the world and rapidly became one of the NU's glamour clubs.

Had things happened differently around the turn of the century and Wigan County been a success, the sporting climate of the town could have been changed forever. As it was by the time another soccer club, Wigan Borough, again playing at Springfield Park, gained admittance to the newly-formed Third Division (North) in 1921, rugby was firmly established as the dominant football code in the town. Borough resigned from the League in October 1931 and it was many years before Wigan Athletic, who bought Springfield Park for £2,850 following their formation a year later, earned Football League membership in 1978.

Latics' remarkable progress up the pyramid in recent seasons, culminating in a ground-share with the rugby club and the earning of a place in the Premier League for 2005/06 is the latest chapter in the town's rich sporting heritage.

But a century or so on from Wigan County, with Rugby League ingrained in the community, it is hard to foresee soccer ever becoming the dominant code of football in the town whatever further success Latics achieve.

In their last match at Springfield Park on 15 May 1999 Wigan Athletic drew 1-1 with Manchester City in a Second Division play-off game before 6,762. A ground record was set when 30,611 saw Wigan Borough's FA Cup-tie against Sheffield Wednesday in 1929. Rugby League briefly returned to the ground during the 1987/88 season following Blackpool Borough's reincarnation as Springfield Borough.

That decision by Wigan back in 1902 to take up a lease on a patch of ground known as Joe Hill's Field, named after a local butcher who used it for grazing purposes, was to

have massive implications for rugby in the town. The area that extended behind the Spion Kop at what became Central Park was known as the "Bloody Mountains" and was the site of the Battle of Wigan Lane in 1651 during the English Civil War.

Nigel Winnard, a distinguished local historian, has watched Wigan for over 70 years and is the foremost authority on the club's past.

"Getting established at Central Park was a turning point in the club's history," Winnard says. "Those early days in the NU had been very unsuccessful. Prescott Street was clearly an unacceptable site. You can still visit the area and see where the ground was. Cricket Street is still there. Springfield Park, though a very upmarket and ambitious project for its day, was relatively inaccessible and lacked the intimacy and facilities required of a successful ground. The club was also faced with a rent demand for £240 per annum had they stayed. Instead, they secured the new ground on a seven-year lease at an annual cost of £50.

"A condition of the lease was that the ground be called Central Park - the vast majority of people think this was because the land was central but it was because the land was owned by the Great Central Railway Company who, when they abandoned the plan to build a line to Blackpool, had no further need of the land.

"By moving back much closer to the centre of town Wigan were not far from their original ground at Folly Field, also known as Upper Dicconson Street. The exact location of the ground has never been satisfactorily pinpointed but it ran roughly where Dicconson Terrace and the lower end of Trafalgar Road is today.

"The club was formed in 1872 but ran into financial problems and the treasurer was jailed for embezzlement. They also suffered a lot of injuries to players during the 1878/79 period. That winter was terrible and little could be done, but then one or two people who had been connected to the club came along with the idea of re-starting things. They deliberately chose the title 'Wigan Wasps' so as not to stand on anyone's toes - a kind of

245

courtesy title that was dropped after one year. They changed at the long-gone Dicconson Arms, opposite Church Street."

An army of volunteers, supervised by Councillor JH Prescott, laid out the new pitch and made the embankments from colliery waste. The original curved wooden stand that ran the full length of the field on the River Douglas side was constructed. This stand was finally demolished in 1973. "Because the ground was originally on a short-term lease there was no point building a permanent pavilion so the teams used to change at a nearby pub, the Princess of Wales that ran by the side of the River Douglas (not the Prince of Wales on Greenhough Street, as often stated) on Water Heys," Winnard continues. "One of the early players, Billy Anderson, changed separately in his own pub on Standishgate and walked to the ground in his football gear.

"It cost the club about £1,000 to get going and an anonymous gentleman, thought to be Mr Fairhurst who lived at Kilhey Court, gave them a grant of £200. One big problem was the drainage because of the water table from the Douglas and that was never solved until the 1980s. The ground soon became waterlogged and because of it being in low-lying land in the valley was prone to mists and fog, even on a decent day."

Central Park was opened for the visit of Batley on Saturday 6 September 1902 when an estimated crowd of 10,000 saw Wigan mark the occasion with a 14-8 victory. Winger Jimmy Barr had the distinction of scoring the first try. "There was no terracing at that time but the ground immediately proved very popular," Winnard says. "But the games were hardly entertaining - in that first season Wigan only scored 14 tries at home all year. The reduction in teams to 13-a-side in 1906 was a massive advancement for the game and sparked Central Park's huge rise in crowds."

Central Park staged the first NU international when England lost 3-9 to Other Nationalities on Tuesday 5 April 1904 before a crowd of 6,000. As a trial the game was played 12-a-side.

The ground's real red-letter day, though, came more than three years later when winger Jimmy Leytham scored a brilliant hat-trick as Wigan defeated the New Zealand All Golds 12-8 before a crowd of 30,000 on 9 November 1907. When Great Britain played the tourists in an international at the ground two months later, however, the attendance was only 10,000 - clearly Wigan fans preferred to watch Wigan. "This was a feature throughout Central Park's history," Winnard says. "The highest crowd for an international at the ground was 27,500 for the England-Wales game in 1950 but there were so many attendances for club games higher than that."

The signing of Leytham from Lancaster, the arrival of other star players such as Bert Jenkins from Wales and Lance Todd from New Zealand and the development of local talent such as winger Joe Miller, saw Wigan become an entertaining side.

"Suddenly Wigan became a force in the land and won their first honour, the Lancashire Cup in 1905," Winnard says. "Todd was a major influence - it is difficult to appreciate in just how high an opinion he was held. In 1909 Wigan played the first Australians who did an Aboriginal war-chant before the game. Wigan responded with a New Zealand haka, which had been coached by Todd.

"Though they had a good team the ground security was an issue until the railway company offered a new 14-year lease and enabled the club to build a pavilion. It was built in 1909 with the familiar headstone that proclaimed: Central Park A1909D Wigan Football Club. It cost £1,246 to build and was finished in five months. The Douglas Stand was now full-length and there was some cover from a wooden shelter at the Spion Kop end. In 1911 they built an 80-yard long Dutch barn, open at the back, on the popular side. They couldn't run this the full way because of the neighbouring St Mary's school and the right of light. An advertisement appeared on this structure for a tailor's shop, who enterprisingly offered an overcoat to any Wigan player to score three tries in a match. In the next game they beat Coventry, 70-0, and four players all qualified - Lewis Bradley, Todd, Dick Ramsdale and Bob Curwen. They all got overcoats. Three days later Bradley and Curwen qualified again during a big win over Runcorn and after that the offer was rescinded."

A new record crowd of 33,000 was established for Huddersfield's visit in March 1913. "Admission was sixpence, but nine pence for the stand," Winnard says. "But then the war started in 1914 and the admission was cut to threepence. Attendances declined and Wigan had to sell the timbered cover at the Kop end to make ends meet.

"When the war was over the finances were in a shocking state and Central Park in a poor state of repair. But there was something of a post-war boom and the crowds began to flock back. They got 33,343 against Huddersfield in 1920, a new ground record, and in 1921 the club was able to buy the ground. The railway company said they would not extend the lease beyond 1923 but that the club could buy the ground for £2,000. Eventually they knocked them down to £500. A limited company was registered with a share capital of £16,000 and the club was now on a much firmer footing."

The signing of Welsh fullback Jim Sullivan in 1921 heralded a glorious new era and Wigan continued to bring in exciting players from all around the globe. "There was hardly a Wiganer in the team," Winnard recalls. "They won the Challenge Cup for the first time in 1924, two championships in five years and then in 1929 beat Dewsbury in the first Wembley final."

Winnard's first memories of going to Central Park were in the early 1930s. "I

Billy Boston

remember all the men wore cloth caps and smoked cigarettes," he says. "The crowds were huge and it was just so exciting for a youngster to see your heroes close-up. Sullivan was absolutely idolised - venerated almost, even more than Billy Boston many years later. But in the 1930s, despite Sullivan's talent, the return in terms of trophies was disappointing and by the start of the Second World War in 1939 the club was in a decline again."

Wigan fans head for the exits following the final game at Central Park

Wigan carried on playing through the war years, setting the foundations for their glorious spell of success when peace returned. "That war-time period brought on so many players," Winnard recalls. "The star turn was Johnny Lawrenson. For the first time for many years the Wigan-born players had a chance to shine. But the ground was even more decrepit and round the Douglas side in particular the conditions were terrible."

The post-war boom after 1945 allowed Wigan to develop the ground, a concrete perimeter wall replacing the wooden railings and the terraces finally being concreted. A new ground record was set on Good Friday 1950 for the visit of St Helens when 44,529 crammed inside. A new stand was built to replace the Dutch Barn and was opened in 1954. It later became the family stand with the Jim Sullivan Bar underneath. In the same year the double-pitched roof over the Kop was completed.

Surprisingly Central Park had to wait until 1956 to be granted a Great Britain-Australia Test match when the new Wigan hero, Welsh winger Boston, scored a memorable try in the hosts' 21-10 victory. And with Boston approaching his peak as a player a new ground record was established on 27 March 1959 when 47,477 (originally stated as 47,747) saw the game against St Helens. Later that year Great Britain last clinched a Test series win over Australia in this country with an 18-12 win, Neil Fox contributing 15 points before a crowd of 26,089.

Ground improvements continued apace as floodlights were introduced in 1967, originally costing £17,000 and being replaced by a new set in 1985 at a cost of £35,000. A new stand on the Douglas side, seating 1,741 at a cost of £100,000, was opened in 1973. The ground also brought in under-soil heating at a cost of £88,000 during the mid-1980s and built a new cantilever stand at the pavilion end after gaining planning approval in 1989. Partly financed by the brewers, Whitbread, the £2m construction (later re-named after Boston) had 2,062 seats and incorporated 16 executive boxes but was plagued by problems with the foundation work and only fully opened in 1991. The 1909 pavilion was

248

encapsulated within the new stand's construction. By 1991 the ground had a capacity of 30,023 including 5,304 seats but by the time of the closure in 1999 this figure had been reduced by safety legislation to 18,500.

Three games in recent memory particularly stand out, topped by the crowd of 36,895 for the inaugural World Club Challenge game against Manly in 1987. In a dramatic floodlit game, which failed to produce a try, Wigan won 8-2. There was the visit of the Kangaroos in 1986 when a crowd of 30,602 saw Wigan go down to a heroic 18-26 defeat in the opening game of the tour. Then there was the ten-try feat by Martin Offiah against Leeds in a Premiership Trophy tie in 1992.

By the late 1990s when Wigan's success began to dry up the continuing rumours about a move from Central Park became reality. Eventually the town's two senior clubs came together for the first time since 1901 as a brand new stadium next to the Robin Park athletics stadium gathered pace under the driving force of Wigan's wealthiest man, Dave Whelan.

Wigan had originally resisted pressure for a ground-share with the Latics but their worsening finances eventually left them with little option. In their last season at Central Park the average league attendance was 9,207 and only three of their 14 league games attracted five-figure crowds.

The curtain was brought down on Central Park when a sell-out crowd of 18,179 saw them defeat old enemy St Helens, 28-20, on a sunny Sunday afternoon, 5 September 1999. The captain, Andrew Farrell, later admitted he was more nervous before that game than for any other in his illustrious Wigan career. "I'd say that game ranks as the most important I've ever played for Wigan," he recalled. "I'd grown up at Central Park, seen my heroes there, got there three hours before kick-off for the Manly game to get a good spot on the wall. I knew what the place meant to Wigan supporters and knew that we simply couldn't afford to lose. We played with great determination that day and it was a very special and emotional occasion. But the over-riding emotion as I remember was one of relief." Four Farrell goals and two Jason Robinson tries helped Wigan's victory push though the honour of scoring the last try on the hallowed turf fell to a Saints player, Tommy Martyn.

The atmosphere built up long before kick-off with a galaxy of Wigan greats paraded before the crowd - Joe Egan, Martin Ryan, Lawrenson, Billy Blan, Colin Clarke, Mick Sullivan, Bill Ashurst, Eric Ashton, Graeme West, Henderson Gill, Dean Bell and John Monie to name a few. But the biggest cheer was reserved for the last man out of the tunnel, the incomparable Boston. He played 487 games for Wigan, scored 478 tries and, most importantly in the fans' eyes, lived in Wigan during and after his career. "There's only one Billy Boston," the faithful chanted and he wiped a tear from his eye. At the end fans embraced and hugged one another, many remaining long after the final whistle, taking in one last long look at the ground that had a special place in their hearts.

Of all the grounds to disappear in recent years Central Park's demise was perhaps the most poignant, the most mourned. Several years on the memories are not dimmed and some Wigan fans have refused to go to the JJB Stadium while others cannot bear to visit the Tesco supermarket than now stands on the site of what was perhaps the world's most instantly-recognisable Rugby League ground.

At the nearby St Mary's Church, Wigan established a memorial garden as a mark of respect for the many hundreds of former players and spectators, including Jim Sullivan, whose ashes were scattered on the Central Park pitch.

No sooner had the last game been played than Central Park was summarily demolished, the familiar landmarks disappearing with almost indecent haste. And a fortnight later Wigan entered their brave new world, playing Castleford in the Super League play-offs at the JJB Stadium on a Sunday evening, 19 September 1999.

Built by Alfred McAlpine plc, the all-seated stadium was officially opened on 4 August 1999 when Wigan Athletic played Manchester United in a high-profile friendly. Heavy afternoon rain had subsided by the time the first Rugby League game there kicked off as expectant fans settled into their opulent new surroundings. But Castleford spoiled the party, as they recorded a 14-10 win before a 13,374 crowd, though Denis Betts did have the distinction of scoring the opening try.

With a seated capacity of 25,004, 5,399 each in the identical North and South Stands, 8,216 in the East and 5,990 in the West and impressive hospitality lounges and suites,

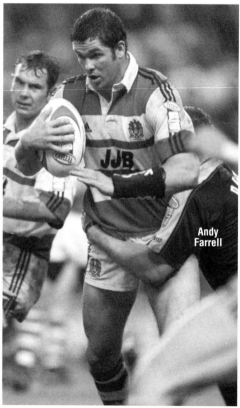

Andy
Farrell

excellent sight-lines and parking for 2,000 cars the stadium grew impressively on the former wasteland site that had the River Douglas and Leeds-Liverpool canal running close-by. That capacity was reached for St Helens' visit on Good Friday, 25 March 2005 when Wigan marked the occasion with a 22-20 victory. But the third and decisive Ashes Test on 24 November 2001, when Australia defeated Great Britain 28-8, saw a recorded attendance of 25,011. And 25,004 saw Great Britain's memorable 24-12 win over the Kangaroos in the Tri-Nations series three years later in what proved to be Farrell's last game at the ground before his move to rugby union.

"The JJB is a beautifully-appointed stadium but should have had the corners filled in to give it a better feel," Winnard maintains. "It could never generate the atmosphere of Central Park. Although the old diehards were dead against the move there were many factors that made it perfect sense. Central Park was the right ground at the right time but had seen its best days. Ground development plans were always hampered by the close proximity of the River Douglas and parking was becoming increasingly difficult. Sadly, it should be remembered for what it was - one of Rugby League's great traditional grounds, one of the most famous if not the most famous in the world.

"Even in the 1970s when the crowds were generally much smaller there was still a great thrill standing on the terraces in the depths of winter and feeling that excitement as the teams ran out to the strains of "Entry of the Gladiators" from the tannoy. They always played that from the time the tannoy system was put up just after the war and must have used the same record throughout. It certainly got very scratched and I always found it amusing they didn't come up with something more modern. Before the war they used to

JJB
Stadium

occasionally rig up a tannoy for the manager, Harry Sunderland, to address the crowd. He'd always say the same thing: 'On Wigan onwards, to Wembley if you can!' That's always stuck in my mind. Then in the 1980s the crowds came back and Wigan enjoyed ten years of the greatest success in its history.

"Central Park generated a feel and atmosphere of its own, even when it was empty. Even though I had never seen them play, the ghosts of Jenkins, Todd, Leytham and so on were always there. They were in-built in the ground's history in the way that later players like Sullivan and Boston were.

"It's easy to overlook the modern players but Farrell was a colossus for Wigan. You look at a player like him and he would have been a great player in any era. The ground took years to evolve, from a simple field to a magnificent stadium that played host to the greatest players ever to grace the game. You name them - they all played there - and the big games staged there: Tests, Challenge Cup semi-finals and finals and so many great Wigan matches too many to mention. Hopefully in time the new ground will develop its own rich history and atmosphere.

"In the week Central Park was a meeting place. People would go down on their own for a chat and a gossip on the car park outside the social club. And you'd see the players - your great heroes arriving and departing. Andy Gregory was truly loved by the Wigan public because he was so friendly and approachable.

"Looking back I suppose that Manly game perhaps holds the greatest memories. It wasn't the game as such but the occasion, seeing a great Australian team come up against our own team that had come on leaps and bounds. And we beat them, the players rising to the occasion magnificently. The ground was absolutely packed and there wasn't a space to be had anywhere. People used every vantage point but the over-riding memory was the friendliness and the great joy at seeing a famous Wigan win."

251

WORKINGTON

Few towns the size of Workington can boast three grounds with such a rich Rugby League heritage. Lonsdale Park, Borough Park and Derwent Park are separated merely by a good old-fashioned punt of a leather ball and all have played their part in the establishment of the game in West Cumberland.

Lonsdale Park was home to the original Workington club, members of the Northern Union from 1898 until 1909, though they never attained senior status. They played Wakefield Trinity at Lonsdale Park in a first round Challenge Cup-tie in 1907, earning a 3-3 draw and losing the replay only 5-16. The ground was regularly used for county and representative games up until the Second World War, the first in December 1898 when Cumberland defeated Lancashire, 13-3, before 4,000. Cumberland played the All Golds there in January 1908, recording a famous 21-9 victory in front of 4,000 spectators. Lonsdale Park also hosted the Kiwi tourists in 1927 and the Kangaroos in 1922 and in 1929 (when the county side won 8-5).

Workington AFC (the Reds) also used the ground from 1890 to 1911 when they folded and then from their reformation in 1921 until 1937 when they moved to the adjacent Borough Park. They staged a famous FA Cup fourth-round tie against Preston North End at the ground on 27 January 1934, losing 1-2, when surviving photographs show scores of spectators perched precariously on the grandstand roof in a scene that would send the ground safety executives of today into apoplexy.

Lonsdale Park also staged speedway meetings in the 1930s and until recently was used for greyhound racing. The Reds returned to play a few games at Lonsdale Park while ground developments rendered Borough Park unusable during the 1986/87 season.

England played Other Nationalities (in all but name Wales) at Lonsdale Park on Saturday 5 February 1921 before a crowd of 10,000, recording a 33-16 win. The England side included greats of the game such as Harold Wagstaff, Billy Batten, Jonty Parkin and Douglas Clark. Four years later England returned, defeating Wales, 27-22, with the famous Huddersfield and Cumberland forward Clark scoring the clinching try in what proved to be his final international, in a game that attracted 14,000 spectators.

The third and final international staged at the venue was in 1933 when a crowd of 11,000 saw England beat Other Nationalities, 34-27.

Walking down by the side of Borough Park to Lonsdale Park in the twilight of a late autumnal evening before the 2004 Cumbria-ANZACs game at Derwent Park was an eerie experience. The ground that once held five-figure crowds is now sadly a pale shadow of its former self, most of the terracing gone, the rusting corrugated iron shelters by the finishing straight and the old football pavilion that housed the bar recently demolished, and the banking overgrown.

It is possible to make out the old speedway track and the playing area still has football

posts standing, but it is impossible to stand and survey the scene for long without feeling you are being touched on the shoulder by the ghosts of the past.

Built with council assistance, Borough Park first hosted Football League games from 1951 after the Reds won election to Division Three (North), replacing New Brighton.

The facilities included a 1,000-seater main stand on the west side, cover for around 3,000 and ash banking around the ground. Terracing and further covers were later added so that by 1957 the ground's capacity was 21,000, with cover for 10,000 and seating for 1,500.

Chesterfield provided the first League opposition before an 11,000 crowd on 22 August 1951, the Reds winning 3-1. The highest League gate was against Carlisle United on Boxing Day 1963 when 18,628 passed through the turnstiles. By contrast just 693 attended a game against Exeter City in December 1973 and the Reds' final home Football League game saw them lose 0-1 to Newport County on 14 May 1977 before 1,285 spectators. A month later they were voted out at the League's AGM, to be replaced by Wimbledon.

Much of the character of the ground was lost when the seating areas and framework of the main stand were largely demolished due to safety measures in 1988, though the social amenities, club offices and dressing rooms underneath were left intact.

Since then the Reds have largely played in the Northern Premier League and an early season run of success in 2004/05 that culminated in promotion to Conference North, saw awakened support. A visit to Borough Park remains one of the most treasured on the groundhopper's list.

The most famous game ever staged there was on 4 January 1958 when a ground record attendance of 21,000 saw a third-round FA Cup-tie against Manchester United, which the visitors won 3-1. This was one of the last games United played before the Munich disaster a month later. Five of the players who had played for United at Borough Park, Roger Byrne, Duncan Edwards, Eddie Colman, Mark Jones and Tommy Taylor were among those who perished.

The first major Rugby League game at Borough Park was on Saturday 18 September 1937 when Lancashire defeated Cumberland, 23-17, before a crowd of 10,200.

Workington Town was registered as a company in December 1944, with directors of the Reds originally holding the majority of shares.

Town's first game was a friendly against Huddersfield on New Year's Day 1945 and in April of that year they were admitted to the Rugby League. In their first game as a senior club they defeated Broughton Rangers, 27-5, before a 4,000 crowd at Borough Park on 25 August 1945. The reserve team played initially at Lonsdale Park.

Tom Mitchell was associated with Town virtually from the outset and went on to give yeoman service as director and benefactor for over 50 years until his death. In his autobiography, 'The Memoirs and Sporting Life of Tom Mitchell', published in 1998 he recalled those early days.

"Town were fortunate in entering the League at a time of austerity," he explained. "Everything was rationed, the war had just ended and people were craving high-class sporting entertainment. Workington vowed from the outset to give the Cumbrian public the best we could possibly afford and that is exactly what we gave them."

Mitchell was a one-man team-building committee and pulled off a masterstroke by recruiting Gus Risman as player-coach on his return from the 1946 Lions tour. "The crowds flocked to the soccer club ground, Borough Park," Mitchell continued, "and the team rewarded them with some wonderful football. The '51/'52 teams are recognised as the best because of the honours they won, but right through the '50s Town matched the best."

In September 1949 England played Other Nationalities there before a crowd of 17,576 on a late Monday afternoon in mid-September. Brian Bevan scored two tries for the

Borough Park

visitors and Pat Devery, Huddersfield's Australian star, was outstanding. A record attendance was set on 8 March 1952, when Town's 15-4 victory over St Helens before a crowd of 20,403 helped them on the way to Wembley.

Eppie Gibson, who was brought up in Ellenborough though he was actually born in Northumberland, turned professional with Town in 1947 and went on to play over three hundred games in a decade's service before moving down the coast to Whitehaven. A talented centre, he remembers his playing days at Workington with affection and pride. So he should, as during his time Town won the Championship and Challenge Cup and were at the forefront of an era when Workington were among the game's elite.

Risman started the revolution, making a huge impact in the town and after his resignation in 1954 Jim Brough, a former Leeds, Cumberland and GB fullback, carried on where Risman left off, taking the team to Wembley again in 1955 and 1958 (when they lost to Barrow and Wigan) and the Championship Final of 1958 (when they lost to Hull).

"Gus was a very nice man and knew what he was doing," Eppie says. "In no time the club went from nowhere to be league champions and cup-winners - they actually held the two trophies concurrently, if only for three weeks or so. At the time they won the cup the championship final had not been played and we were still the holders.

"I'd have loved to see him play in his prime, for even at the end of his playing career he was capable of flashes of brilliance. He believed in the players and allowed them to think for themselves. In training he'd set us a task or a move and then sit and watch the players. Then he'd step in and, gently, remark: 'Can we try this?' He'd encourage the players at decision-making and all the players knew one another well. Playing at fullback he was in the right position to point us in the right direction and he was very effective at that."

Risman, though, could hardly be accused of molly-coddling his players. "For away games the team bus always left from Cockermouth, where Gus lived, and we had to make our own way there by public transport," Eppie recalls. "I'd catch the 7.20 bus from Maryport in order to get the team bus at 8.30 and we'd dropped off in Cockermouth after the match in time to catch the last bus home. We'd have long journeys to every away game, bar Whitehaven, and you'd just sit quietly and relax and prepare yourself for the game. On the other side of the coin, opposing teams never liked coming to Workington. We used to say that the only thing they got out of it was the ride up."

Eppie remembers well the excitement in Workington when they were admitted to the Rugby League. "It was just after the war and there was a lot of deprivation," he recalls. "There was no television in those days and people in the town had read about the players or heard about them on the radio. Suddenly they were seeing the stars of the game, either on the Town side or in the opposing ranks, with their own eyes.

"Men were coming back from the war after serving in the forces and there was great excitement. It was a boom period for the game as a whole and we were disappointed if we got crowds of less than 10,000."

Town started off ground-sharing with Workington Reds, at Borough Park, while Derwent Park was developed. The two club's home fixtures usually alternated each Saturday, though there were occasions when both clubs were at home on the same day - one of them switching to an early kick-off.

After the first game all the spectators were required to leave the ground and were re-admitted later should they so wish. The ground-staff had to quickly re-mark the pitch and change the posts and flags.

The most famous occurrence of this ground-sharing phenomenon came on 15 March 1952 when the Reds, in their first Football League season, played Oldham Athletic before a 5,352 crowd with a 2pm kick-off. Town then played Warrington at 4.45pm before an all-ticket 20,000 crowd in a third-round Challenge Cup-tie.

"Borough Park was a very good ground for the players. The spectators were right on top of the action and it created an intimate, special atmosphere that you didn't get at many grounds," Eppie recalls. "I remember, by contrast, playing at Odsal, a vast bowl of a place. Even though there was a decent crowd it felt when we were playing that there was hardly anyone there and you could almost go to sleep.

"West Cumberland is a real rugby area and we were doing well so the crowds were good. There were people that watched both soccer and rugby but we had the majority of the spectators.

"Risman brought in players from all over, including a few Australians. He also had a Midas touch at bringing in class players that had maybe not had too many chances at their former clubs, and resurrecting their careers. We were a happy team, we had a lot of local lads and we were friends without being too close. We weren't in each other's pockets all the time but we enjoyed one another's company, though people would speak their minds.

"But Risman's biggest secret was the way he kept a settled team. In the year we won the championship we only used around 20 players and that enabled us to build a really good team spirit and understanding."

The legendary Bill Shankly was once the Reds' manager, though his stay at Borough Park was comparatively short, lasting from January 1954 until November 1955. The Rugby League boys used to come across a man who went on to achieve such success as a manager at Liverpool.

"On training nights we'd often see him sat watching from a bench and I soon realised that his command of the English language was quite something," Eppie smiles. "Let's say he tolerated Rugby League on his beloved pitch. But people from Workington are very proud that, for all he achieved in the game, he was associated with the Reds. Another famous Reds manager was Joe Harvey (who went on to manage Newcastle United with distinction). I knew him well, much better than Shankly.

"Actually the relationship between the clubs was pretty good. There was no great animosity and the directors got along well. When the Reds applied for membership of the Football League they produced a brochure that showed a photograph of a packed Town End at Borough Park in an attempt to show the support for soccer in the town. The photograph had actually been taken at a Rugby League game. We always used to tease them that we had helped them achieve their Football League status."

Eppie recalls with particular pride the 1952 Wembley win, when Town defeated Featherstone Rovers 18-10, even more so than the 1951 Championship Final defeat of Warrington at Maine Road (when he scored two tries in a 26-11 win).

"That was my outstanding memory of my time at Town," he says. "Virtually everyone from Workington travelled down to London for the game. I remember there was a sign that someone put up on the road out of the town that read: 'Will the last one out please switch off the lights!' The Championship win was spectacular but Wembley had even greater glamour attached to it and the exodus of thousands of people was something special.

"I remember the homecoming when we toured the villages on an open top bus before ending up in the town centre. We even went through Whitehaven - we thought they'd appreciate that, the chance to see the cup. All the Whitehaven fans could do was wave, smile and wish. I don't recall any particular animosity."

Whitehaven's entry into the Northern Rugby League in 1948 provided one of the game's most keenly-fought rivalries, one that still exists just as intensely today. Eppie saw the derby from both sides, initially as a player at Town then at 'Haven, where he became their player-coach. "The first time I went back to Workington there was a lot of booing when we took to the pitch," he says. "I looked around and suddenly realised they were booing me. They felt I should have stayed at Town but though it was meant it was also good humoured and I was always made welcome after that.

"The animosity between the two clubs at times, though, is incredible. There is an intense rivalry. At times when we played one another you could have taken the referee off the field and just let the players settle things between themselves. It was hard rugby, with no quarter asked or given and a case of the best team won."

Eppie has lived in Whitehaven since 1958 but is not regarded as a Marra. "Even my oldest friends call me a Townie or a jam-eater," he shrugs. "It's just a shame that at the moment there is no Town-'Haven derby game with the clubs being in different divisions. The fans love those games and they do so much for the area. It would be nice if both clubs were in the first division and it's a big loss to Town that they're not."

The departure of Risman was the end of an era at Workington, even though the team continued to be successful under his successor, Brough. "He had been there virtually since the beginning and had brought honour to the town and everyone was sorry to see him go," Eppie says. "It was just the nature of things that it was time to move on and the incoming manager had his own ideas.

"But the influence of Risman and the great players of that era are still remembered with great affection in the town, especially among the older end. There are only seven of the 1952 Wembley side still living. I was asked to speak at a reunion recently, the reason given that I was one of those still alive."

The legendary Mitchell was one of the driving forces behind Town, single-handedly at times driving forward the development of the Derwent Park ground. But Eppie recalls, too, the influence of then chairman Jim Graves. "He was a very quiet man but he was the boss," Eppie recalls. "He used to come in to see the players before the start of each season and reveal the playing terms. That was it and if any player disagreed it was a case of: "Which other club would you like to play for?" He used to come down for training and after the match, if you fancied a quick half, he'd be there in the bar and you could approach him for a word."

Eppie had mixed feelings about the move to Derwent Park. "I think the soccer club had their concerns about the pitch at Borough Park and the two clubs felt they could each sustain their own ground," he says. "It was a popular move at the time. Derwent Park was much more open and in the depths of winter a fair old wind used to whistle from one end to another. The playing area felt and looked bigger, even though it wasn't. We lost that personal feeling and in recent times, when the numbers coming through the gates haven't been as good, the open-ness of the ground detracts from the atmosphere."

Derwent Park, the site of an old council rubbish tip, was constructed on eleven feet of ash and rubble with the council granting Town a 199-year lease for a peppercorn amount on the 18-acre site. Hundreds of wagon-loads of colliery shale helped form the distinctive oval. The site had formerly been owned by the Lowther Estates.

Although the ground was first used for reserve team games in the 1947/48 season, the scarcity of building permits, the shortage of building materials after the war and drainage problems meant that Town's inaugural first team game there was delayed until 11 February 1956 when they beat Salford, 16-0, in a Challenge Cup first round-tie.

As the dressing rooms and grandstand were not completed the teams changed at Siddick pit baths and travelled the half-mile to the ground.

Town's first league game there was on 27 August 1956 when they entertained Wigan, losing 0-24, before a crowd of 5,000.

Wigan provided the opposition for the ground record attendance, when 17,741 saw a third round Challenge Cup-tie in 1965, the visitors winning 10-4.

The grandstand at Derwent Park is built on what was until around 1900 a tidal creek known as the Saltings where fishing boats used to moor.

It holds 1,700 and was designed and built by Mitchell, who utilised a £13,000 loan from the RFL. The ground was mostly financed by £19,000 loans in total. On Mitchell's instigation the sides of the grandstand were built at 45 degrees instead of 90 at most other grounds, allowing stand patrons a perfect view of both ends. If only the architects of St Helens' main stand at Knowsley Road, to name but one example, had been blessed with equal foresight. Mitchell was given overall responsibility for the construction of Derwent Park and his farming and land-owning experience proved invaluable.

Mitchell recalled the doubts that many people had over Derwent Park: "My memory takes me back to one dismal Jimmy - a very prominent citizen (long since deceased), looking over the uneven wasteland opposite the Reds ground at Borough Park with its rusty oil drums, briars and other debris of all kinds. I pointed out the vision of a stadium reaching across to the LMS Railway Track: 'Well, Tom, that's a red herring if ever there was one'. He was not alone. It was meant to be a thumbs down sign all right.

"I can say now that it wasn't at all easy to obtain planning consent. There was a suspicion that it was "pie in the sky". I fought a strong, personal rearguard action and turned the corner by goodwill at several levels (including RLHQ itself) but the main argument I advanced was that Rugby League was coming to an enforced ending on Borough Park. Stark realism took hold!"

Keighley became the first senior side to play at Derwent Park, losing 2-10 to local amateurs Risehow and Gillhead before a crowd of 3,231 in a Challenge Cup-tie on 14 February 1948. That game kicked-off at 11am; later in the day Town were defeated by Warrington before 19,478 at Borough Park.

Town returned to Borough Park for games against Bramley and Batley in March 1984, both played on Friday evenings under floodlights, and in January 1986 the ground again staged Rugby League. Wigan beat Town 56-12 in a first round Challenge Cup-tie that attracted a crowd of 6,346, with Derwent Park ruled out by the wave of ground safety legislation in the wake of the Valley Parade disaster. A ground that once had held 20,000 saw its capacity temporarily reduced to 986.

In 1987 Town were again drawn at home to Wigan in the competition but this time switched the game to Central Park - a move that proved very unpopular with supporters. Town had to spend over £100,000 on essential safety work to enable their ground to continue to stage matches and the sale of the training ground for a supermarket, that realised £450,000 in 1989, was a big help in this respect. Part of the windfall was used to install the ground's first floodlights, officially inaugurated at the Cumbria-Australians tour game in 1990.

Derwent Park has been a regular venue for county games, including Cumberland's famous 17-15 win (attendance: 7,545) over the Australians in November 1967 and in 2004

attracted a crowd of over 4,000 for Cumbria's game with the ANZACs, roughly five times Town's recent average gates. One of the most famous games staged there was in the 2000 World Cup when the Samoa-New Zealand Maori game attracted a captivated crowd of 4,107, Samoa winning 21-16.

Town enjoyed a glorious spell in the early 1990s, winning the second division title in 1993/94 and later earning a place in the inaugural Super League. But what a disastrous season that was - Town finished bottom in 1996 with only five points from 22 games and their gates were down 739 from the Centenary season to 2,332. Apparently in freefall, Town entered administration in June 1997 and it has been a long haul back ever since.

Speedway was first staged at Derwent Park in 1970 and though the sport has had a chequered existence in the town, it is currently enjoying something of a boom period since its return in 1999.

Eppie has observed Town's decline in recent years with sadness but feels that there is genuine hope of a revival. "A big blow for the town was the soccer club losing its Football League status. Originally people say Workington was more a soccer town than a rugby town but Rugby League is very strong all along the West Cumbrian coast and has a good base in the amateur ranks," he says. "I don't think it will ever get back to the point where they have 10,000 crowds for home games but there is still definitely a nucleus of support there. If they can build on that the club can certainly keep going and the speedway helps financially. But it is a very steep climb for them."

Allerdale Council, who own Lonsdale Park, Borough Park and Derwent Park have recently floated the idea of redeveloping all three grounds and building a new 10,000 capacity stadium to house both the football and Rugby League clubs, with the speedway staying at Derwent Park. This groundhopper's tale looks far from over.

YORK

The sports grounds safety legislation that followed in the wake of the tragedy of the 1985 Valley Parade fire had so many ramifications for Rugby League clubs.

For York it effectively spelled the end of their tenure at one of the game's most loved grounds.

Ideally located close to the city centre, Clarence Street was a wonderful, traditional venue and had been home to York rugby for over a century. Many a tear was shed when the final game was staged there against Hunslet on Sunday 26 March 1989.

York had been Hunslet's last opponents at their beloved Parkside ground in 1973 and also the last visitors to the Greyhound Stadium seven years later before Hunslet moved up Elland Road to share with Leeds United. Now it was the turn for the tables to be reversed. Before a crowd of 2,904 York ran out 26-17 winners of the last game at Clarence Street. York's last home game of that season - a Second Division Premiership tie against Swinton - was staged at Castleford and attracted a crowd of only 1,000.

With the bulldozers revved up and waiting to transform the site into yet another housing development the arguments raged. Supporters claimed that the York City Council had not provided enough help to the club and a major sporting amenity for the city was lost that had been home to generations of supporters of the Wasps. It was a claim the council flatly denied.

York had been informed they had to spend £100,000 on safety measures at Clarence Street or face the ground being closed. It was money the club simply did not possess, so they turned to the council for help, arguing that the city could ill-afford to lose a club that provided such good publicity and a professional sport followed by many of its residents. Several meetings between the parties took place but nothing could be agreed.

The council maintained they would like to help but were legally prevented from spending money in an irresponsible manner. In the summer of 1988 a meeting of the council's Leisure Services committee decided that it could not provide financial assistance, either by grant or loan, as the York club was run by a limited company whose finances were far from healthy. Later there was talk of a £60,000 payment so long as the ground was freely allowed to be used for community use, but by then the club, with the deadline for the completion of the safety work looming, was well down the road of negotiations to sell the ground and move to Ryedale Council's new development at Monks Cross in Huntington.

York had carried on talks with their soccer neighbours, York City AFC, with a view to ground-sharing and with the council on jointly purchasing and developing a sporting facility at Thanet Road. But both of those schemes broke down. York had staged a first round Challenge Cup-tie against Leeds at City's Bootham Crescent on 29 January 1989 that attracted a highly encouraging gate of 11,347 but it progressed no further than that. With time not on the club's side, the Monks Cross scheme began to look more and more

The Huntington Stadium

appealing and the decision was taken to take the club's home out of the city centre and move to Ryedale.

The then York chairman, Ted Tebbutt, explained at the time: "As chairman of the club I had to take the best offer and that was a multi-million pound venture where we were welcomed. York could offer nothing in comparison and there was so much opposition to Thanet Road, some of it from inside the council. We will have a brand new modern stadium with first class facilities and some money to build a team to go with it. At the end of the day York council did not once came to us and offered us a penny nor even hinted at the possibility."

York fans pointed to the help that Wakefield Council gave its local club, purchasing the Belle Vue ground for £120,000, granting a further £80,000 loan to pay off debts and then meeting a £100,000 bill for safety work at the ground. But it was pointed out that the Wakefield club was then run as a non-profit making members' club, instead of a limited company like York and that Wakefield, as a metropolitan authority, had far greater budgets and powers than the district council of York.

With that, 104 years of rugby at Clarence Street was brought to a close.

York, formed in 1868 by ex-pupils of St Peter's School as York Amateurs RFC, played their early games on the bank of the River Ouse and on the Knavesmire opposite the famous racecourse. Their only major asset in those days was a pair of portable goalposts. From their early days the club acquired the nickname of the Wasps due to their amber and black hooped jerseys. They then moved to the Yorkshire Gentlemen's Cricket Ground at Wigginton Road (which was built over by the northern half of the District Hospital in the late 1960s and was opposite the location of the Clarence Street ground) before merging

261

with the Melbourne Club and playing from 1883 at a ground at Poad's Field, off Fulford Road near to Grange Street.

In 1885 they reached agreement to rent the Clarence Street ground, staging their first trial game there on 19 September of that year before Thornes became the first visitors a week later. The Yorkshire Evening Press reported: "The ground, although rather small, is well adapted for the purpose of football. A small stand has been erected and there is no doubt that it will be well patronised and the desire to afford accommodation to the public appreciated."

When it opened, the ground had a small open stand on the Wigginton Road side but there was no cover on any side. The dressing rooms were at the nearby Castle Howard Ox. The ground was in close proximity to the York Workhouse and the Bootham Park Lunatic Asylum. Local residents appeared quite happy with the latter two organisations but launched an objection to the lease for the rugby ground being renewed in 1886. which was perhaps a reflection on the behaviour of some rugby supporters in those days.

One of the most famous games staged at Clarence Street came on 20 March 1889 when the New Zealand Maoris, in the 71st of their 74-match tour of the British Isles, attracted a then ground record crowd of 4,200, producing receipts of £115, despite heavy rain. Special excursions were organised to bring in supporters from neighbouring towns and villages for the occasion. The Maoris ran out narrow winners over York by a try and a goal to a try.

In 1896 the club bought the Watermen's Mission Hut, which had previously been sited in Fishergate, and turned it into a small grandstand and dressing rooms on the Haxby Road side of the ground. Behind the stand was the Asylum Cottage - one of the boundaries to York Workhouse. The hut boasted three tin baths for the convenience of the players and was destroyed by fire in 1928.

York initially stayed loyal to rugby union after the 1895 split but then took the decision to join the Northern Union in 1898, finally achieving senior status in 1901.

Ground improvements continued, with the stand on the Wigginton Road side being rebuilt. Capable of providing cover for 1,200 spectators it was opened by John G Butcher, MP prior to the home game with Wakefield Trinity on 20 September 1902. This stand was destroyed by fire in 1922 and the same gentleman, now with a knighthood, again performed the opening ceremony prior to the home game with Leigh on 7 October 1922. New dressing rooms and offices were built in this stand in 1927 which survived until the ground's closure.

In 1903 York attracted then record home crowds for home Challenge Cup-ties against Hunslet (8,000) and Salford (11,000).

On a Wednesday afternoon, 29 January 1908 the Wasps hosted the New Zealand All Golds and ran out 5-3 winners before a 5,000 crowd.

Nearly nine months later they played the first Kangaroos at Clarence Street, again in a midweek encounter, in the fourth game of their tour and shared a 5-5 draw in front of a 3,000 crowd. Another great day came in 1921 when they beat the touring Australians 9-3 before 5,000. Three days later the Australians won the first Test with four of the team that faced the Wasps.

York fans of a more recent vintage still savour the visit of the 1971 Kiwis when an injury-ravaged home side produced a famous 11-5 victory.

The last tourists to play at Clarence Street were the 1978 Kangaroos, who ran out 29-2 winners before a 5,155 crowd on 14 November of that year. The penultimate game of the British part of the tour was played on a Tuesday evening, York hiring portable floodlights for the occasion. The club never erected permanent floodlights at the ground, though temporary lights were again used in the 1985/86 season.

York's first major honour in the professional ranks (they had won the Yorkshire Cup in rugby union way back in 1877) came when they won the Yorkshire Cup in 1922, defeating Batley, 5-0, before a 33,719 crowd at Headingley.

A limited company was formed in 1928 and the ground purchased for £5,300 three years later from the Bootham Park (Lunatic Asylum) governors, including former allotments that became the training pitch. A new popular stand on the Haxby Road side, that survived until the ground's closure, was then constructed, providing cover for 2,000. The two ends remained uncovered but both provided a good view of the action, many York fans preferring to switch ends at half-time to where their favourites were attacking.

From its earliest days the ground was known as Clarence Street, though later it became referred to as Wigginton Road in some circles.

At the time of the ground's opening, Clarence Street actually came up to the ground and was the main entrance, but later the street came to an end at traffic lights to the south of the ground. When the limited company was formed the club's registered office was on Wigginton Road, where the office itself actually stood, but traditionalists always knew the ground as Clarence Street right up until its death throes.

York's glory days were in the 1930s when they reached Wembley for the first and only time and also attained a top-four finish in the Championship in 1932/33, finishing third and losing at Swinton in the play-off semi-final.

York's Wembley Final came in 1931 when they lost 22-8 to Halifax, hampered by an injury to their halfback, Arthur Lloyd, long before the days of substitutes.

Along the way York defeated Huddersfield in a second round-tie before a new record home crowd of 12,943.

In 1933 York won the Yorkshire Cup for a second time, defeating Hull KR, 10-5, before 22,222 at Headingley. Two years later they lost 3-0 to Leeds in the final at Halifax but a year later earned another triumph, with a 9-2 win over Wakefield Trinity, again at their lucky ground of Headingley (19,000). York made only two more Yorkshire Cup Final appearances, losing to Huddersfield in 1957 and Bradford Northern in 1978.

The 1930s saw Clarence Street pull in some big gates, including 14,000 for a Yorkshire Cup-tie against Leeds on 19 October 1932. The ground record was set when 14,689 saw a first round Challenge Cup-tie against Swinton on 10 February 1934 when the sides fought out a 0-0 draw.

Clarence Street also staged a Yorkshire county game for the first time - against Cumberland in October 1931. A record home league attendance was established when 13,116 attended the game against Castleford on Boxing Day 1936.

York's only league honour, until 2005, came in the 1980/81 season when they lifted the second division title on the back of the 35 tries of club record-breaking stand-off John Crossley, seeing off the challenge of newly-relegated Wigan and newcomers Fulham. York defeated the Londoners 15-10 in March 1981 before a Clarence Street crowd of 7,351 - a figure that would now be regarded as remarkable for a second division game.

Fifty-three years after gracing Wembley, York got so near to visiting the Twin Towers again in 1984. They were a second division side but lost only 8-14 to Wigan at Elland Road. On the way to the semi-final York had beaten Castleford, 14-12, in a third-round tie before a crowd of 8,529 at Clarence Street - a game still remembered fondly in the city.

York stand-off Graham Steadman was the hero that day, ironically against the club for whom he would later play and coach. He scored all his side's points with two tries and three goals, the match-winning converted try coming midway through the second half.

York coach Phil Lowe injured his pelvis in a car crash after that game and returned for the semi-final on crutches. A Wigan side packed with internationals, including the influential Gary Stephens, who ironically soon after became York player-coach, had a hard-earned win on a waterlogged pitch and York have never reached that stage since.

"At the time I played for York they were known as a yo-yo club," Steadman recalls. "They were a good second division side but could never consolidate their place in the first division. But they had a good support base, attracting 2,500 to 3,000 for games against Lancashire clubs and 4-6,000 when they played the top Yorkshire clubs.

"There was a cracking atmosphere at Clarence Street, even with 2,000 on. One game I'll never forget is that quarter-final against Cas - that was a special game with a great atmosphere and I was lucky enough to be in a position to score a few points that day. For the semi-final Phil Lowe had been involved in that nasty accident and he was effectively ruled out for three months. If he'd stayed healthy maybe the game would have turned out differently. The game should never have been played due to the conditions, but Wigan just had that extra class and played the elements well on the back of our errors."

Steadman often looks back on that game and considers what might have happened had York reached Wembley. Maybe they would still have had the financial resources to stay at Clarence Street. "Tommy Harris was one of the directors and he said to me that if we win we'd get part of the Minster," Steadman recalls. "York was a city crying out for success - it still is. We still had a heroes' welcome when we got back home.

"From the people of York to the board of directors, everyone had a passion for the old ground. It was a crying shame when they had to move on. The day of the last game there was a very sad one - there had been so many memorable games and occasions at the ground. Without being too critical, the new ground would never have the same feel and atmosphere as the old one. It's a multi-purpose stadium and when games are played at an athletics track the atmosphere is not the same. The dimensions of the field also limit expansive football."

Within two years of nearly reaching Wembley for a second time York sold the training pitch for housing for £200,000 to stave off the threat of bankruptcy and the end of Clarence Street as a rugby ground was not far away.

St John Ellis, the current Doncaster coach, is York born and bred and was making his way in the game at the time the Wasps moved grounds. "There was a fantastic atmosphere at Clarence Street," he recalls. "The crowd was nice and close and we used to get good gates. They'd pile out of the pubs - there were so many in the vicinity - at five to three and come to the game. I loved playing there. The playing surface was a bit woolly and the changing rooms were old but the passionate crowd more than made up for that.

"I was a Fulford lad but was a bit of a latecomer to the game. The first time I saw York was in the semi-final at Elland Road. All the lads from the pub ran a coach-trip to the game. Then the first house I bought was near to the ground. I'd jump over the wall and be into training. I was a local kid and just wanted to perform the best I could. It was great to pick up the local paper when we'd had a good performance.

"The last match there was a very sad occasion. I remember having a good drink afterwards with Stewart Horton. I had so many good memories of the place."

Singe then played in a trial game against Castleford and impressed them that much they signed him. As a result he never played for York at their new ground.

York's new home at the Monks Cross development, with Birse Construction Ltd the contractors, was situated about two miles from Clarence Street. Birse had also been contractors for Scunthorpe United, who became the first Football League club to open a new ground since 1955 when their Glandford Park ground was inaugurated in 1988.

York's stadium, initially known as Ryedale Stadium but now referred to as Huntington Stadium, also hosts a multi-purpose sports hall and a 400-metre athletics track, opened in October 1989 by Olympic athletes Tessa Sanderson and Steve Ovett, as part of a huge complex, including a huge shopping area and light industrial site.

Capacity was originally set at 5,500 with plans to increase this to 8,000 by terracing the grass bankings at either end. The complex cost around £2m, with the club contributing £730,000 (far greater than the £450,000 originally planned, with the floodlights and popular side stand not included in the original budget) which was more than the £705,000 they received from the sale of Clarence Street.

York secured a 66-year licence to use the ground rent-free with exclusive rights to ground advertising and the provision of a social club. The club also changed its name to Ryedale-York before reverting to York in 1995.

York-born Graham Sullivan, having scored the last points at Clarence Street, had the distinction of being the first scorer on the new ground as York defeated Keighley, 16-6, before 4,803 on Sunday 8 October 1989, after playing their first six games of that season away from home.

He was one of six players to play in the last match at Clarence Street and the first at the Ryedale Stadium.

Nearly 2,000 more people watched the first match at the new ground than the last at the old one and the seasonal average was up 474 at 2,495 - the best since the 1985/86 season.

But in the Centenary season of 1995/96 the average was down to 642, rising only by 26 for the first summer campaign of 1996.

Completely different in character to Clarence Street, York's new ground was built on what had been farmland in the lowest point of the city. On one side was a propped cantilever stand with ten rows of 74 seats, eight hospitality boxes, police control room and a vice-presidents lounge that doubled as a boardroom. On the opposite side was a £155,000 full length covered terrace capable of holding 2,700. But for those used to the intimacy and accessibility of Clarence Street the new ground, with its location outside the city centre, low viewing angles and distance from the pitch came as quite a culture shock.

Letters from supporters to the Evening Press frequently described the new ground as cold and soulless. "Huntington Stadium is the most sparse, cold and horrible place to go and watch a match," wrote one. "There is no atmosphere at all." Another fan wrote: "The

heart of the club was ripped out when they left Clarence Street and the nucleus of support was lost." One fan stated: "A running track is anathema to the spirit of watching the game at close quarters."

A ground record for the new ground was set when 4,977 saw a league game against Halifax on 5 January 1990.

The following season the Ryedale Stadium was unavailable due to an athletics meeting so York staged their play-off game with Leigh at Scarborough AFC on 21 April 1991, losing 6-11 before a crowd of 956. On 25 August 1991 with the stadium again unavailable, they played Hunslet in a Yorkshire Cup preliminary round-tie at Heworth ARL's Elm Park Way ground, winning 36-8 before a crowd of 707.

On 19 March 2002 the directors closed the club, blaming dwindling crowds and lower than expected sponsorship. Seven days later their resignation from the Rugby League was accepted after a week of efforts to save the club failed. Just 280 had attended what proved to be their final home game, against Chorley on 10 March 2003.

But a "Kick-Start York RL" campaign headed by supporters Gary Hall, Mike Miller and Roger Dixon ensured that the professional game was not lost to the Minster City and a new club, York City Knights, entered the RL the following season, abandoning any link with the Wasps and playing in a new dark and light blue and white strip.

The Knights' first campaign was a great success in re-generating support for the professional game in the city and average crowds of 1,365 were achieved, up nearly 700 on the Wasps' truncated last season. The Knights' opening game against Hull KR on 19 January 2003 attracted a crowd of 3,105.

Afterwards, chief executive Steve Ferres remarked: "The people of York have today shown they want professional Rugby League in the city."

In 2004 York have continued their hard work, attracting 1,520 to an Arriva Trains Cup-tie against Gateshead, staged in midweek, switched to Bootham Crescent and 2,519 for a home league game against the same opponents after heavily promoting the game

York City Knights formed from the ashes of the old Wasps club, and gained promotion to National League One in 2005 *(right)*

among local schools.

At one time it looked as though York City FC, faced with losing Bootham Crescent for housing, would move in at Huntington Stadium and the ground would be brought up to Football League standards. But the tireless work of their supporters' trust has ensured that the Minstermen, as the soccer club is known, will continue in the short term at Bootham Crescent, while exploring the possibility of moving to a new ground within the next five years.

The soccer club has now ruled out a move to the Huntington Stadium and if the Knights are to aspire to Super League status in the future they will either have to develop their own ground, build a new one or enter into a ground-sharing agreement with the soccer club. Recently there was a suggestion the Knights could be involved in the latter, the leader of York City Council, Steve Galloway, commenting: "Discussions are only starting but the working assumption is that if we're going to have a purpose-built stadium it would be used by the Rugby League club as well as the football club."

Time will tell.

POT POURRI

Any serious groundhopper searching for traces of long defunct clubs can often have a fruitless or frustrating hunt, save for digging up old match reports from newspapers in dusty libraries.

It is a lonely and often sad quest, reading about great deeds of the past, stirring encounters, and the great wafts of optimism that greeted each new season only to then discover those hopes being dashed and the clubs sliding into oblivion. Visiting the sites of the grounds that once resonated to the sounds of the greatest game of all, most now developed for housing or industrial use, can also often be an emotional experience with few, if any, remaining signs of the site's historical importance.

It was only recently that Tyldesley's Well Street ground was built upon, the rugby union club moving a few hundred yards to new headquarters at St George's Park in 2001. Situated at the bottom of the hill leading to the town, Well Street was an atmospheric ground often echoing to the ghosts of the past, notably the team known as "The Mighty Bongers" that was one of the foremost rugby teams in the north in the 1890s and founder members of the Northern Union (NU) in 1895.

Located next to the cricket field the Well Street ground had rather rudimentary facilities and the teams and officials changed at a nearby public house before being transported to the match by horse-drawn wagonnettes. There was one main grandstand but the rest of the ground was mostly open standing.

Tyldesley had one of the game's most recognisable halfbacks in John "Buff" Berry, who won England RU honours in the early 1890s, and their forward pack was feared. Derby games against local rivals Leigh, both before and after the "split", usually attracted Tyldesley's biggest gates of the season, but with Wigan, St Helens, Salford and Swinton also close by there was no shortage of local interest.

The Wigan Examiner reporter graphically described Wigan's visit there in 1888. "Wigan explored the barbaric regions of prehistoric Lancashire," he stated. "It is a village where the houses seem creeping up slopes and in the midst of the cotton spinning institutions and mines there is a devouring appetite for football food."

Well Street's record crowd of 7,000 saw Tyldesley clinch the Lancashire Senior Competition with a victory over Saints in the last season before the breakaway and the Bongers finished sixth in the first season of the NU before entering a steep decline. They lacked the financial clout of many of their local rivals and the onset of professionalism invariably damaged those clubs with limited resources - a tale often repeated elsewhere.

Crowds fell to a few hundred by the time Tyldesley lost their senior status in 1900 and they folded after one season in the Second Competition. Bailiffs, acting on behalf of the Inland Revenue authorities, took control of the turnstiles at what proved to be the club's final home game, against Birkenhead Wanderers, and the club's effects were later sold at auction for £30 to recover some of the unpaid rent and income tax.

The Leigh Journal's post-mortem could have been applied to many other clubs who folded around this time. Though there was "not the slightest doubt" that payments to players had been made before 1895 the practice now became "general and undisguised, and many leading clubs were soon engaged in a fierce and costly competition for the services of well-known players. The inevitable result of this was to cripple and finally crush out of all existence the football organisations in relatively small centres."

The amateur game continued to flourish in the town and Well Street's future was secured when a local coal mine owner, William Ramsden, passed the ground over to the Tyldesley RU club formed just after the First World War. Until recently a visit there was a rewarding one and it was easy to imagine the days when the Bongers were a force in the game.

Other ill-fated founder members included Liversedge, Manningham, Stockport and Brighouse Rangers. Runcorn (folded 1916) and Broughton Rangers (1955) have been covered elsewhere in this book.

Liversedge, formed in 1877, first played at a field in Hightown before moving to another enclosure in the same area, now part of the George V Playing Fields. Their headquarters were initially at the Shoulder of Mutton, but club rooms were then constructed at the ground. Though competing against neighbouring clubs in Cleckheaton and Heckmondwike, Liversedge earned the title of the leading club in the Spen Valley and had the finance to erect a new stand at a cost of £300 in 1892. Two of their players, Harry Varley and Bob Wood, played for England.

Liversedge entered the NU as reigning champions of the Yorkshire Senior Competition but soon encountered financial problems, similar to those of other smaller clubs. They merged with Cleckheaton in 1901 and though continuing under the name of Liversedge for a while played at Cleckheaton's ground at Whitcliffe Road, opposite West End Park. The club lost its senior status in 1902 but continued under the name of Cleckheaton until folding in 1906.

Manningham, based at Valley Parade, were inaugural champions of both the Northern Rugby League and Yorkshire Senior Competition in 1895/96 but entered a decline, switching to soccer after the end of the 1902/03 season in an act known to local rugby followers as "The Great Betrayal."

At the Manningham annual general meeting on 29 May 1903 an earlier resolution to play both codes passed at the previous meeting was over-ruled and it was decided that the club "abandon the rugby code for the present." A gloom seemed to settle over the club following the tragic death of their star fullback, George Lorimer, from typhoid fever at the age of only 24 in 1897. Such was the eagerness of the Football Association authorities to establish the round ball game in a previously rugby stronghold the newly-formed Bradford City were elected into the League without playing a game. Rugby League did return to Valley Parade, though, in 1920 when a crowd of 20,318 saw Bradford Northern draw 2-2 against Oldham in the Challenge Cup and has been played there many times since.

Formed in 1876 as Manningham Albion, dropping the suffix four years later, the club moved to Valley Parade, the site of a former quarry, in 1886, leasing the ground from the Midland Railway Company. They re-erected a 50-yard stand that was transported from their previous ground at Carlisle Road. With a paddock area in front the stand could accommodate 2,500 spectators and the ground, which had a capacity of 18,000 and excellent viewing from the steep slopes on three sides, also incorporated a 400-yard cinder track which was used for the very popular athletics festivals that many clubs promoted around this time.

Stockport, a sufficiently senior club to be granted a fixture against the 1888/89 Maori tourists, joined the NU immediately after it was formed, playing at Edgeley Park until 1902/03. Stockport moved to Edgeley Park in 1891 when they vacated the nearby Cale Green ground they shared with the town's cricket club. Edgeley Park also regularly hosted Cheshire's County Championship games. The tour game at Cale Green was perhaps the most memorable in the club's history as a crowd of 4,000 saw the home side put up what was described as a "gallant fight" against the Maoris to earn a creditable draw. The visitors were also taken on a tour of a local hat-making factory prior to the commencement of the game.

After finishing bottom of the second division in what proved to be their final season Stockport disbanded in August 1903 and Stockport County FC, who had been sharing the ground since leaving Green Lane in 1902, gained sole control. County had been junior partners and had to revert to Green Lane if the fixtures clashed. Elected to the Football League in 1900 County became the first League club to groundshare with a rugby club. After gaining sole tenancy County then made substantial ground improvements. The groundshare was repeated a century later when Sale Sharks RU moved from Heywood Road. Broughton Rangers staged some of their home fixtures at Edgeley Park during the second world war.

Brighouse Rangers, winners of the Yorkshire Senior Competition in 1896/97, folded after the 1905/06 season after finishing bottom of the 31-team Northern Rugby League. Formed in 1878 by Harry Waller, who became the first Chairman of the NU, Rangers first played at Fink Hill before moving to the Lane Head ground on Waterloo Road by the 1883/84 season. They soon erected a new grandstand and enlarged the ground. When Rangers lost to the Maoris in January 1889 there was a 4,000 crowd in attendance.

In 1895, when Rangers joined the NU, the ground was purchased by the Council from Barron Piggott for £2,800. Rangers remained at Lane Head but encountered problems paying their rent, and their assets, which consisted of two stands, five turnstiles and a wooden dressing tent, were sold at auction in August 1906, fetching around £50. A Brighouse Rangers team was briefly revived in 1913, playing in the Yorkshire Combination, and the grounds were taken over by the Council for the library and art gallery during the second world war years.

Edgeley Park, home of Stockport until 1902/03

Other clubs that quickly disappeared in those early pioneering years of the breakaway were Leeds Parish Church, Heckmondwike, Goole, Sowerby Bridge, Altrincham and Radcliffe.

Leeds Parish Church, formed around 1874 as a section of the church recreation club as part of the "Muscular Christianity" movement, played at Clarence Field. The ground was situated over Crown Point bridge between the tow-path of the Aire & Calder Navigation and Clarendon Road, just behind Leeds locks in what was then a deprived and highly-populated area. In 1899 a crowd of 12,000 saw Yorkshire clinch the County Championship with an 8-5 win over Cumberland and a record crowd of 20,000 saw the club's Challenge Cup fourth-round tie against Runcorn in 1900. The Churchmen drew 5-5 but won the replay before losing 0-8 to Swinton in the semi-final at Watersheddings. But a year later they were given notice to quit the ground and decided to abandon NU football in the summer of 1901.

Heckmondwike, formed during the early 1870s, played at Beck Lane, a ground later taken over in the 1930s by Huddersfield Town FC's junior sides. After joining the NU in 1896 they struggled for three seasons in the Yorkshire Senior Competition before losing their senior status in 1899 after going down to Hull KR in a promotion/relegation test match. In 1903 the rugby section was closed and the club went over to the round ball game.

In its early days the ground had ash banks on three sides and railway sleeper terracing. Heckmondwike's most famous player was John Sutcliffe, who won caps for England at rugby union and soccer, going on to make 332 league appearances for Bolton Wanderers where his rugby skills were utilised in a goal-keeping role. He later played for Manchester United.

After a gap of over 100 years rugby almost returned to Beck Lane in 2005, but plans by Huddersfield Giants to stage two Academy games there were thwarted by pitch renovation works. Beck Lane also hosted the longest penalty shoot-out in soccer history in 2001 when the West Riding Amateur Cup-tie between Littletown FC and Storthes Hall was level at 17-17 when the game was abandoned due to the failing light.

A rugby club was established in Goole, a purpose built town to serve the terminus of the Aire & Calder Canal Company, in 1879. Known as the "Seaporters" they played at the Victoria Pleasure Grounds, Carter Street. The ground is currently home to Goole FC, who recently won promotion from the Northern Counties (East) League to the Unibond League. The soccer club was re-formed in 1997 after Goole Town (formed 1900) went defunct due to financial problems in the 1996 and they began to fight their way back up the football pyramid.

Goole joined the NU in 1898 and gained senior status in 1901/02, finishing 12th out of 14 clubs in the Yorkshire Senior Competition and losing 0-67 at Salford in the Challenge Cup. But after failing to win a place in the newly-formed second division for the 1902/03 season they disbanded.

The amateur game continued in the town for a period and Goole reached the first round proper of the Challenge Cup in 1937, losing 2-14 at home to Broughton Rangers before 2,500 people. In 1990 Rugby League returned when Hull played a reserve game at Carter Street against Leeds before Scarborough Pirates based their "A" team there during their one season in the League.

Also a past venue for galas, wrestling matches, sports days and heavy horse shows Carter Street lies in the shadow of the town's famous 145-foot water tower, which can be clearly seen when travelling past on the M62 motorway.

Sowerby Bridge (formed c1886) joined the NU in 1899 when they were holders of rugby union's Yorkshire Cup. Nicknamed "Tups" or "Tuppers" and playing in red, based at the Beech Road recreation ground they attained senior status in 1901/02, finishing one place above bottom club Liversedge in the Yorkshire Senior Competition. But after failing to win a place in the second division for 1902/03 (when they lost 5-14 at home to Batley in the Challenge Cup) they folded before the start of the following season due to mounting debts.

Altrincham's home was at Devisdale, a large piece of spare land actually situated in neighbouring Bowdon. The land was owned by the Earl of Stamford who let it to the Altrincham Agricultural Society and the rugby club was a sub-tenant. Some of the Society members objected to "the coarse language of the footballers and their followers" and the ground was only free for rugby once the last of the summer shows had been completed. Occasionally they played some games on a field off Stockport Road.

A ground record crowd of 3,000 saw Altrincham lose 0-16 to Salford in the Challenge Cup in 1898. Altrincham had only one season as a senior club, in 1901/02 when they finished next-to-bottom of the Lancashire Senior Competition, and then folded due to financial problems and the club's meagre assets were sold at auction in November 1902.

Radcliffe, founded 1878, were one of the oldest rugby organisations in Lancashire. A local man, Mr Lawrence Ashworth, was the club's founder. The story went that one day, tired of seeing a group of local lads loitering about the area, he bought them a ball and provided them with a field. "The founders of the Radcliffe club," reported the Radcliffe Times, "were soon engaged in running in tries, dropping goals and scoring that relic of the past, the minor point." Their most famous player, Tom Kent, also associated with Salford, won England RU honours and toured Australia in 1888. Later that year he persuaded one of the touring New Zealand Maori side, Joseph Warbrick, to turn out for Radcliffe against Tyldesley - one of the first instances of an overseas player playing for an English club.

Despite having two prominent soccer towns, Bolton and Bury, in close proximity Radcliffe was regarded as a rugby town until the club was formally wound up in 1903. For their last 13 years they played at Peel Park, in the centre of the town, sharing their facilities with the cricket club. There were few facilities at the ground apart from a pavilion and a small stand.

After joining the NU in 1896, Radcliffe had the distinction of becoming Wigan's first-ever opponents in a Challenge Cup-tie, losing only 3-0.

Despite gaining senior status in 1901 Radcliffe suffered from the growing popularity of soccer, with Bury, FA Cup winners in 1900 and 1903, attracting average home gates of around 8,000. By contrast, for the home game against Barrow in December 1901 the receipts at Peel Park were only one pound. Radcliffe could only muster eleven players for their game against Wigan (this, at a time when the game was still 15-a-side) and played their final game against Barrow in April 1902 when the gate money was just sufficient to pay the referee's travelling expenses. Peel Park was later taken over by the Manchester Welsh RU side. A local junior side, Radcliffe Rangers, carried on the code for a few years and reached the first round of the Challenge Cup in 1907, losing 0-13 at home to York.

In north-west Lancashire, Morecambe and Lancaster flew the NU flag until the early 1900s. Lancaster folded in 1905 while neighbours Morecambe lasted another year.

Rugby was the dominant code of football in Lancaster in the late 19th century following the formation of the club around 1877 and a healthy rivalry was established with Morecambe. After leaving their original home at the Giant Axe Field (now home to

Lancaster City FC) the club moved 400 yards across the railway line to the picturesque Quay Meadow ground, overlooked by the castle and St Mary's church. There their reputation grew and one of their players, John Pinch, earned England RU honours.

Despite that, Pinch was an influential figure in the decision to join the NU in 1897 when the club played in the Lancashire Second Competition before attaining senior status in 1901. The club's finances were helped no end when a local benefactor, Lord Ashton, wiped off their debts of £100 "to show his appreciation of the management of the club steering clear of the close affinity with public houses that marks some clubs".

An emerging local talent, Jimmy Leytham, blossomed after Lancaster entered the second division before being transferred to Wigan and becoming one of the great wingers of the Edwardian era. Struggling with poor home gates, not helped by the increase in popularity in the area of soccer, and large travelling expenses, Lancaster's debts soon mounted again. With no-one prepared to stand for the committee, the club folded in June 1905 with debts of around £100.

Morecambe leased a field off Moss Lane from the railway company from their formation in 1876 and had their headquarters at the King's Arms Hotel in the Lancashire seaside resort. The ground, which had a grandstand along one side with the other three sides being uncovered standing areas, was to the south of the railway line near the town's gas works.

The "Seasiders" became one of the most prominent clubs in the north of the county and became a senior club straight after joining the NU in 1896. But after three seasons of struggle they were relegated and spent two years in the backwaters of the Lancashire Second Competition before regaining their status.

Perennially near the bottom of the table Morecambe's problems were made worse by their geographical isolation and consequent high travelling expenses. With gates falling after many seasons of poor results they played their final game at Widnes in April 1906 and folded with debts of £40. At the meeting that decided the club's fate, the town's Mayor stated that the big clubs "had no sympathy for the smaller ones" and the chairman said "it was useless continuing as they would only run head-over-heels in debt." As a postscript he added: "The NU has ruined us. They are all for themselves."

Further north, Millom was another outpost of the game but rather than fold reverted to the amateur ranks in 1906.

One of the oldest and most successful clubs in Cumberland, Millom switched codes in 1897 at a time when they boasted two England RU internationals in Edward Knowles and Sam Northmore and had a host of county players in their ranks. Playing at the Salthouse ground, which was located next to a field that formerly was used for public executions, Millom's facilities were somewhat sparse. Contemporary reports describe a small grandstand as the ground's only feature. A ground record gate of £111 was taken from the 4,000 crowd that attended the game against local rivals Barrow in 1898 and Millom earned senior status after beating Morecambe in a test match a year later.

"The Blues" enjoyed their best season in 1902/03, finishing third in the second division, but the signs of the financial pressures of competing against teams in Yorkshire on falling gates often numbered in their hundreds were becoming marked.

The re-organisation of the leagues for the 1905/06 season sounded the death knell for Millom. Secretaries were left to organise their own fixtures in the 31-club competition with positions to be decided on a percentage basis on the proviso that a minimum of 20 fixtures were played.

Millom had enormous difficulties in persuading the requisite number of teams to make the long and costly journey to the north-west coast in return for a home fixture against a club regarded as unfashionable and hence unlikely to attract a big gate. Significantly Millom played only 20 games - the bare minimum - and their fixture against their only opponents from Yorkshire, Pontefract, in April 1906 was their last as a senior club. Millom's win, by 10-5, meant they won 75 of their 188 league games - a respectable record. From the 1906/07 season Millom competed in the Cumberland Senior League, and fortunately the town remains a stronghold of the game, albeit at an amateur level.

In Cheshire Birkenhead Wanderers resigned after four Second Division games in the 1904/05 season. In the shadow of their more illustrious neighbours, Birkenhead Park RU, the premier Wirral club, Wanderers joined the NU in 1897 and achieved senior status in 1901/02.

Wanderers played at the St Anne's Enclosure, about half-a-mile from the Park ground. Due to its close proximity to the station the venue was often referred to as the Park Station ground. Owned by the local council the ground had one main stand with spectators also standing around the other three banked cindered sides. One the club's major signings was a former Welsh RU international, Tom Pook. Not only was Pook a useful operator on the field he was an ingenious one off it, rigging up an electrical system at the ground so the players could train in the winter evenings.

Though geographically out on a limb, Wanderers competed profitably until they left the Lancashire Second Competition to join the Northern League. They had to finance long trips into Yorkshire and the north-east and lost many of their local fixtures. Their closest rivals were Rochdale and Stockport and many of the Yorkshire clubs they faced were not considered attractive opposition. As a result home crowds fell from a few thousand to a few hundred in a short space of time.

In a bid to boost support Birkenhead dropped their Wanderers tag and moved to a new ground at Prenton Park in 1903, which they shared with Tranmere Rovers FC.

They took with them a 250-seater stand from their old ground. Rovers, who went on to achieve Football League status in 1921, moved ground a few yards away in 1912 and their new home was also called Prenton Park. The original ground was then referred to as Old Prenton Park.

Ground-sharing had its problems and Rovers had preference if fixtures clashed, so the rugby team had to play some home games at the Docks Station enclosure, owned by the Wirral Railway Company. But the finances of the club were now so parlous they held two midweek games, against Holbeck and Wakefield Trinity, at Wigan's Central Park ground.

Despite beginning the 1904/05 season the club's finances were described as being at "breaking point" and they fulfilled only a handful of fixtures before folding in October 1904. Once lost, the game of NU, or Rugby League as it became, at a senior level never returned to the area.

In Yorkshire Holbeck (folded 1904) was covered in the Hunslet section, while Normanton's last senior season was in 1905/06, though the area remained a stronghold of the amateur game.

Formed around 1880, Normanton joined the NU in 1898. Known as the Colliers and playing in black and white stripes they won the Yorkshire Second Competition in 1899/1900 and also defeated Leeds 5-0 at home in a Challenge Cup first-round tie that season before losing 0-3 to Batley in the next round.

Their former ground, known as Horsfalls Paddock, is now covered by a housing estate, though a road through it is called The Paddock. In 1901 Normanton achieved senior status and moved to a new ground at Mopsey Garth, previous home to the defunct Normanton St John's club. The club folded after the 1905/06 season when they finished 26th out of 31 teams in the Northern Rugby League. Their last game, against Huddersfield, was switched to Wakefield and resulted in a 0-5 defeat.

Neighbouring Pontefract lasted one more season, resigning after the 1906/07 campaign, but established something of a record for their bewildering change of home venues in such a short membership.

Rising out of the ashes of the old Pontefract club (formed c1880 and winners of the Yorkshire Cup in 1891) in the mid-1890s and known as "the Liquoricemen" Pontefract played in blue and white colours at Halfpenny Lane Cricket Ground before moving to a new ground at Skinner Lane. They joined the NU in 1898 and became a senior club in 1903/04 after the resignation of Manningham, moving to a new ground at Park Avenue.

But soon after the club hit financial problems and a re-formed organisation rented a new ground from the local army barracks at Garrison Field where they erected a temporary stand. Agreement was then reached with the Duchy of Lancaster estates to rent a new ground along Halfpenny Lane. The first game staged here was on Christmas Eve 1904 when Pontefract defeated Bramley, 10-6.

Despite several respectable mid-table finishes the club announced in December 1906 that they would fold due to financial problems after fulfilling only eight of their fixtures during the 1906/07 season. Their final game was a 5-11 defeat at home to Dewsbury on 8 December 1906. They complained that the League had imposed repeated fines on them for petty offences and it was suggested outside the club that due to county court summonses on the committee for outstanding debts it had been decided to cease playing while there was still a balance in hand.

The grounds of South Shields and Newcastle, Liverpool City (the 1906/07 version), St Helens Recreation and Welsh clubs Merthyr Tydfil, Ebbw Vale, Aberdare, Barry, Mid-Rhondda, Treherbert, Pontypridd and Cardiff together with London clubs Acton & Willesden and Streatham & Mitcham have also been covered elsewhere in this book.

Coventry had three seasons in the league before folding after the 1912/13 campaign. Though they won only 12 of 93 league matches and resigned soon after losing 102-0 to Leeds at Headingley in what proved to be their final game on 12 April 1913, it was a brave if failed attempt to establish the NU code in virgin territory. Formed in November 1909 Coventry took over the tenancy of the Butts Stadium three months later. The former home of the suspended Coventry RU club, the ground was owned by the Coventry Cricket Grounds company and boasted two stands with the playing area surrounded by an athletics track and a banked cycle track.

Coventry attracted 3,500 for their first competitive home game, a 3-15 defeat against Runcorn in September 1910, and later had several crowds of around the 5,000 mark in their first season before enthusiasm waned. Their last home game against York saw a mere handful of spectators trickle through the turnstiles. After they went defunct the stadium was re-let to the rugby union club. Later used for soccer and athletics, the ground again hosted Rugby League from 2003 when NL3 side Coventry began playing at the well-appointed and modernised arena, raising hopes that the senior game may one day return to the city.

The Butts staged an international in February 1910 when England defeated Wales 39-13 before 4,500 and the following year the second Kangaroos opened their tour there with a 20-11 defeat of a Midlands & South selection before 2,000 spectators.

The loss of Bramley's McLaren Field was much lamented among groundhoppers - a relatively new venue, opened in 1966, but one still full of character and charm.

Bramley had previously played next door at the old Barley Mow ground back to 1881 and Maurice Bamford, who coached the Villagers in two spells, was captivated by both places.

"As a small boy I was taken along to watch Rugby League by my father," Bamford explains. "We went to Leeds one week, where I used to marvel at seeing all the stars and great teams, and to Bramley the next. Bramley were a struggling outfit but it was there that I developed my love of the game and began to get a feel for its unique character.

"At the old ground the players used to strip in the pub, named the Barley Mow, behind the posts. It was one of the old Northern Union stripping holes - and had links right back to the early days of the game. Round the back of the pub (now re-named the Villager) was a little fence with a wicker gate and the players used to go through that and out onto the field. On the right-hand side was a small stand with a half-rounded roof.

"Barley Mow was far from being a Wembley, but it was a grand little ground. As a youngster going to watch Leeds the terraces seemed a mile high and thronging with people; the following week you could stand a yard or so from a scrum, see and feel the steam from the props writhing in the mud and smell the liniment mixed with the beer from the night before. Wintergreen, olive oil and beer mixed together is a lovely smell and remains a vivid memory.

"There was a gnarled, timber staircase up to the back of the pub where the players changed in a whitewashed room with wall pegs. Wigan, Australia, Bramley - they all stripped there and it was amazing to think that some of the pioneers from the game's great history had changed there in exactly the same facilities. They stripped there in the 1890s and were still doing so in the 1960s. There was a scalding hot bath on the ground floor and if you didn't open the door outside the steam used to rise and you'd go back upstairs to find your clothes running with whitewash. Even on the coldest of winter days the players would forget about their modesty and keep that door open for that reason. Then they'd go to the Barley Mow pub for a beer and a sandwich before making their way home.

"In the mid-1960s Mrs McLaren who owned the field behind the stand died and gave it to Bramley in her will. Bill Norfolk, the Bramley chairman, was a potato man and one Saturday he and Ernest Humphreys, another club director, set out the new pitch and marked the lines with sawdust. They built a nice grandstand with a bar underneath and a terrace with a cover at the back of the old parabolic stand at the old ground.

"Bramley was such a friendly club and they kept to the old ways in an endearing fashion. The team would be picked after training on a Thursday and the secretary, Les Phillips, would then send out cards to the players and the coach with instructions for the game. If it was away he'd always write: "You are asked to bring clean boots and laces and are reminded that there is no smoking in the saloon."

The Barley Mow ground hosted the first club game against a touring team when the 1907/08 New Zealand "All Golds" began their tour with a 25-6 victory before a crowd of 6,000 on a Wednesday afternoon, 9 October 1907. Bramley put up a terrific fight before the tourists scored five second-half tries. When the 1921 Australians visited, though, Bramley were swamped 92-7 before a crowd of only 1,500. The record attendance at the ground was established in May 1947 when 12,600 saw the local derby with Leeds. It was only during the 1952/53 season that the covered stand was equipped with seating for the first time.

The death of Bramley's neighbour, Mrs Edith McLaren, coincided with notice from

McLaren Field, Bramley's home from 1966-1995 and
(below) Clarence Field, one of the club's temporary bases

the brewery that they required part of the Barley Mow ground to build a car-park. Hastily moving next door, named McLaren Field according to the proviso in the will, Bramley opened up with a heroic 11-16 defeat against Leeds on 20 August, 1966. The new £35,000 seated main stand, with dressing rooms and bars underneath, was much admired and considered a remarkable improvement on the old Barley Mow facility.

The record attendance at McLaren Field was an estimated 7,500 (£2,257) to see Bramley defeat Bradford Northern in a Challenge Cup-tie in February 1972. Floodlights were installed in time for Bramley to host the Roses match in 1973 and this enabled the Villagers to compete in the popular BBC2 Floodlit Trophy competition for the first time, culminating in the club's greatest moment.

"At the time the power cuts were on during the miners' strike and so they were unable to use the floodlights," Bamford recalls. "They beat St Helens at home in the semi-final one Tuesday afternoon with the highlights later being shown on television and then travelled to

Widnes for the final. Though they were the underdogs Bramley pulled off a famous win, 15-7. Again the match was played in the afternoon and highlights later shown on television. Arthur Keegan was the player-coach. It was the first honour in the club's long history.

"When I was coach we had some good players and there was always a tremendous community feel to the club though money was always tight. We considered running a car-boot sale or market at the ground to help raise funds, but Leeds council were dead against it. One day I got a furtive 'phone call from a council member sympathetic to our cause. "Go to Bramley library," he said, "and enquire about when Bramley saved Leeds."

"I went to the library and did some research. I found out that in the 1600s the plague hit Leeds and carts were carrying the dead away in droves. They tried to re-locate the market to Rothwell, Castleford and Horsforth but none of those places would entertain the idea. But Bramley said "yes" and Bramley ran Leeds City Market for three months and saved all the jobs and businesses of the market traders. I mentioned this in my letter to the council and explained it was time for Leeds to reciprocate. They agreed and we took £4,000 in the first week, then a steady £3,300 for six months. That saved the club at that time."

McLaren Field also briefly hosted an American Football team and the re-formed Bradford Park Avenue FC played at the ground from 1989 to 1993.

After the sale of McLaren Field greatly saddened their loyal band of followers, the site was developed for private dwellings, though a strip of nearby land still provides for some recreational space for local children.

The final home game at the ground was attended by 538 who saw Rochdale Hornets run out 40-20 victors in April 1995. Bramley then moved briefly to play at the rugby union ground at Clarence Field, Kirkstall, where they achieved a club record victory, 74-0 against Chorley in September 1995. But only 212 could say "they were there." After taking up residence at Headingley in 1997 Bramley suffered a lingering and agonising death, leaving the RL after a creditable 11th-placed finish in the Northern Ford Premiership in 1999. Just 300 saw their final home game, against York and the season ended a week later in a 12-28 defeat at Dewsbury.

After 103 years membership of the RL their passing created little more than a stir at the time though was lamented by true followers of the game's rich heritage who believed that without the smaller clubs the game would not flourish. The reformation of Bramley, now known as the Buffaloes and playing in NL3 at Stanningley ARLFC gives hope that one day Bramley will return to the senior ranks.

A much more recent convert to the professional game, though in an area seemingly with rich potential was Carlisle. A professional game had been staged in the city on the Australians' tour of 1908/09 when they played Cumberland at Devonshire Park, the former home of Carlisle United FC and now the Trinity School Playing Fields, the county side recording an 11-2 victory before 2,000. In 1928 a Carlisle City team entered the league, playing at the Harraby Park Stadium, a greyhound and speedway racing venue that the promoters claimed would hold 70,000 spectators with 5,000 seated. But those claims were never tested as the club resigned after fulfilling only ten league games with just one victory and home gates down to the low hundreds. They were hampered by the fact that Carlisle United had joined the Football League that season and attracted average crowds of nearly 8,000 in the Third Division North. The greyhound company was wound up in March 1929 and the grandstand transported by rail to Redheugh Park, Gateshead.

Carlisle then entered the league in 1981, in what became a boom period for new clubs and just a year after Fulham's spectacular entry into the sport. Like Fulham, Carlisle shared their facilities with a soccer club, playing at Carlisle United's Brunton Park and they emulated their achievement in finishing in the promotion places in their first season, achieving an average home gate of 2,950. They then recruited a young New Zealander, Dean Bell, to join them for what proved to be their only season in the top flight.

Bell looks back fondly at what was starting point of an illustrious playing career. "Brunton Park was a terrific place and my introduction to the English game was playing on that ground," he recalls. "I later found out that not all the grounds were like that. They got their turf from the same place as Wembley and it was a fantastic pitch, like playing on a carpet. They pitches in New Zealand were very different.

"We had a good following and the ground was great for Rugby League. It had a big main stand and was then a typical old soccer stadium, though it has been developed since, with a lot of atmosphere. The team was Yorkshire based and, living in Carlisle, I had a 250-mile round-trip for training. But I had the bonus of not having to travel for home games. They were happy times - the catalyst of my professional career. There was many a wily old professional in that team so it was the ideal learning ground for me. It helped me a lot."

After seven seasons Carlisle left Brunton Park, unable to afford the rent, and took up residence in far less salubrious surroundings at Gillford Park, part of the ground being built on the old Harraby Park Stadium that had previously housed the professional game.

"When I first joined Carlisle there was that uniqueness to Rugby League in the city and that sustained interest for a while," Bell adds. "But after that they needed a winning team and, if they'd had that, I'm sure the crowds would have stayed with them. But Carlisle is dominated by soccer, shown by the crowds United have attracted in recent years, despite having a struggling team."

Carlisle's opening game at Brunton Park, against Wigan in the Lancashire Cup, attracted 2,779 and they had 5,903 for their opening league game against Workington Town, a record that remained until the club's demise. Carlisle briefly returned to Brunton Park for a Lancashire Cup-tie against Widnes in September 1989 when the turn-out, 4,329, was further proof of the potential for the game in the border city.

Gillford Park was leased from the Carlisle & District Railwaymen's Sports and Athletic Club and was an open field before the rugby club developed two stands, one of them seated. After their reserve team played there in 1987/88 the first first-team game took place on 4 September 1988 when Batley shared the spoils in a 17-17 draw.

Though the ground had limited development potential and an estimated capacity of

Gillford Park, Carlisle

John Play

only 3,000, for Simon Knox it was an ideal place to launch his career as a professional. He played for Carlisle for four years before being snapped up by Bradford.

"Gillford Park was a very small, close-knit stadium," Knox recalls. "Everyone was cramped in on the touchlines and there was a small main stand. For the players it wasn't the best ground for facilities - the dressing rooms were rickety and makeshift and you were lucky if there was any hot water. There was so little space you had to take turns to dress, with four or five showers for 30 players and the officials.

"But the pitch conditions were very good and there was always a good atmosphere, even with only a few hundred on. When teams like Widnes, Leigh or Castleford came with a good following the atmosphere was fantastic. Carlisle had about 400 loyal supporters and they were very vocal and passionate. They certainly let you know what they thought about your performance, either during the game or afterwards in the bar."

Carlisle added six more grounds to the groundhoppers' list before leaving the RFL at the end of the 1997 season after "merging" with Barrow. During their second season, 1982/83, they played "home" games at Wakefield and Huddersfield and in 1986/87 took two first team games, against Keighley and Sheffield, 15 miles down the M6 to Penrith FC's Southend Road ground, also the venue of their reserve team games for a while. In April 1995 they played York at Gateshead International Stadium and during the centenary season they played three games at Carlisle RU's ground on Warwick Road, next door to Brunton Park. In their last season they took the high road to the Scottish borders play Lancashire Lynx one Friday evening at Hawick RUFC's Mansfield Park ground, attracting a crowd of 424. In their final game Carlisle lost 24-34 to Workington before 453 at Gillford Park.

"I was very saddened when the professional game left the city," Knox adds. "But I could see the reasons why. Rugby League was always going to be third after soccer and then union. But I felt it had its place at Gillford Park. We had some real characters in the side. Kevin Pape was a terrific centre who took me under his wing and really taught me about the rights and wrongs of being a professional player. And the prop, Steve Brierley, was a Carlisle resident who just loved turning out for the club. Steve was a postman in the city and they used to say he finished his round about an hour-and-a-half after everyone else because he spent that much amount of time talking about Rugby League."

If Rugby League was not to be successful in Carlisle the chances of sustaining a club far from the heartlands in an entirely virgin area were far from promising. But Kent Invicta's launch into the senior ranks in 1983, playing at Maidstone United FC's ground on London Road was accompanied by more than the usual hype.

United's home since the 1890s and formerly a hop garden and orchard, the ground (renamed the Maidstone Stadium in the 1970s) was shaped like an amphitheatre and also staged greyhound racing. United at that time were knocking on the door of the Football League, finally joining in 1989 after their second Conference title. By then they had been forced to play their home games at Dartford after their much loved ground was sold in 1988 for development and they left the league after being unable to give guarantees they could fulfil the 1992/93 season.

Invicta hosted another new club, Cardiff Blue Dragons, in their first game on a stiflingly hot summer's afternoon in the "Garden of England" on 21st August 1983. But financial problems soon surfaced and the running of the club was taken over by the soccer club. Invicta's record crowd was 2,107 for the visit of St Helens in the JPS Trophy and they later attracted a crowd of 1,643 when hosting Castleford in front of the BBC Grandstand television cameras in the Challenge Cup. Though they lost, 20-42, a Londoner, Frank Feighan, scored a memorable solo try that day - his long-range effort being judged good enough to later win "Try of the Season" on the BBC.

Gary Hetherington, then in the throes of organising Sheffield Eagles, entry into the RL a year later, joined Invicta, travelling from Yorkshire with a car-load of experienced professionals to help add some know-how and guile. He looks back on his short time with the club with affection.

"I joined in the knowledge my time at the club would be short but I really enjoyed it there," Hetherington says. "It wasn't a big ground but it was a pretty good place; the pitch was OK and the environment was fine. The people involved in the running of the club were very enthusiastic and bubbling with ideas. The Yorkshire lads trained together in the north and we'd maybe go down a day early before the game for a training session with the rest of the players. We had some good New Zealand players in the team - Gary Freeman played, as did Mark Elia and a few former rugby union players who tried League, like Adrian Alexander and Bob Mordell. I managed to feature on the video of the Feighan try - it was me who played the ball. As I later told Ray French (commentating for the BBC that day), if I hadn't played the ball properly then Frank wouldn't have been able to do what he did!"

After one year Invicta were on the move, re-launching as Southend Invicta for the following season. Whereas their time in Kent had seen some respectable crowds and a league average of 731, there appeared to be little or no enthusiasm for Rugby League on the Essex coast. Playing at Roots Hall, home of Southend United FC, Invicta averaged only 216 and had some of the lowest recorded gates for a professional club game in history. Their final home game, against Huddersfield, was watched by just 85. Their highest gate was 504 against Fulham on New Year's Day. Bizarrely, the former Australian prop, the late John "Dallas" Donnelly, was persuaded to see out his career with the club and after one year they folded.

Mansfield Marksman came into the RL in 1984, taking their name from the sponsorship of a local brewery who had a Marksman lager brand. Playing initially at Field Mill, home of Mansfield Town FC since 1919, there were initial hopes that the game could be established in the East Midlands. Dave Parker was heavily involved with Mansfield's formation.

"At first things looked promising," Parker says. "The ground has been changed out of all recognition now but then it was still a decent stadium with a big main stand (purchased from Hurst Park Racecourse in 1966). For the first game, against Wakefield, we had over 2,000 packed in that stand and there was a good atmosphere. There was a real buzz going there - it was a good venue for the game." Mansfield got off to a flying start, beating Wakefield 15-0 before 2,291 but the first season's average was only 1,020, falling to 487 in the second.

"We got a few locals on board and they were very enthusiastic. We had people coming to watch us from Derbyshire, South Yorkshire, Leicestershire and even Skegness," Parker adds. "We got good backing from Mansfield Brewery and people used to call us Marksmen instead of Marksmen. The famous pop star Alvin Stardust, who was born in Mansfield, was the Club President.

"The groundsman was very good and never complained. Winters twenty years ago were different to how they are now and he used to tell me that there was no high land between Mansfield and the Urals so we used to get some of the worst of the weather with some icy blasts of sleet and snow. It was a really cold spot and many a time he'd ring me on a Sunday morning to say the pitch was covered in an inch of snow. But we always seemed to play. I thought it was going well but then the soccer club got greedy and upped the rent. There was no way we could survive on the new terms so had to go somewhere else."

Marksman played their final game at Field Mill against Leigh on a bitterly cold afternoon with snow on the ground in February 1986, by which time they had slumped to the bottom of the table. They then moved a few miles into Derbyshire to ground-share with Alfreton Town.

"North Street was very stark compared to Mansfield," Parker adds. "There was a small open stand and open standing on the other sides. It took us a long time to drill the holes in the ground sufficient to put in the posts. I went there with the late Brian Cartwright, the famous RL groundsman, who very kindly helped us out many-a-time."

A cup-tie against Hull gave Mansfield their biggest payday since leaving Field Mill, with 1,579 in attendance. North Street has since been redeveloped considerably as the ambitious soccer club aim for a spot in the Conference and is virtually unrecognisable from the ground that once staged Rugby League.

Mansfield staged one game at Notts County FC's Meadow Lane ground (that hosted England's 5-3 victory over Australia before 3,000 in December 1911) having put on an exhibition game at their neighbours Nottingham Forest's City Ground between Hull KR and Cardiff City in May 1983 before their formation. Mansfield defeated Fulham, 32-18, before 950 at Meadow Lane in September 1986.

But their next home was another non-league soccer ground, Sutton Town's Lowmoor Road ground at Kirkby-in-Ashfield, since demolished. With seated capacity of only 150 and a small covered area for another 300 the ground was one of the smallest to host the professional game. The average crowd during their one season there in 1988/89 was 560. "That was even more stark and bare than Alfreton," Parker recalls. "It was bereft of facilities and not what I had aspired towards."

For the 1989/90 season after a boardroom split Mansfield lost their brewery sponsorship, changed their name to Nottingham City and moved to play at the Harvey Hadden Stadium in the city. Named after a local man, who bequeathed the land in his will "to benefit the inhabitants of Nottingham," the stadium, within Bilborough Park, is a pleasant tree-lined athletics and cycling arena, first opened in 1959. The only cover was provided by a cantilevered stand with seats for nearly 700.

City's first official game there saw 902 attend a Yorkshire Cup-tie against Hull and

Mansfield to Nottingham - the Harvey Hadden Stadium hosted Rugby League from 1989-1993

2,545 attended for the visit of Halifax, then one of the game's best supported clubs. City had to move their Yorkshire Cup-tie against Hull KR in August 1990 to Tattersfield due to work being carried out at the stadium and the locals were spared seeing their team annihilated 100-6.

City's fortunes slumped and after losing every game during the 1991/92 season they were thrown out of the league at the end of the following season. Their final game, against Highfield, did attract a crowd of 851 with fans descending on the ground from many different clubs in an organised protest at the decision of the RFL to demote three clubs, with the visitors retaining their senior status after their 39-6 victory. But earlier that season the home game against Barrow attracted only 101.

Another ambitious project to launch a professional club - and in a holiday resort at that - came in 1991 when Scarborough Pirates entered the league, co-sharing the McCain Stadium on Seamer Road (formerly known as the Athletic Ground until a sponsorship deal in 1988 and the football club's home since 1898) with the town's soccer club who, from 1987 to 1999, were members of the Football League. York had switched their play-off game with Leigh to Scarborough in April 1991 as a taster, attracting a crowd of 956, and the interest for the Pirates was encouraging. Geoffrey Richmond, the soccer club's chairman, was the principal shareholder in the independent Rugby League club.

With former GB international Len Casey as coach Pirates recruited an experienced squad, with many of the players coming from the Humberside and East Yorkshire area, including Ray Stead who was the only ever-present. And the fledging club hit the headlines when it was announced that a local theme park would sponsor the club to the tune of £1m if they won promotion at the first attempt.

The much-respected RL administrator Roland Davis was recruited as chief executive and he looks back on the Pirates' days with a feeling that the club was never allowed to take root. "We built a useful team but needed more players if we were to chase promotion that first season," he recalls. "Everything seemed to hinge around that £1m but it soon became apparent we weren't going to achieve that. We had a lot of bad luck in close finishes but by Christmas the prospect of the £1m had disappeared and Casey was sacked.

"We had a keen bunch of supporters and they tried everything to help the club. We signed some good players - some at the start of their careers like Jason Ramshaw and Martyn Wood and some nearing the end like Bob Beardmore, Peter Smith, Gary Pearce and Garry Clark. We had a fair budget for team-strengthening but a lot of the deals we tried to put in place just wouldn't go through. After Len was sacked a lot of the impetus was lost and it was a case of just going through the motions and seeing out the season. Crowds diminished and there was no chance of keeping going for another year. Things hadn't been thought through long-term.

"There had been a lot of interest in RL in the town with an active schools programme before the Pirates were started and in many ways the area had a lot going for it. The ground has since been developed considerably, with two big stands at either end, but even then it was more than adequate for watching Rugby League and created a good atmosphere. We played our reserve games at Goole and built up quite a decent following on a Friday night. One day we played Hull in the Cup and had a crowd of about 1,000 which was terrific."

The Pirates' opening home game, against Huddersfield, attracted a crowd of 1,402 and the average for the season was a respectable 777. Their last game was on 17 April 1992 when they lost 12-24 at home to Barrow before 463. High hopes were soon quashed and another venue was lost to the game.

SENIOR GROUNDS

TOWN/CITY	GROUND	FIRST YEAR	FIRST GAME
Aberavon	Talbot Athletic Ground	1996	South Wales 8-70 Hull KR (League)
Aberdare	Ynys Field (Athletic Ground)	1908	Wales 9-8 New Zealand (Tour game)
Abertillery	Park Ground	1949	Wales 5-6 Other Nationalities (International)
Alfreton	North Street	1986	Mansfield 18-42 Workington (League)
Altrincham	Devisdale	1901	Altrincham 0-13 Millom (League)
Altrincham	Moss Lane	1989	Trafford Borough 18-33 Swinton (League)
Ashton-u-Lyne	Hurst Cross	2002	Oldham 32-16 York (League)
Barnsley	Oakwell	1990	Sheffield Eagles 24-10 Wakefield Trinity (League)
Barrow	Cavendish Park	1900	Barrow 3-6 Oldham (League)
Barrow	Craven Park	1931	Barrow 7-30 Swinton (League)
Barrow	Little Park	1914	Barrow 31-2 Bramley (League)
Barry	Trinity Street	1908	Barry 6-3 Treherbert (League)
Batley	Mount Pleasant	1895	Batley 7-3 Hull (League)
Belfast	Windsor Park	2000	Ireland 30-16 Samoa (World Cup)
Birkenhead	Docks Station Enclosure	1904	Birkenhead 0-3 Castleford (League)
Birkenhead	Old Prenton Park	1903	Birkenhead 0-35 St Helens (League)
Birkenhead	Park Station	1901	Birkenhead 16-0 Radcliffe (League)
Birmingham	Villa Park	1909	Great Britain 6-5 Australia (Test)
Blackburn	Ewood Park	1911	Lancashire 12-25 Australia (Tour game)
Blackpool	Bloomfield Road	1955	Blackpool Borough 24-24 New Zealand (Tour game)
Blackpool	Borough Park	1963	Blackpool Borough 36-16 Salford (League)
Blackpool	Common Edge Road	1992	Blackpool Gladiators 8-22 Workington Town (Lancashire Cup)
Blackpool	St Annes Road Stadium	1954	Blackpool Borough 7-10 Batley (League)
Bolton	Burnden Park	1985	Swinton 14-8 Sheffield Eagles (League)
Bolton	Reebok Stadium	1998	Great Britain 16-36 New Zealand (Test)
Bradford	Birch Lane	1908	Bradford Northern 11-14 Huddersfield (League)
Bradford	Greenfield Athletic Ground, Dudley Hill	1907	Bradford Northern 5-8 Huddersfield (League)
Bradford	Odsal Stadium	1934	Bradford Northern 16-31 (Huddersfield)
Bradford	Park Avenue	1895	Bradford 11-0 Wakefield (League)
Bradford	Valley Parade	1895	Manningham 5-3 Batley (League)
Bridgend	Brewery Field	2003	Wales 4-76 Australia (Tour game)
Bridgend	Coychurch Road	1984	Bridgend 16-28 Swinton (League)
Brighouse	Lane Head	1895	Brighouse Rangers 13-0 Rochdale (League)
Bristol	Ashton Gate	1911	Wales & West 3-23 Australia (Tour game)
Bury	Gigg Lane	1992	Swinton 10-14 Rochdale Hornets (League)
Cardiff	Cardiff Arms Park	1996	South Wales 8-26 Swinton Lions (League)
Cardiff	Mainde Stadium	1952	Cardiff 14-59 Wigan (League)
Cardiff	Millennium Stadium	2000	Cook Islands 22-22 Lebanon (World Cup)
Cardiff	Ninian Park	1981	Cardiff City 21-26 Salford (League)
Cardiff	Penarth Road Stadium	1951	Cardiff 10-27 Widnes (Cardiff)
Cardiff	Sloper Road Greyhound Stadium	1928	Wales 15-39 England (International)
Carlisle	Brunton Park	1981	Carlisle 6-9 Wigan (Lancashire Cup)
Carlisle	Devonshire Park	1909	Cumberland 11-2 Australia (Tour game)
Carlisle	Gillford Park	1988	Carlisle 17-17 Batley (League)
Carlisle	Greystone Road, Carlisle RUFC	1995	Carlisle 40-8 York (League)
Carlisle	Harraby Park Stadium	1928	Carlisle City 3-10 Wigan Highfield (League)
Castleford	Sandy Desert	1896	Castleford 4-6 Brighouse Rangers (League)
Castleford	Wheldon Road	1926	Castleford 12-18 St Helens Recs (Challenge Cup)
Cheltenham	Athletic Ground	1908	Great Britain 5-8 New Zealand (Test)
Chesterfield	Saltergate	1989	Sheffield Eagles 16-27 Leeds (League)
Chorley	Victory Park	1988	Chorley Borough 8-22 Workington Town (League)
Cleckheaton	Whitcliffe Road	1901	Liversedge 0-24 Normanton (League)

TOWN/CITY	GROUND	FIRST YEAR	FIRST GAME
Coventry	Butts Stadium	1910	Coventry 3-15 Runcorn (League)
Crawley	Broadfield Stadium	2001	London Broncos 44-6 Batley Bulldogs (Challenge Cup)
Dewsbury	Crown Flatt	1901	Dewsbury 3-0 Sowerby Bridge (League)
Dewsbury	Owl Lane	1994	Dewsbury 76-8 Barrow (League)
Doncaster	Belle Vue (Earth Stadium)	1983	Doncaster 10-33 Cardiff City (League)
Doncaster	Tattersfield	1953	Doncaster 11-34 Keighley (League)
Doncaster	York Road Greyhound Stadium	1951	Doncaster 10-3 Wakefield Trinity (League)
Douglas, Isle of Man	Douglas Bowl	1985	Wigan 34-6 Hull KR (Charity Shield)
Ebbw Vale	Bridge End Field (Eugene Cross Park)	1907	Ebbw Vale 0-29 Salford (League)
Edinburgh	Murrayfield	2000	Bradford Bulls 24-18 Leeds Rhinos (Challenge Cup Final)
Edinburgh	Tynecastle Stadium	1911	Great Britain 11-11 Australia (Test)
Featherstone	Post Office Road	1921	Featherstone Rovers 9-21 Hull (League)
Gateshead	Gateshead International Stadium	1991	Hull 8-22 Wigan (Charity Shield)
Gateshead	Hedley Lawson Park, Gateshead Fell RUFC	2003	Gateshead Thunder 42-12 Workington Town (National League Cup)
Gateshead	Redheugh Park	1934	England 19-14 Australia (International)
Gateshead	White City Stadium	1937	Newcastle 3-17 Featherstone Rovers (League)
Glasgow	Celtic Park	1909	England 17-17 Australia (International)
Glasgow	Firhill	1996	Scotland 26-6 Ireland (International)
Glasgow	Old Anniesland	2003	Scotland 22-24 Ireland (International)
Gloucester	Kingsholm	2000	New Zealand 64-0 Lebanon (World Cup)
Goole	Carter Street	1901	Goole 3-10 Dewsbury (League)
Halifax	The Shay	1986	Halifax 8-15 Widnes (League)
Halifax	Thrum Hall	1895	Halifax 6-0 Widnes (League)
Halifax	Thrum Hall cricket ground	1904	Halifax 8-5 Leigh (League)
Hawick	Mansfield Park	1997	Carlisle Border Raiders 32-6 Lancashire Lynx (Divisional Premiership)
Heckmondwike	Beck Lane	1896	Heckmondwike 0-0 Bramley (League)
Horwich	Grundy Hill	1992	Chorley 13-23 Ryedale-York (League)
Huddersfield	Fartown	1895	Huddersfield 10-0 Wakefield Trinity(League)
Huddersfield	Fartown cricket ground	1914	Huddersfield 20-10 Hull (League)
Huddersfield	Leeds Road	1952	Wigan 13-6 Bradford Northern (Championship Final)
Huddersfield	McAlpine Stadium (Galpharm Stadium)	1994	Huddersfield 50-12 Barrow (League)
Hull	"New" Craven Park	1989	Hull KR 48-8 Trafford Borough (League)
Hull	Boothferry Park	1953	Hull 13-2 Hull KR (League)
Hull	Boulevard	1895	Hull 3-0 Liversedge (League)
Hull	Craven Park	1922	Hull KR 0-3 Wakefield Trinity (League)
Hull	Craven Street	1899	Hull KR 8-2 Hull (League)
Hull	Kingston Communications Stadium	2003	Hull FC 24-16 Halifax (Challenge Cup)
Hyde	Ewen Fields	1997	Oldham Bears 20-21 Sheffield Eagles (League)
Jarrow	Monkton Stadium	2003	Gateshead Thunder 18-18 Workington Town (League)
Keighley	Lawkholme Lane (Cougar Park)	1901	Keighley 7-6 Wakefield Trinity (League)
Kirkby-in-Ashfield	Lowmoor Road	1988	Mansfield Marksman 24-11 Huddersfield (League)
Lancaster	Quay Meadow	1901	Lancaster 4-5 Millom (League)
Leeds	Barley Mow, Bramley	1896	Bramley 10-5 Batley (League)
Leeds	Clarence Field	1995	Bramley 16-30 Swinton (League)
Leeds	Clarence Field, Crown Point	1896	Leeds Parish Church 7-10 Bradford (League)
Leeds	Elland Road	1897	Holbeck 8-4 Manningham (League)
Leeds	Elland Road Greyhound Stadium	1973	New Hunslet 23-0 Huyton (League)
Leeds	Headingley	1895	Leeds 3-0 Brighouse Rangers (League)
Leeds	Headingley cricket ground	1938	Leeds 5-0 Salford (League)
Leeds	McLaren Field, Bramley	1966	Bramley 11-16 Leeds (League)
Leeds	Parkside	1895	Hunslet 16-8 Oldham (League)
Leeds	Recreation Ground	1896	Holbeck 4-5 Bradford (League)
Leeds	South Leeds Stadium	1995	Hunslet 37-10 Leigh (League)
Leicester	Welford Road	1999	London Broncos 16-19 Bradford Bulls (League)
Leigh	Charles Street	1946	Leigh 17-4 St Helens (Lancashire Cup)
Leigh	Kirkhall Lane (Hilton Park)	1947	Leigh 0-15 St Helens (Lancashire Cup)
Leigh	Mather Lane	1895	Leigh 3-6 Leeds (League)
Liverpool	Alt Park, Huyton	1969	Huyton 5-60 Salford (League)
Liverpool	Anfield	1989	Widnes 27-22 Wigan (Charity Shield)
Liverpool	Goodison Park	1908	Northern Rugby League 9-10 Australia (Tour game)
Liverpool	Knotty Ash	1950	Liverpool Stanley 2-36 St Helens (League)
Liverpool	Stanley Athletic Grounds	1906	Liverpool City 8-41 Wigan (League)
Liverpool	Stanley Greyhound Track	1934	Liverpool Stanley 21-5 St Helens Recs (League)

285

Senior grounds

TOWN/CITY	GROUND	FIRST YEAR	FIRST GAME
Liversedge	Hightown	1895	Liversedge 0-3 Wigan (League)
Llanelli	Stebonheath Park	1935	Wales 41-7 France (International)
Llanelli	Stradey Park	2000	Wales 24-22 Lebanon (World Cup)
London	Claremont Road, Hendon	1989	Fulham 4-34 Wigan (Lancashire Cup)
London	Copthall Stadium, Barnet	1993	London Crusaders 40-6 Batley (League)
London	Craven Cottage	1911	England 6-11 Australia (International)
London	Crystal Palace National Sports Centre	1965	Commonwealth XIII 7-15 New Zealand (Tour game)
London	Griffin Park	1995	London Broncos 26-12 Leeds (League)
London	Herne Hill Stadium	1922	England 12-7 Wales (International)
London	Highbury Stadium	1921	England 5-4 Australia (International)
London	Kingsmeadow	2000	London Broncos 44-18 Wath Brow Hornets (Challenge Cup)
London	Loftus Road	1955	Leigh 46-20 Hunslet (Independent Television Trophy)
London	Lower Mead	1985	Fulham 10-10 Whitehaven (League)
London	Mitcham Stadium	1935	Streatham & Mitcham 5-10 Oldham (League)
London	New River Stadium	2003	London Skolars 10-22 Dewsbury Rams (National League Cup)
London	Park Royal Stadium	1935	Acton & Willesden 17-17 York (League)
London	Park Royal, Willesden	1908	Great Britain 22-22 Australia (Test)
London	Polytechnic of Central London Stadium, Chiswick	1985	Fulham 17-16 Runcorn Highfield (League)
London	Stamford Bridge	1908	Great Britain 6-18 New Zealand (Test)
London	The Stoop Memorial Ground	1995	London Broncos 34-50 St Helens (League)
London	The Valley	1995	London Broncos 46-14 Oldham Bears (League)
London	Twickenham	2000	England 2-22 Australia (World Cup)
London	Wembley Stadium	1929	Dewsbury 2-13 Wigan (Challenge Cup Final)
London	White City Stadium	1933	London Highfield 8-9 Wakefield (League)
London	Woolwich Stadium	1955	Huddersfield 33-11 Wigan (Independent Television Trophy)
Maidstone	London Road Stadium	1983	Kent Invicta 12-31 Cardiff City (League)
Manchester/ Salford	Belle Vue Zoological Gardens	1933	Broughton Rangers 8-14 Warrington (League)
Manchester/ Salford	Chorley Road, Swinton	1896	Swinton 17-6 Warrington (League)
Manchester/ Salford	City of Manchester Stadium	2004	Great Britain 8-12 Australia (Tri-Nations Series)
Manchester/ Salford	Fallowfield Stadium	1899	Oldham 19-9 Hunslet (Challenge Cup Final)
Manchester/ Salford	Maine Road	1939	Salford 8-6 Castleford (Championship Final)
Manchester/ Salford	Moor Lane, Kersal	2002	Swinton Lions 12-29 Doncaster Dragons (League)
Manchester/ Salford	New Barnes	1896	Salford 0-9 Oldham (League)
Manchester/ Salford	Old Trafford	1958	Salford 17-22 Leeds (League)
Manchester/ Salford	Park Lane, Whitefield	2004	Swinton Lions 6-22 Leigh Centurions (National League Cup)
Manchester/ Salford	Station Road, Swinton	1929	Swinton 9-3 Wigan (League)
Manchester/ Salford	The Cliff, Broughton	1913	Broughton Rangers 0-14 Swinton (League)
Manchester/ Salford	The Willows, Weaste	1901	Salford 2-0 Swinton (League)
Manchester/ Salford	Wheater's Field	1895	Broughton Rangers 0-9 Wigan (League)
Manchester/ Salford	White City Stadium	1961	Rugby League XIII 22-20 New Zealand (Tour game)
Mansfield	Field Mill	1984	Mansfield Marksman 15-0 Wakefield Trinity (League)
Maryport	Athletic Ground	1901	Cumberland 5-16 Yorkshire (County Championship)
Maryport	Sandy Lonning	1920	Cumberland 6-27 Yorkshire (County Championship)
Merthyr Tydfil	College Field	1907	Merthyr Tydfil 6-25 Oldham (League)
Merthyr Tydfil	Penydarren Park	1909	Welsh League 14-13 Australia (Tour game)
Merthyr Tydfil	Rhydycar Road	1909	Merthyr Tydfil 0-4 Hull (League)
Millom	Salthouse	1899	Millom 5-13 Oldham (League)
Morecambe	Moss Lane	1896	Morecambe 3-6 Wigan (League)
Newcastle-u-Tyne	Brough Park	1936	Newcastle 12-33 Huddersfield (League)
Newcastle-u-Tyne	Kingston Park	2005	Gateshead Thunder 16-24 York City Knights (League)
Newcastle-u-Tyne	St James' Park	1909	Great Britain 15-5 Australia (Test)
Newport	Rodney Parade	2000	London Broncos 18-28 Warrington Wolves (League)
Normanton	Mopsey Garth	1901	Normanton 9-0 Castleford (League)
North Shields	Preston Avenue, Percy Park RUFC	2004	Gateshead Thunder 24-40 Barrow Raiders (League)
Northampton	Sixfields Stadium	1998	Halifax Blue Sox 32-10 Sheffield Eagles (League)
Nottingham	Harvey Hadden Stadium	1989	Nottingham City 6-56 Hull (Yorkshire Cup)
Nottingham	Meadow Lane	1911	England 5-3 Australia (International)
Oldham	Boundary Park	1982	Oldham 17-9 Batley (League)
Oldham	Watersheddings	1895	Oldham 3-11 Tyldesley (League)
Penrith	Southend Road	1986	Carlisle 8-2 Keighley (League)
Plymouth	South Devon Place	1913	England 40-16 Wales (International)
Pontefract	Garrison Field	1904	Pontefract 13-0 Morecambe (League)
Pontefract	Halfpenny Lane	1904	Pontefract 10-6 Bramley (League)
Pontefract	Park Avenue	1903	Pontefract 8-0 Morecambe (League)
Pontypridd	Taff Vale Park	1921	Wales 16-21 Australia (International)

TOWN/CITY	GROUND	FIRST YEAR	FIRST GAME
Prescot	Hope Street	1940	Liverpool Stanley 8-8 Oldham (League)
Preston	Deepdale	1997	Lancashire Lynx 5-48 London Broncos (Challenge Cup)
Preston	Lightfoot Green	1998	Lancashire Lynx 18-18 Oldham (League)
Radcliffe	Peel Park	1901	Radcliffe 13-2 Altrincham (League)
Reading	Madejski Stadium	2000	New Zealand 84-10 Cook Islands (World Cup)
Rochdale	Athletic Grounds	1896	Rochdale Hornets 0-23 Runcorn (League)
Rochdale	Dane Street	1895	Rochdale Hornets 3-14 Bradford (League)
Rochdale	Spotland	1954	Rochdale Hornets 13-13 Keighley (League)
Rotherham	Clifton Lane	2005	Sheffield Eagles 20-38 Doncaster Dragons (National League Cup)
Rotherham	Millmoor	1985	Sheffield Eagles 2-34 Swinton (League)
Runcorn	Irwell Lane (Canal Street)	1895	Runcorn 15-4 Widnes (League)
Scarborough	McCain Stadium	1991	Ryedale-York 6-11 Leigh (Second Division Premiership)
Sheffield	Bramall Lane	1911	Yorkshire 13-33 Australia (Tour game)
Sheffield	Don Valley Stadium	1990	Sheffield Eagles 34-6 Wakefield Trinity (League)
Sheffield	Hillsborough	1989	Sheffield Eagles 20-36 St Helens (League)
Sheffield	Owlerton Sports Stadium	1984	Sheffield Eagles 29-10 Rochdale Hornets (League)
Sheffield	Woodbourn Athletics Stadium	2005	Sheffield Eagles 31-28 Workington Town (League) check
South Shields	Horsley Hill	1902	South Shields 0-16 Lancaster (League)
Southend	Roots Hall	1984	Southend Invicta 14-17 Bramley (League)
Sowerby Bridge	Beech Road	1901	Sowerby Bridge 2-4 Heckmondwike (League)
St Helens	City Road	1919	St Helens Recs 5-2 Widnes (League)
St Helens	Hoghton Road	1990	Runcorn Highfield 10-22 Ryedale-York (League)
St Helens	Knowsley Road	1895	St Helens 8-3 Rochdale Hornets (League)
Stainforth	Meadowcourt Greyhound Stadium	1995	Doncaster 31-8 York (League)
Stalybridge	Bower Fold	2002	Oldham 6-40 St Helens (Challenge Cup)
Stockport	Edgeley Park	1895	Stockport 0-5 Brighouse Rangers (League)
Swansea	Morfa Stadium	1996	South Wales 22-18 Bramley (League)
Swansea	St Helen's	1945	Wales 11-3 England (International)
Swansea	Vetch Field	1990	Widnes 24-8 Wigan (Charity Shield)
Tonypandy	Athletic Ground	1908	Wales 35-18 England (International)
Treherbert	Athletic Ground	1908	Treherbert 6-29 Halifax (League)
Tyldesley	Well Street	1895	Tyldesley 6-0 Manningham (League)
Wakefield	Belle Vue	1895	Wakefield Trinity 13-9 Wigan (League)
Warrington	Halliwell Jones Stadium	2004	Warrington Wolves 34-20 Wakefield Trinity Wildcats (League)
Warrington	Wilderspool	1898	Warrington 3-3 Swinton (League)
Warrington	Wilderspool Road (Fletcher Street)	1895	Warrington 5-4 Hunslet (League)
Watford	Vicarage Road	1998	Great Britain 23-23 New Zealand (Test)
Whitehaven	Recreation Ground	1899	Cumberland 3-0 Cheshire (County Championship)
Whitehaven	The Playground, Whitehaven CC	1924	Cumberland 20-0 Yorkshire (County Championship)
Widnes	Lowerhouse Lane/ Naughton Park (Halton Stadium)	1895	Widnes 11-8 Leeds (League)
Wigan	Central Park	1902	Wigan 14-8 Batley (League)
Wigan	Edge Hall Road, Orrell	2000	Swinton Lions 28-28 Whitehaven (League)
Wigan	JJB Stadium	1999	Wigan Warriors 10-14 Castleford Tigers (Play-offs)
Wigan	Prescott Street	1895	Wigan 0-0 Tyldesley (League)
Wigan	Springfield Park	1901	Wigan 12-0 Morecambe (League)
Wigan	Tunstall Lane, Pemberton	1922	Wigan Highfield 10-25 Wigan (League)
Workington	Borough Park	1937	Cumberland 17-23 Lancashire (County Championship)
Workington	Derwent Park	1956	Workington Town 0-24 Wigan (League)
Workington	Lonsdale Park	1898	Cumberland 13-3 Lancashire (County Championship)
Wrexham	Racecourse Ground	2000	Wales 38-6 Cook Islands (World Cup)
York	Bootham Crescent	1989	York 9-28 Leeds (Challenge Cup)
York	Clarence Street	1901	York 15-3 Goole (League)
York	Elm Park Way, Heworth	1991	York 36-8 Hunslet (Yorkshire Cup)
York	Ryedale (Huntington) Stadium	1989	Ryedale-York 16-6 Keighley (League)